We Never Learn

[x]

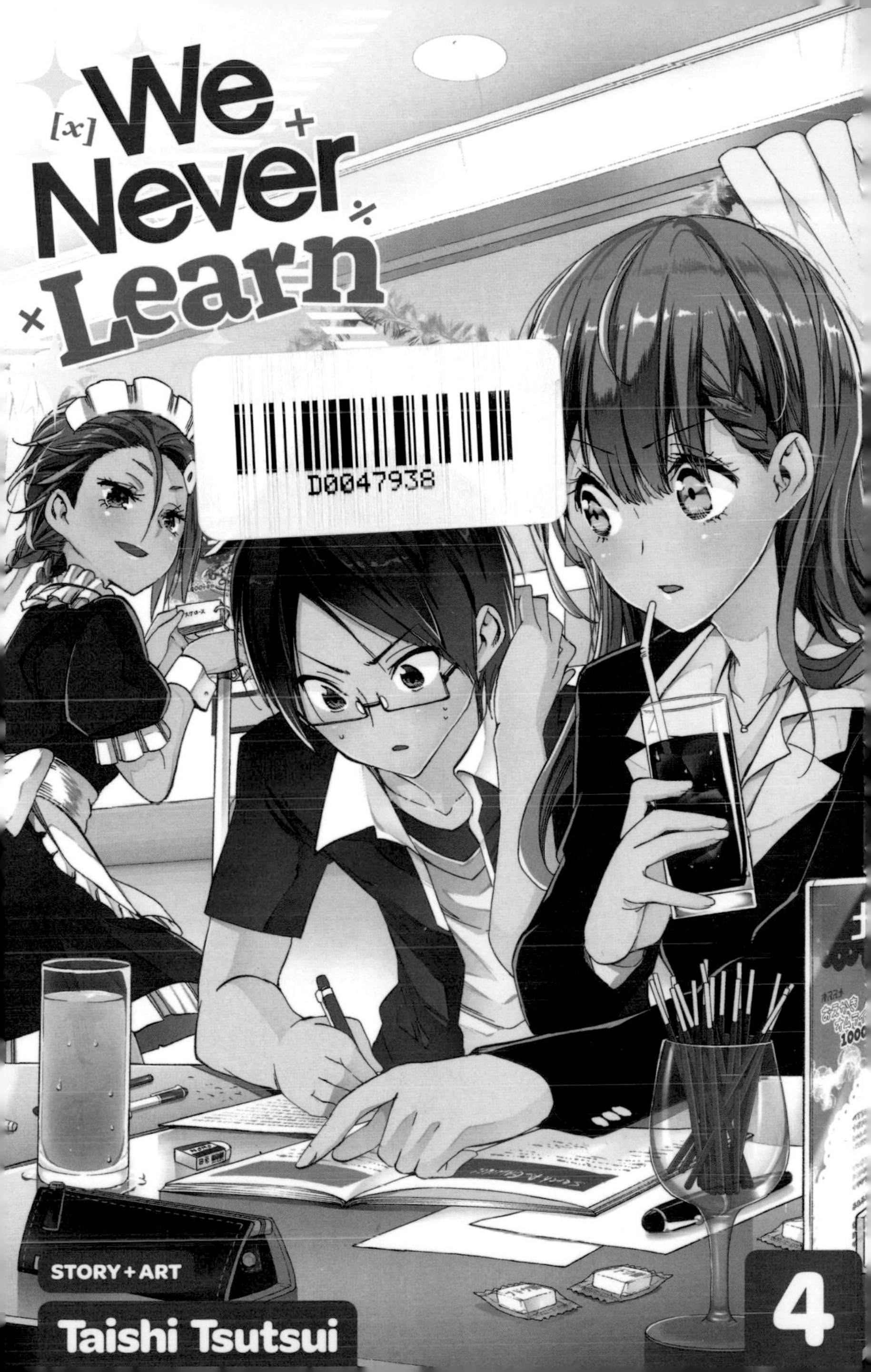

STORY + ART

Taishi Tsutsui

4

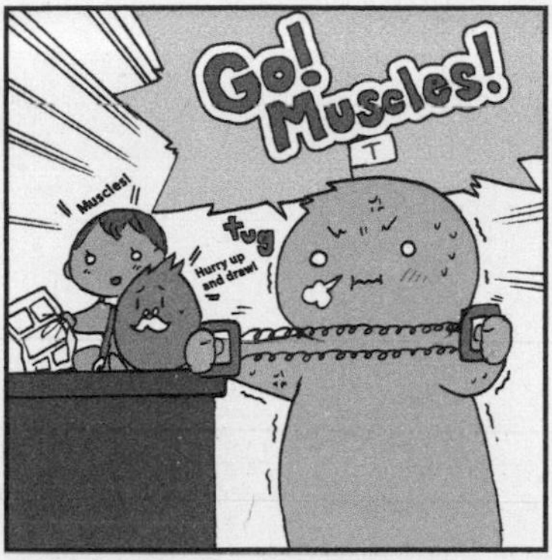
Go! Muscles!
Muscles!
tug
Hurry up and draw!

This is Tsutsui. I'm so happy! We're on volume 4 already! Thank you so much for supporting the series for four volumes! Last time, I wrote about joining a gym. Well, the other day a friend gave me a bodybuilding device called an expander. Right on! I've decided to work out hard in between drawing my manga pages to see if I can get ripped! My assistants think I'm an idiot, but I don't care! When I overdo it, my hands get so exhausted that they start shaking and I can't hold a pen. It makes it hard to get my manga pages done... (Don't tell anyone!!) So, if you're tired from working out with an expander too, this is for you! This is the fourth volume of a slightly strange exam-prep romance comic, and I hope you enjoy it!

Taishi Tsutsui

We Never Learn

We Never Learn

Volume 4 • SHONEN JUMP Manga Edition

STORY AND ART **Taishi Tsutsui**

TRANSLATION Camellia Nieh
SHONEN JUMP SERIES LETTERING Snir Aharon
GRAPHIC NOVEL TOUCH-UP ART & LETTERING Erika Terriquez
DESIGN Shawn Carrico
SHONEN JUMP SERIES EDITOR John Bae
GRAPHIC NOVEL EDITOR David Brothers

Printed in the U.S.A.

Published by VIZ Media, LLC
P.O. Box 77010
San Francisco, CA 94107

10 9 8 7 6 5 4 3 2 1
First printing, June 2019

VIZ MEDIA
viz.com

SHONEN JUMP
shonenjump.com

ratings.viz.com
RATED T+ OLDER TEEN

PARENTAL ADVISORY
WE NEVER LEARN is rated T+ for Older Teen and is recommended for ages 16 and up. This volume contains mild language and sexual themes.

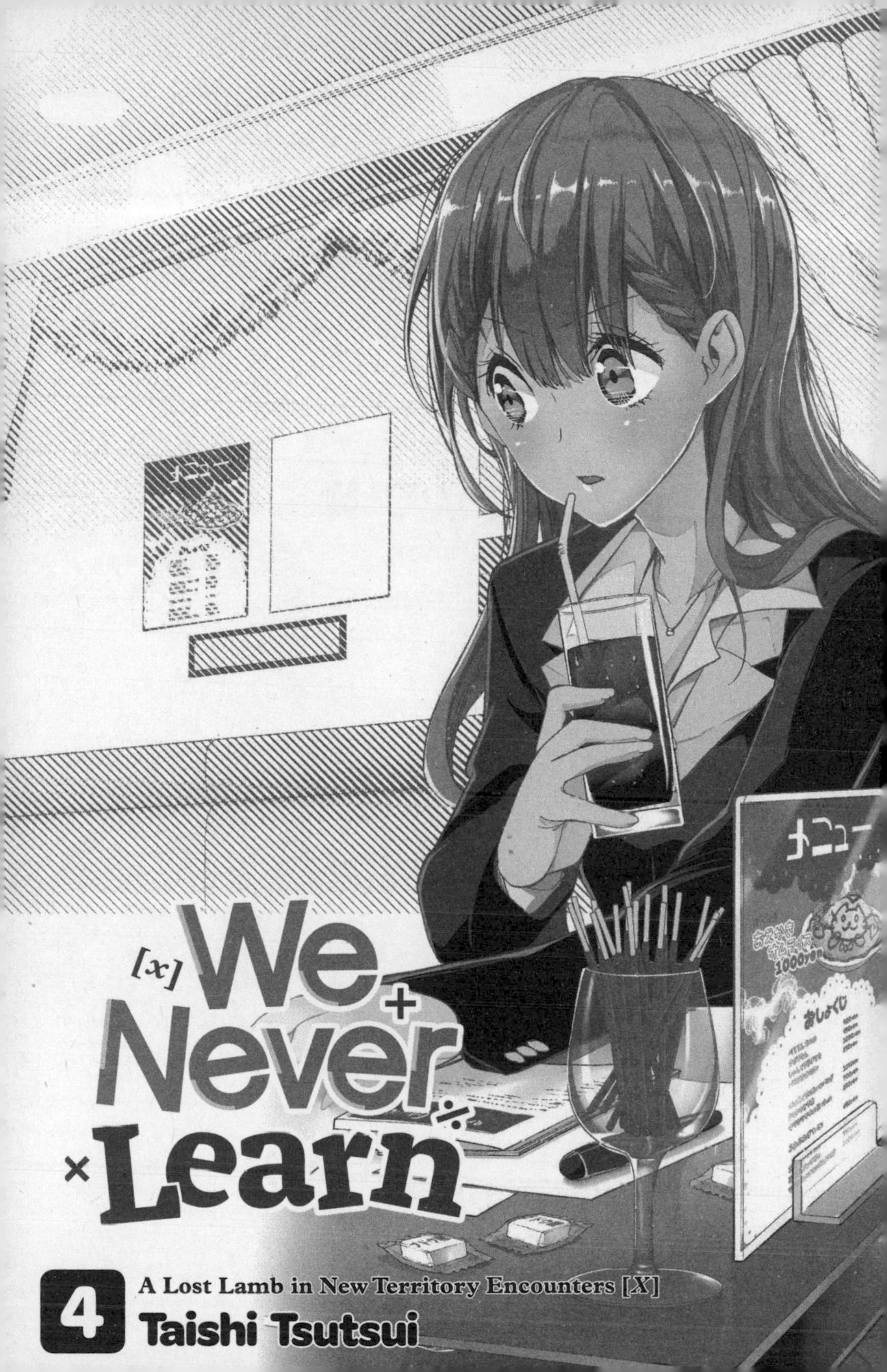
メニュー
おしょくじ
1000yen
[x] We + Never ÷ × Learn
4
A Lost Lamb in New Territory Encounters [X]
Taishi Tsutsui

We Never Learn

Characters & Story

Nariyuki Yuiga and his family have led a humble life since his father passed away, with Yuiga doing everything he can to support his siblings. So when the principal of his school agrees to grant Nariyuki the school's special VIP recommendation for a full scholarship to college, he leaps at the opportunity. However, the principal's offer comes with one condition: Yuiga must serve as the tutor of Rizu Ogata, Fumino Furuhashi and Uruka Takemoto, the three girl geniuses who are the pride of Ichinose Academy! Unfortunately, the girls, while extremely talented in certain ways, all have subjects where their grades are absolutely rock-bottom. How will these three struggling students ever manage to pass their college entrance exams?!

When a rumor circulates that Yuiga kissed someone, both Uruka's and Rizu's grades plummet! Fumino notices her friends' feelings and tries to advise Nariyuki about how to treat a lady while at the same time ignoring her own heart. But what will happen when Nariyuki accidentally overhears that he's Uruka's crush?!

NARIYUKI YUIGA

CLASS:3-B

☺ Liberal Arts
☺ STEM
☹ Athletics

A bright student from an ordinary family. Nariyuki lacks genius in any one subject but manages to maintain stellar grades through hard work. Agrees to take on the role of tutor in return for the school's special VIP recommendation.

The Yuiga Family

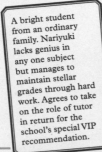

A family of five consisting of Nariyuki, his mother and his siblings, Mizuki, Hazuki and Kazuki.

Sawako Sekijo

The head of the science club and a rival of Rizu's, but she secretly adores her.

Kawase and Umihara

Uruka's friends.

Ogata (Father)

Runs an udon shop. Dotes on his daughter.

RIZU OGATA

CLASS:3-F

☹ Liberal Arts
☺ STEM
☹ Athletics

Known as the Thumbelina Supercomputer, Rizu is a math and science genius, but she's a dunce at literature, especially when human emotions come into play. She chooses a literary path to learn about human psychology—partially because she wants to learn how to be better at board games.

FUMINO FURUHASHI

CLASS:3-A

☺ Liberal Arts
☹ STEM
☺ Athletics

Known as the Sleeping Beauty of the Literary Forest, Fumino is a literary wiz whose mind goes completely blank when she sees numbers. She chooses a STEM path because she wants to study the stars.

URUKA TAKEMOTO

CLASS:3-D

☹ Liberal Arts
☹ STEM
☺ Athletics

Known as the Shimmering Ebony Mermaid Princess, Uruka is a swimming prodigy but is terrible at academics. In order to get an athletic scholarship, she needs to meet certain academic standards. She's had a crush on Nariyuki since junior high.

MAFUYU KIRISU

TEACHER

☺ Pedagogy
☹ Home Economics

A teacher at Ichinose Academy, and Rizu and Fumino's previous tutor. She believes people should choose their path according to their talents and pressures Rizu and Fumino to change course. However, deep down, she's a caring person. She's also surprisingly slovenly for a teacher!

TITLE
We Never Learn

CONTENTS

VOLUME **4** A Lost Lamb in New Territory Encounters [X] NAME **Taishi Tsutsui**

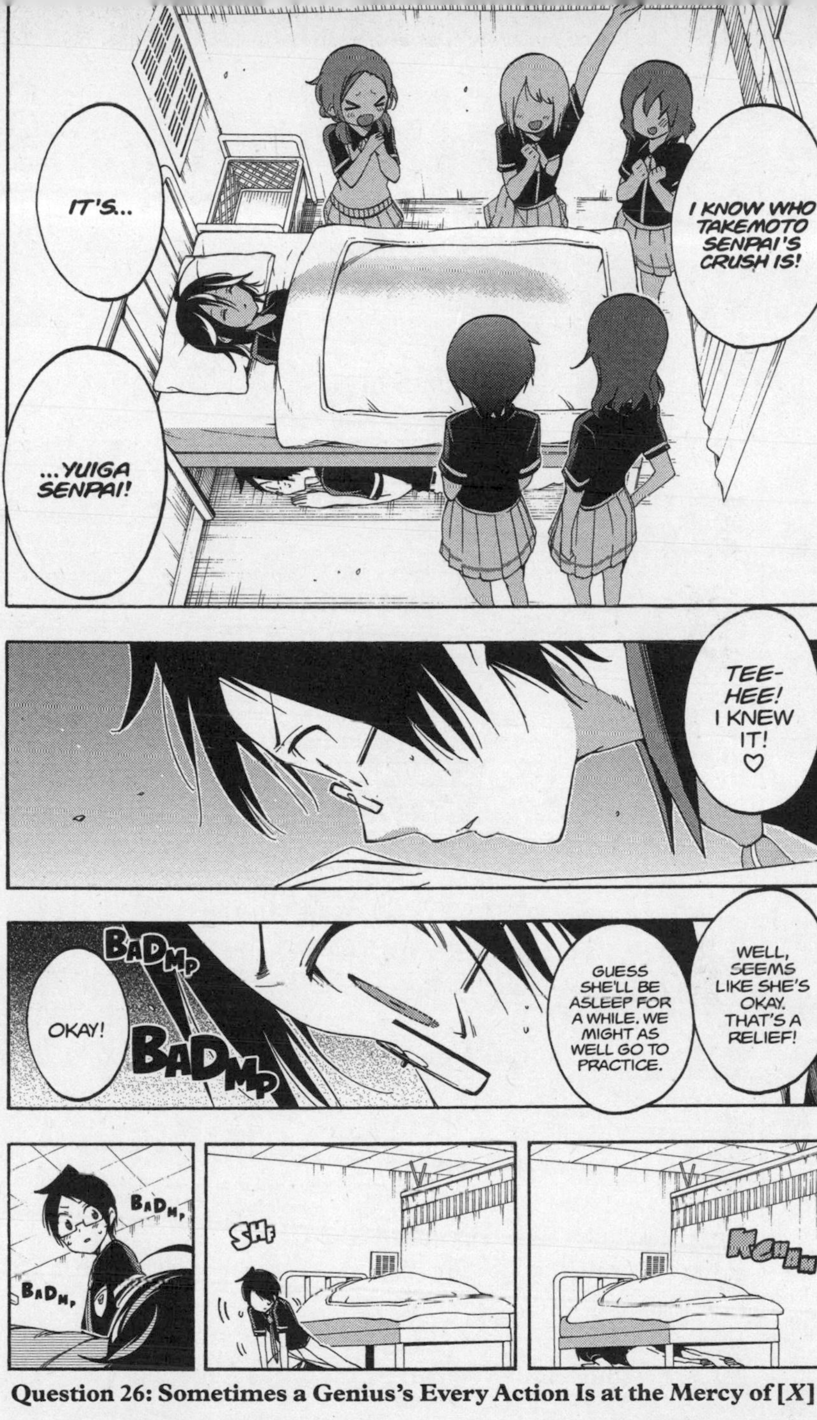
I KNOW WHO TAKEMOTO SENPAI'S CRUSH IS!
IT'S...
...YUIGA SENPAI!
TEE-HEE! I KNEW IT! ♡
WELL, SEEMS LIKE SHE'S OKAY. THAT'S A RELIEF!
GUESS SHE'LL BE ASLEEP FOR A WHILE. WE MIGHT AS WELL GO TO PRACTICE.
BADMP
OKAY!
BADMP
SHF
BADMP
BADMP

Question 26: Sometimes a Genius's Every Action Is at the Mercy of [*X*]

Question 26: Sometimes a Genius's Every Action Is at the Mercy of [X]

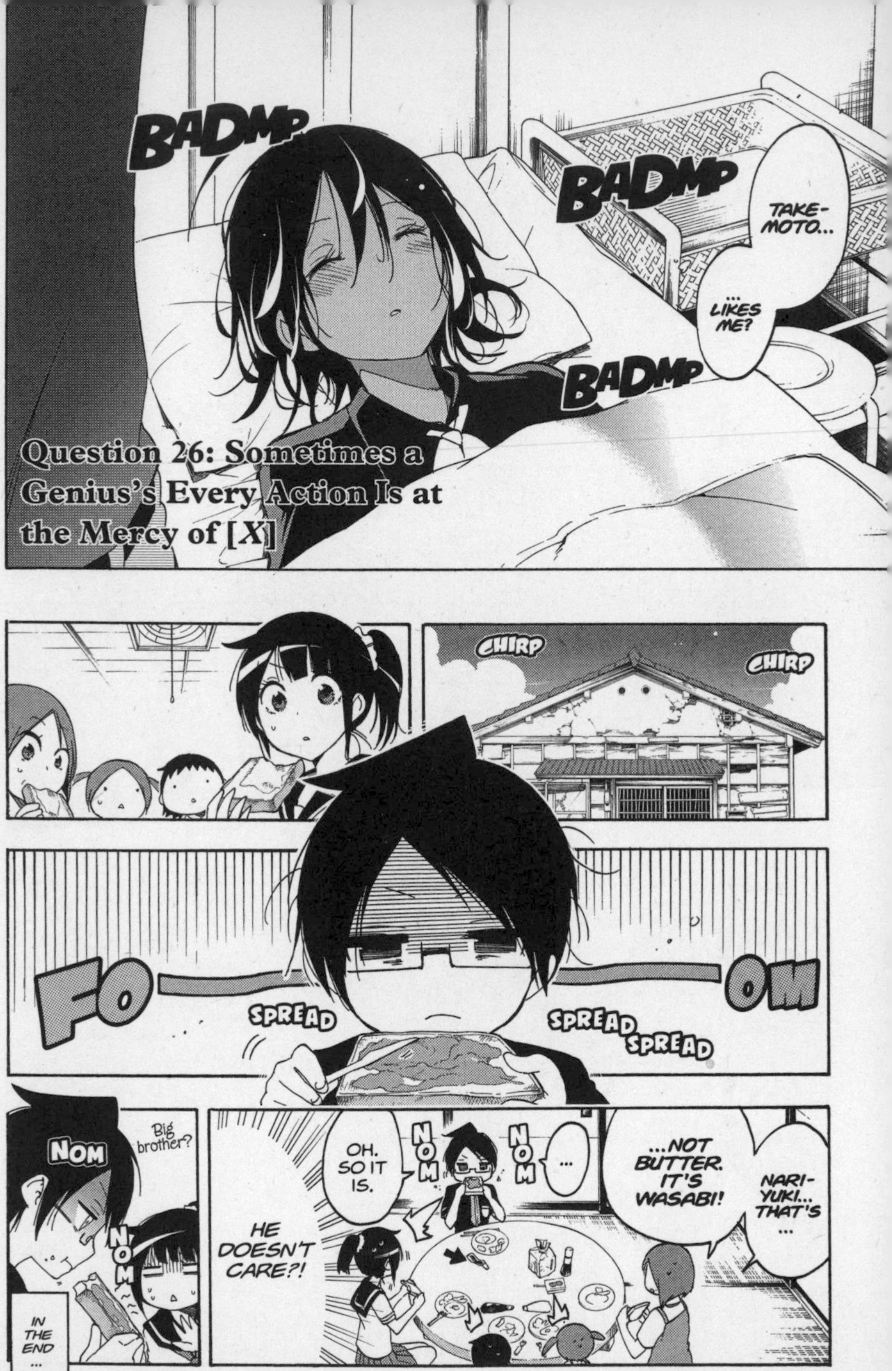
BADMP
BADMP
BADMP
TAKE-MOTO...
...LIKES ME?
CHIRP
CHIRP
FO————OM
SPREAD
SPREAD SPREAD
NARI-YUKI... THAT'S ...
...NOT BUTTER. IT'S WASABI!
...
NOM
NOM
OH. SO IT IS.
HE DOESN'T CARE?!
Big brother?
NOM
NOM
IN THE END ...

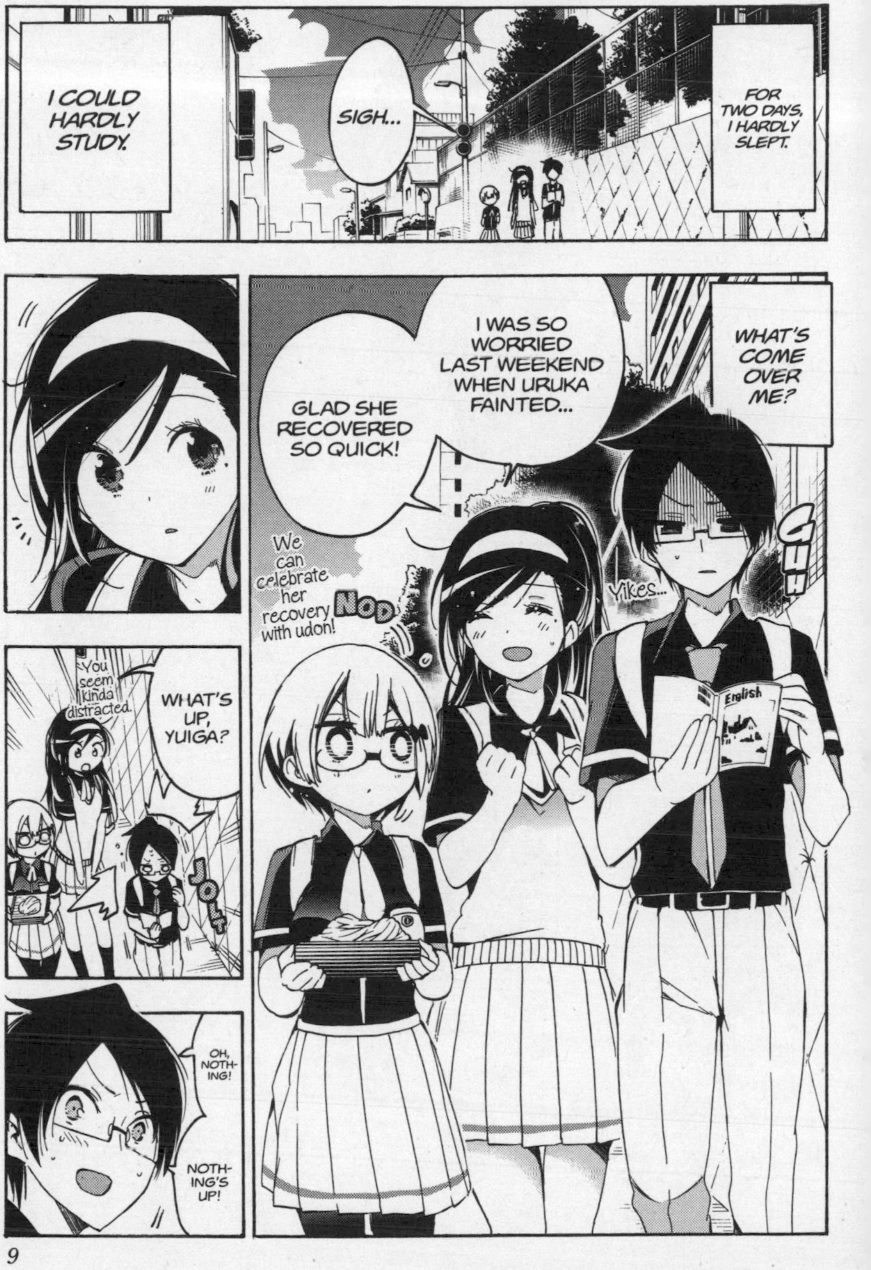
FOR TWO DAYS, I HARDLY SLEPT.
SIGH...
I COULD HARDLY STUDY.
WHAT'S COME OVER ME?
I WAS SO WORRIED LAST WEEKEND WHEN URUKA FAINTED...
GLAD SHE RECOVERED SO QUICK!
GUH
Yikes...
We can celebrate her recovery with udon!
NOD
English
WHAT'S UP, YUIGA?
You seem kinda distracted.
JOLT
OH, NOTHING!
NOTHING'S UP!

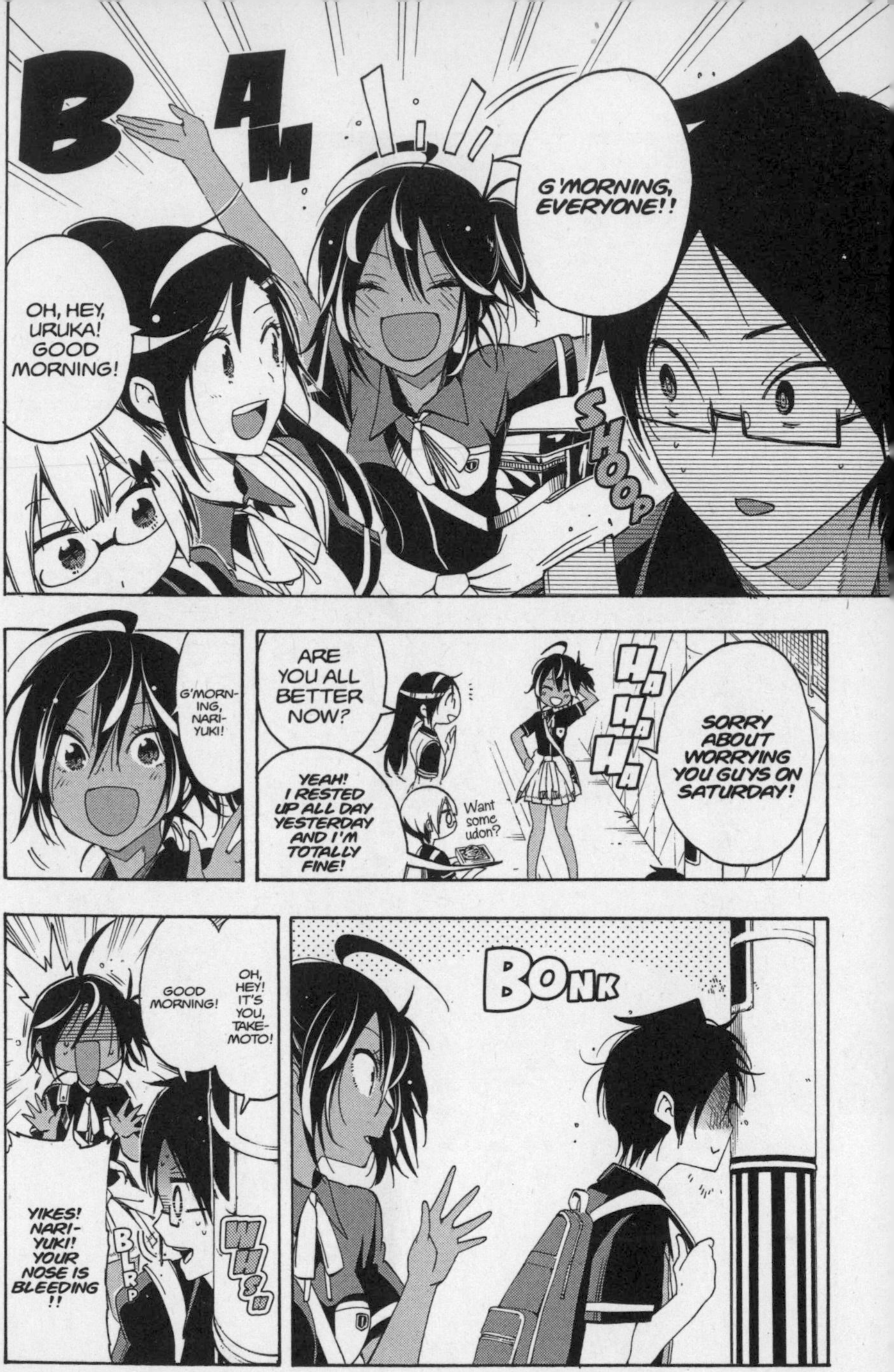
G'MORNING, EVERYONE!!
BAM
SHOOP
OH, HEY, URUKA! GOOD MORNING!
SORRY ABOUT WORRYING YOU GUYS ON SATURDAY!
HA HA HA HA
ARE YOU ALL BETTER NOW?
YEAH! I RESTED UP ALL DAY YESTERDAY AND I'M TOTALLY FINE!
Want some udon?
G'MORN-ING, NARI-YUKI!
BONK
OH, HEY! IT'S YOU, TAKE-MOTO!
GOOD MORNING!
WHSH
BLRP
YIKES! NARI-YUKI! YOUR NOSE IS BLEEDING!!

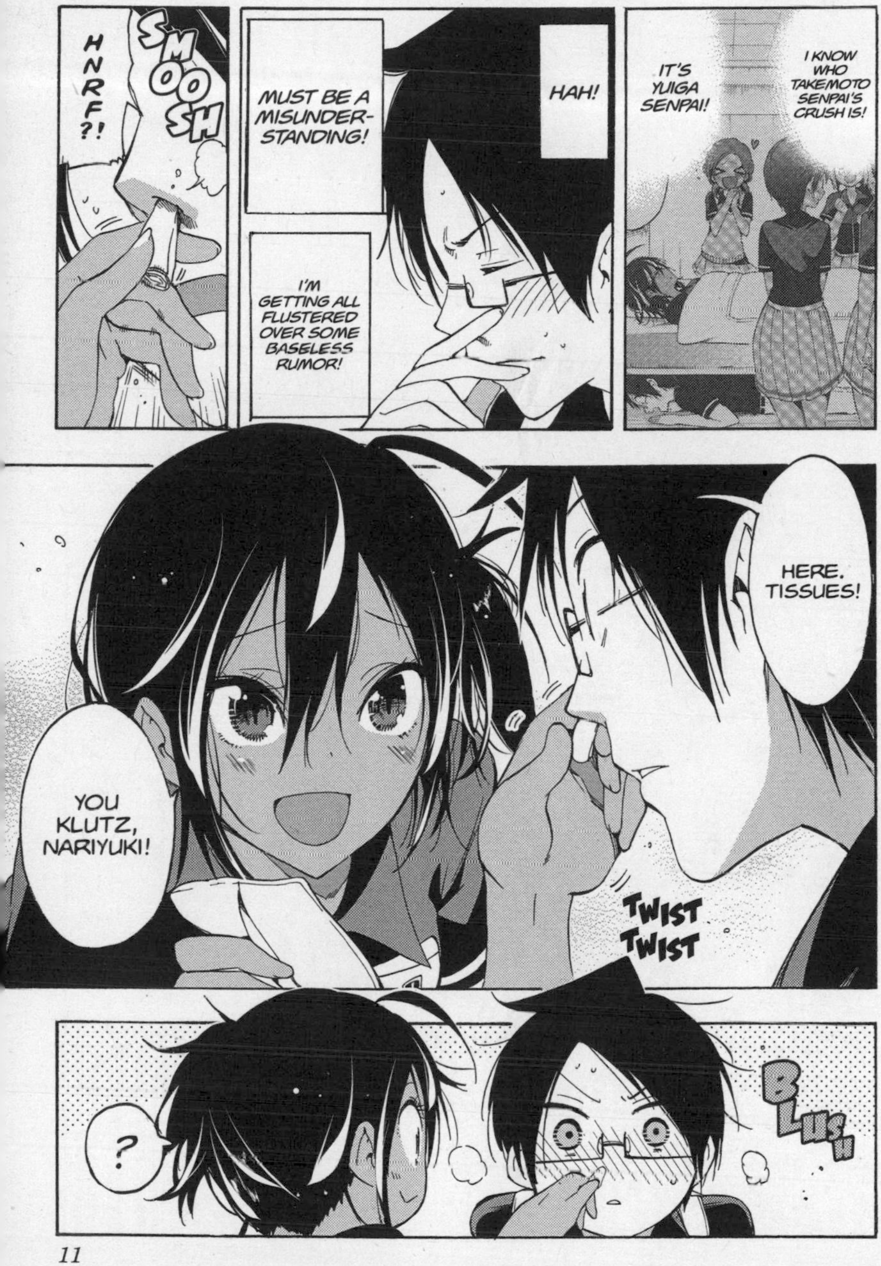
I KNOW WHO TAKEMOTO SENPAI'S CRUSH IS!
IT'S YUIGA SENPAI!
HAH!
MUST BE A MISUNDER-STANDING!
I'M GETTING ALL FLUSTERED OVER SOME BASELESS RUMOR!
SMOOSH
HNRF?!
HERE. TISSUES!
TWIST TWIST
YOU KLUTZ, NARIYUKI!
BLUSH
?

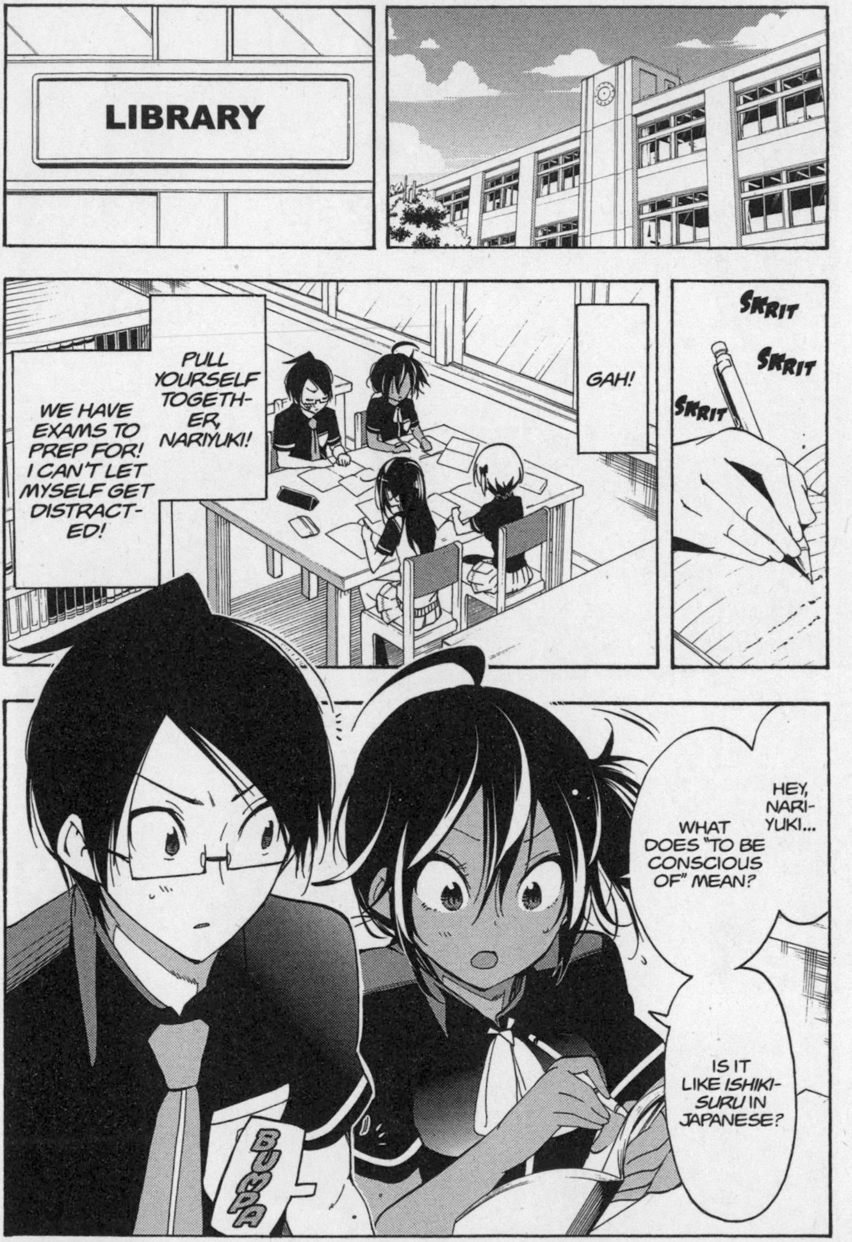
LIBRARY
SKRIT
SKRIT
SKRIT
GAH!
PULL YOURSELF TOGETH-ER, NARIYUKI!
WE HAVE EXAMS TO PREP FOR! I CAN'T LET MYSELF GET DISTRACT-ED!
HEY, NARI-YUKI...
WHAT DOES "TO BE CONSCIOUS OF" MEAN?
IS IT LIKE *ISHIKI-SURU* IN JAPANESE?
BUMPA

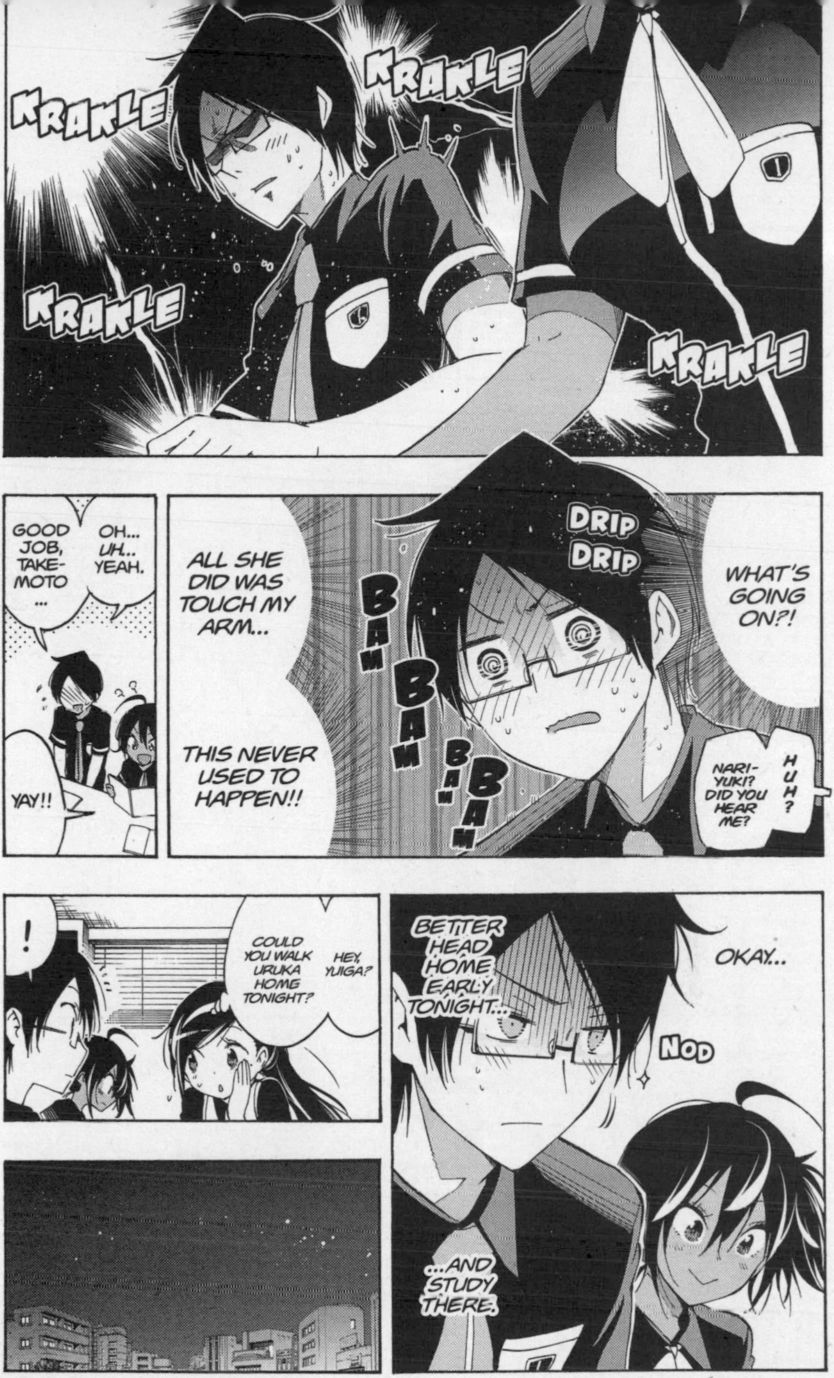
KRAKLE
KRAKLE
KRAKLE
KRAKLE
WHAT'S GOING ON?!
DRIP DRIP
ALL SHE DID WAS TOUCH MY ARM...
HUH?
NARI-YUKI? DID YOU HEAR ME?
BAM BAM BAM BAM
THIS NEVER USED TO HAPPEN!!
OH... UH... YEAH.
GOOD JOB, TAKE-MOTO ...
YAY!!
OKAY...
BETTER HEAD HOME EARLY TONIGHT...
NOD
...AND STUDY THERE.
HEY, YUIGA?
COULD YOU WALK URUKA HOME TONIGHT?
!

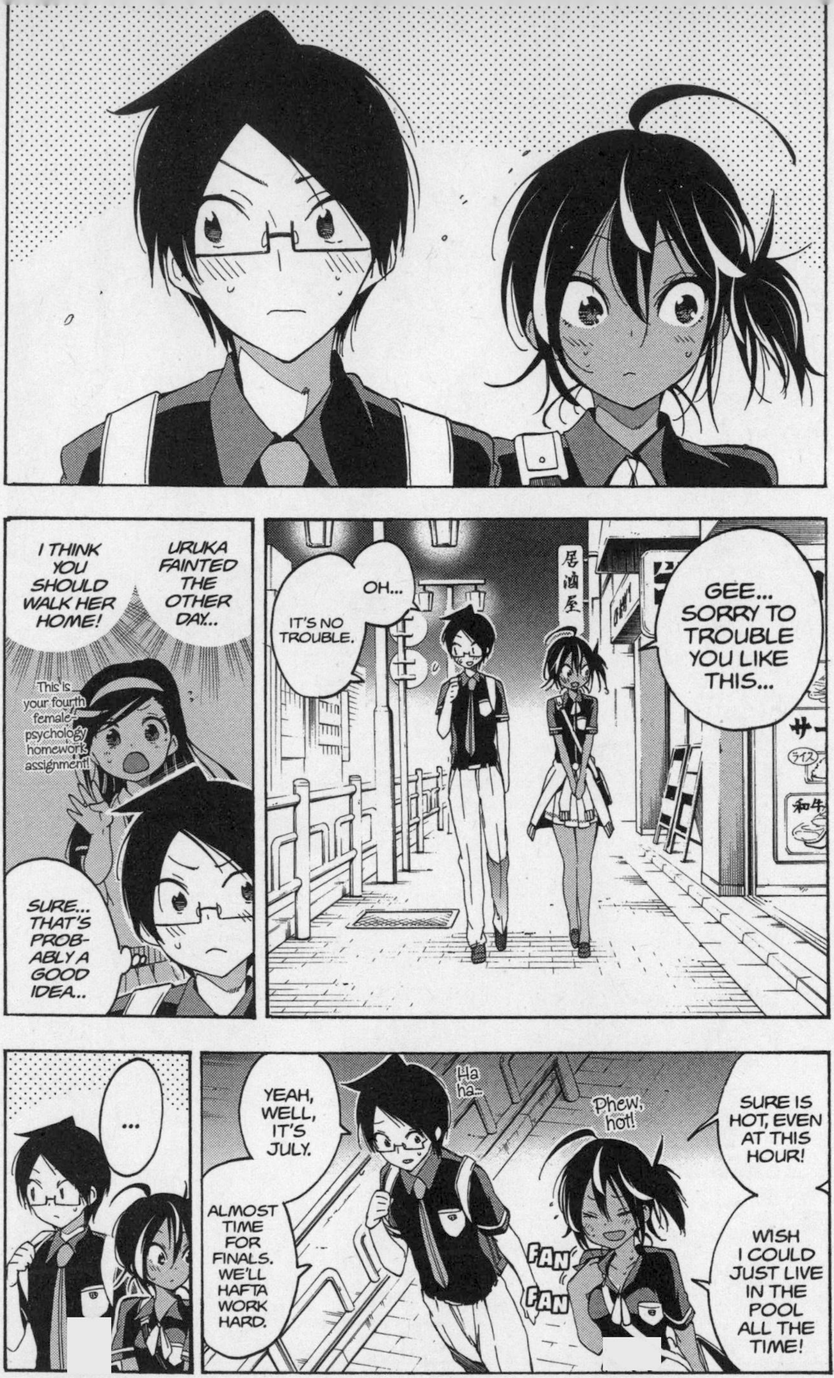
GEE... SORRY TO TROUBLE YOU LIKE THIS...
OH...
IT'S NO TROUBLE.
居酒屋
URUKA FAINTED THE OTHER DAY...
I THINK YOU SHOULD WALK HER HOME!
This is your fourth female-psychology homework assignment!
SURE... THAT'S PROBABLY A GOOD IDEA...
SURE IS HOT, EVEN AT THIS HOUR!
Phew, hot!
Ha ha...
YEAH, WELL, IT'S JULY.
WISH I COULD JUST LIVE IN THE POOL ALL THE TIME!
FAN
FAN
ALMOST TIME FOR FINALS. WE'LL HAFTA WORK HARD.
...

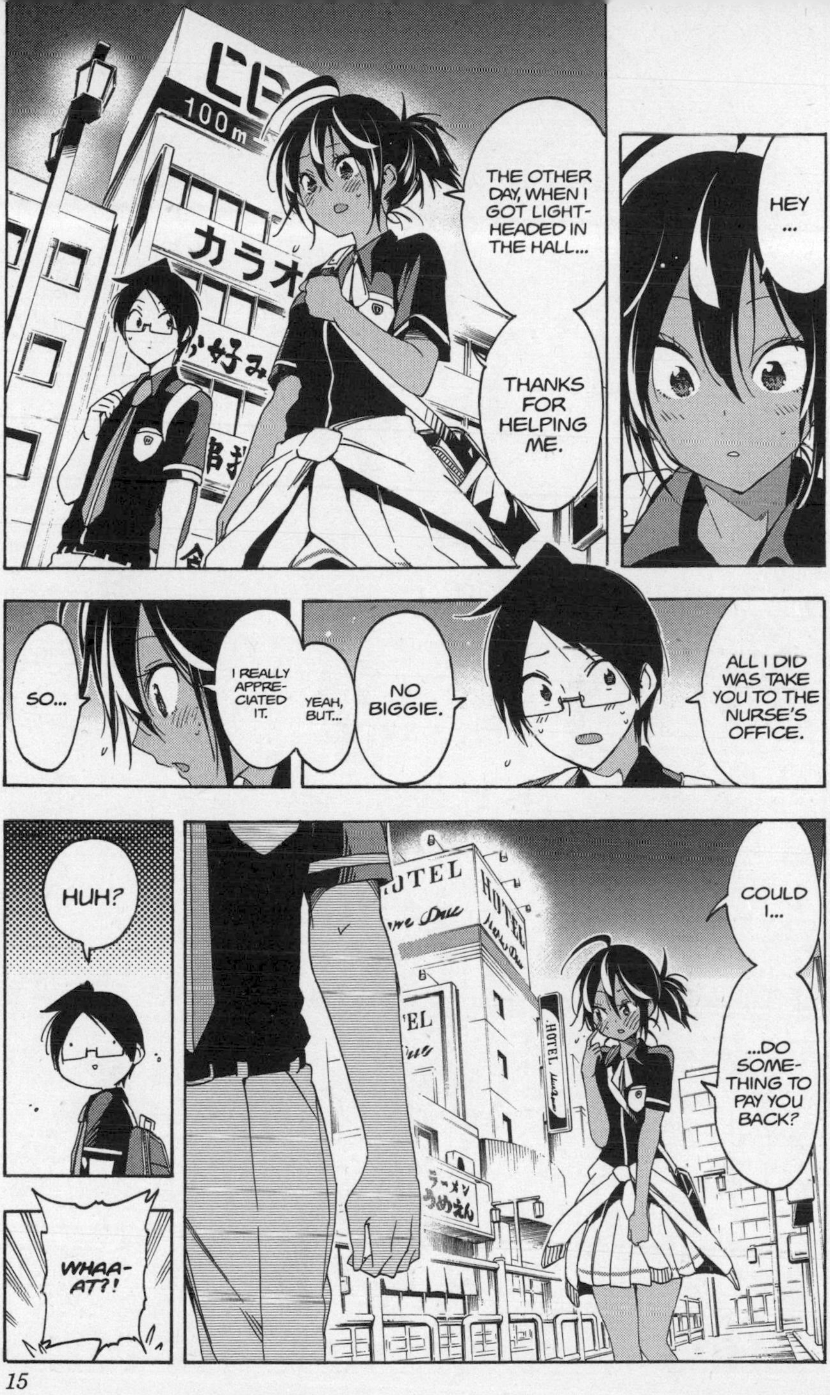
HEY ...
100m
カラオ
THE OTHER DAY, WHEN I GOT LIGHT-HEADED IN THE HALL...
THANKS FOR HELPING ME.
ALL I DID WAS TAKE YOU TO THE NURSE'S OFFICE.
NO BIGGIE.
YEAH, BUT...
I REALLY APPRECIATED IT.
SO...
HOTEL
COULD I...
...DO SOMETHING TO PAY YOU BACK?
HUH?
WHAA-AT?!

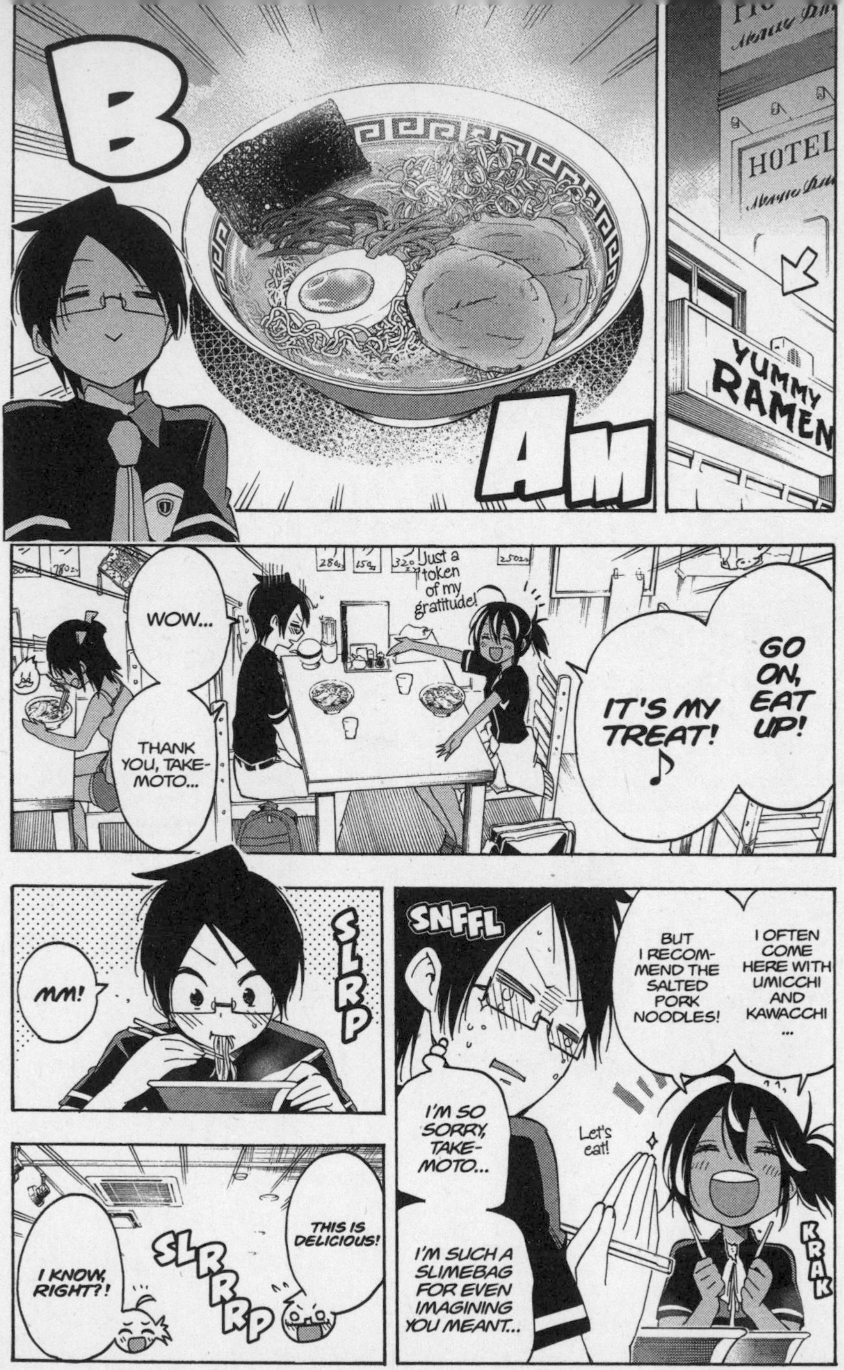
HOTEL
YUMMY RAMEN
B
AM
GO ON, EAT UP!
IT'S MY TREAT! ♪
Just a token of my gratitude!
WOW...
THANK YOU, TAKEMOTO...
I OFTEN COME HERE WITH UMICCHI AND KAWACCHI ...
BUT I RECOMMEND THE SALTED PORK NOODLES!
SNFFL
Let's eat!
KRAK
I'M SO SORRY, TAKEMOTO...
I'M SUCH A SLIMEBAG FOR EVEN IMAGINING YOU MEANT...
SLRP
MM!
THIS IS DELICIOUS!
SLRRRP
I KNOW, RIGHT?!

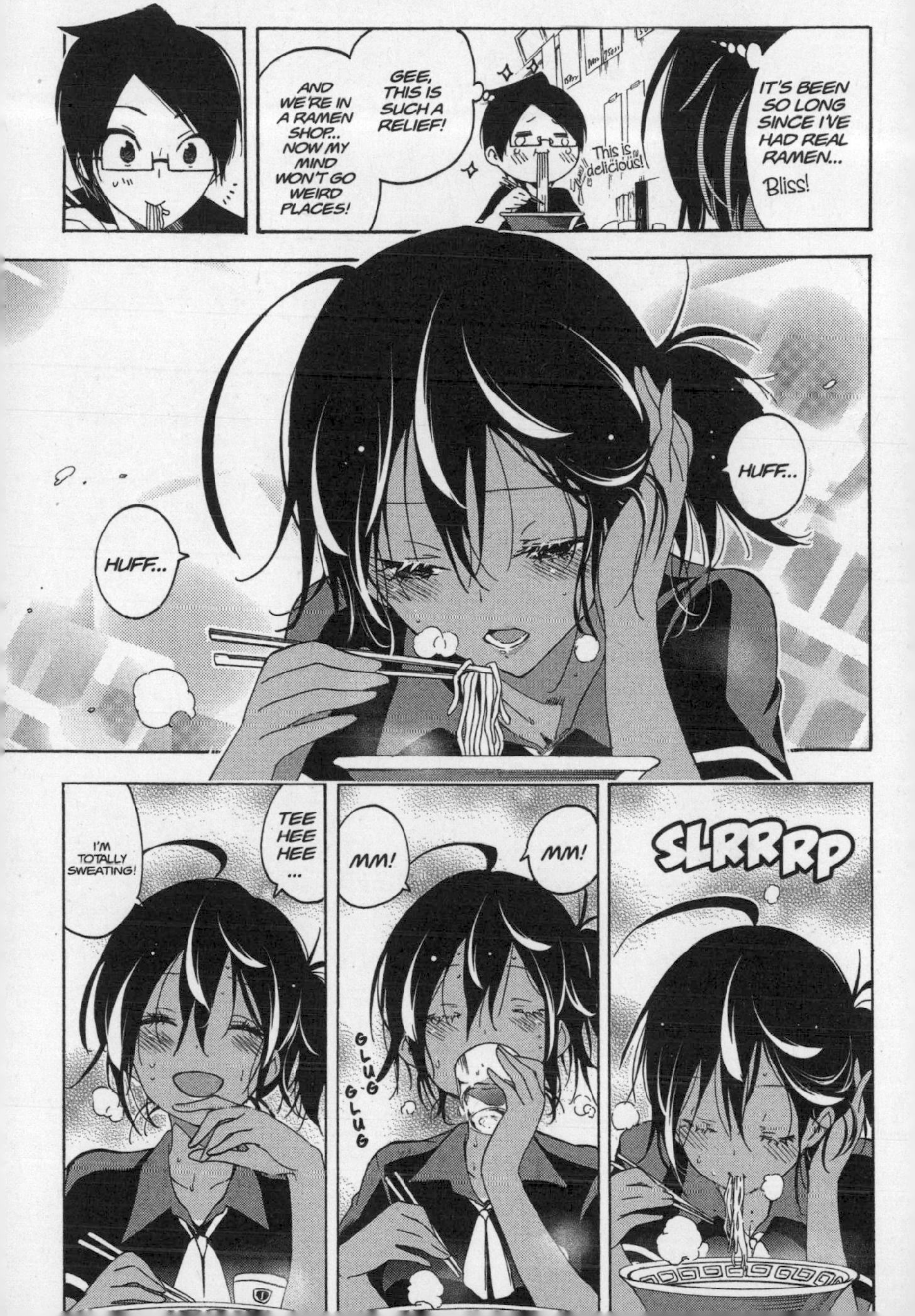
IT'S BEEN SO LONG SINCE I'VE HAD REAL RAMEN...
Bliss!
This is delicious!
GEE, THIS IS SUCH A RELIEF!
AND WE'RE IN A RAMEN SHOP... NOW MY MIND WON'T GO WEIRD PLACES!
HUFF...
HUFF...
SLRRRP
MM!
MM!
GLUG GLUG
GLUG GLUG
TEE HEE HEE ...
I'M TOTALLY SWEATING!

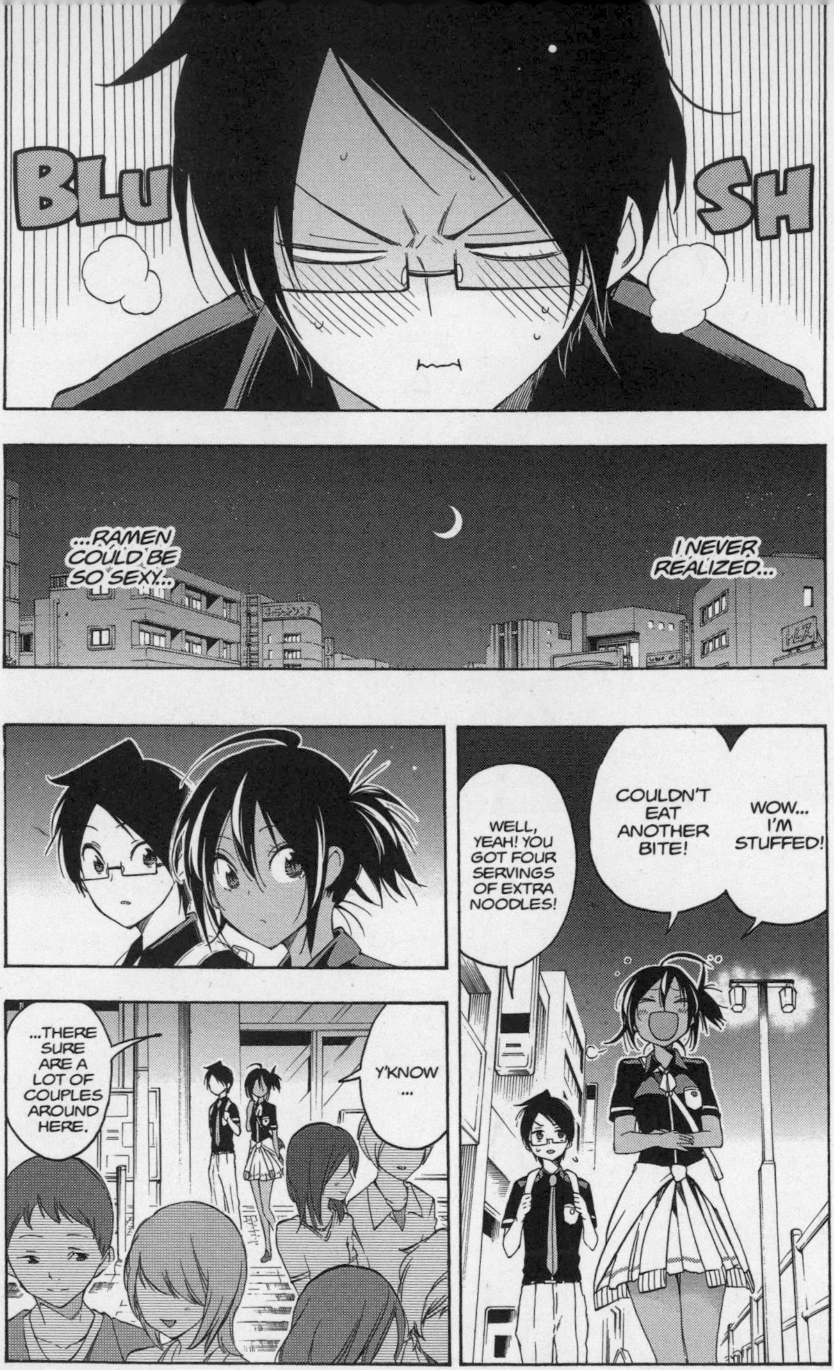
BLU
SH
I NEVER REALIZED...
...RAMEN COULD BE SO SEXY...
WOW... I'M STUFFED!
COULDN'T EAT ANOTHER BITE!
WELL, YEAH! YOU GOT FOUR SERVINGS OF EXTRA NOODLES!
Y'KNOW ...
...THERE SURE ARE A LOT OF COUPLES AROUND HERE.

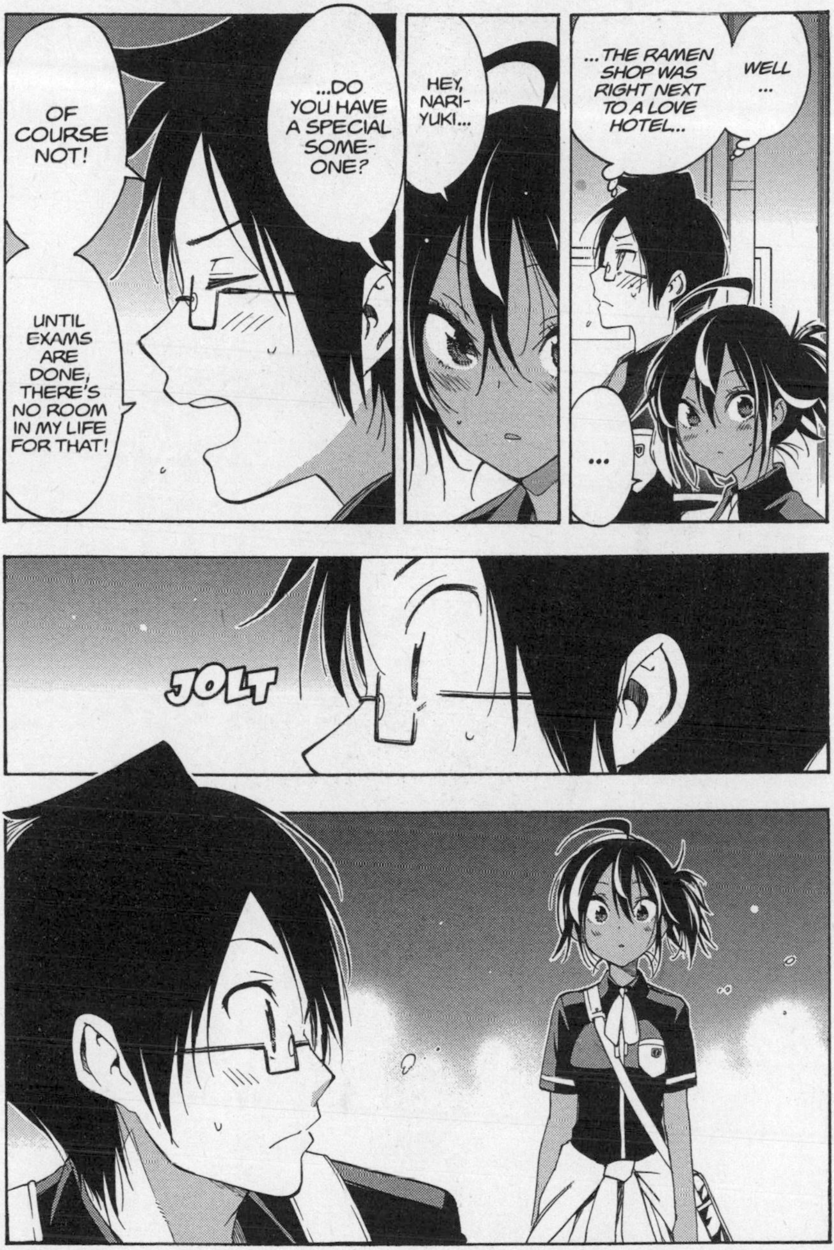
WELL ...
...THE RAMEN SHOP WAS RIGHT NEXT TO A LOVE HOTEL...
...
HEY, NARI-YUKI...
...DO YOU HAVE A SPECIAL SOME-ONE?
OF COURSE NOT!
UNTIL EXAMS ARE DONE, THERE'S NO ROOM IN MY LIFE FOR THAT!
JOLT

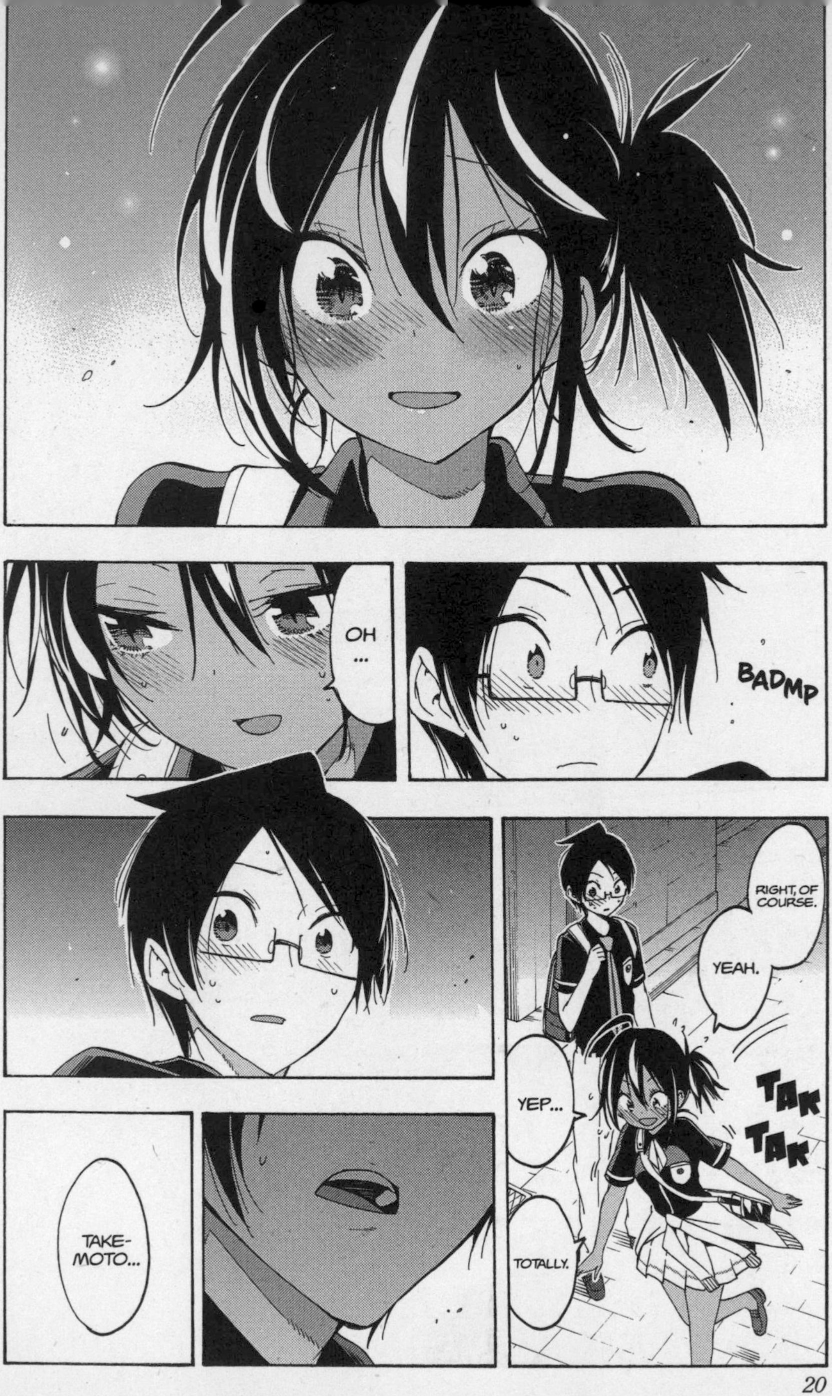
BADMP
OH ...
RIGHT, OF COURSE.
YEAH.
TAK TAK
YEP...
TOTALLY.
...
TAKE-MOTO...

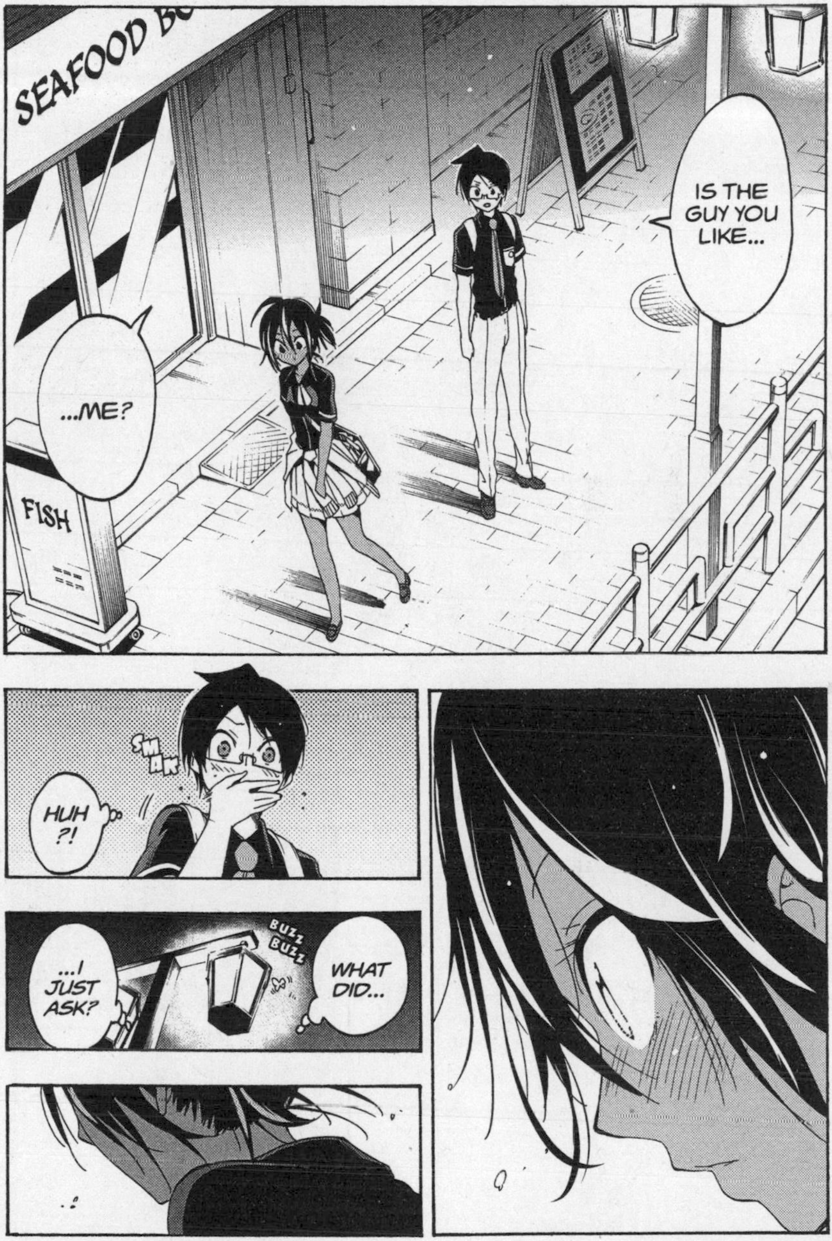
SEAFOOD B
IS THE GUY YOU LIKE...
...ME?
FISH
SMAK
HUH ?!
BUZZ BUZZ
WHAT DID...
...I JUST ASK?

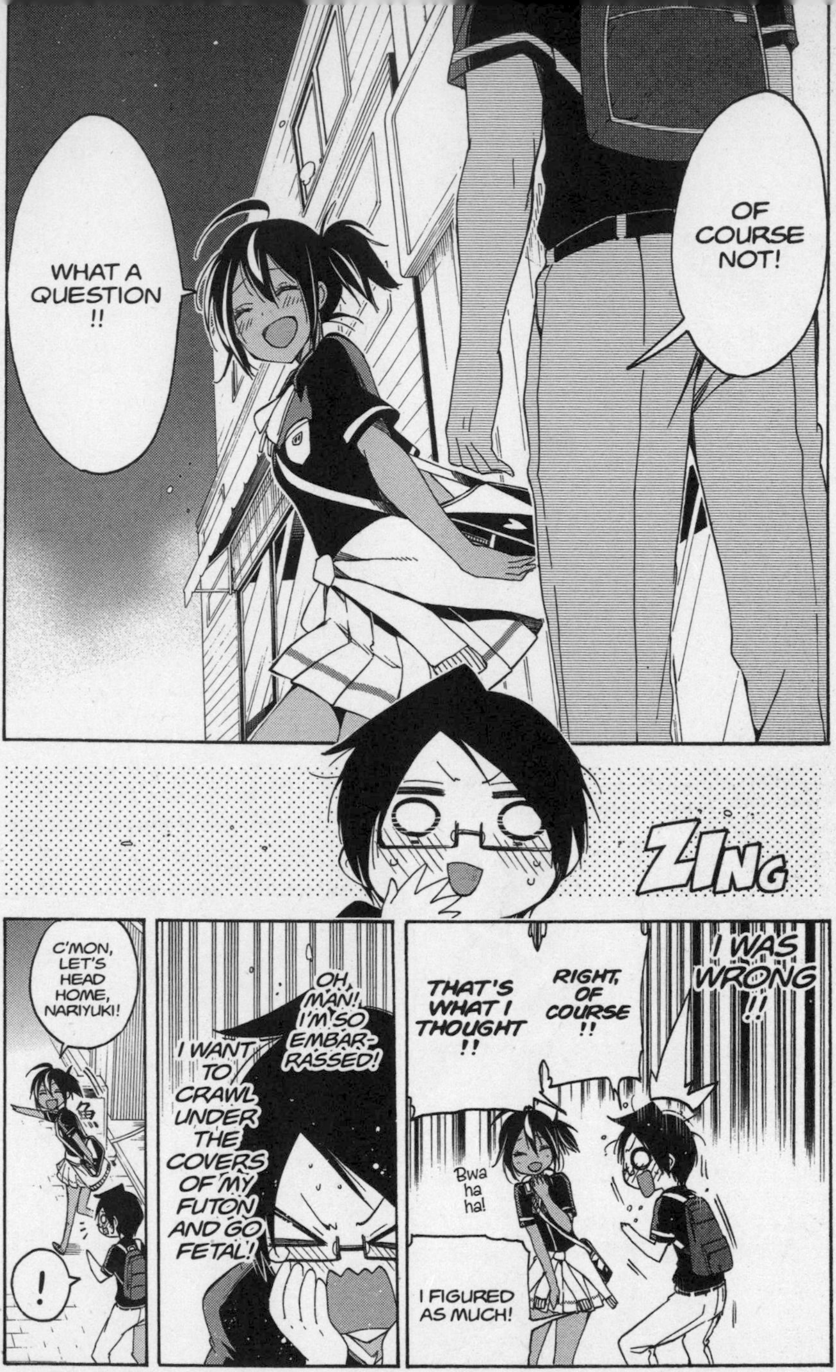
OF COURSE NOT!
WHAT A QUESTION !!
ZING
I WAS WRONG !!
RIGHT, OF COURSE !!
THAT'S WHAT I THOUGHT !!
Bwa ha ha!
I FIGURED AS MUCH!
OH, MAN! I'M SO EMBARRASSED!
I WANT TO CRAWL UNDER THE COVERS OF MY FUTON AND GO FETAL!
C'MON, LET'S HEAD HOME, NARIYUKI!
!

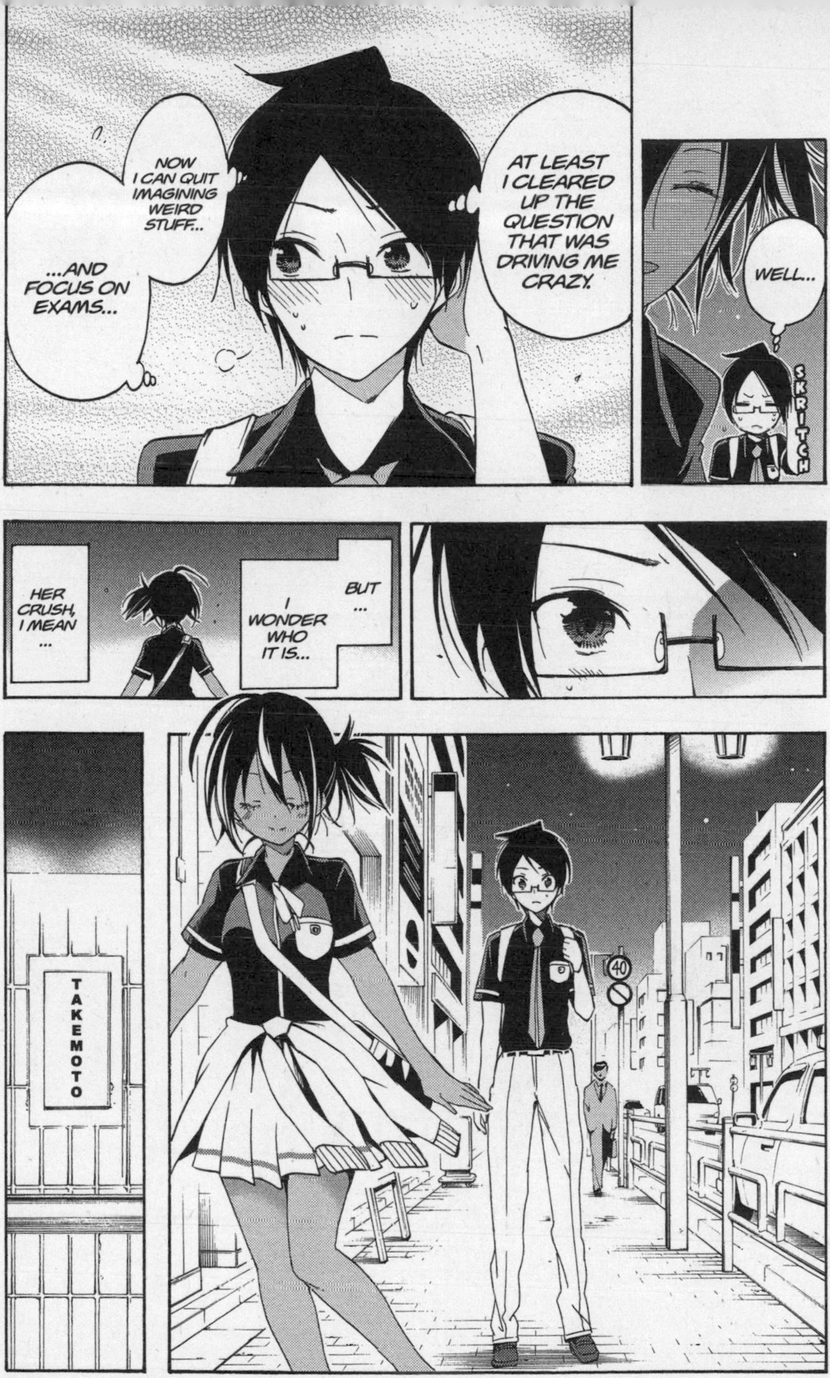
WELL...
SKRITCH
AT LEAST I CLEARED UP THE QUESTION THAT WAS DRIVING ME CRAZY.
NOW I CAN QUIT IMAGINING WEIRD STUFF...
...AND FOCUS ON EXAMS...
BUT ...
I WONDER WHO IT IS...
HER CRUSH, I MEAN ...
40
TAKEMOTO

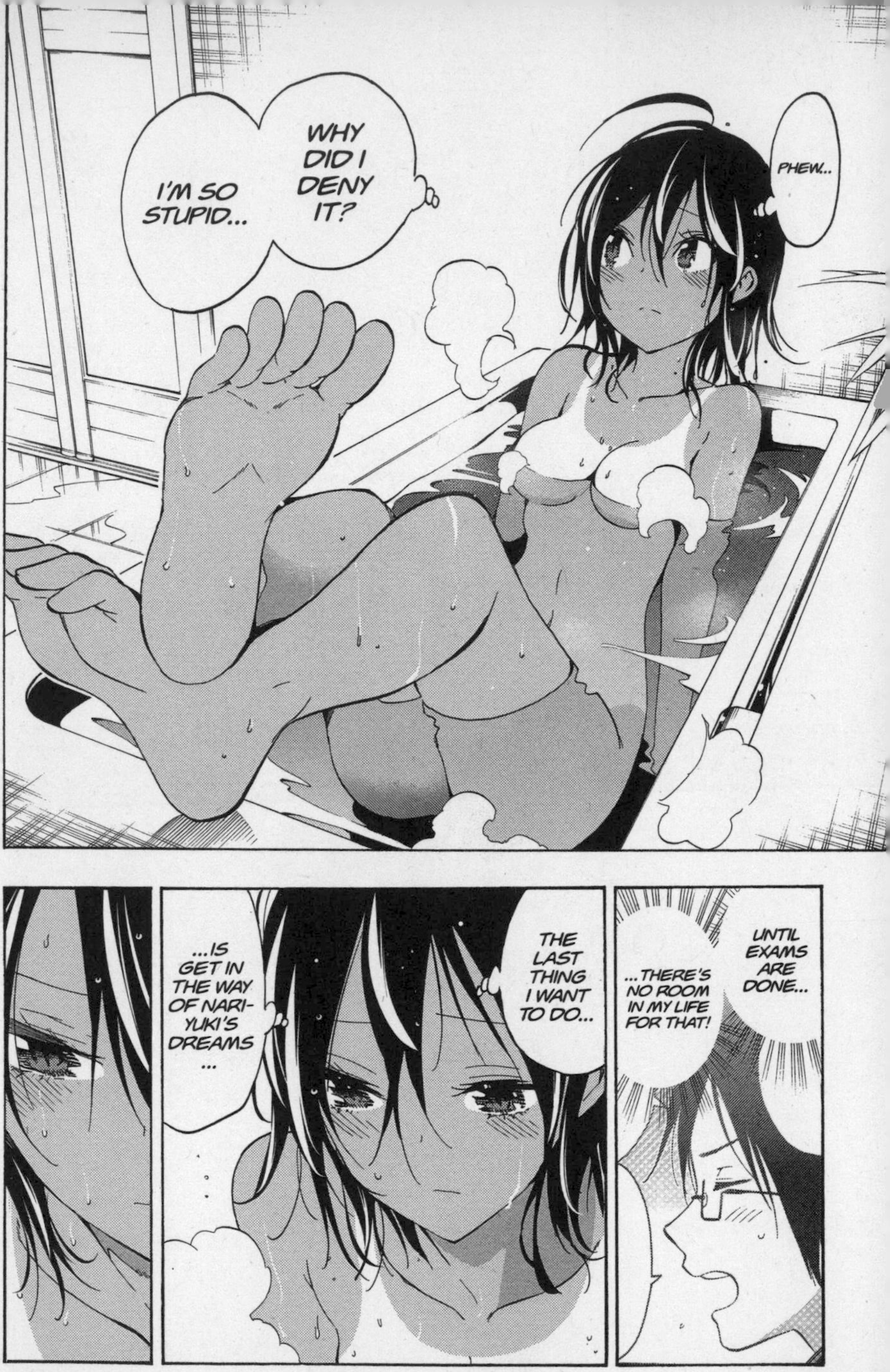
PHEW...
WHY DID I DENY IT?
I'M SO STUPID...
UNTIL EXAMS ARE DONE...
...THERE'S NO ROOM IN MY LIFE FOR THAT!
THE LAST THING I WANT TO DO...
...IS GET IN THE WAY OF NARI-YUKI'S DREAMS ...

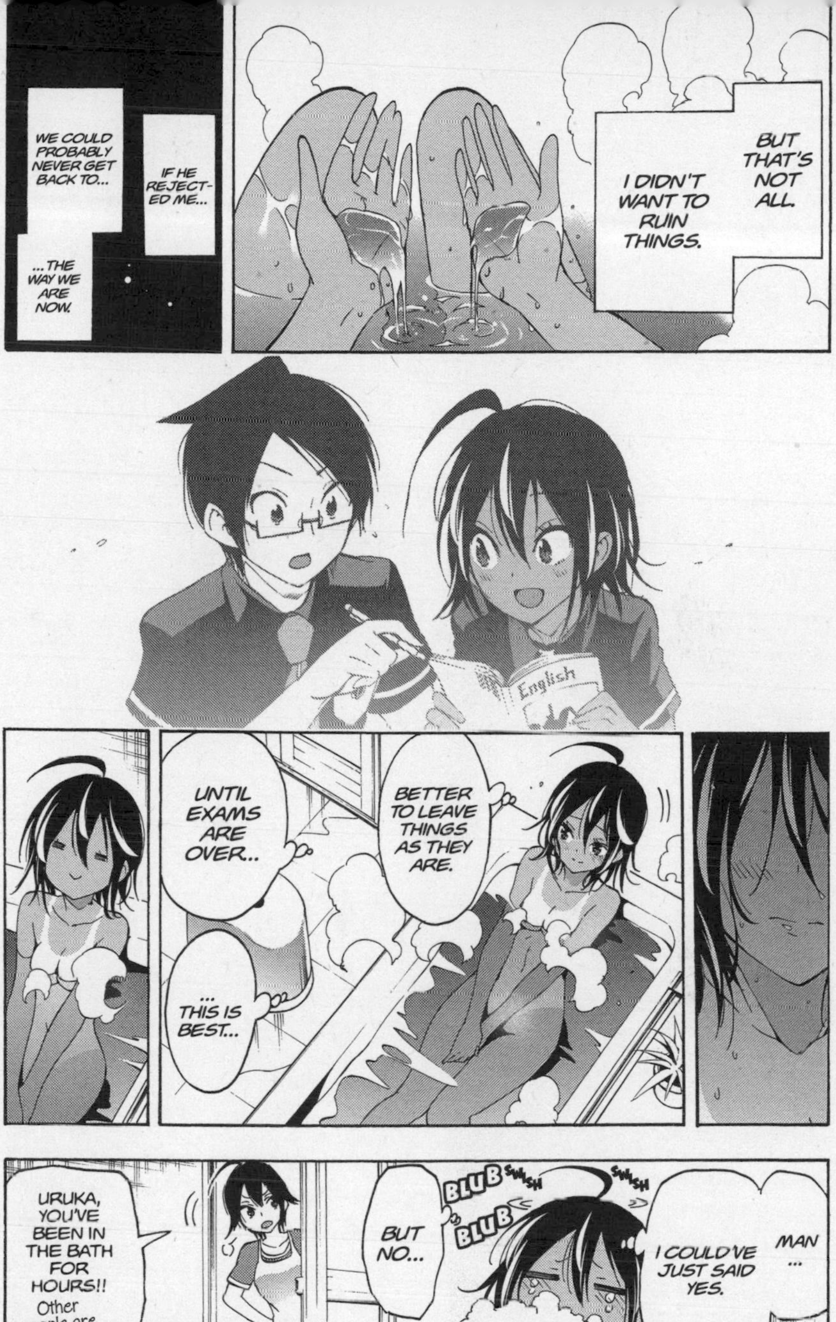
BUT THAT'S NOT ALL.
I DIDN'T WANT TO RUIN THINGS.
IF HE REJECTED ME...
WE COULD PROBABLY NEVER GET BACK TO...
...THE WAY WE ARE NOW.
English
BETTER TO LEAVE THINGS AS THEY ARE.
UNTIL EXAMS ARE OVER...
...THIS IS BEST...
MAN...
I COULD'VE JUST SAID YES.
SWISH
SWISH
BLUB
BLUB
BUT NO...
URUKA, YOU'VE BEEN IN THE BATH FOR HOURS!!
Other people are waiting!

Example of rolling all wrapped up in a futon

AAAAAAH

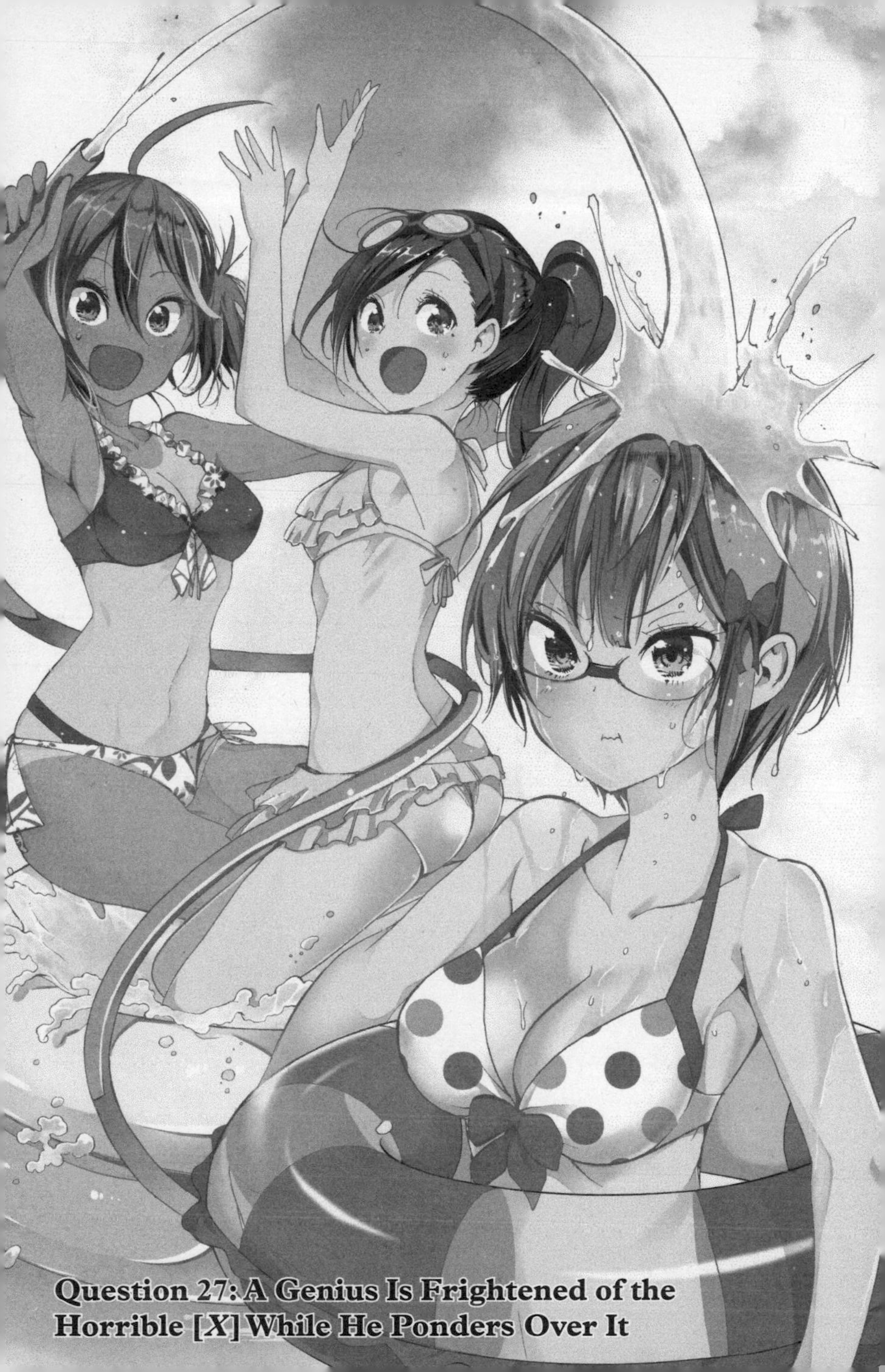

Question 27: A Genius Is Frightened of the Horrible [X] While He Ponders Over It

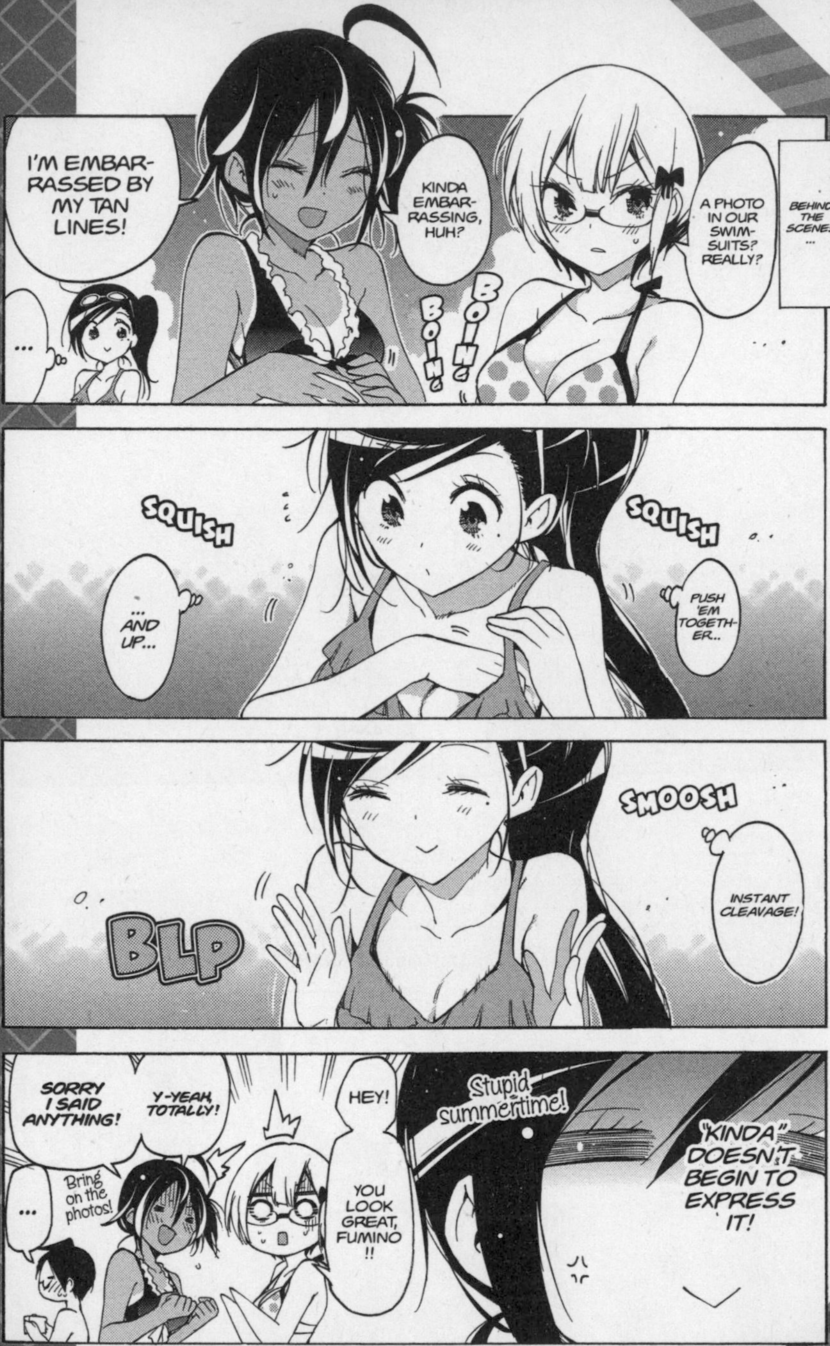
BEHIND THE SCENES ...
A PHOTO IN OUR SWIM-SUITS? REALLY?
BOING
BOING
KINDA EMBAR-RASSING, HUH?
I'M EMBAR-RASSED BY MY TAN LINES!
...
SQUISH
PUSH 'EM TOGETH-ER...
SQUISH
... AND UP...
SMOOSH
INSTANT CLEAVAGE!
BLP
"KINDA" DOESN'T BEGIN TO EXPRESS IT!
Stupid summertime!
HEY!
YOU LOOK GREAT, FUMINO !!
Y-YEAH, TOTALLY!
SORRY I SAID ANYTHING!
Bring on the photos!
...

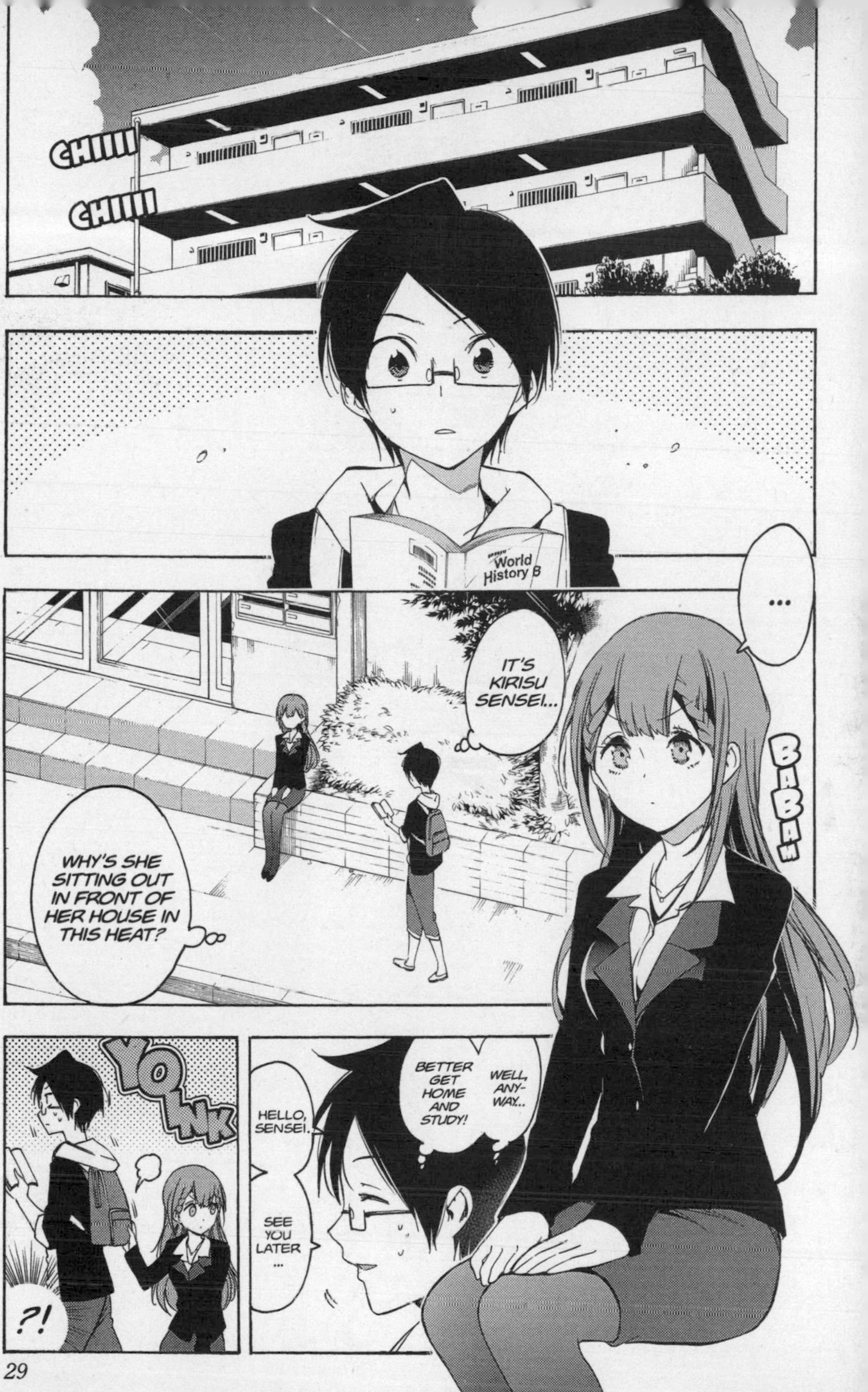
CHIIII
CHIIII
World History B
...
BABAM
IT'S KIRISU SENSEI...
WHY'S SHE SITTING OUT IN FRONT OF HER HOUSE IN THIS HEAT?
WELL, ANYWAY...
BETTER GET HOME AND STUDY!
HELLO, SENSEI...
SEE YOU LATER...
YOINK
?!

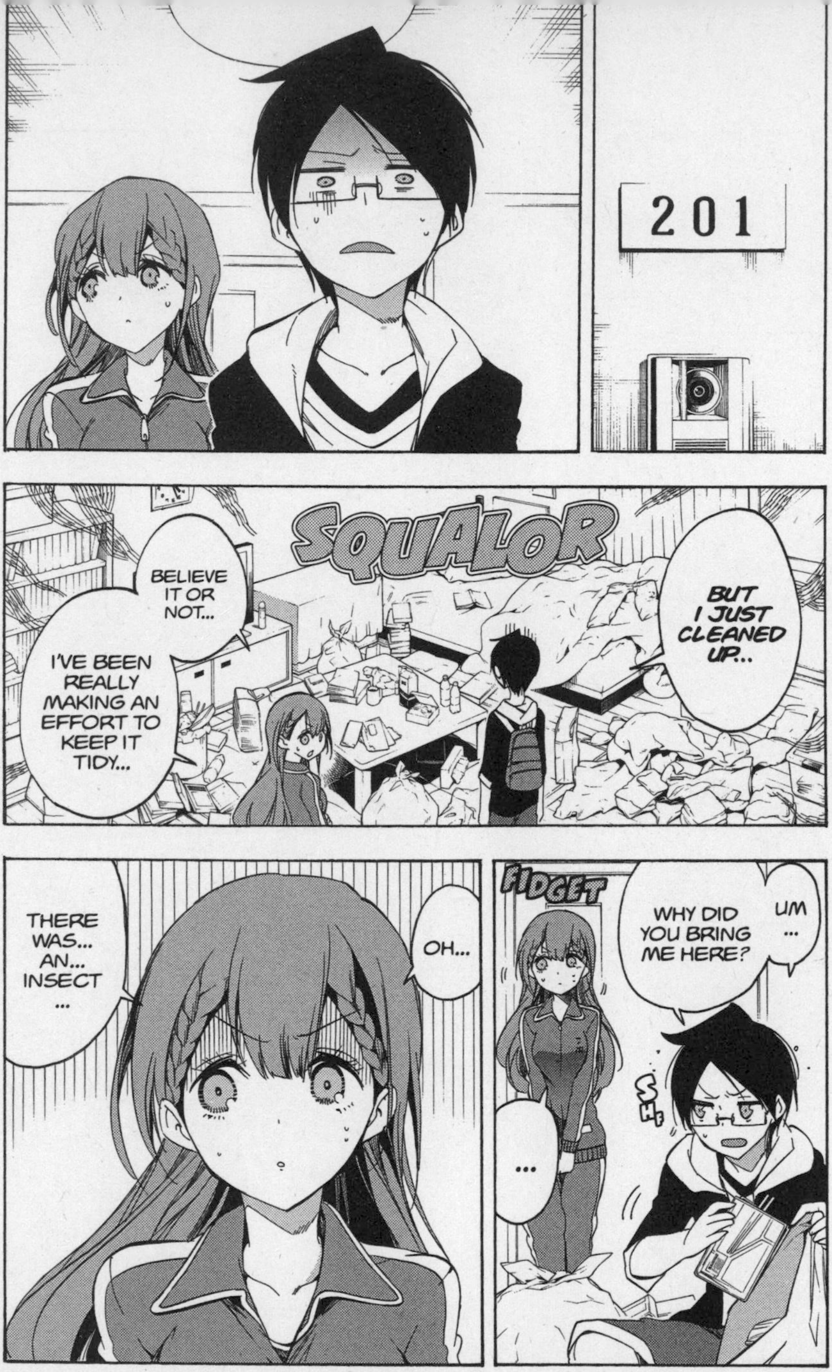
201
BUT I JUST CLEANED UP...
SQUALOR
BELIEVE IT OR NOT...
I'VE BEEN REALLY MAKING AN EFFORT TO KEEP IT TIDY...
UM ...
WHY DID YOU BRING ME HERE?
FIDGET
SHF
...
OH...
THERE WAS... AN... INSECT ...

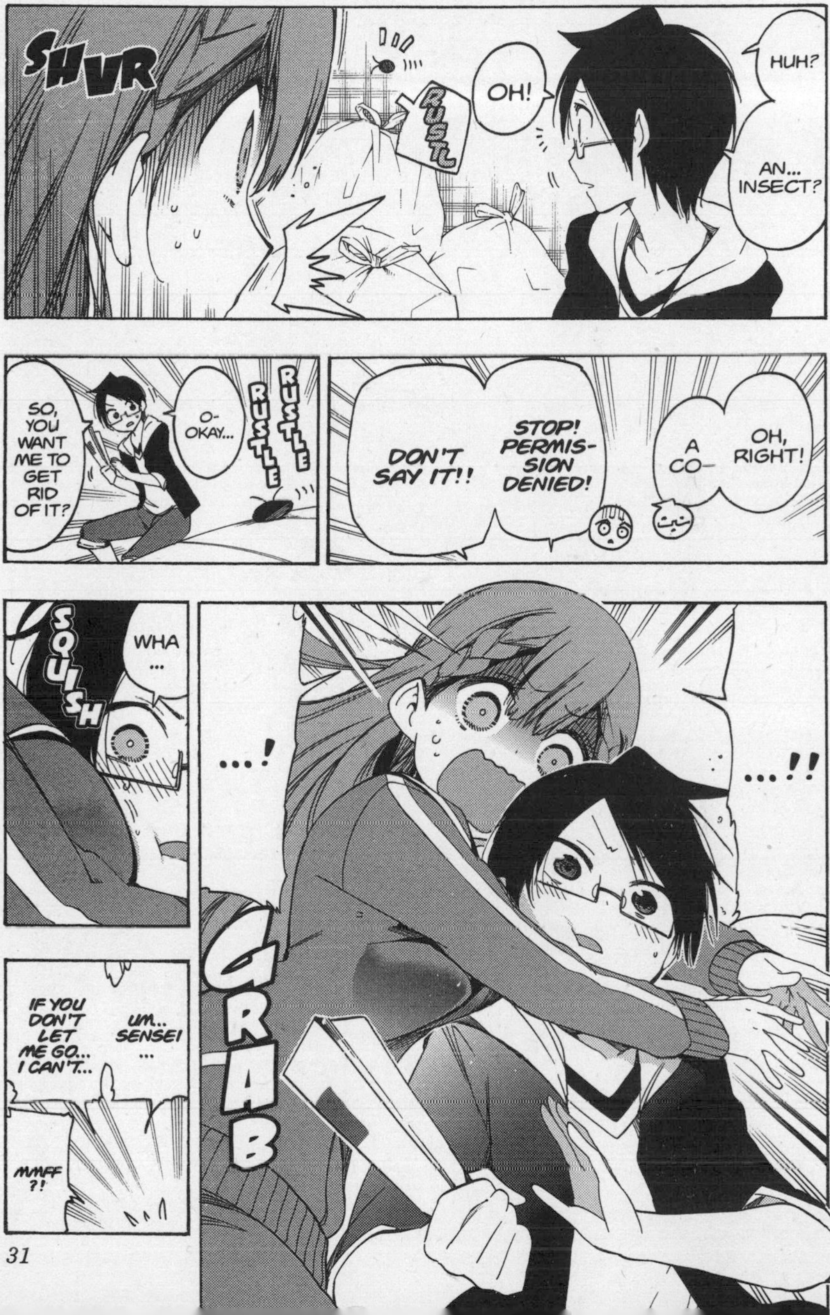
HUH?
AN... INSECT?
OH!
RUSTL
SHVR
OH, RIGHT!
A CO—
STOP! PERMISSION DENIED!
DON'T SAY IT!!
RUSTLE
RUSTLE
O-OKAY...
SO, YOU WANT ME TO GET RID OF IT?
...!!
...!
GRAB
WHA ...
SQUISH
UM... SENSEI ...
IF YOU DON'T LET ME GO... I CAN'T...
MMFF ?!

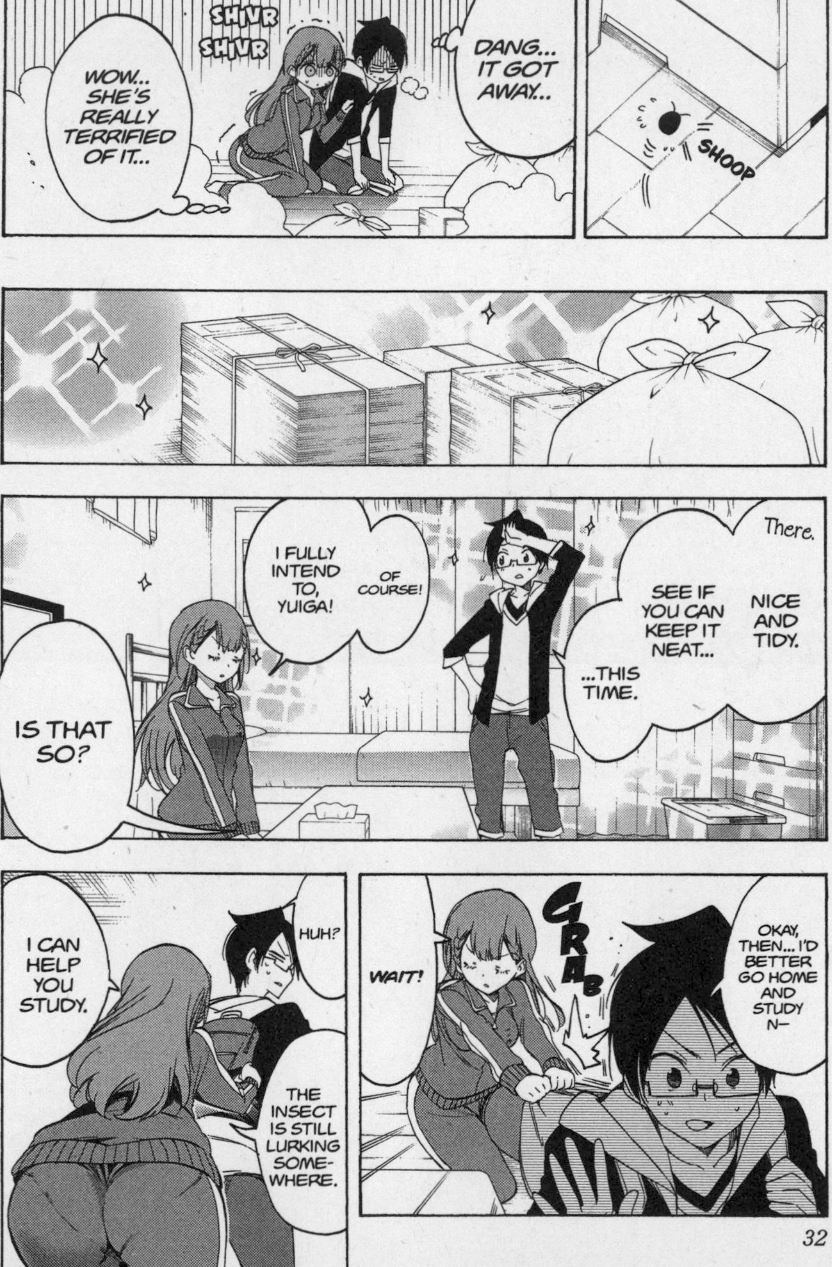
SHOOP
DANG... IT GOT AWAY...
SHIVR SHIVR
WOW... SHE'S REALLY TERRIFIED OF IT...
There.
NICE AND TIDY.
SEE IF YOU CAN KEEP IT NEAT...
...THIS TIME.
OF COURSE!
I FULLY INTEND TO, YUIGA!
IS THAT SO?
OKAY, THEN... I'D BETTER GO HOME AND STUDY N—
GRAB
WAIT!
HUH?
I CAN HELP YOU STUDY.
THE INSECT IS STILL LURKING SOMEWHERE.

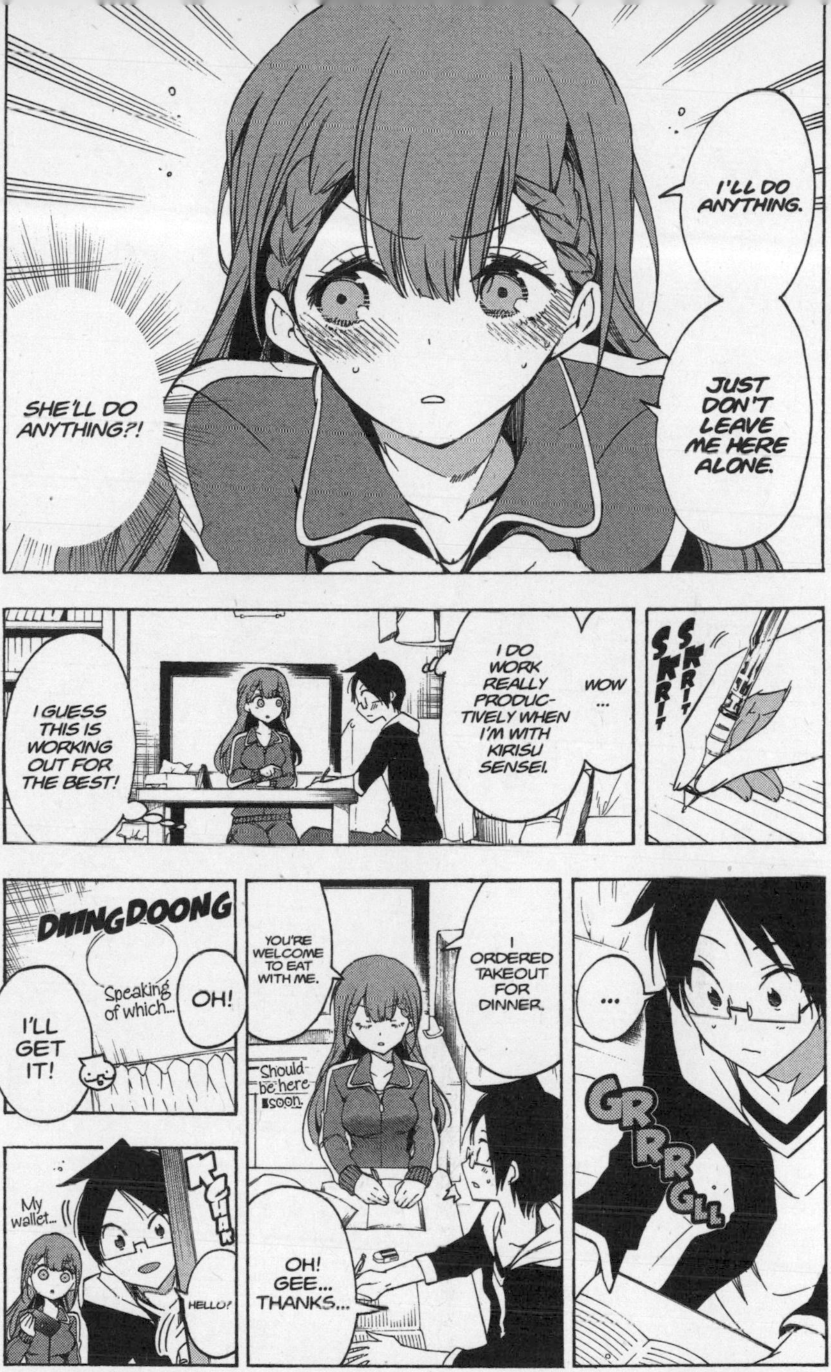
I'LL DO ANYTHING.
JUST DON'T LEAVE ME HERE ALONE.
SHE'LL DO ANYTHING?!
SKRIT SKRIT
WOW ...
I DO WORK REALLY PRODUCTIVELY WHEN I'M WITH KIRISU SENSEI.
I GUESS THIS IS WORKING OUT FOR THE BEST!
...
GRRRGLL
I ORDERED TAKEOUT FOR DINNER.
YOU'RE WELCOME TO EAT WITH ME.
Should be here soon.
OH! GEE... THANKS...
DIIINGDOONG
OH!
Speaking of which...
I'LL GET IT!
KCHAK
My wallet...
HELLO?

OGATA UDON DELIVERY!

TWO LARGE ORDERS OF SHISO LEAF TEMPURA UDON.

THAT'S ¥1,280...

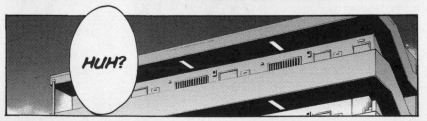

HUH?

34

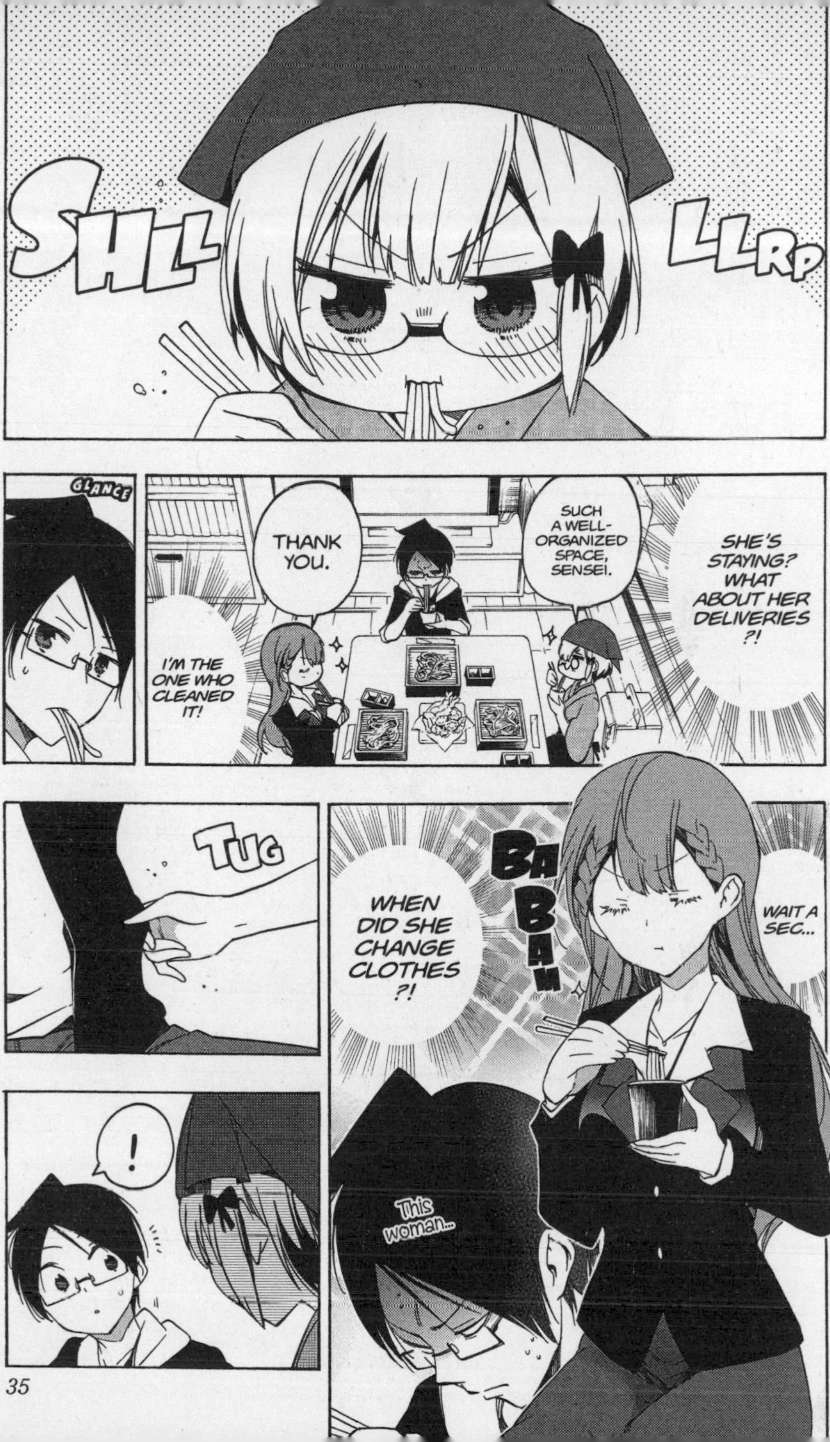

SHLL
LLRP
SHE'S STAYING? WHAT ABOUT HER DELIVERIES?!
SUCH A WELL-ORGANIZED SPACE, SENSEI.
THANK YOU.
I'M THE ONE WHO CLEANED IT!
GLANCE
WAIT A SEC...
BA BA BAM
WHEN DID SHE CHANGE CLOTHES?!
This woman...
TUG
!

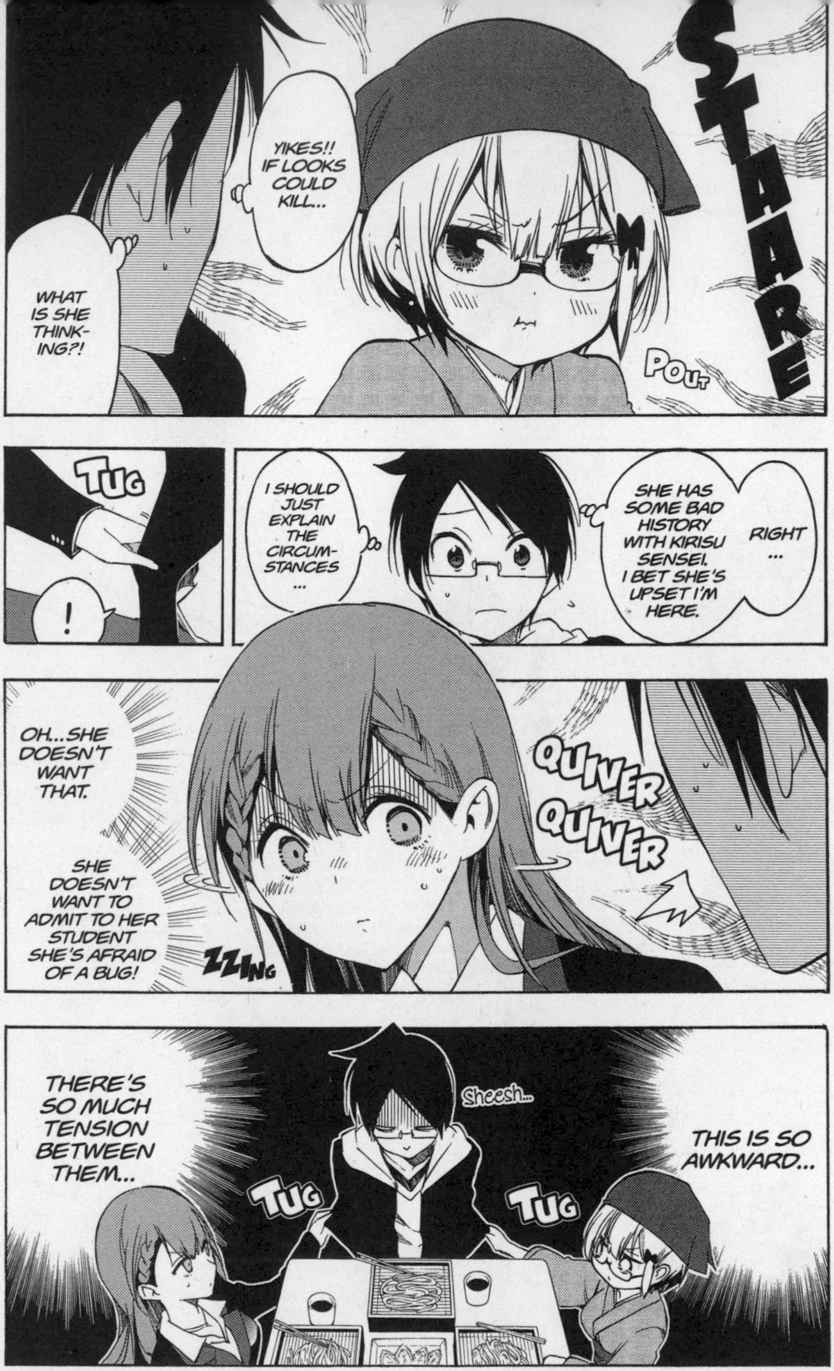
STARE
POUT
YIKES!! IF LOOKS COULD KILL...
WHAT IS SHE THINKING?!
RIGHT...
SHE HAS SOME BAD HISTORY WITH KIRISU SENSEI. I BET SHE'S UPSET I'M HERE.
I SHOULD JUST EXPLAIN THE CIRCUM-STANCES...
TUG
!
QUIVER QUIVER
OH...SHE DOESN'T WANT THAT.
SHE DOESN'T WANT TO ADMIT TO HER STUDENT SHE'S AFRAID OF A BUG!
ZZING
THIS IS SO AWKWARD...
TUG
Sheesh...
TUG
THERE'S SO MUCH TENSION BETWEEN THEM...

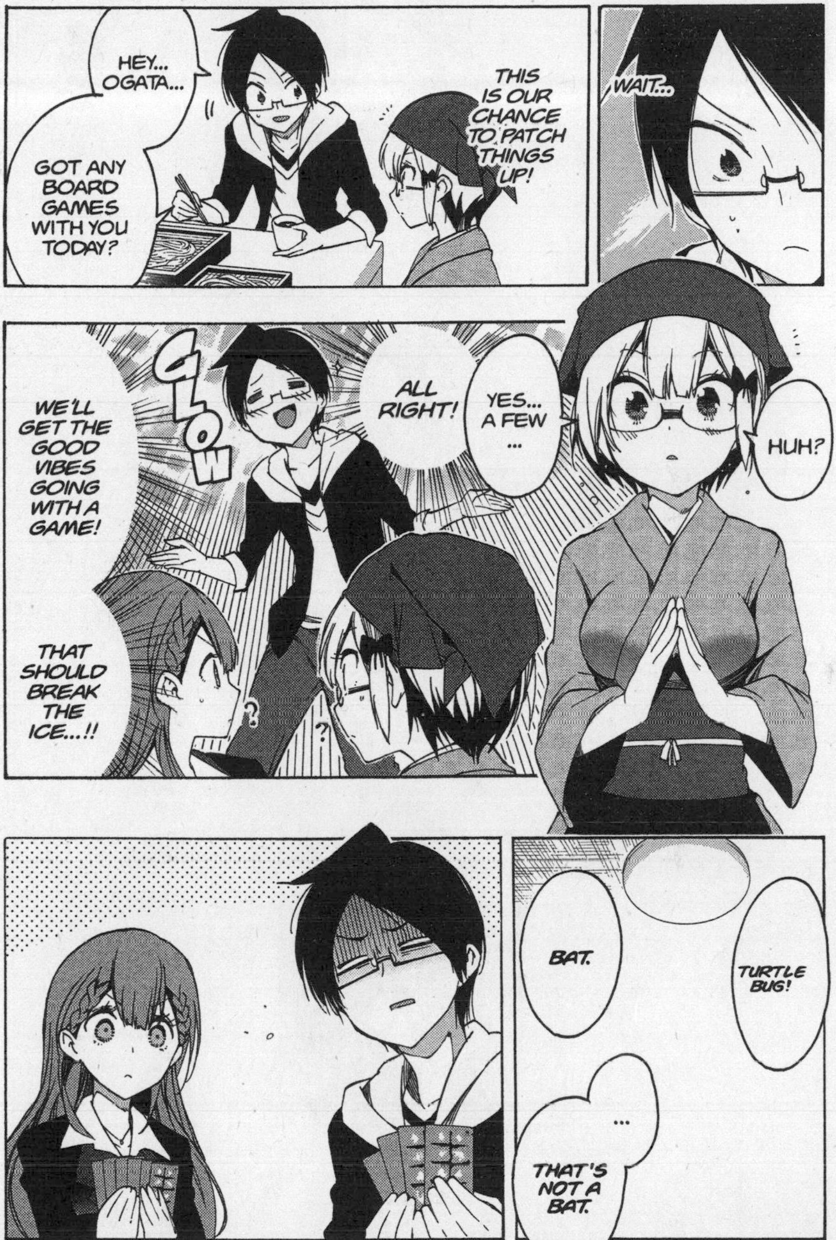
WAIT...
THIS IS OUR CHANCE TO PATCH THINGS UP!
HEY... OGATA...
GOT ANY BOARD GAMES WITH YOU TODAY?
HUH?
YES... A FEW ...
ALL RIGHT!
GLOW
WE'LL GET THE GOOD VIBES GOING WITH A GAME!
THAT SHOULD BREAK THE ICE...!!
BAT.
TURTLE BUG!
...
THAT'S NOT A BAT.

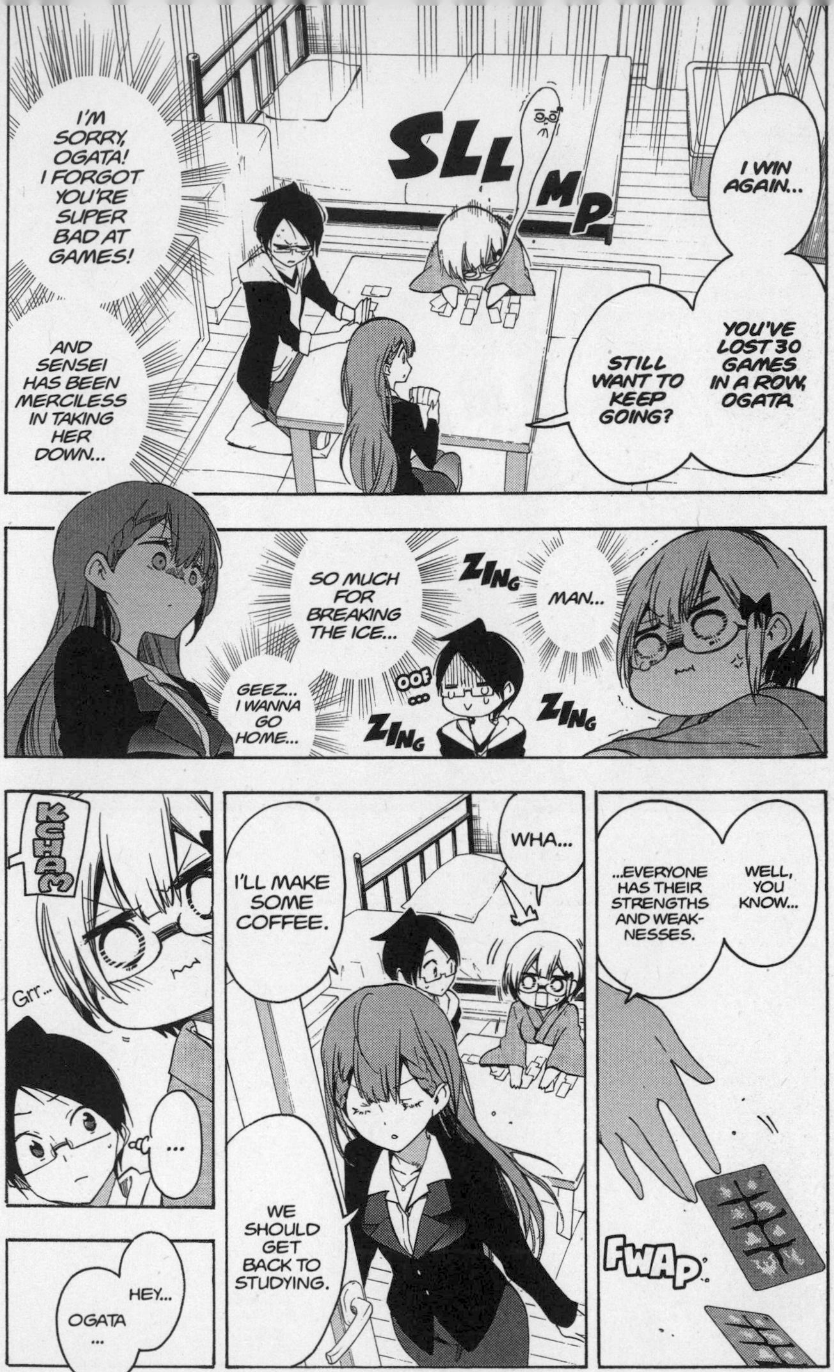
I WIN AGAIN...
YOU'VE LOST 30 GAMES IN A ROW, OGATA.
STILL WANT TO KEEP GOING?
SLLMP
I'M SORRY, OGATA! I FORGOT YOU'RE SUPER BAD AT GAMES!
AND SENSEI HAS BEEN MERCILESS IN TAKING HER DOWN...
MAN...
ZING
SO MUCH FOR BREAKING THE ICE...
OOF...
ZING
ZING
GEEZ... I WANNA GO HOME...
WELL, YOU KNOW...
...EVERYONE HAS THEIR STRENGTHS AND WEAK-NESSES.
FWAP
WHA...
I'LL MAKE SOME COFFEE.
WE SHOULD GET BACK TO STUDYING.
KCHAM
Grr...
...
HEY... OGATA ...

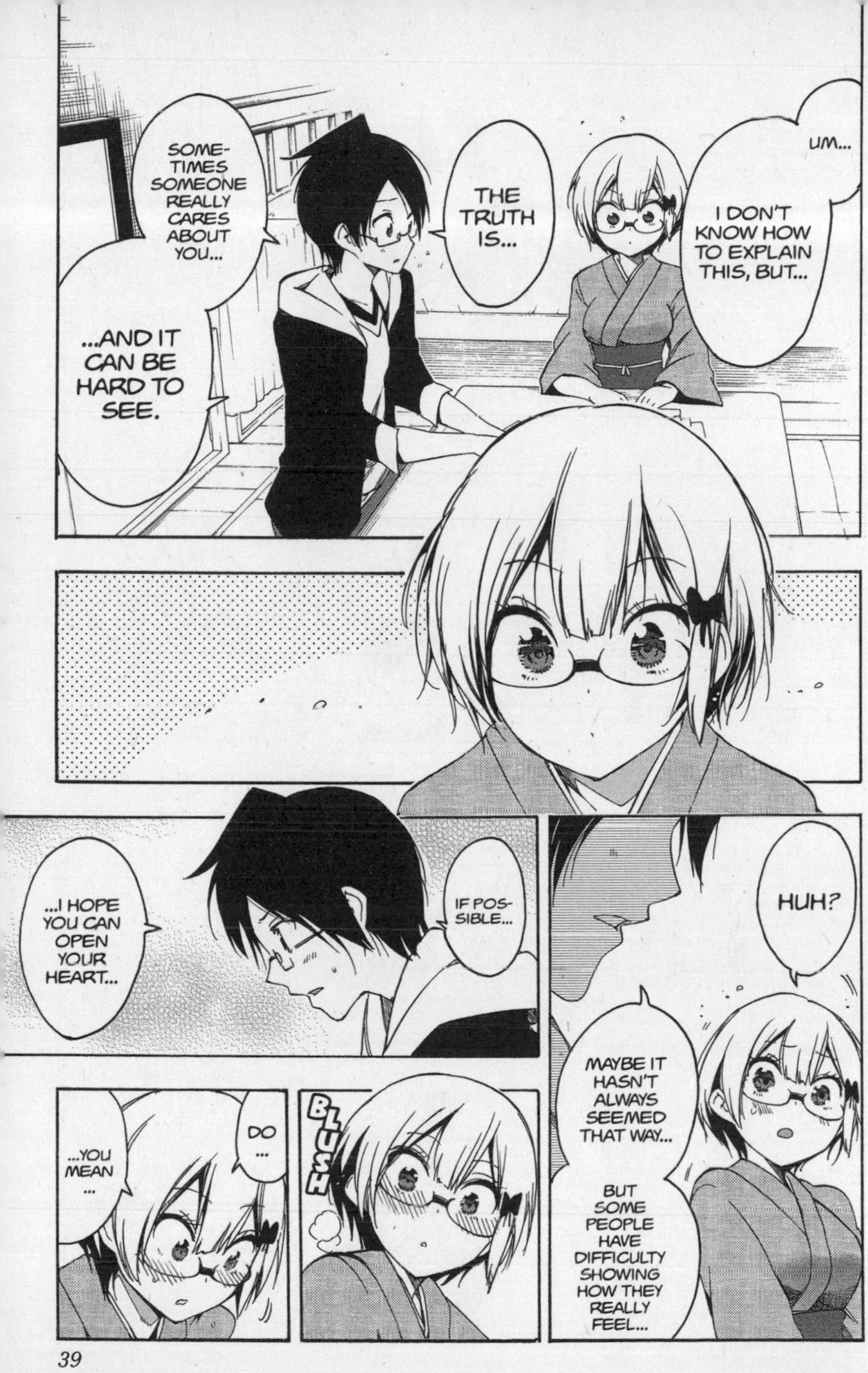
UM... I DON'T KNOW HOW TO EXPLAIN THIS, BUT...
THE TRUTH IS...
SOME-TIMES SOMEONE REALLY CARES ABOUT YOU...
...AND IT CAN BE HARD TO SEE.
HUH?
MAYBE IT HASN'T ALWAYS SEEMED THAT WAY...
BUT SOME PEOPLE HAVE DIFFICULTY SHOWING HOW THEY REALLY FEEL...
IF POS-SIBLE...
...I HOPE YOU CAN OPEN YOUR HEART...
BLUSH
DO...
...YOU MEAN...

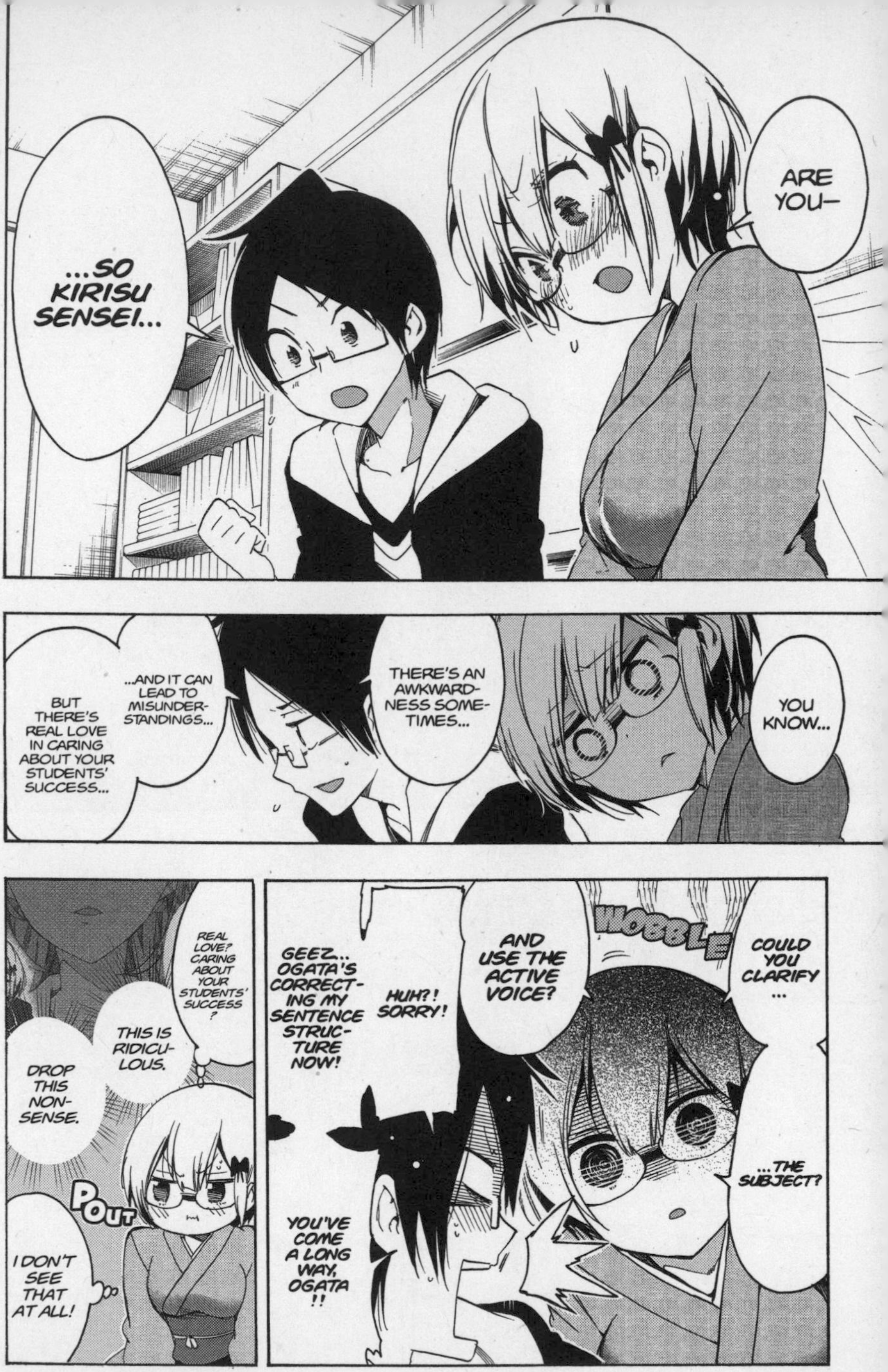
ARE YOU—
...SO KIRISU SENSEI...
YOU KNOW...
THERE'S AN AWKWARDNESS SOMETIMES...
...AND IT CAN LEAD TO MISUNDERSTANDINGS...
BUT THERE'S REAL LOVE IN CARING ABOUT YOUR STUDENTS' SUCCESS...
COULD YOU CLARIFY ...
...THE SUBJECT?
WOBBLE
AND USE THE ACTIVE VOICE?
HUH?! SORRY!
GEEZ... OGATA'S CORRECTING MY SENTENCE STRUCTURE NOW!
YOU'VE COME A LONG WAY, OGATA!!
REAL LOVE? CARING ABOUT YOUR STUDENTS' SUCCESS?
THIS IS RIDICULOUS.
DROP THIS NONSENSE.
POUT
I DON'T SEE THAT AT ALL!

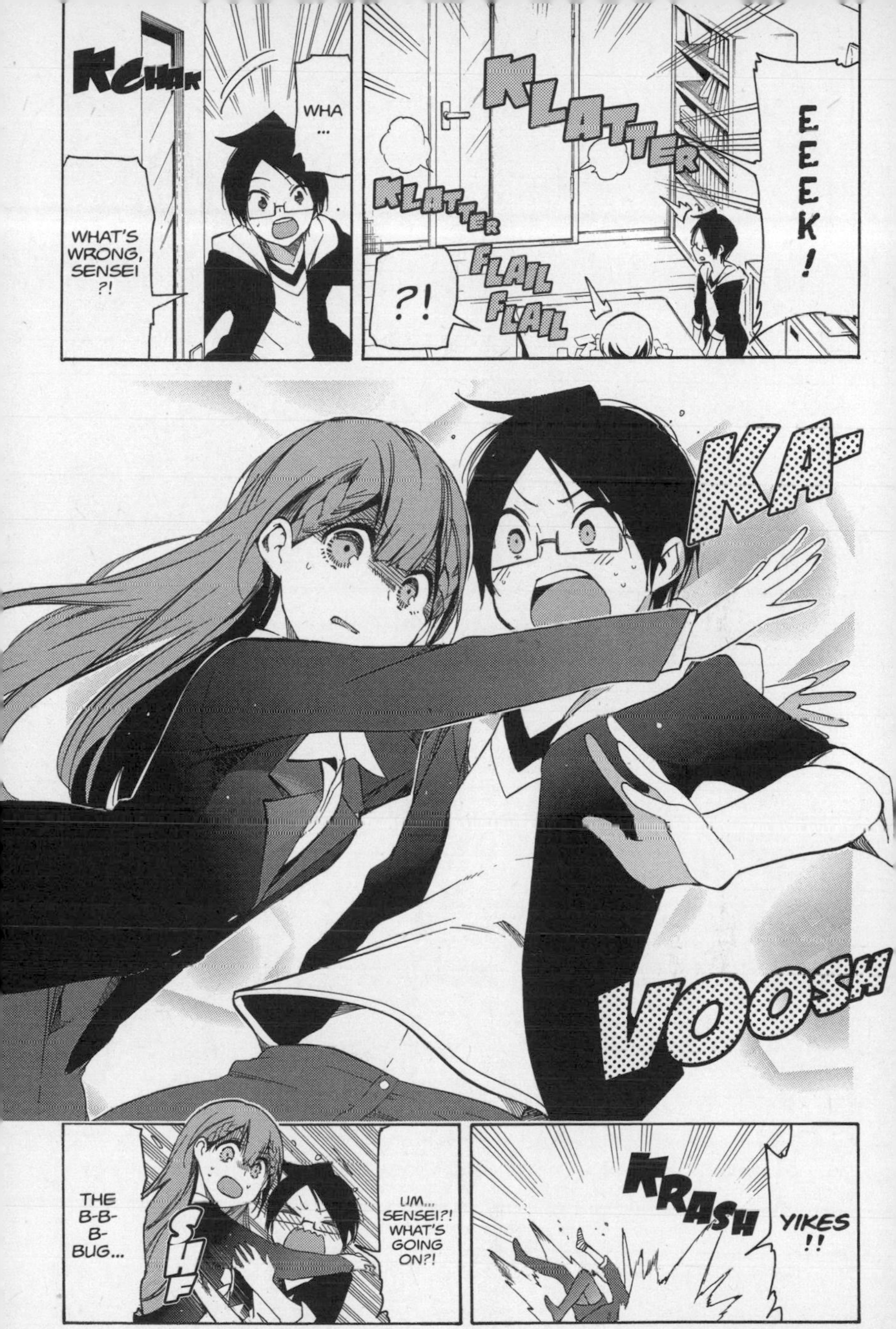
EEEEK!
KLATTER
KLATTER
FLAIL FLAIL
?!
WHA...
KCHAK
WHAT'S WRONG, SENSEI?!
KA-
VOOSH
YIKES!!
KRASH
UM... SENSEI?! WHAT'S GOING ON?!
SHF
THE B-B-B-BUG...

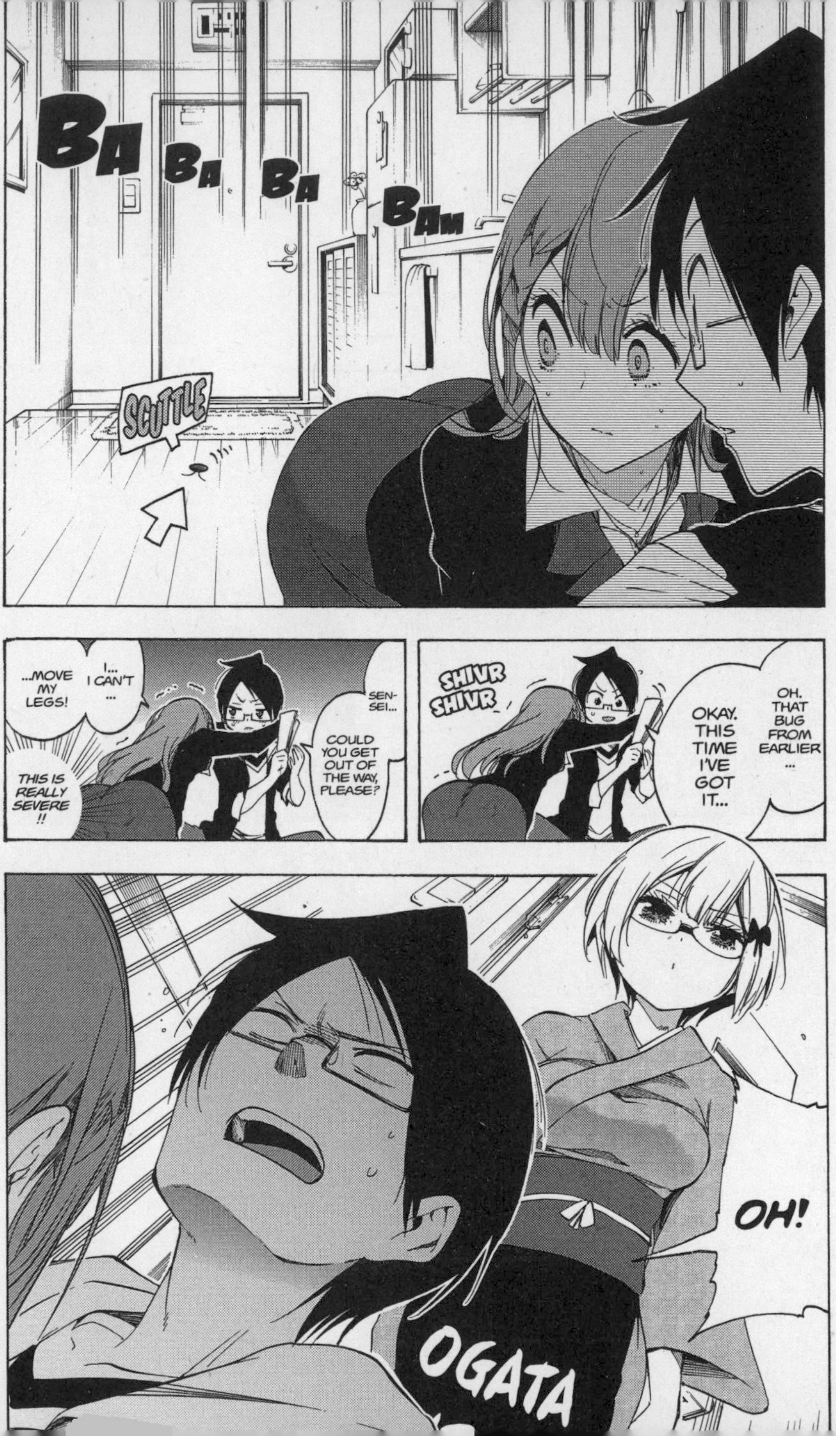
BA BA BA BAM
SCUTTLE
OH. THAT BUG FROM EARLIER ...
OKAY. THIS TIME I'VE GOT IT...
SHIVR SHIVR
SEN-SEI...
COULD YOU GET OUT OF THE WAY, PLEASE?
I... I CAN'T ...
...MOVE MY LEGS!
THIS IS REALLY SEVERE !!
OH!
OGATA

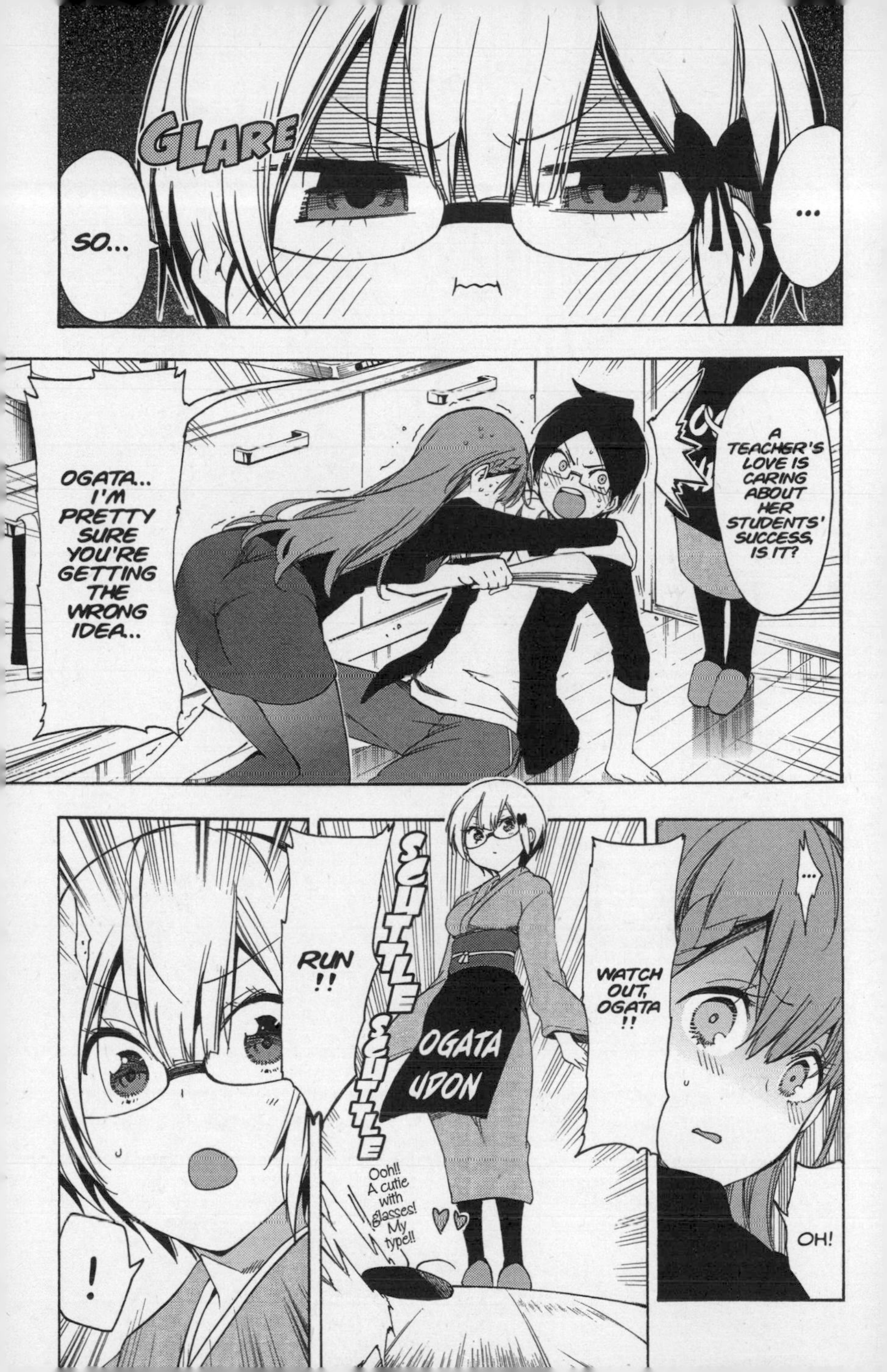
...
GLARE
SO...
A TEACHER'S LOVE IS CARING ABOUT HER STUDENTS' SUCCESS, IS IT?
OGATA... I'M PRETTY SURE YOU'RE GETTING THE WRONG IDEA...
...
WATCH OUT, OGATA!!
OH!
SCUTTLE SCUTTLE
OGATA UDON
Ooh!! A cutie with glasses! My type!!
RUN!!
!

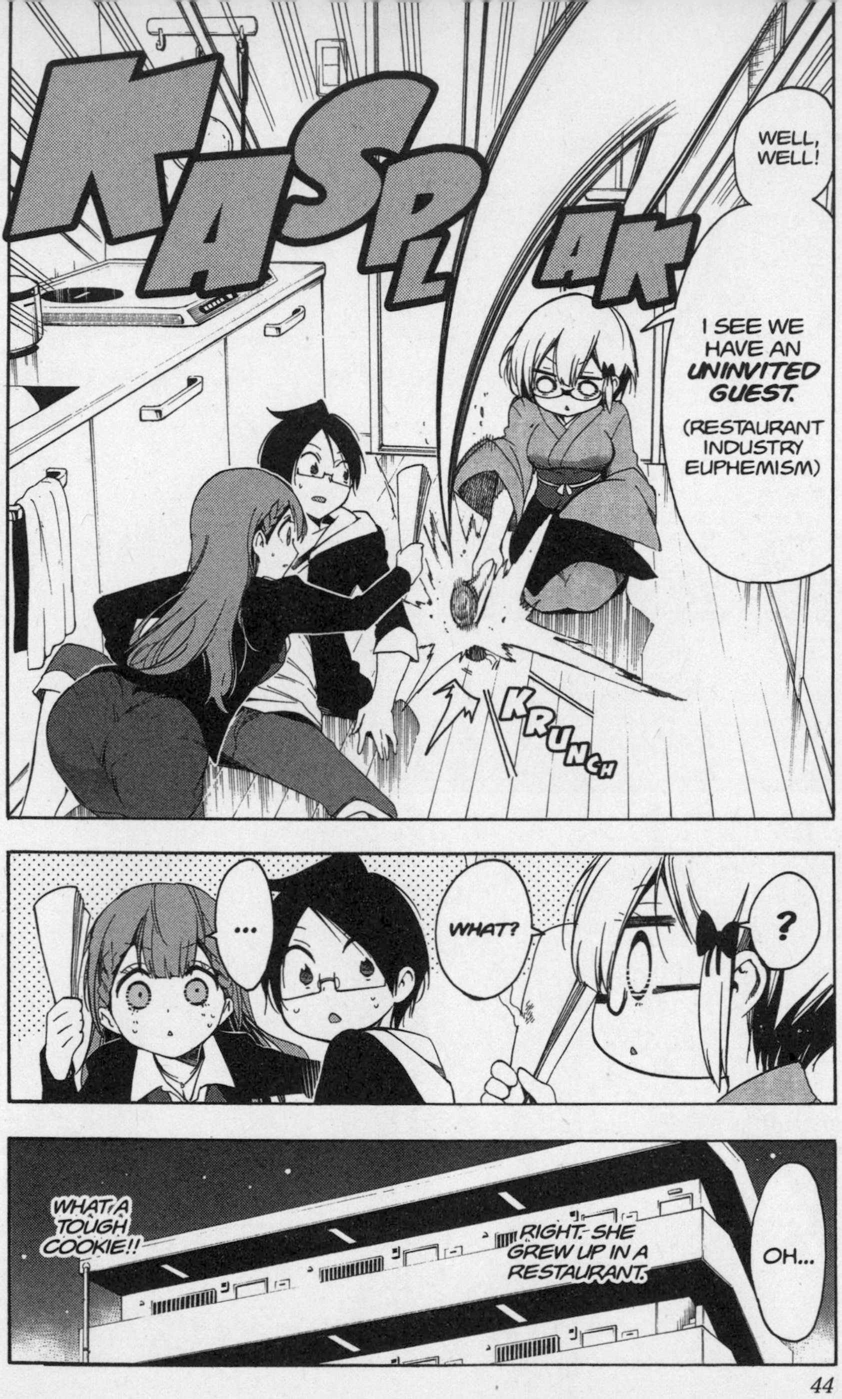
KASPLAK
WELL, WELL!
I SEE WE HAVE AN *UNINVITED GUEST.*
(RESTAURANT INDUSTRY EUPHEMISM)
KRUNCH
?
WHAT?
...
OH...
RIGHT. SHE GREW UP IN A RESTAURANT.
WHAT A TOUGH COOKIE!!

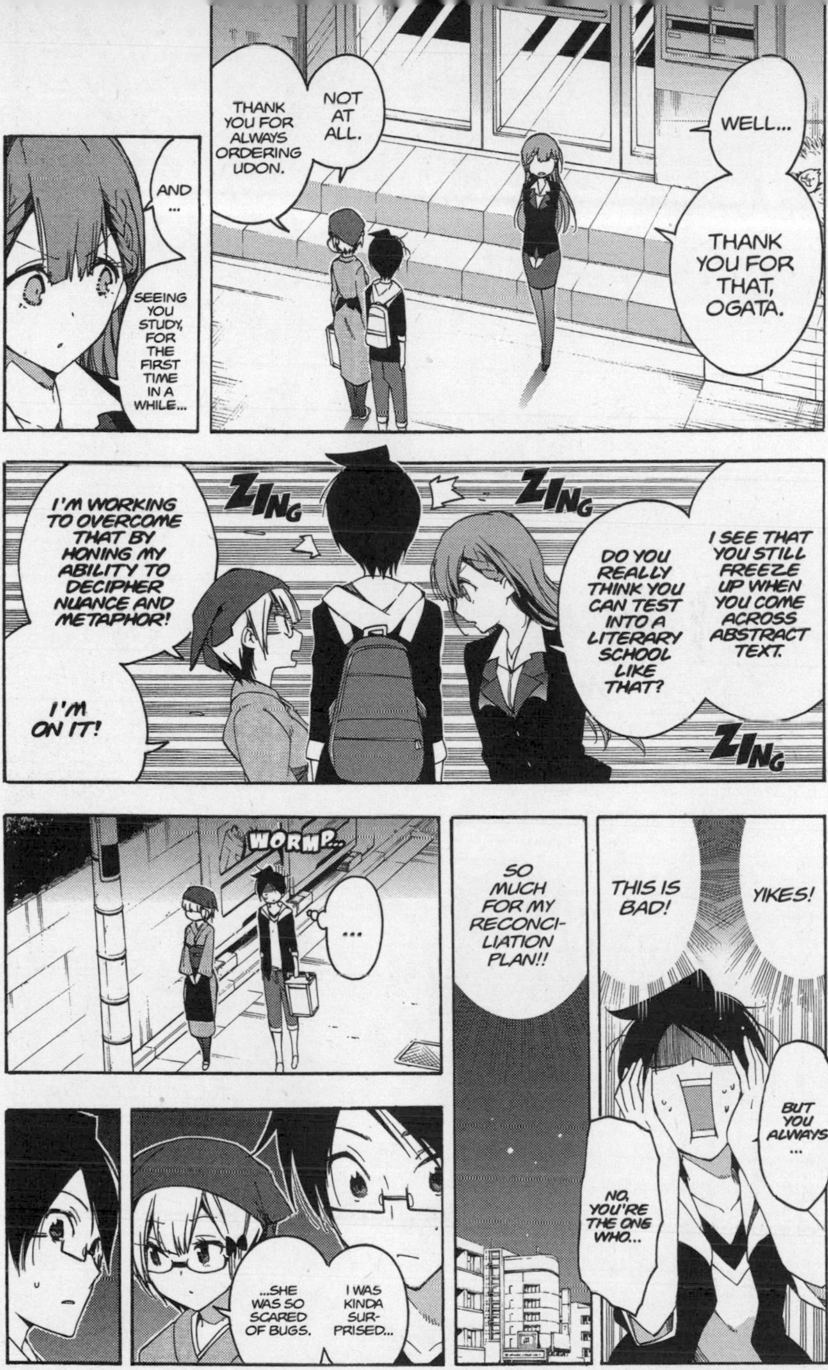
WELL...
THANK YOU FOR THAT, OGATA.
NOT AT ALL.
THANK YOU FOR ALWAYS ORDERING UDON.
AND ...
SEEING YOU STUDY, FOR THE FIRST TIME IN A WHILE...
ZING
ZING
I SEE THAT YOU STILL FREEZE UP WHEN YOU COME ACROSS ABSTRACT TEXT.
DO YOU REALLY THINK YOU CAN TEST INTO A LITERARY SCHOOL LIKE THAT?
ZING
I'M WORKING TO OVERCOME THAT BY HONING MY ABILITY TO DECIPHER NUANCE AND METAPHOR!
I'M ON IT!
YIKES!
THIS IS BAD!
BUT YOU ALWAYS ...
NO, YOU'RE THE ONE WHO...
SO MUCH FOR MY RECONCILIATION PLAN!!
WORMP...
...
I WAS KINDA SUR-PRISED...
...SHE WAS SO SCARED OF BUGS.

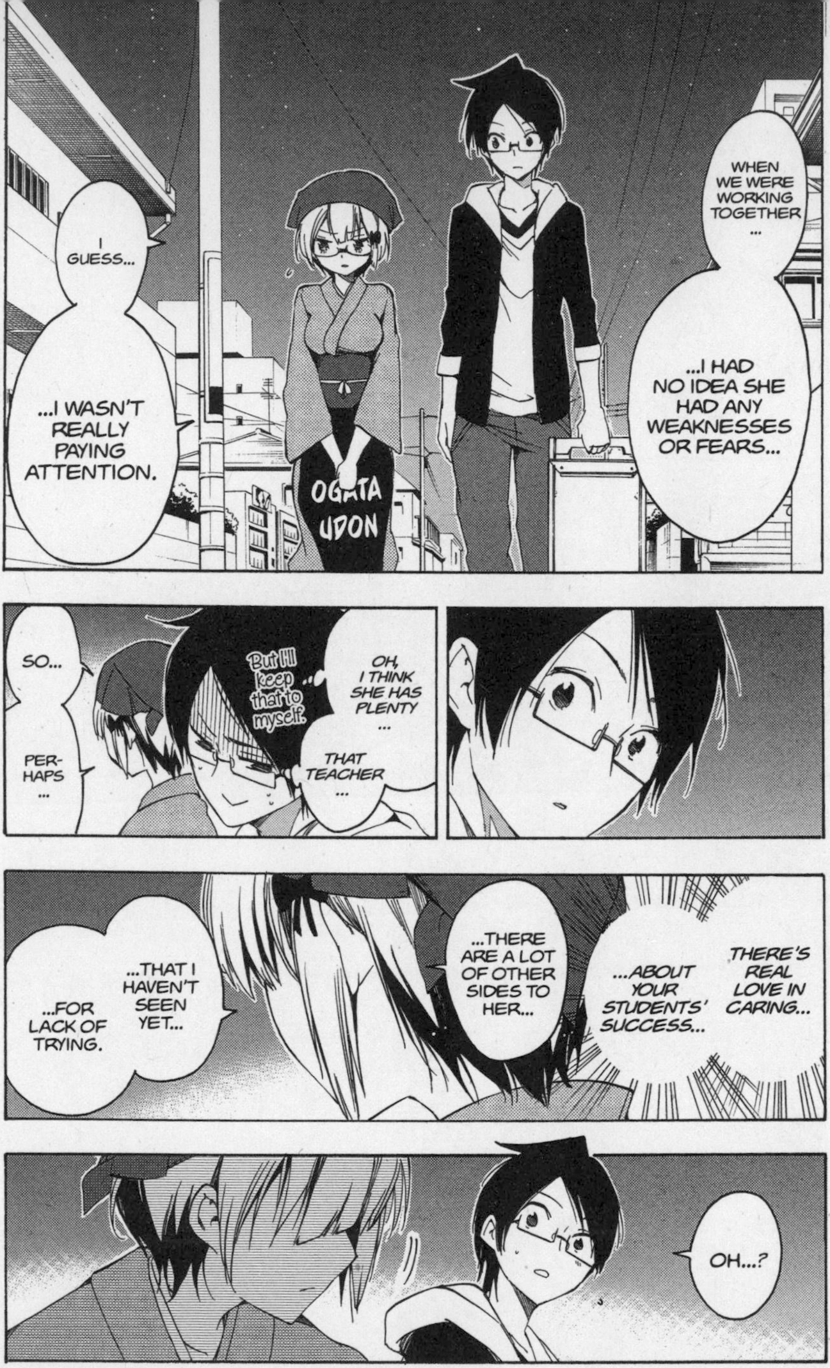
WHEN WE WERE WORKING TOGETHER ...
...I HAD NO IDEA SHE HAD ANY WEAKNESSES OR FEARS...
I GUESS...
...I WASN'T REALLY PAYING ATTENTION.
OGATA UDON
OH, I THINK SHE HAS PLENTY ...
THAT TEACHER ...
But I'll keep that to myself.
SO...
PER-HAPS ...
THERE'S REAL LOVE IN CARING...
...ABOUT YOUR STUDENTS' SUCCESS...
...THERE ARE A LOT OF OTHER SIDES TO HER...
...THAT I HAVEN'T SEEN YET...
...FOR LACK OF TRYING.
OH...?

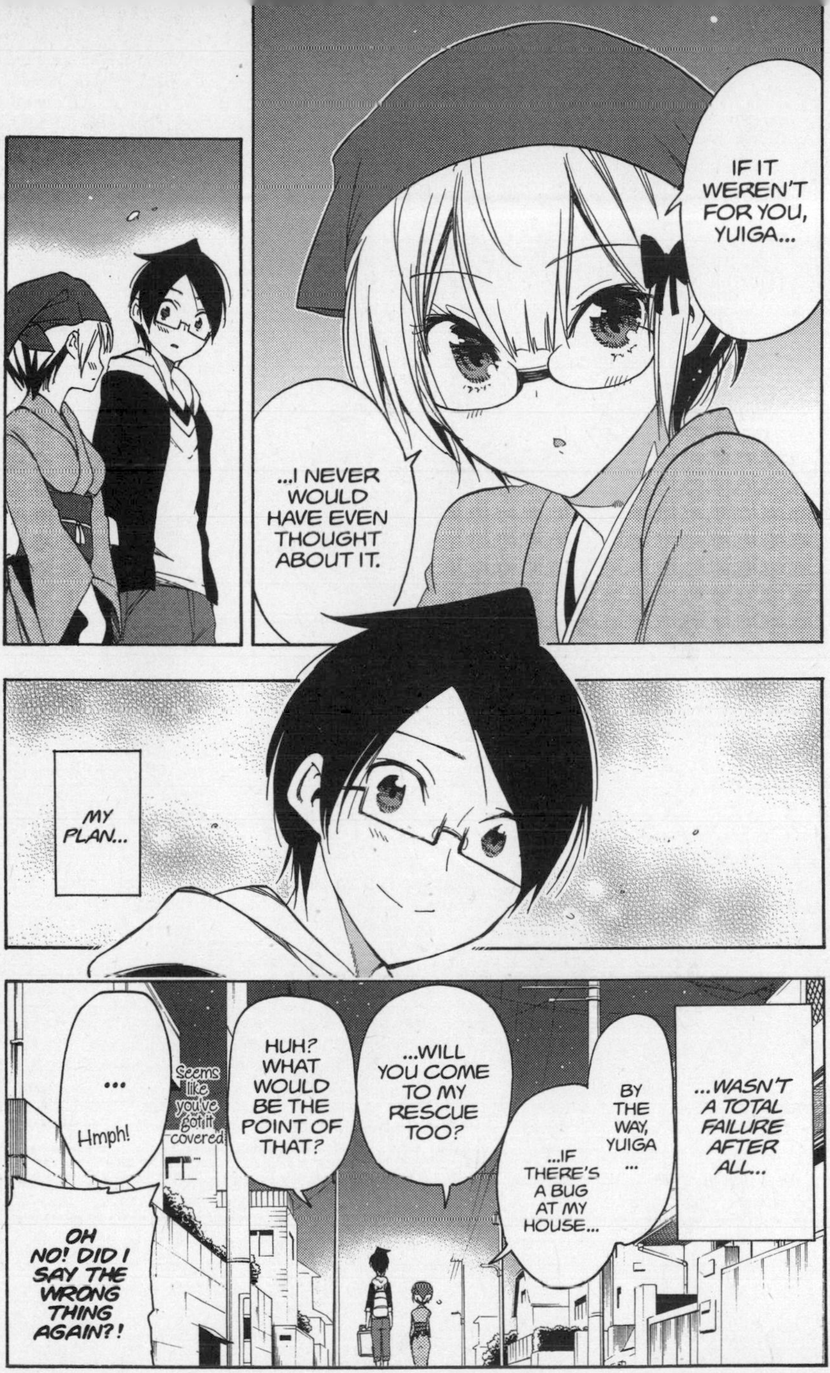
IF IT WEREN'T FOR YOU, YUIGA...
...I NEVER WOULD HAVE EVEN THOUGHT ABOUT IT.
MY PLAN...
...WASN'T A TOTAL FAILURE AFTER ALL...
BY THE WAY, YUIGA ...
...IF THERE'S A BUG AT MY HOUSE...
...WILL YOU COME TO MY RESCUE TOO?
HUH? WHAT WOULD BE THE POINT OF THAT?
Seems like you've got it covered...
...
Hmph!
OH NO! DID I SAY THE WRONG THING AGAIN?!

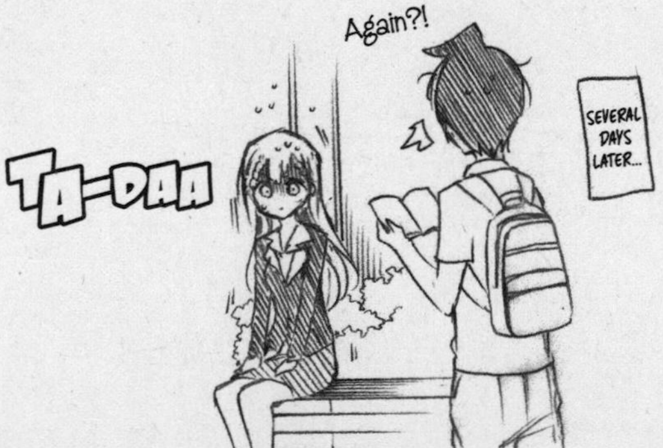
SEVERAL DAYS LATER...
Again?!
TA-DAA

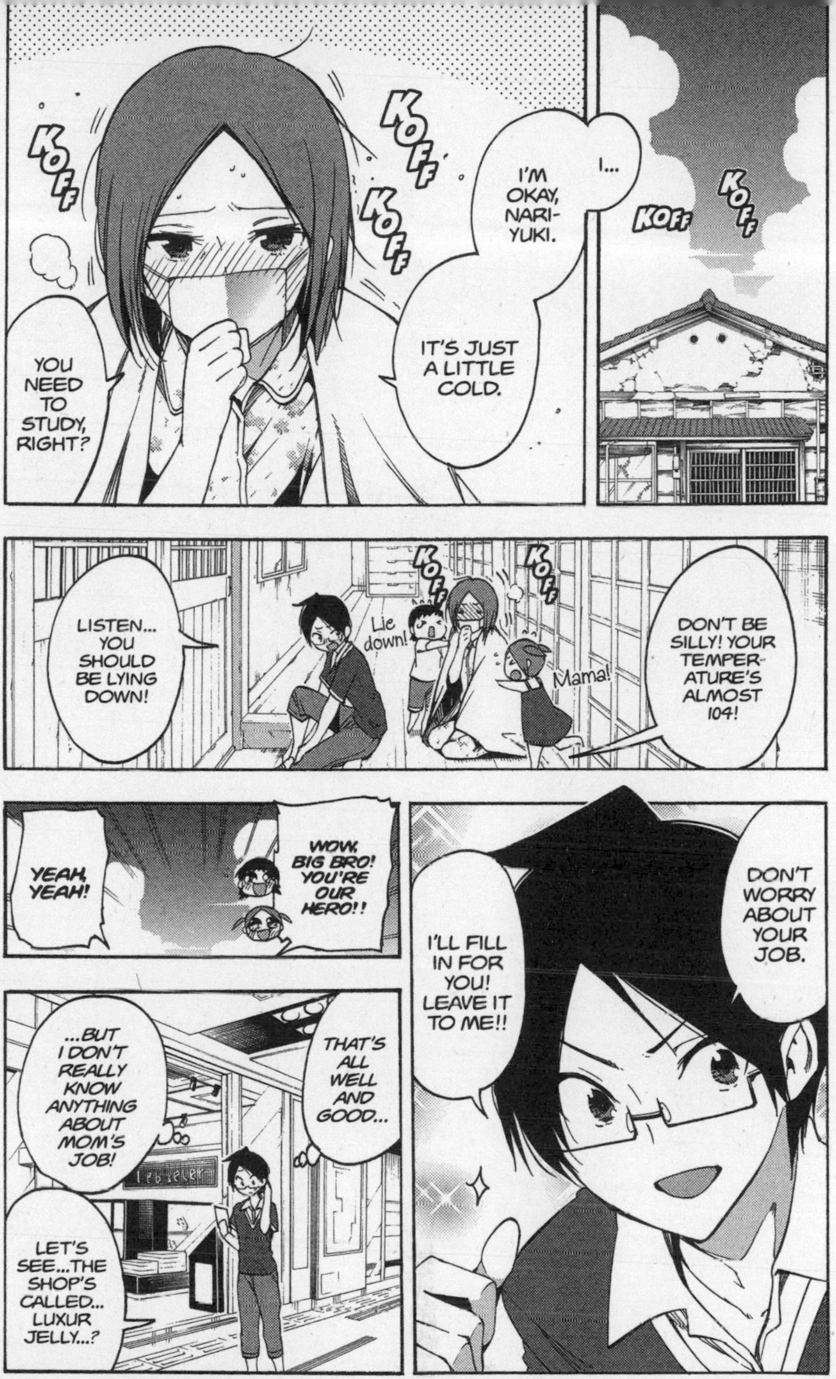
I...
KOFF
KOFF
I'M OKAY, NARI-YUKI.
IT'S JUST A LITTLE COLD.
KOFF
KOFF
KOFF
YOU NEED TO STUDY, RIGHT?
DON'T BE SILLY! YOUR TEMPER-ATURE'S ALMOST 104!
KOFF
Mama!
KOFF
Lie down!
LISTEN... YOU SHOULD BE LYING DOWN!
DON'T WORRY ABOUT YOUR JOB.
I'LL FILL IN FOR YOU! LEAVE IT TO ME!!
WOW, BIG BRO! YOU'RE OUR HERO!!
YEAH, YEAH!
THAT'S ALL WELL AND GOOD...
...BUT I DON'T REALLY KNOW ANYTHING ABOUT MOM'S JOB!
LET'S SEE...THE SHOP'S CALLED... LUXUR JELLY...?

Question 28: He Struggles with [*X*] in a Forbidden Zone

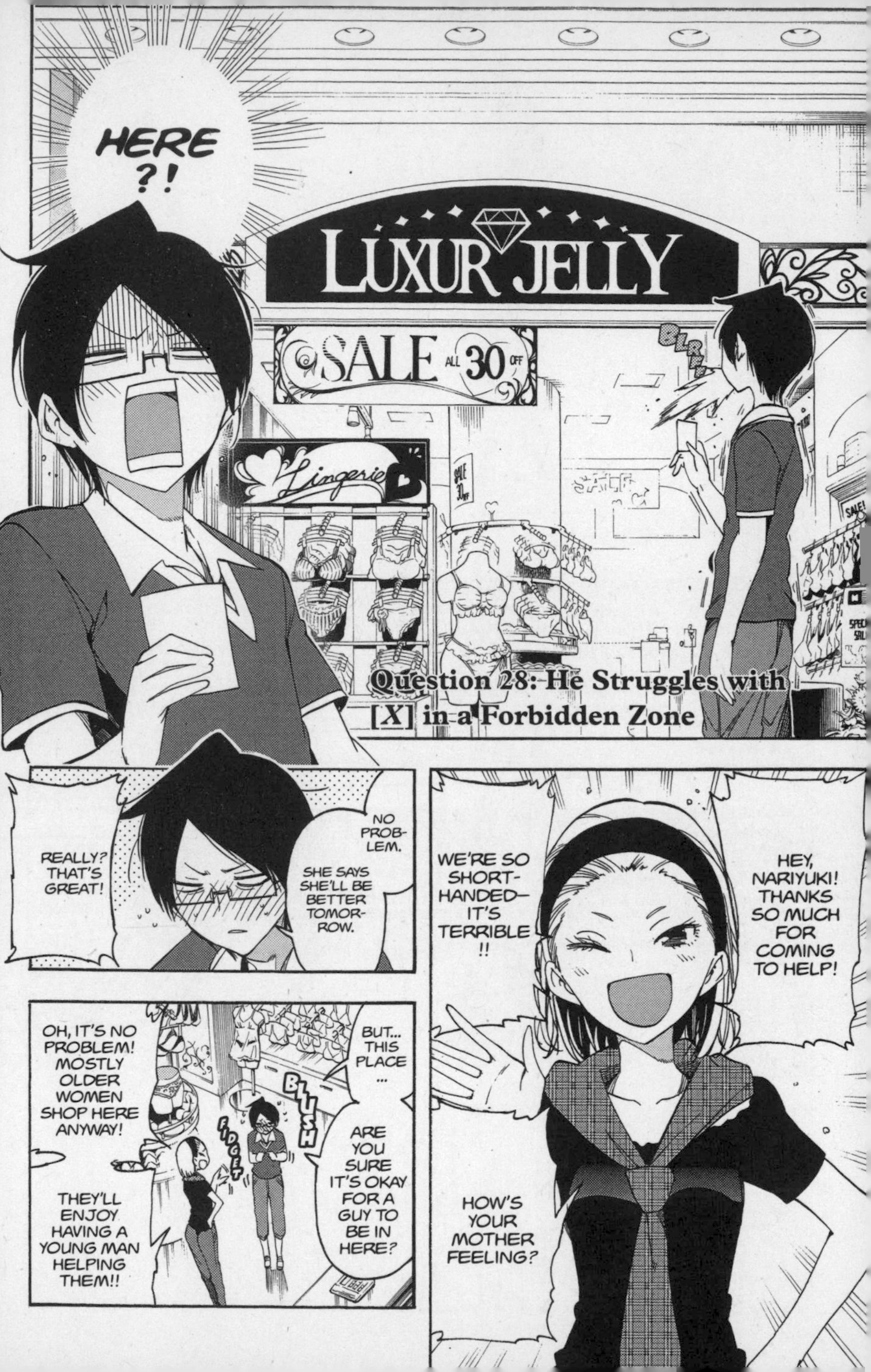
HERE ?!
LUXUR JELLY
SALE ALL 30 OFF
Lingerie
Question 28: He Struggles with [X] in a Forbidden Zone
HEY, NARIYUKI! THANKS SO MUCH FOR COMING TO HELP!
WE'RE SO SHORT-HANDED— IT'S TERRIBLE !!
HOW'S YOUR MOTHER FEELING?
NO PROB-LEM.
SHE SAYS SHE'LL BE BETTER TOMOR-ROW.
REALLY? THAT'S GREAT!
BUT... THIS PLACE ...
ARE YOU SURE IT'S OKAY FOR A GUY TO BE IN HERE?
BLUSH
FIDGET
OH, IT'S NO PROBLEM! MOSTLY OLDER WOMEN SHOP HERE ANYWAY!
THEY'LL ENJOY HAVING A YOUNG MAN HELPING THEM!!

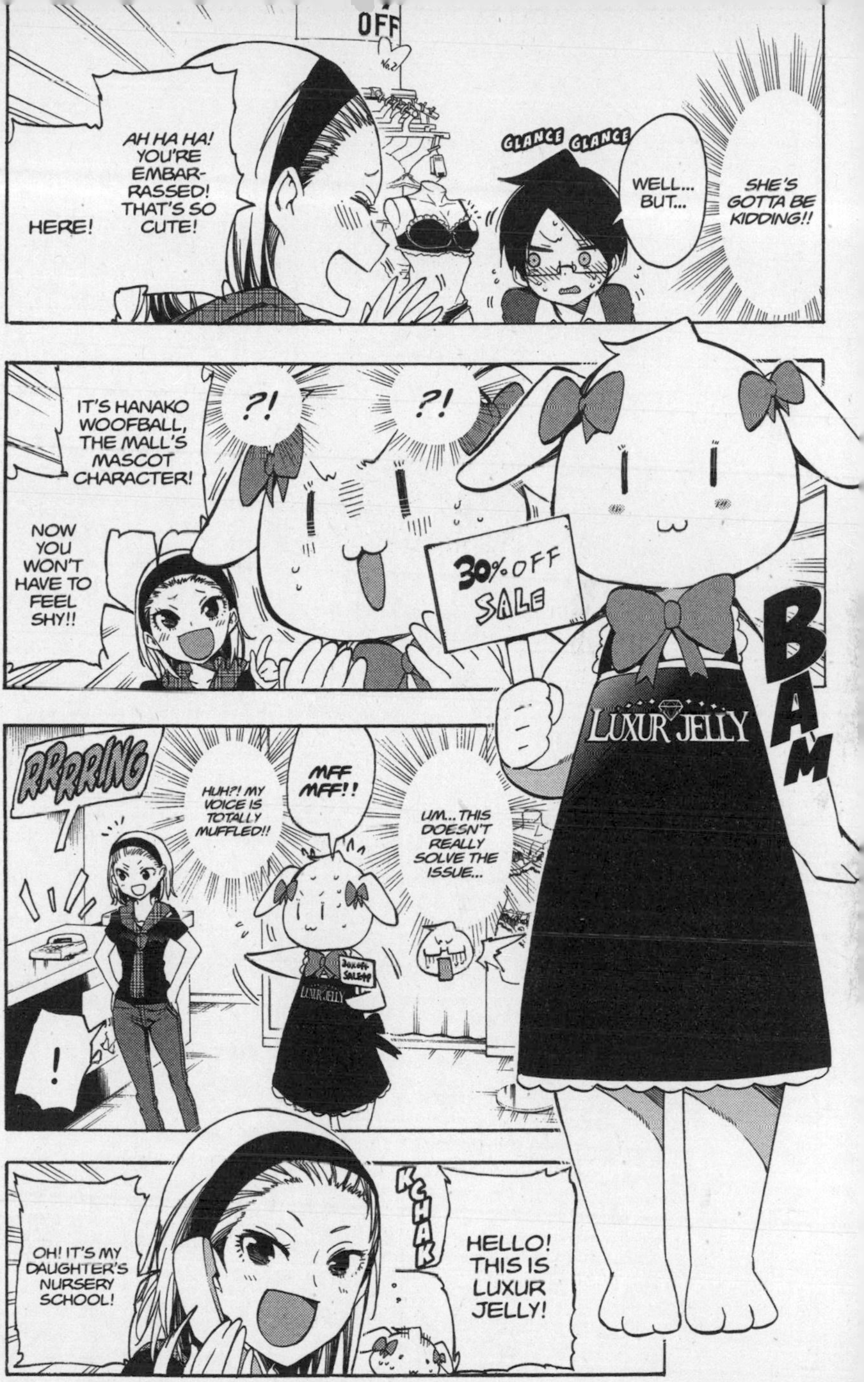
OFF
SHE'S GOTTA BE KIDDING!!
WELL... BUT...
GLANCE GLANCE
AH HA HA! YOU'RE EMBAR-RASSED! THAT'S SO CUTE!
HERE!
BAM
30% OFF SALE
LUXUR JELLY
?!
?!
IT'S HANAKO WOOFBALL, THE MALL'S MASCOT CHARACTER!
NOW YOU WON'T HAVE TO FEEL SHY!!
UM... THIS DOESN'T REALLY SOLVE THE ISSUE...
MFF MFF!!
HUH?! MY VOICE IS TOTALLY MUFFLED!!
RRRRING
!
HELLO! THIS IS LUXUR JELLY!
KCHAK
OH! IT'S MY DAUGHTER'S NURSERY SCHOOL!

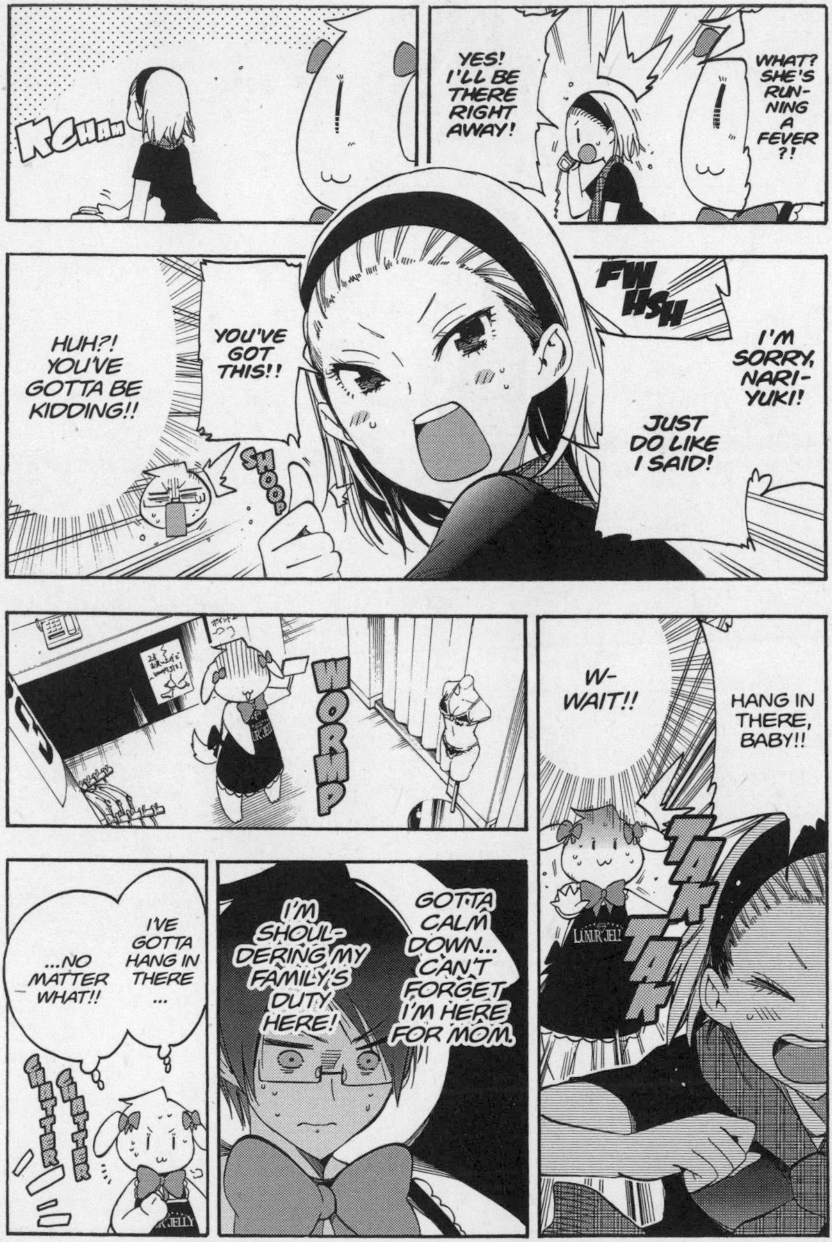
WHAT? SHE'S RUN-NING A FEVER?!
YES! I'LL BE THERE RIGHT AWAY!
KCHAM
FWHSH
I'M SORRY, NARI-YUKI!
JUST DO LIKE I SAID!
YOU'VE GOT THIS!!
SHOOP
HUH?! YOU'VE GOTTA BE KIDDING!!
HANG IN THERE, BABY!!
W-WAIT!!
TAK TAK
WORMP
GOTTA CALM DOWN... CAN'T FORGET I'M HERE FOR MOM.
I'M SHOUL-DERING MY FAMILY'S DUTY HERE!
I'VE GOTTA HANG IN THERE ...
...NO MATTER WHAT!!
CHITTER CHITTER
LUXUR JELLY

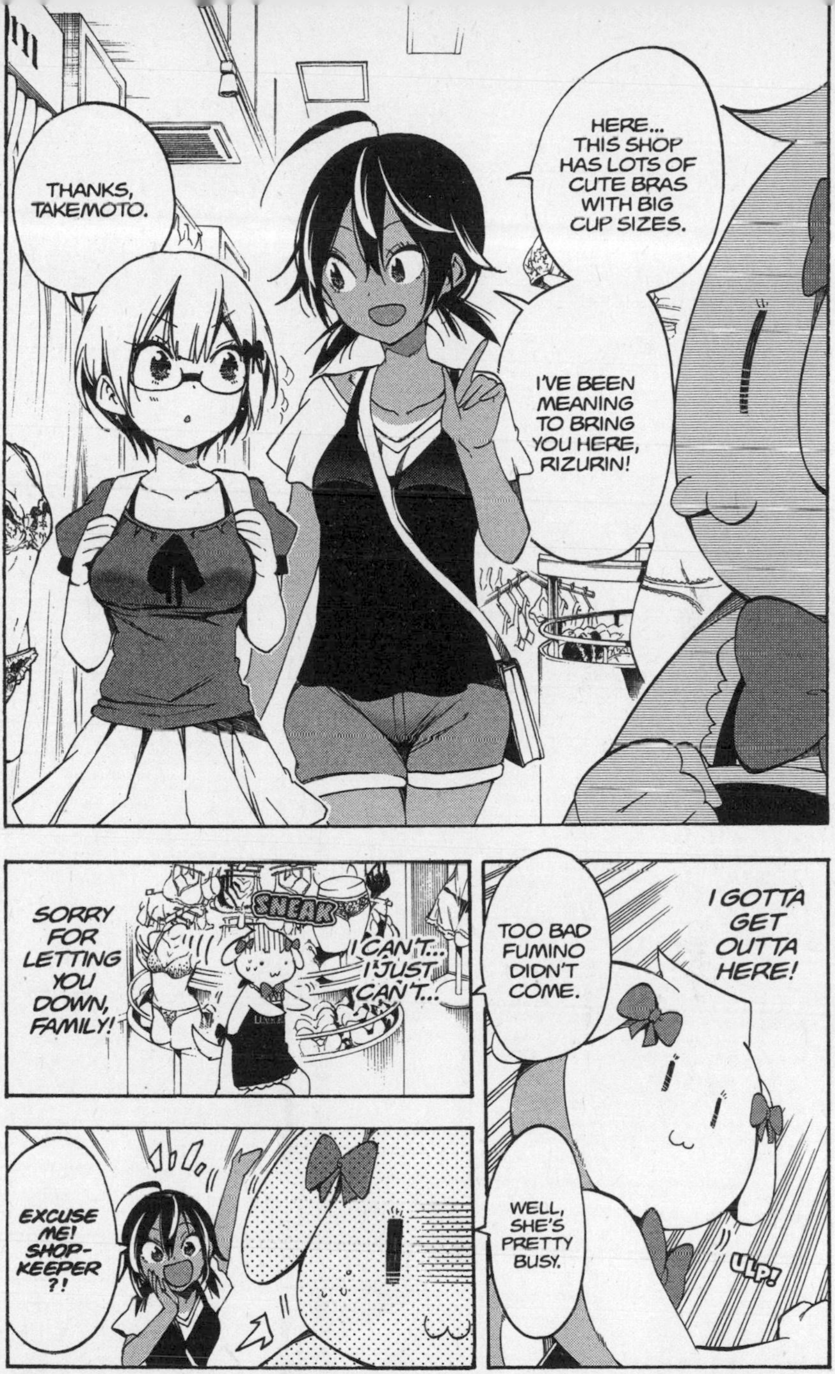
HERE... THIS SHOP HAS LOTS OF CUTE BRAS WITH BIG CUP SIZES.
I'VE BEEN MEANING TO BRING YOU HERE, RIZURIN!
THANKS, TAKEMOTO.
I GOTTA GET OUTTA HERE!
TOO BAD FUMINO DIDN'T COME.
WELL, SHE'S PRETTY BUSY.
ULP!
I CAN'T... I JUST CAN'T...
SNEAK
SORRY FOR LETTING YOU DOWN, FAMILY!
EXCUSE ME! SHOP-KEEPER?!

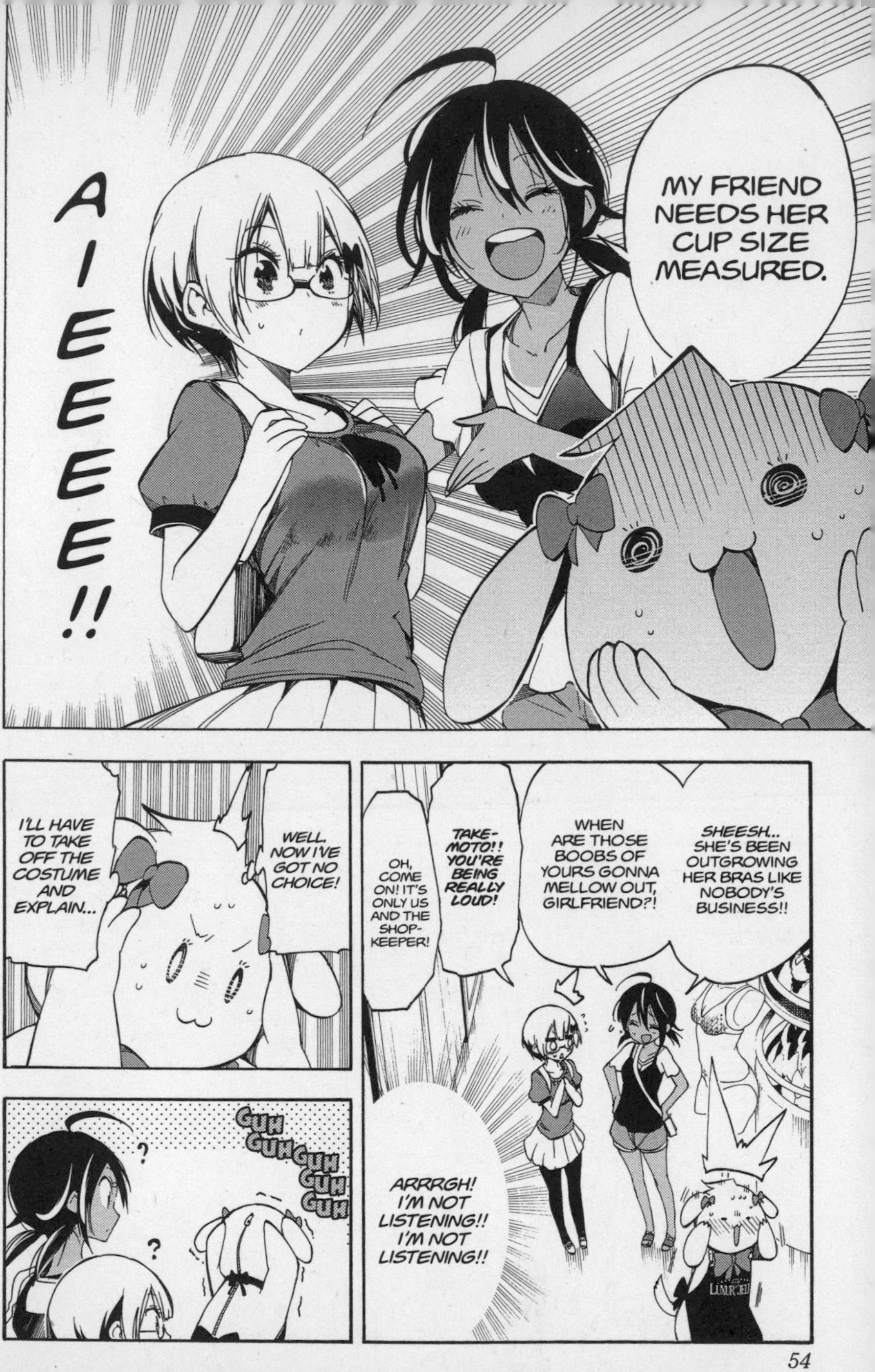
MY FRIEND NEEDS HER CUP SIZE MEASURED.
AIEEEEE!!
SHEESH... SHE'S BEEN OUTGROWING HER BRAS LIKE NOBODY'S BUSINESS!!
WHEN ARE THOSE BOOBS OF YOURS GONNA MELLOW OUT, GIRLFRIEND?!
TAKEMOTO!! YOU'RE BEING REALLY LOUD!
OH, COME ON! IT'S ONLY US AND THE SHOPKEEPER!
ARRRGH! I'M NOT LISTENING!! I'M NOT LISTENING!!
WELL. NOW I'VE GOT NO CHOICE!
I'LL HAVE TO TAKE OFF THE COSTUME AND EXPLAIN...
GUH GUH GUH GUH GUH

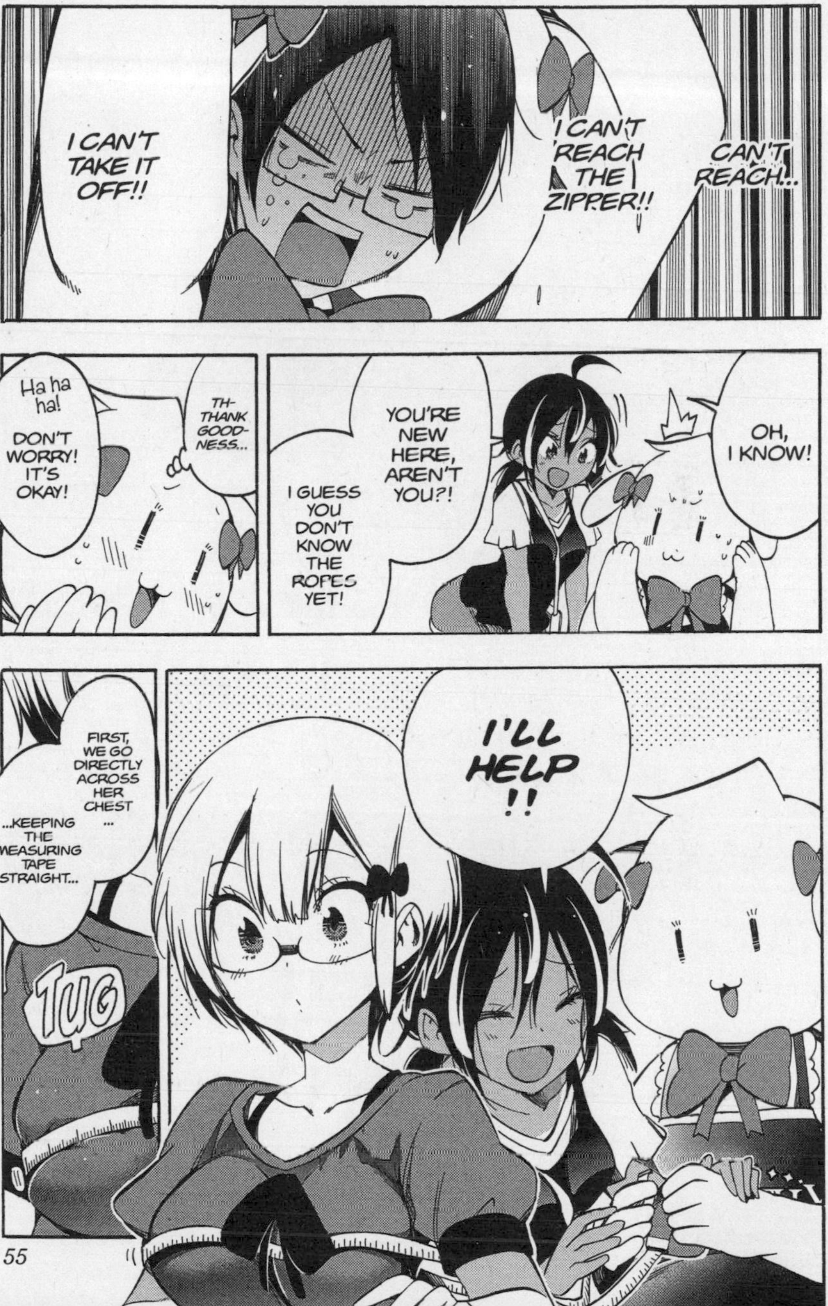
CAN'T REACH...
I CAN'T REACH THE ZIPPER!!
I CAN'T TAKE IT OFF!!
OH, I KNOW!
YOU'RE NEW HERE, AREN'T YOU?!
I GUESS YOU DON'T KNOW THE ROPES YET!
TH-THANK GOODNESS...
Ha ha ha!
DON'T WORRY! IT'S OKAY!
I'LL HELP!!
FIRST, WE GO DIRECTLY ACROSS HER CHEST...
...KEEPING THE MEASURING TAPE STRAIGHT...
TUG

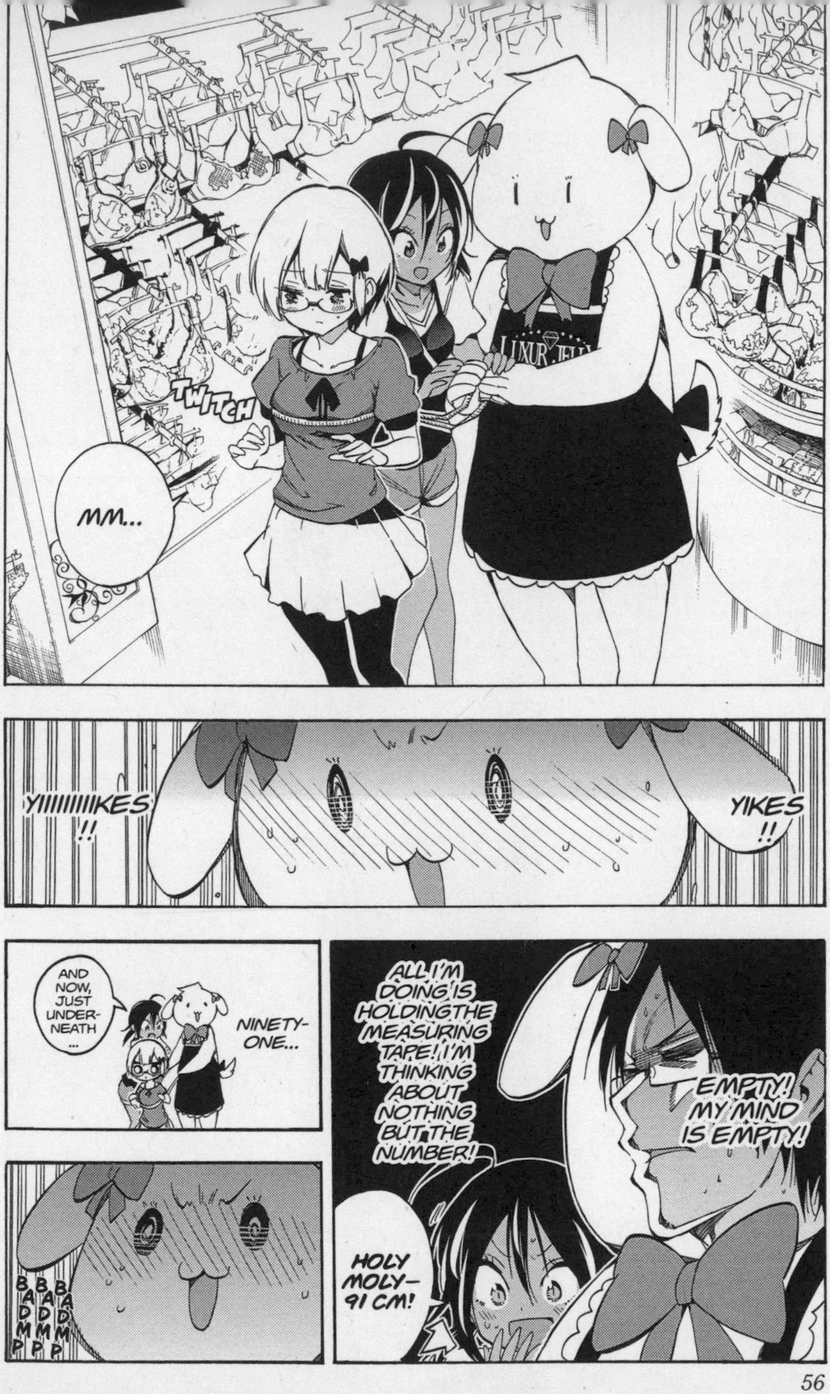
TWITCH
MM...
YIKES !!
YIIIIIIIIIKES !!
ALL I'M DOING IS HOLDING THE MEASURING TAPE! I'M THINKING ABOUT NOTHING BUT THE NUMBER!
EMPTY! MY MIND IS EMPTY!
HOLY MOLY— 91 CM!
NINETY-ONE...
AND NOW, JUST UNDER-NEATH ...
BADMP BADMP BADMP

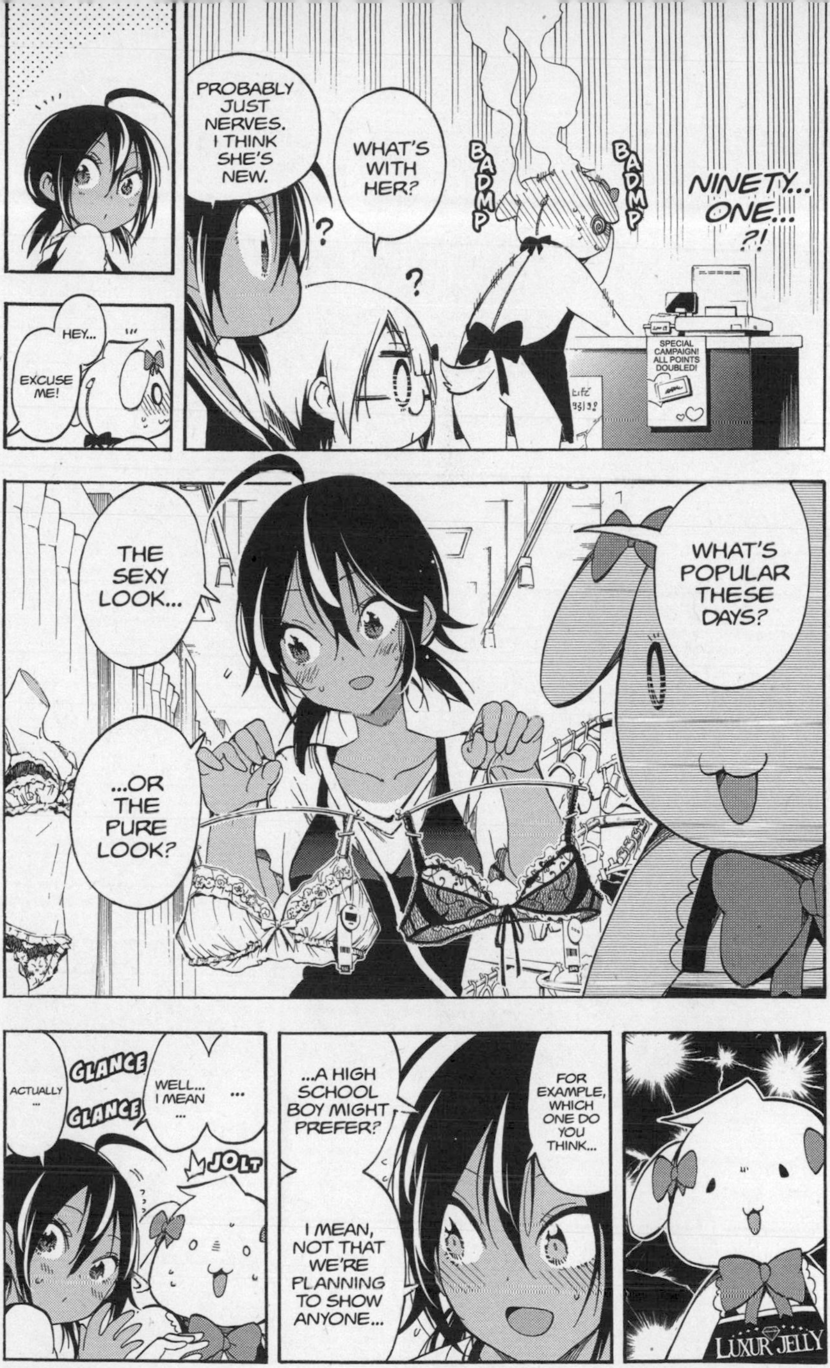
NINETY... ONE... ?!
BADMP
BADMP
WHAT'S WITH HER?
PROBABLY JUST NERVES. I THINK SHE'S NEW.
SPECIAL CAMPAIGN! ALL POINTS DOUBLED!
HEY...
EXCUSE ME!
WHAT'S POPULAR THESE DAYS?
THE SEXY LOOK...
...OR THE PURE LOOK?
FOR EXAMPLE, WHICH ONE DO YOU THINK...
LUXUR JELLY
...A HIGH SCHOOL BOY MIGHT PREFER?
I MEAN, NOT THAT WE'RE PLANNING TO SHOW ANYONE...
WELL... I MEAN ...
...
GLANCE
GLANCE
ACTUALLY ...
JOLT

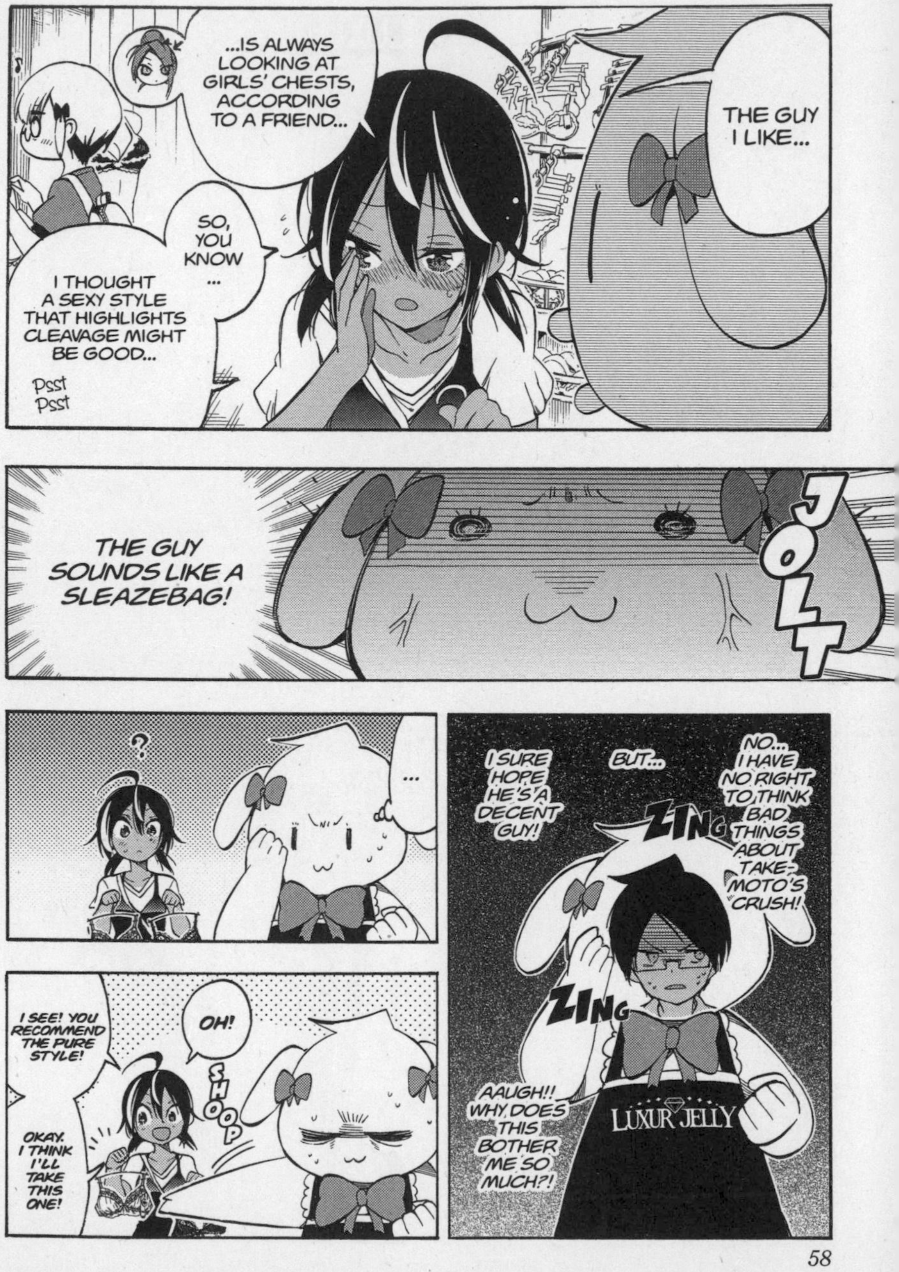
THE GUY I LIKE...
...IS ALWAYS LOOKING AT GIRLS' CHESTS, ACCORDING TO A FRIEND...
SO, YOU KNOW ...
I THOUGHT A SEXY STYLE THAT HIGHLIGHTS CLEAVAGE MIGHT BE GOOD...
Psst Psst
JOLT
THE GUY SOUNDS LIKE A SLEAZEBAG!
NO... I HAVE NO RIGHT TO THINK BAD THINGS ABOUT TAKE-MOTO'S CRUSH!
BUT...
I SURE HOPE HE'S A DECENT GUY!
ZING
ZING
AAUGH!! WHY DOES THIS BOTHER ME SO MUCH?!
LUXUR JELLY
...
?
OH!
SHOOP
I SEE! YOU RECOMMEND THE PURE STYLE!
OKAY. I THINK I'LL TAKE THIS ONE!

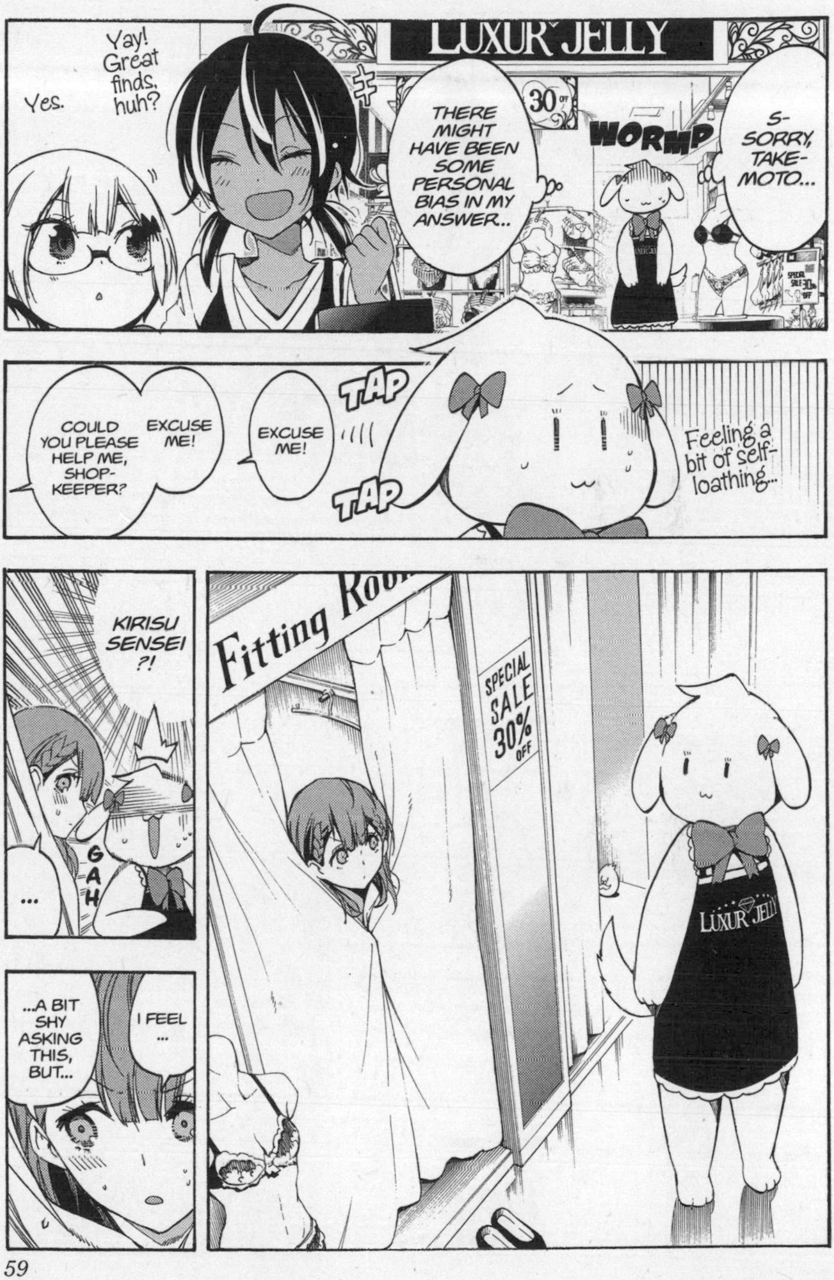
LUXUR JELLY
S-SORRY, TAKEMOTO...
WORMP
30 OFF
THERE MIGHT HAVE BEEN SOME PERSONAL BIAS IN MY ANSWER...
Yay! Great finds, huh?
Yes.
Feeling a bit of self-loathing...
TAP
TAP
EXCUSE ME!
EXCUSE ME!
COULD YOU PLEASE HELP ME, SHOP-KEEPER?
Fitting Roo
SPECIAL SALE 30% OFF
LUXUR JELLY
KIRISU SENSEI ?!
GAH
...
I FEEL ...
...A BIT SHY ASKING THIS, BUT...

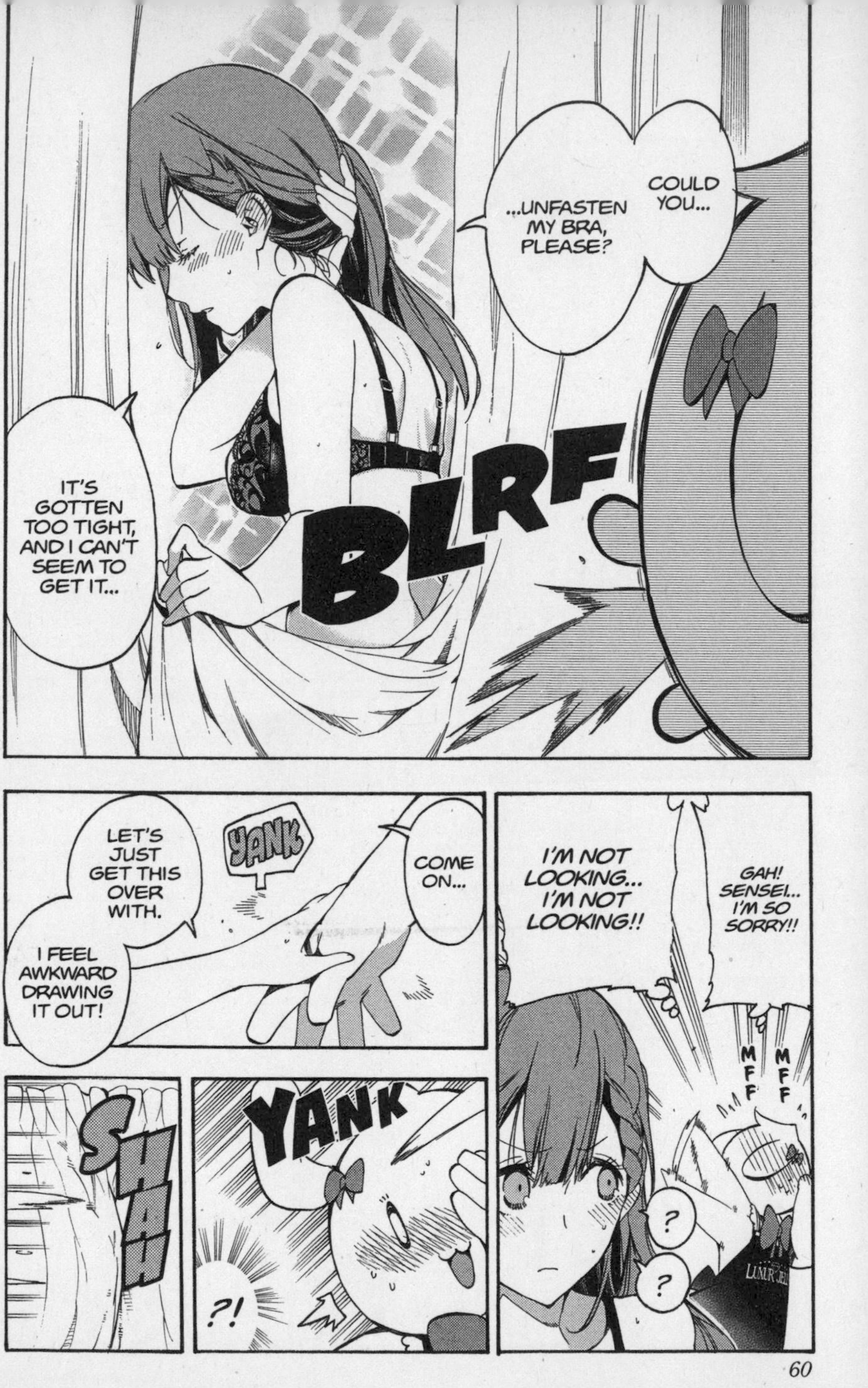
COULD YOU...
...UNFASTEN MY BRA, PLEASE?
BLRF
IT'S GOTTEN TOO TIGHT, AND I CAN'T SEEM TO GET IT...
GAH! SENSEI... I'M SO SORRY!!
I'M NOT LOOKING... I'M NOT LOOKING!!
MFF MFF
?
?
COME ON...
YANK
LET'S JUST GET THIS OVER WITH.
I FEEL AWKWARD DRAWING IT OUT!
YANK
?!
SHAA

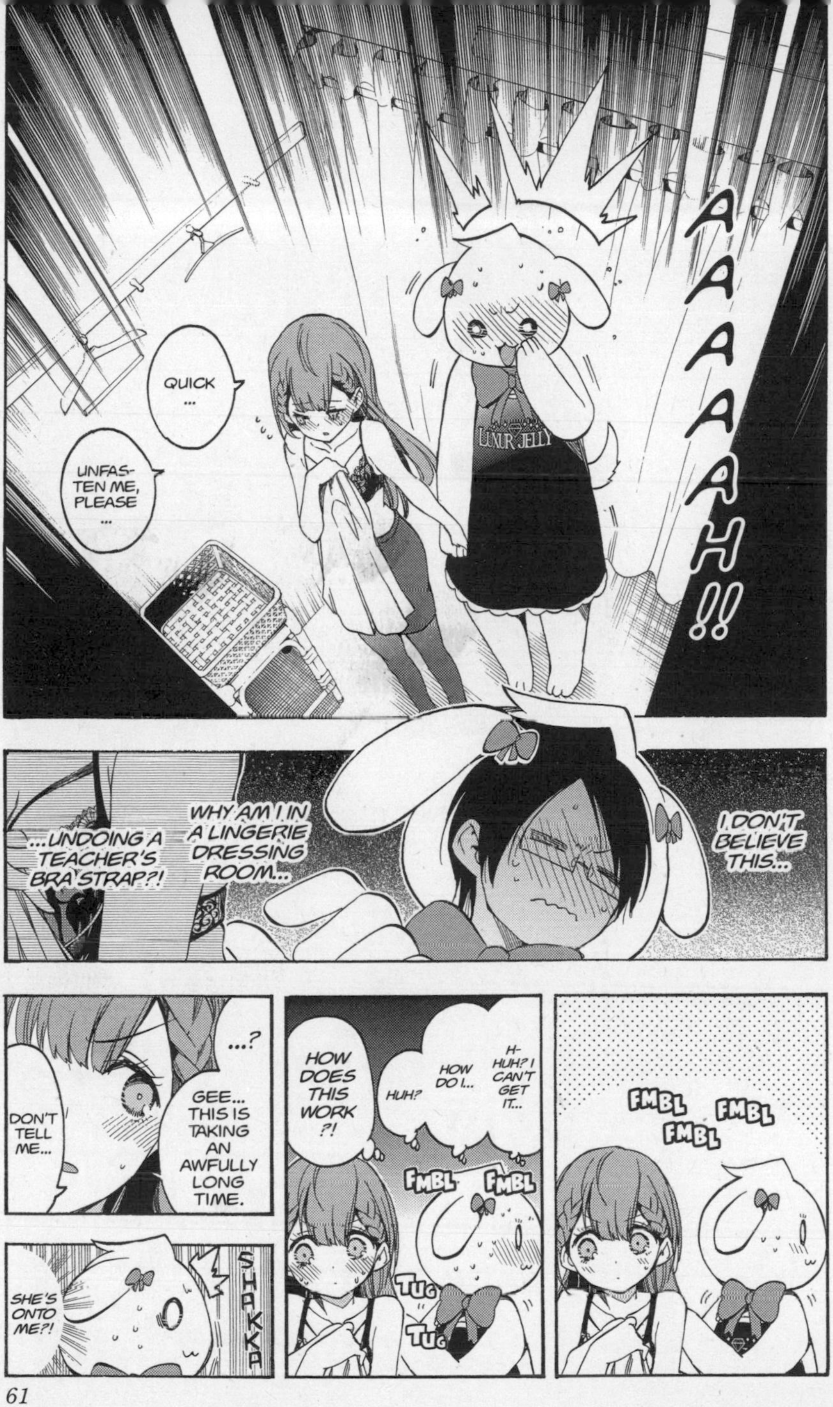
AAAAAAH!!
QUICK...
UNFASTEN ME, PLEASE...
I DON'T BELIEVE THIS...
WHY AM I IN A LINGERIE DRESSING ROOM...
...UNDOING A TEACHER'S BRA STRAP?!
FMBL FMBL FMBL
H-HUH? I CAN'T GET IT...
HOW DO I...
HUH?
HOW DOES THIS WORK?!
FMBL FMBL
TUG TUG
...?
GEE... THIS IS TAKING AN AWFULLY LONG TIME.
DON'T TELL ME...
SHAKKA
SHE'S ONTO ME?!

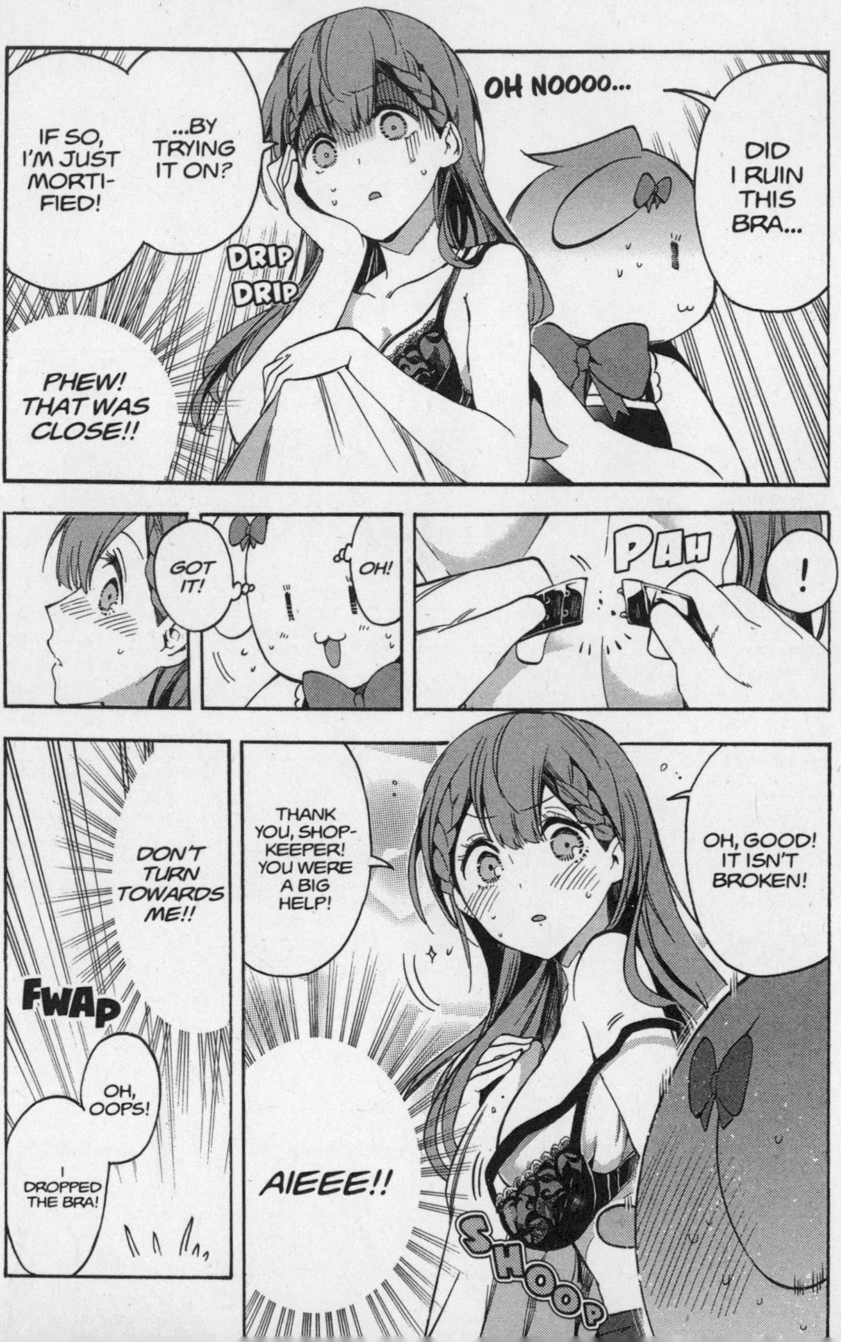
DID I RUIN THIS BRA...
OH NOOOO...
...BY TRYING IT ON?
IF SO, I'M JUST MORTI-FIED!
DRIP DRIP
PHEW! THAT WAS CLOSE!!
!
PAH
OH!
GOT IT!
OH, GOOD! IT ISN'T BROKEN!
THANK YOU, SHOP-KEEPER! YOU WERE A BIG HELP!
AIEEE!!
SHOOP
DON'T TURN TOWARDS ME!!
FWAP
OH, OOPS!
I DROPPED THE BRA!

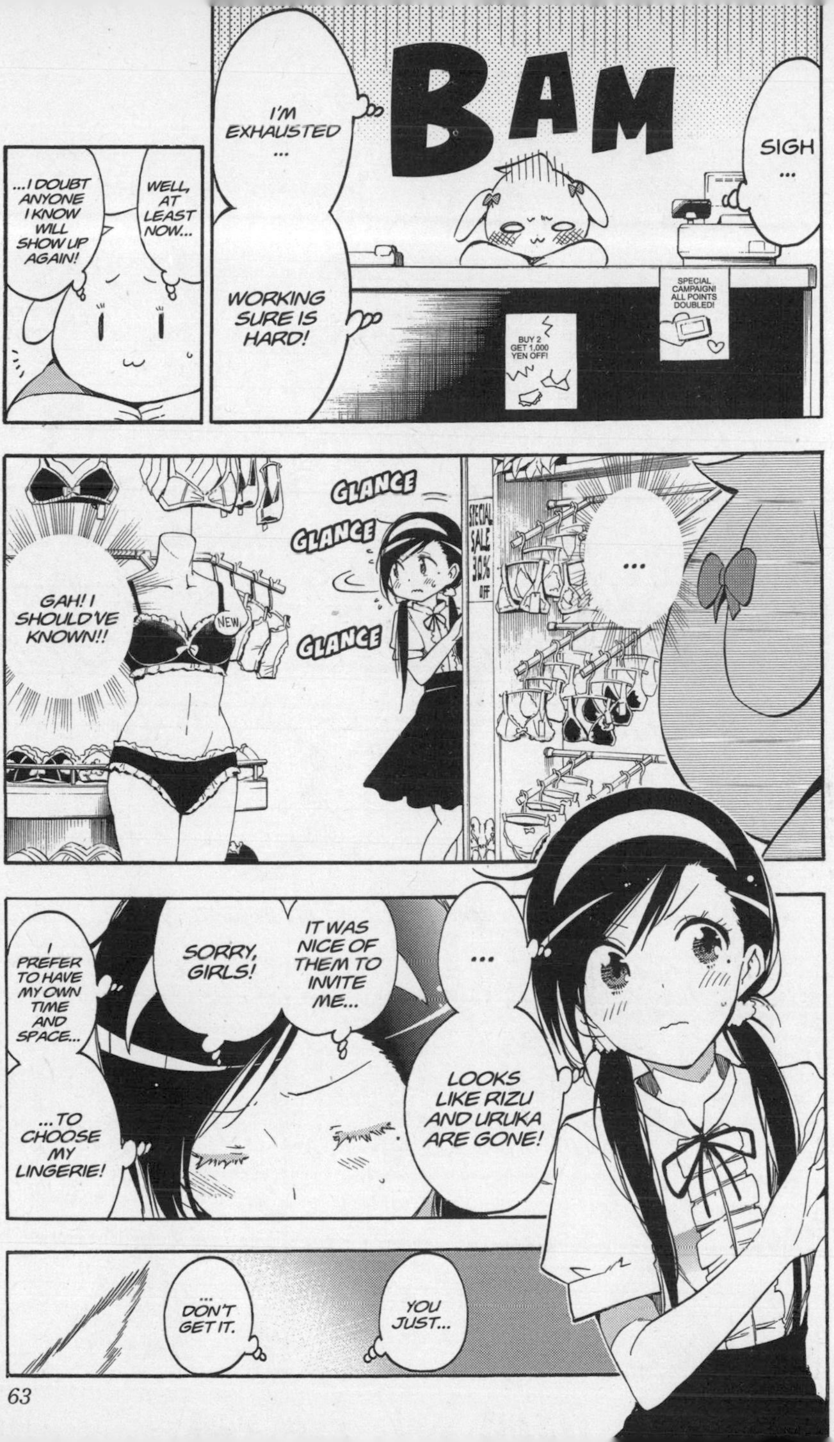
SIGH ...
BAM
I'M EXHAUSTED ...
SPECIAL CAMPAIGN! ALL POINTS DOUBLED!
BUY 2 GET 1,000 YEN OFF!
WORKING SURE IS HARD!
WELL, AT LEAST NOW...
...I DOUBT ANYONE I KNOW WILL SHOW UP AGAIN!
...
SPECIAL SALE 30% OFF
GLANCE
GLANCE
GLANCE
GAH! I SHOULD'VE KNOWN!!
NEW
...
LOOKS LIKE RIZU AND URUKA ARE GONE!
IT WAS NICE OF THEM TO INVITE ME...
SORRY, GIRLS!
I PREFER TO HAVE MY OWN TIME AND SPACE...
...TO CHOOSE MY LINGERIE!
YOU JUST...
... DON'T GET IT.

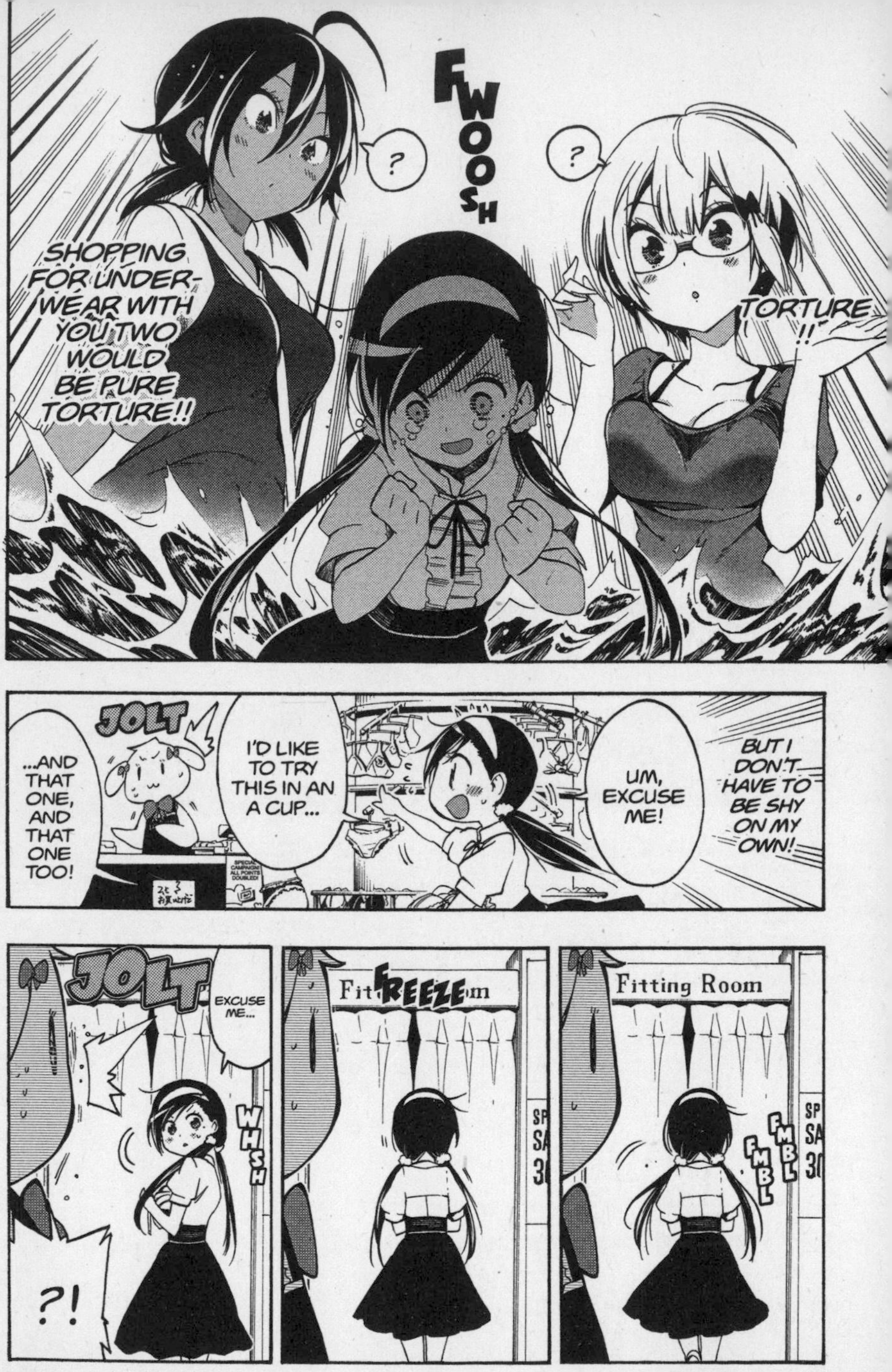
?
FWOOSH
?
TORTURE!!
SHOPPING FOR UNDERWEAR WITH YOU TWO WOULD BE PURE TORTURE!!
BUT I DON'T HAVE TO BE SHY ON MY OWN!
UM, EXCUSE ME!
I'D LIKE TO TRY THIS IN AN A CUP...
SPECIAL CAMPAIGN! ALL POINTS DOUBLED!
JOLT
...AND THAT ONE, AND THAT ONE TOO!
Fitting Room
FMBL
FMBL
FREEZE
JOLT
EXCUSE ME...
WHSH
?!

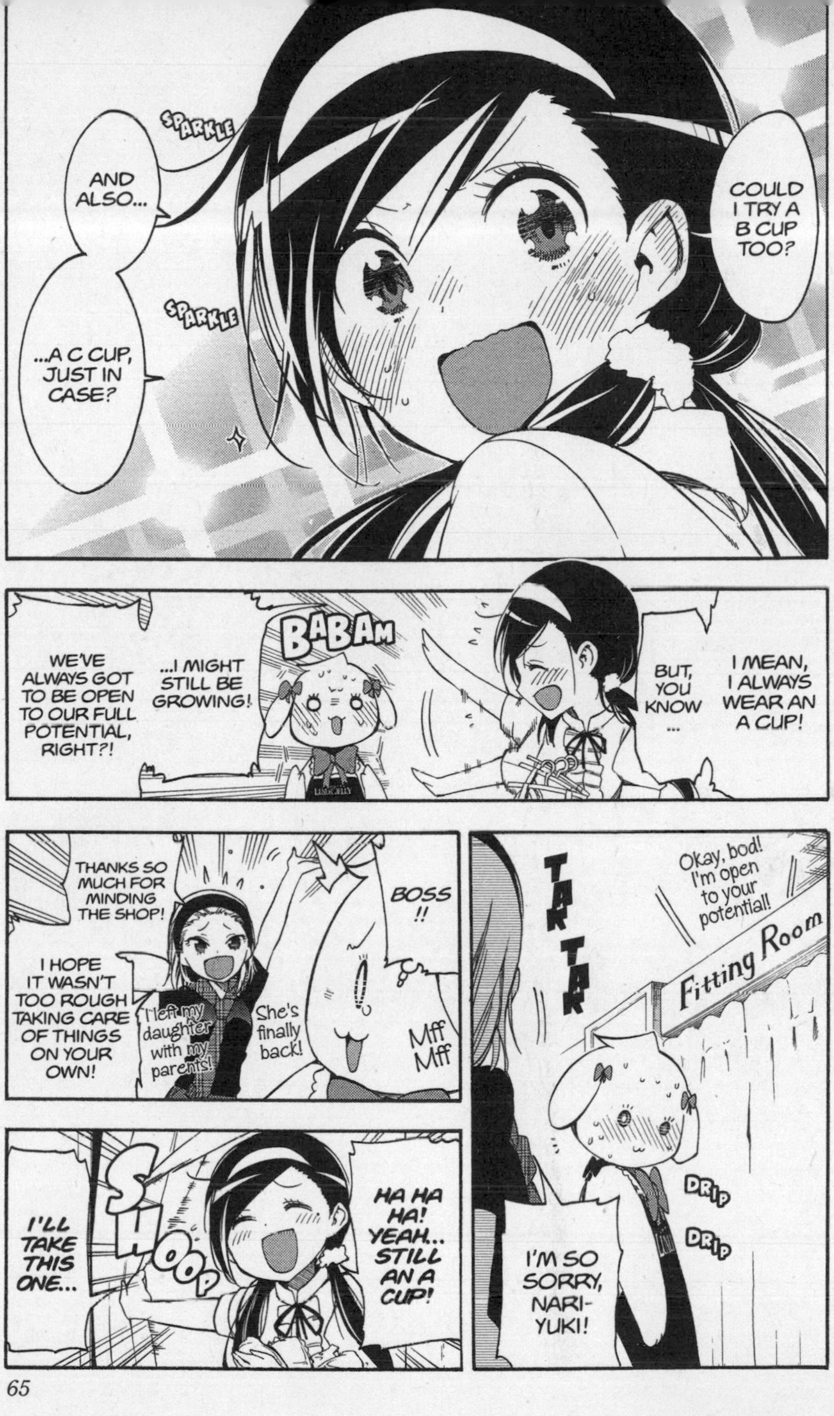
COULD I TRY A B CUP TOO?
SPARKLE
AND ALSO...
SPARKLE
...A C CUP, JUST IN CASE?
I MEAN, I ALWAYS WEAR AN A CUP!
BUT, YOU KNOW...
BABAM
...I MIGHT STILL BE GROWING!
WE'VE ALWAYS GOT TO BE OPEN TO OUR FULL POTENTIAL, RIGHT?!
BOSS!!
Mff Mff
She's finally back!
THANKS SO MUCH FOR MINDING THE SHOP!
I HOPE IT WASN'T TOO ROUGH TAKING CARE OF THINGS ON YOUR OWN!
I left my daughter with my parents!
HA HA HA! YEAH... STILL AN A CUP!
SHOOP
I'LL TAKE THIS ONE...
Okay, bod! I'm open to your potential!
TAK TAK
Fitting Room
DRIP
DRIP
I'M SO SORRY, NARI-YUKI!

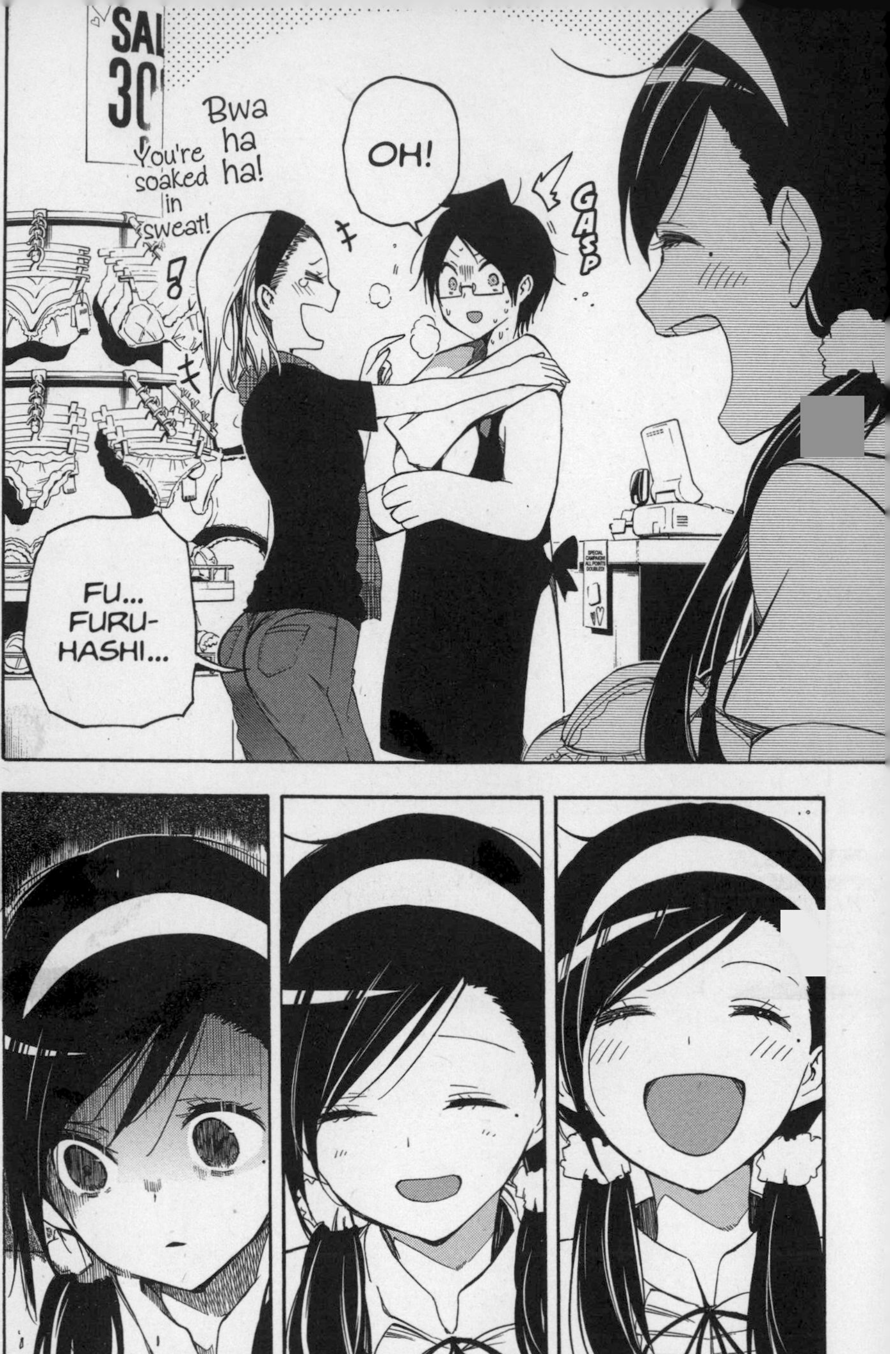
GASP
OH!
Bwa ha ha!
You're soaked in sweat!
FU... FURU-HASHI...

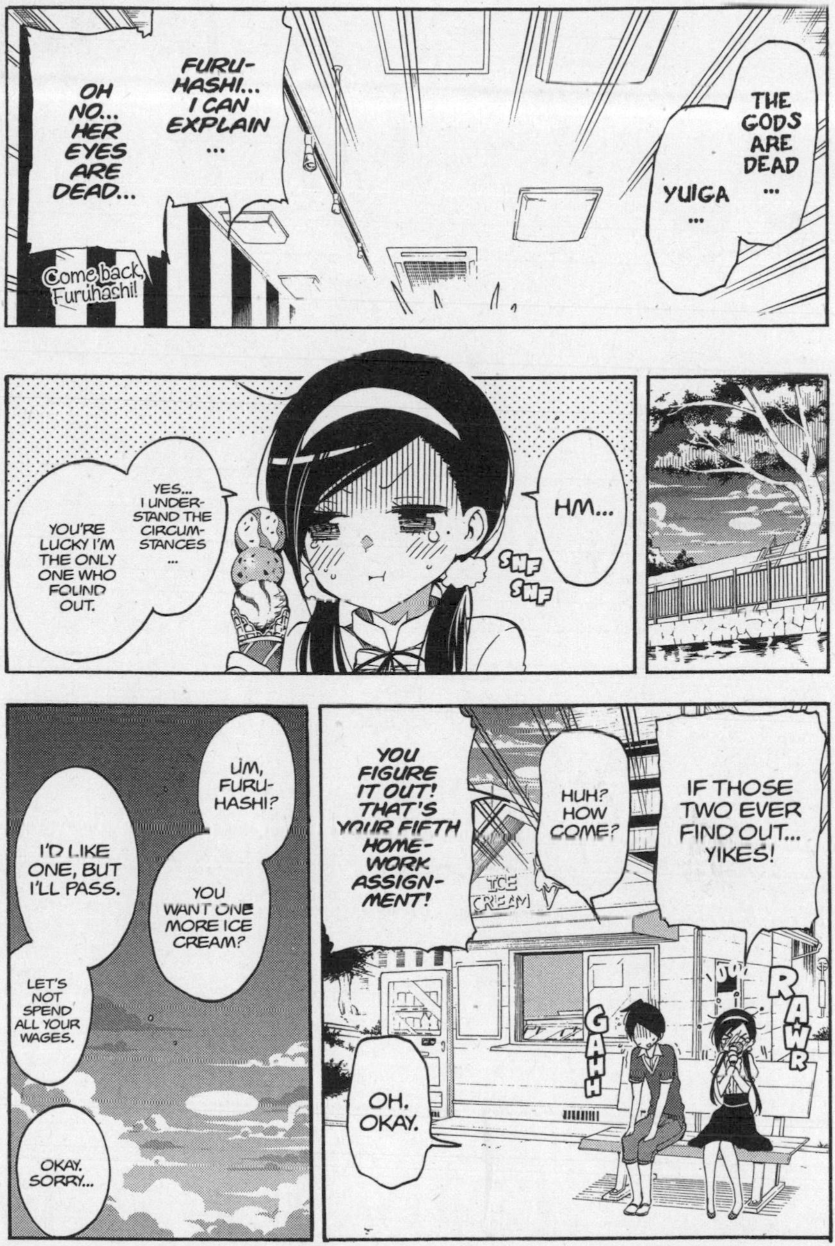
THE GODS ARE DEAD...
YUIGA...
FURU-HASHI... I CAN EXPLAIN...
OH NO... HER EYES ARE DEAD...
Come back, Furuhashi!
HM...
SNF SNF
YES... I UNDER-STAND THE CIRCUM-STANCES...
YOU'RE LUCKY I'M THE ONLY ONE WHO FOUND OUT.
IF THOSE TWO EVER FIND OUT... YIKES!
HUH? HOW COME?
YOU FIGURE IT OUT! THAT'S YOUR FIFTH HOME-WORK ASSIGN-MENT!
ICE CREAM
RAWR
GAHH
OH. OKAY.
UM, FURU-HASHI?
YOU WANT ONE MORE ICE CREAM?
I'D LIKE ONE, BUT I'LL PASS.
LET'S NOT SPEND ALL YOUR WAGES.
OKAY. SORRY...

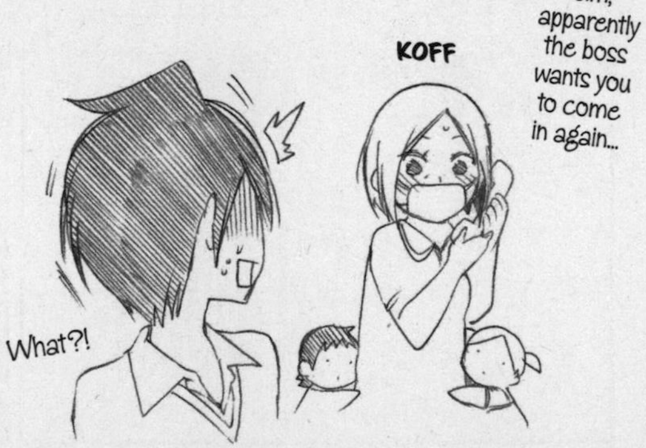
Um, apparently the boss wants you to come in again...
KOFF
What?!

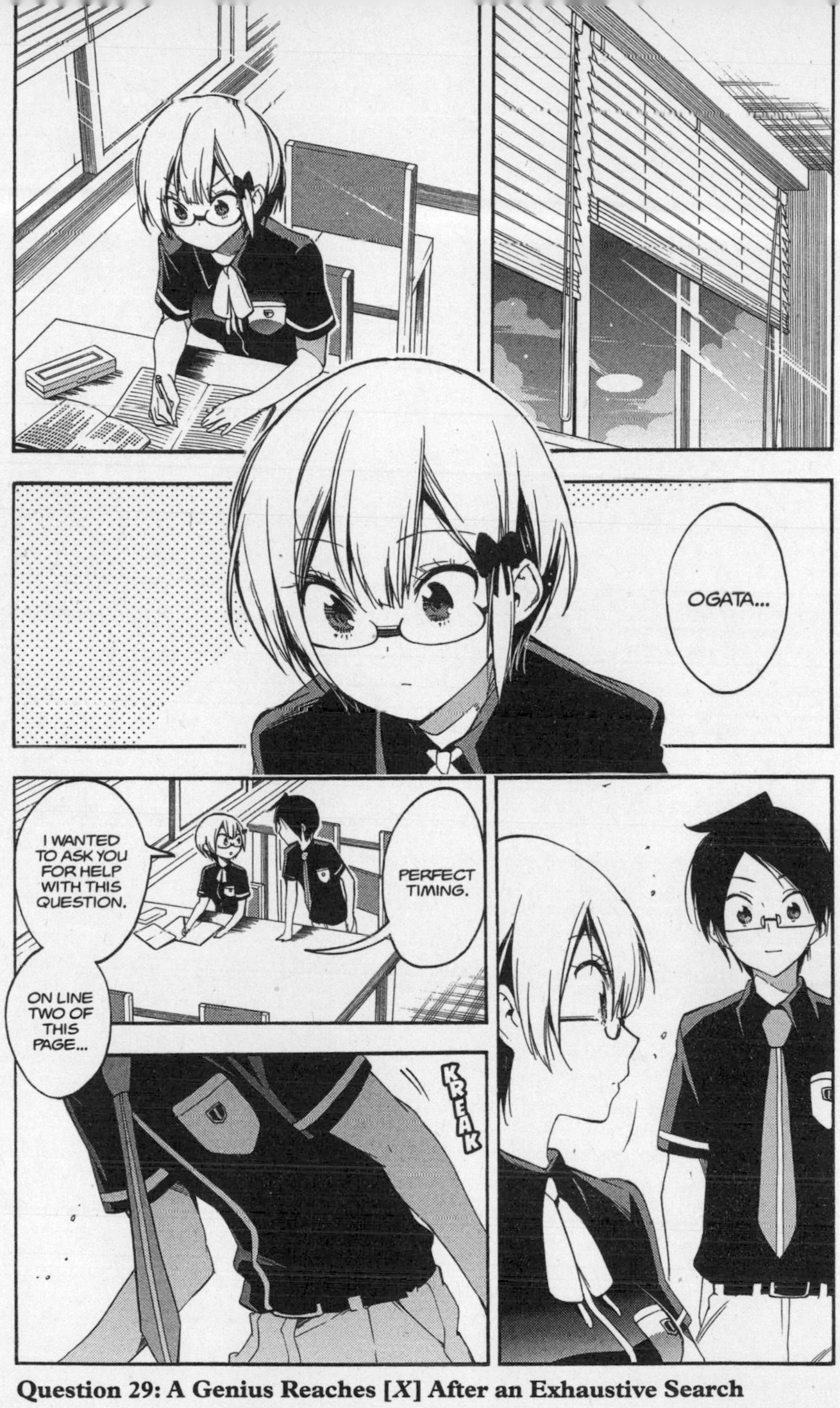
OGATA...
PERFECT TIMING.
I WANTED TO ASK YOU FOR HELP WITH THIS QUESTION.
ON LINE TWO OF THIS PAGE...
KREAK

Question 29: A Genius Reaches [*X*] After an Exhaustive Search

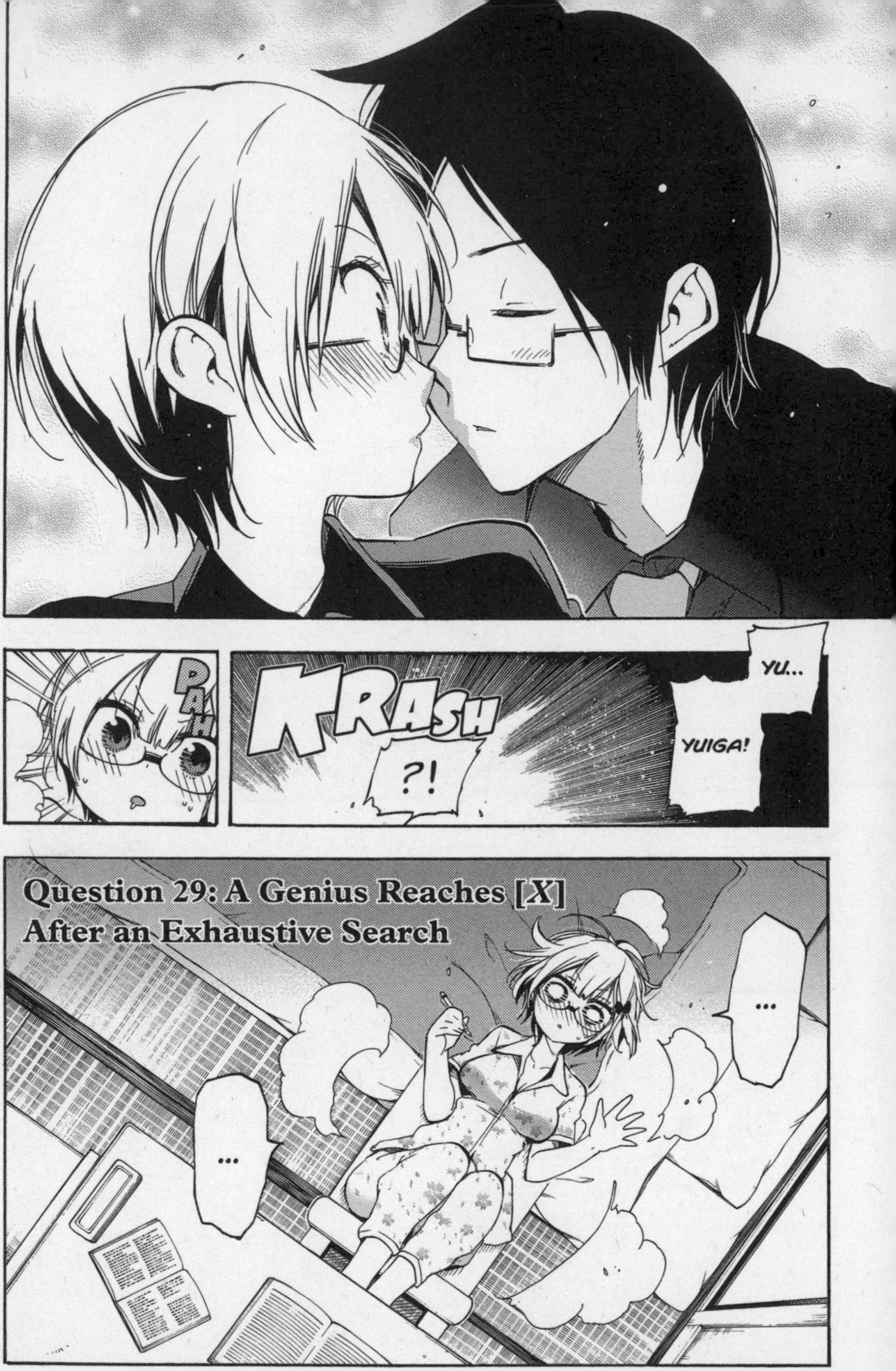
YU...
YUIGA!
KRASH
?!
PAH
Question 29: A Genius Reaches [X] After an Exhaustive Search
...
...

TAKA TAKA TAKA

OGATA UDON

CHAK

Kiss meaning 🔍

• Kiss – peck, smack, smooch
A touch with the lips to the lips, cheek, hand, etc. as an expression of love or respect.

• Indirect kiss – A type of kiss in which a person's lips touch an object that has been touched by another person's lips.

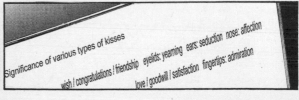

Significance of various types of kisses

wish / congratulations / friendship eyelids: yearning ears: seduction nose: affection
love / goodwill / satisfaction fingertips: admiration

71

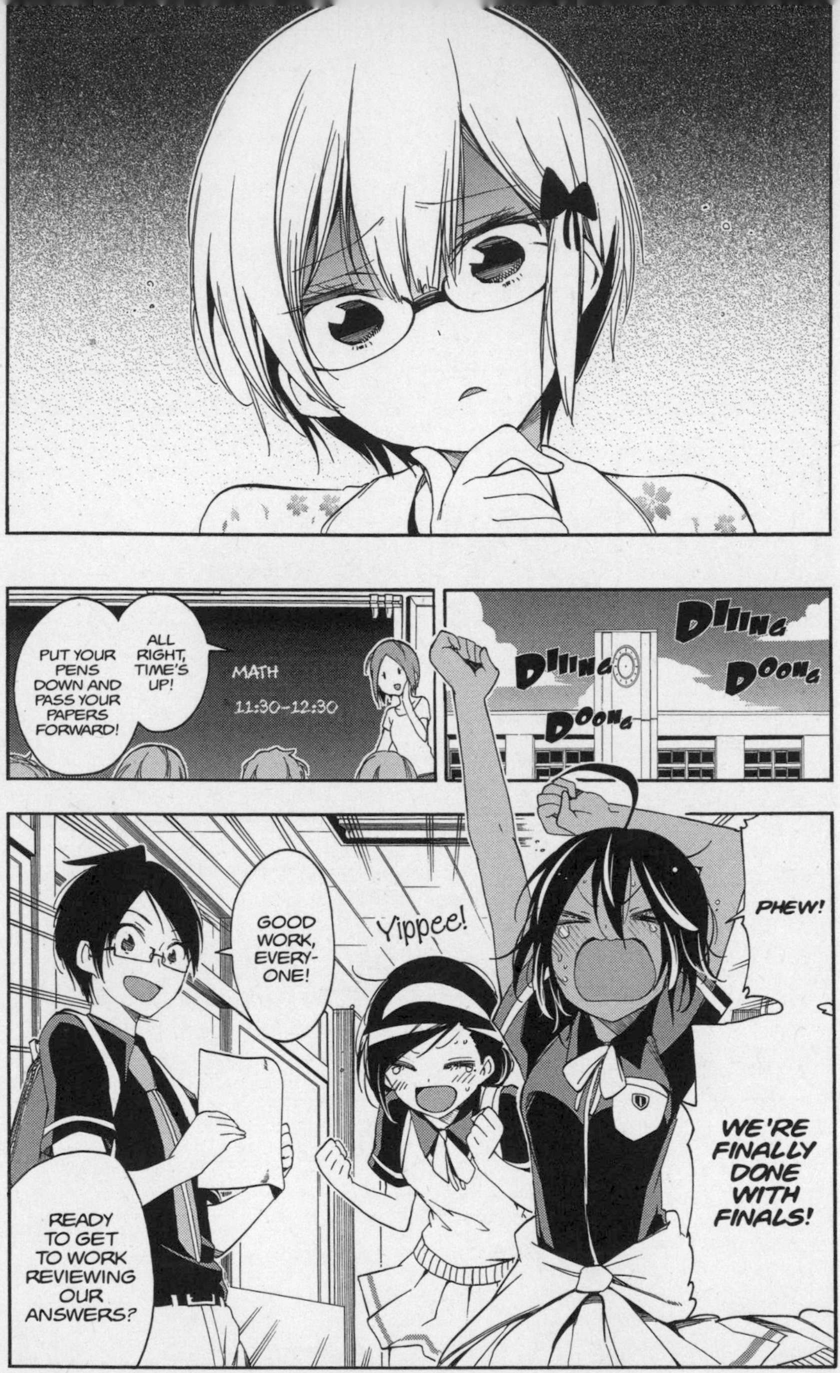
DIIING
DOOONG
DIIING
DOOONG
ALL RIGHT, TIME'S UP!
PUT YOUR PENS DOWN AND PASS YOUR PAPERS FORWARD!
MATH
11:30-12:30
PHEW!
WE'RE FINALLY DONE WITH FINALS!
Yippee!
GOOD WORK, EVERY-ONE!
READY TO GET TO WORK REVIEWING OUR ANSWERS?

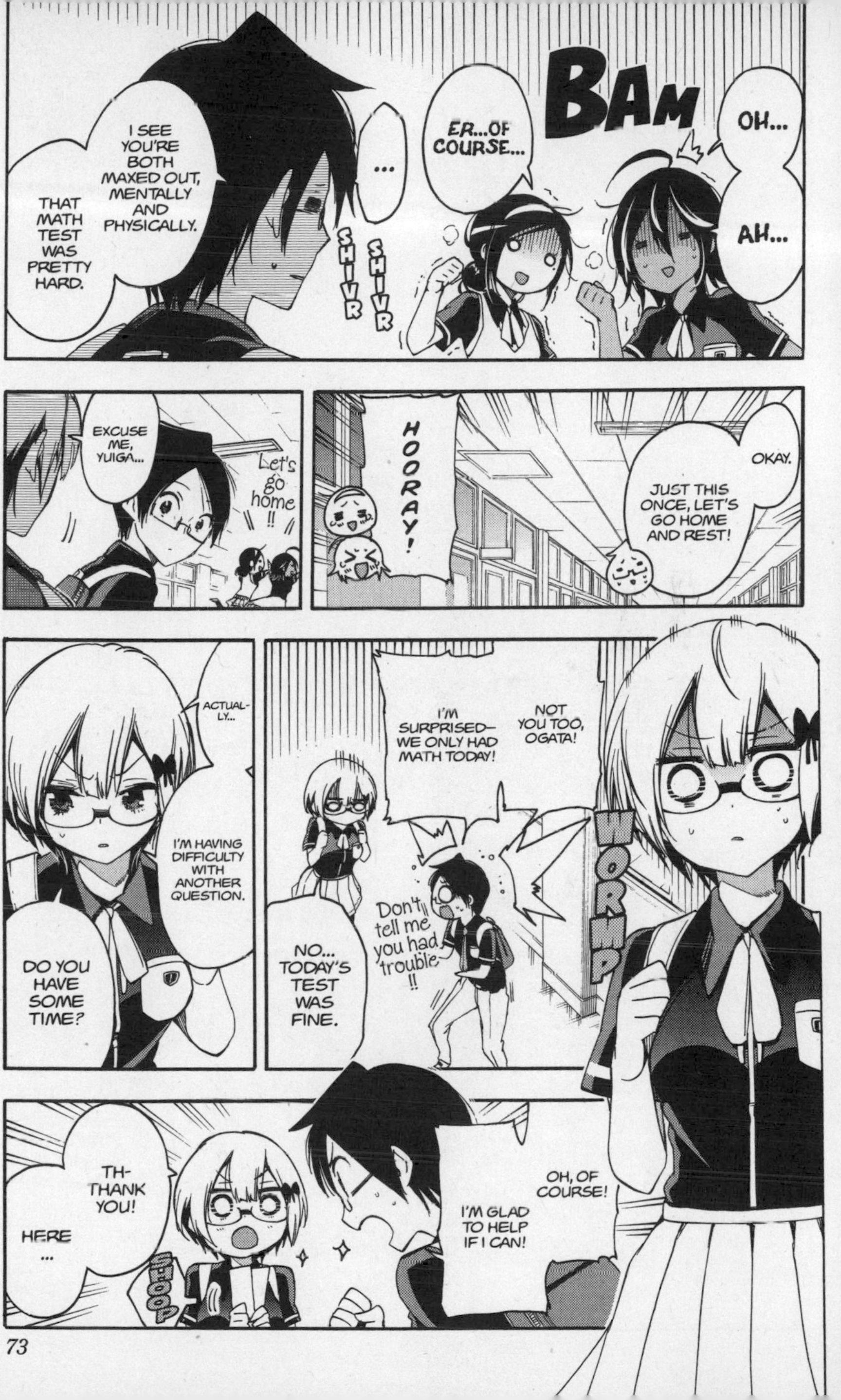
OH...
AH...
BAM
ER...OF COURSE...
...
SHIVR SHIVR
I SEE YOU'RE BOTH MAXED OUT, MENTALLY AND PHYSICALLY.
THAT MATH TEST WAS PRETTY HARD.
OKAY.
JUST THIS ONCE, LET'S GO HOME AND REST!
HOORAY!
Let's go home!!
EXCUSE ME, YUIGA...
WORMP
NOT YOU TOO, OGATA!
I'M SURPRISED—WE ONLY HAD MATH TODAY!
Don't tell me you had trouble!!
NO... TODAY'S TEST WAS FINE.
ACTUAL-LY...
I'M HAVING DIFFICULTY WITH ANOTHER QUESTION.
DO YOU HAVE SOME TIME?
OH, OF COURSE!
I'M GLAD TO HELP IF I CAN!
TH-THANK YOU!
HERE...
SHOOP

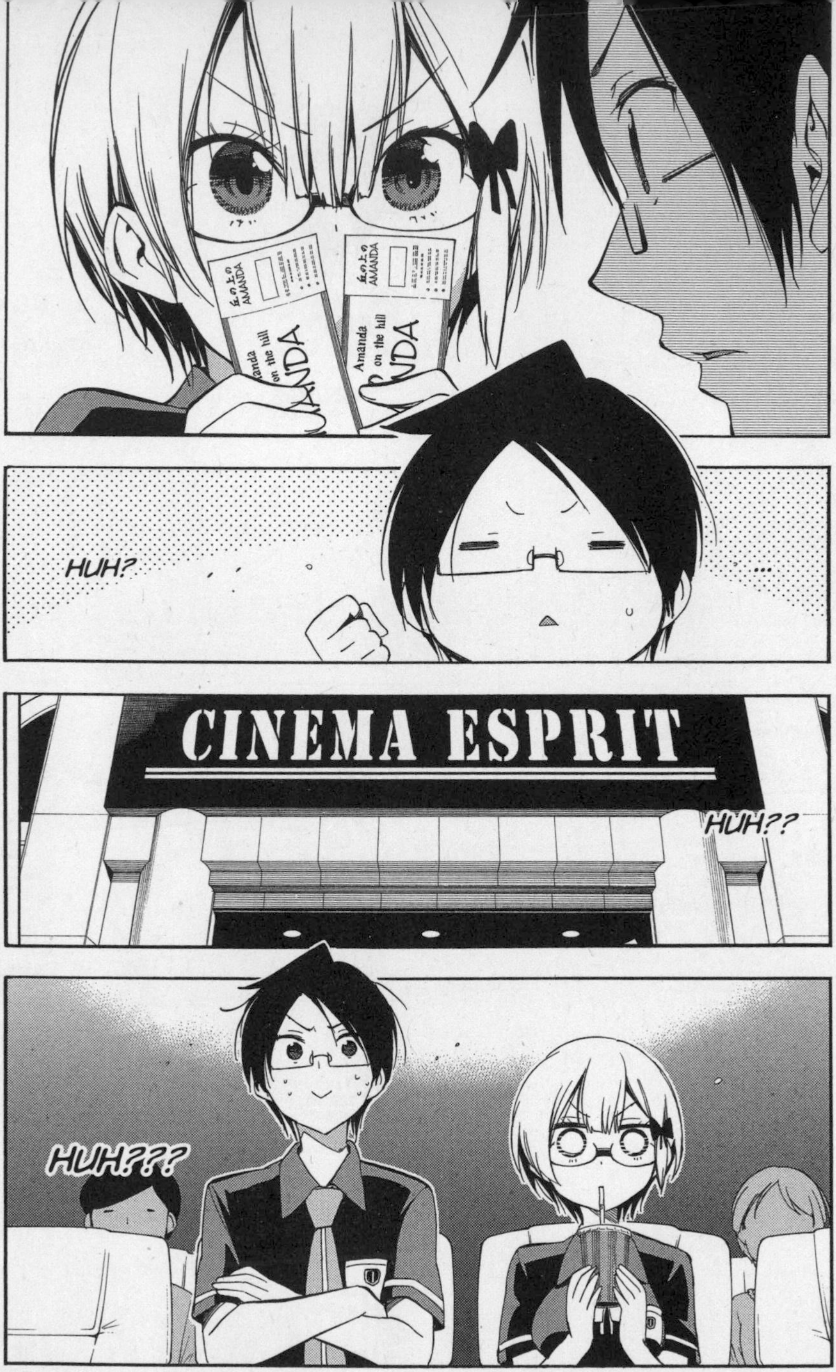
丘の上の AMANDA
Amanda on the hill
丘の上の AMANDA
Amanda on the hill
...
HUH?
CINEMA ESPRIT
HUH??
HUH???

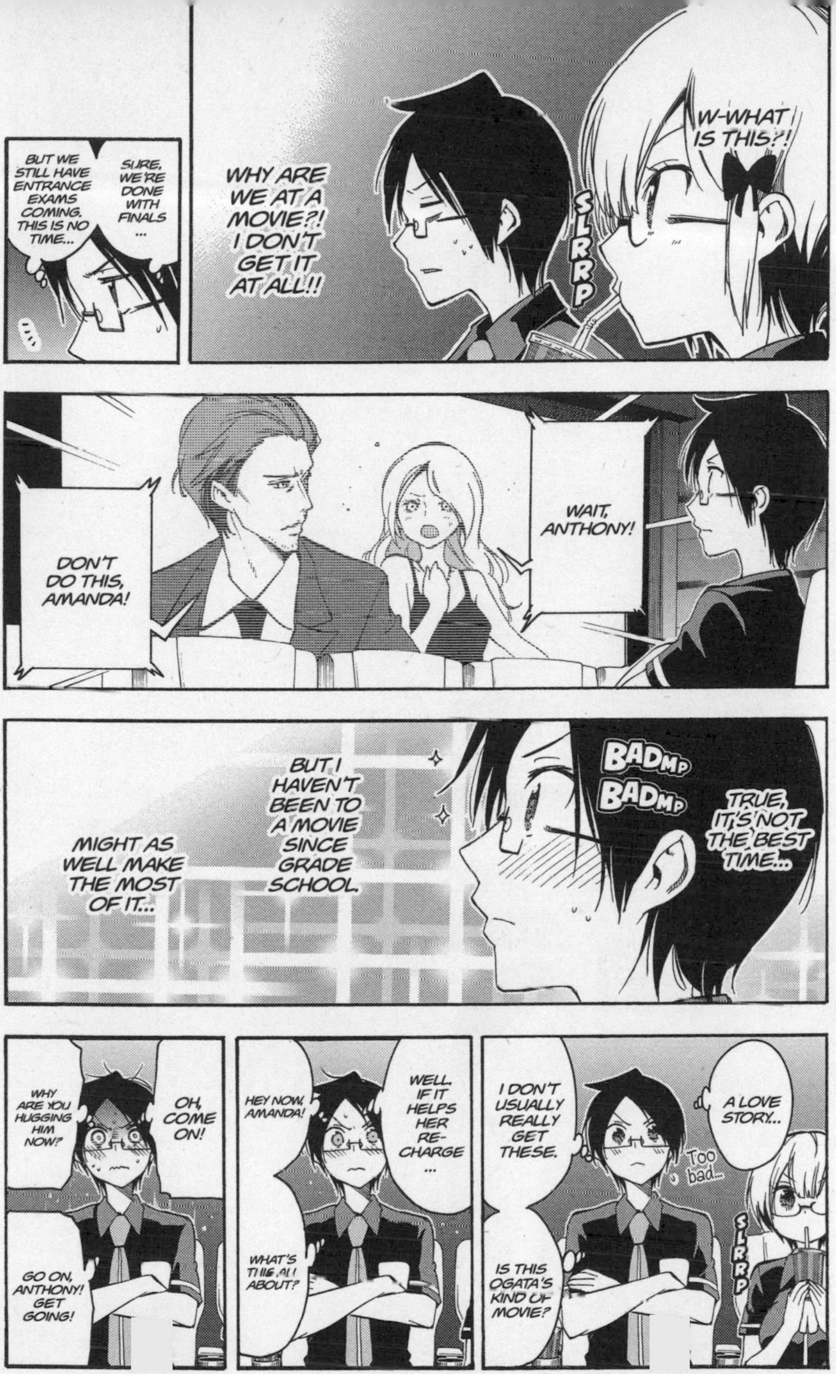
W-WHAT IS THIS?!
SLRRP
WHY ARE WE AT A MOVIE?! I DON'T GET IT AT ALL!!
SURE, WE'RE DONE WITH FINALS...
BUT WE STILL HAVE ENTRANCE EXAMS COMING. THIS IS NO TIME...
.....
WAIT, ANTHONY!
DON'T DO THIS, AMANDA!
BADMP
BADMP
TRUE, IT'S NOT THE BEST TIME...
BUT I HAVEN'T BEEN TO A MOVIE SINCE GRADE SCHOOL.
MIGHT AS WELL MAKE THE MOST OF IT...
A LOVE STORY...
Too bad...
SLRRP
I DON'T USUALLY REALLY GET THESE.
IS THIS OGATA'S KIND OF MOVIE?
WELL, IF IT HELPS HER RE-CHARGE...
HEY NOW, AMANDA!
WHAT'S THIS ALL ABOUT?
OH, COME ON!
WHY ARE YOU HUGGING HIM NOW?
GO ON, ANTHONY! GET GOING!

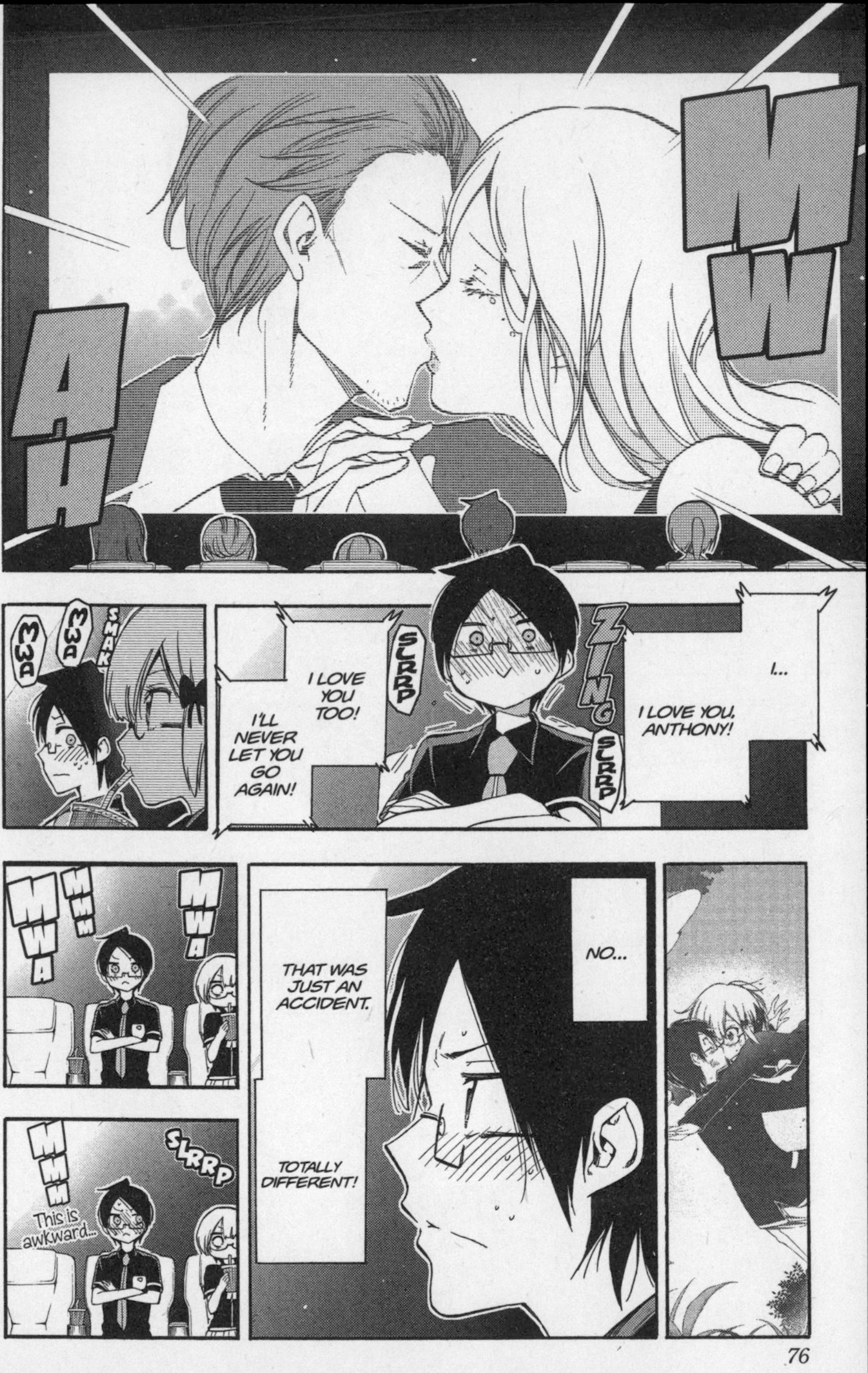
MW
AH
I...
I LOVE YOU, ANTHONY!
SLRRP
ZING
I LOVE YOU TOO!
I'LL NEVER LET YOU GO AGAIN!
SLRRP
SMAK
MWA
MWA
NO...
THAT WAS JUST AN ACCIDENT.
TOTALLY DIFFERENT!
MWA
MMM
MWA
SLRRP
MMM
This is awkward...

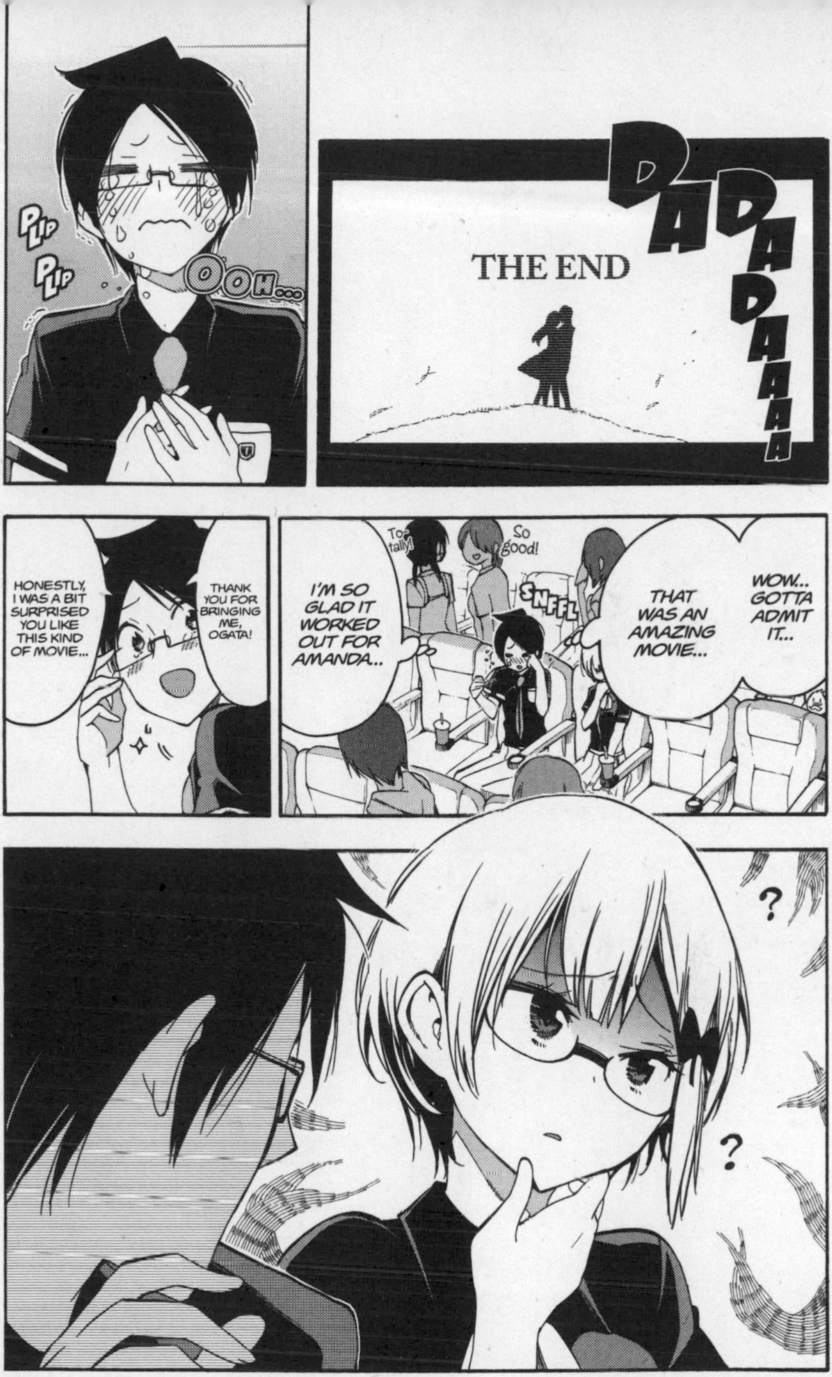
THE END
DADADAAAA
PLIP PLIP
OOH...
WOW... GOTTA ADMIT IT...
THAT WAS AN AMAZING MOVIE...
SNFFL
So good!
To- tally!
I'M SO GLAD IT WORKED OUT FOR AMANDA...
THANK YOU FOR BRINGING ME, OGATA!
HONESTLY, I WAS A BIT SURPRISED YOU LIKE THIS KIND OF MOVIE...
?
?

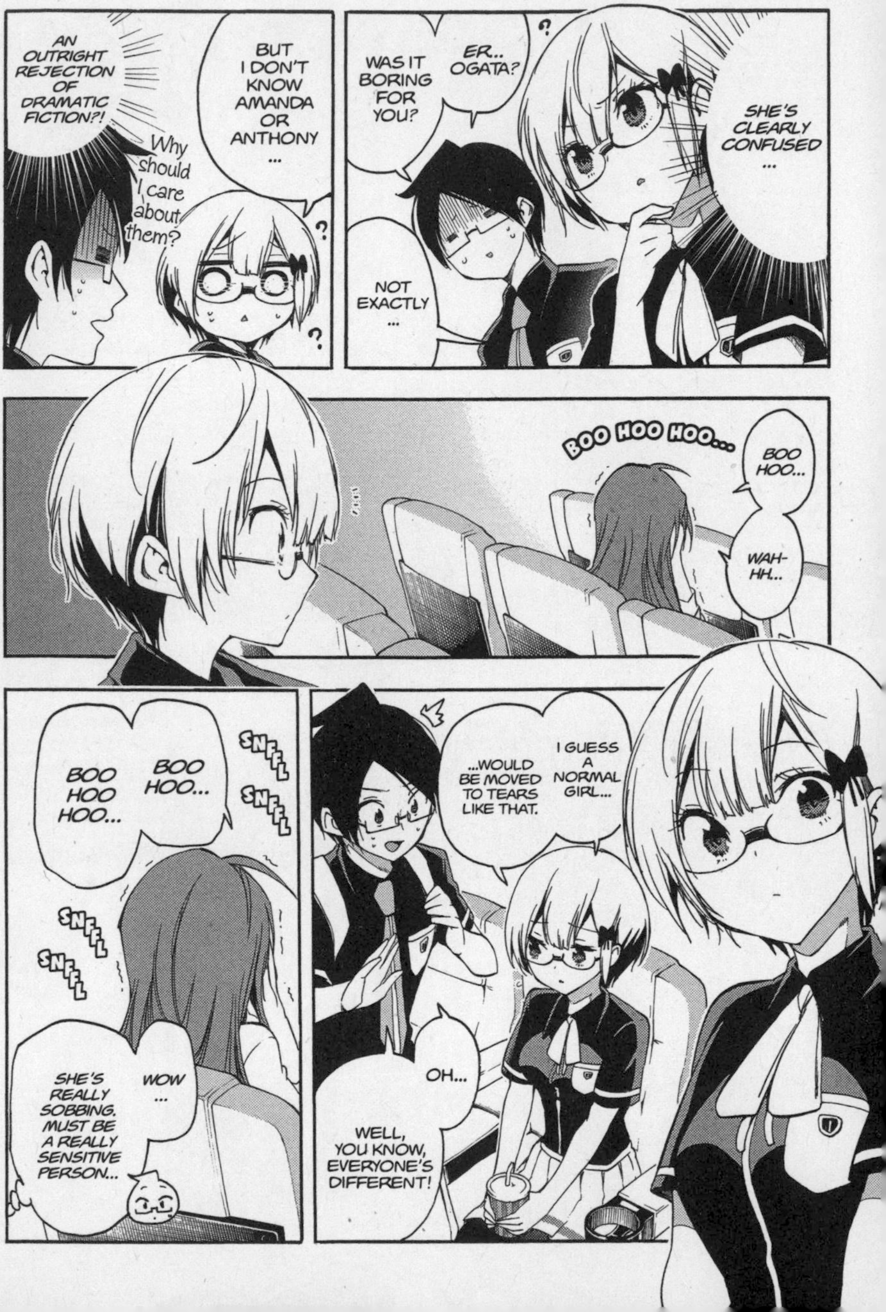
ER.. OGATA?
WAS IT BORING FOR YOU?
NOT EXACTLY ...
SHE'S CLEARLY CONFUSED ...
BUT I DON'T KNOW AMANDA OR ANTHONY ...
Why should I care about them?
AN OUTRIGHT REJECTION OF DRAMATIC FICTION?!
BOO HOO HOO...
BOO HOO...
WAH-HH...
I GUESS A NORMAL GIRL...
...WOULD BE MOVED TO TEARS LIKE THAT.
OH...
WELL, YOU KNOW, EVERYONE'S DIFFERENT!
BOO HOO...
BOO HOO HOO...
SNFFL
SNFFL
SNFFL
SNFFL
WOW ...
SHE'S REALLY SOBBING. MUST BE A REALLY SENSITIVE PERSON...

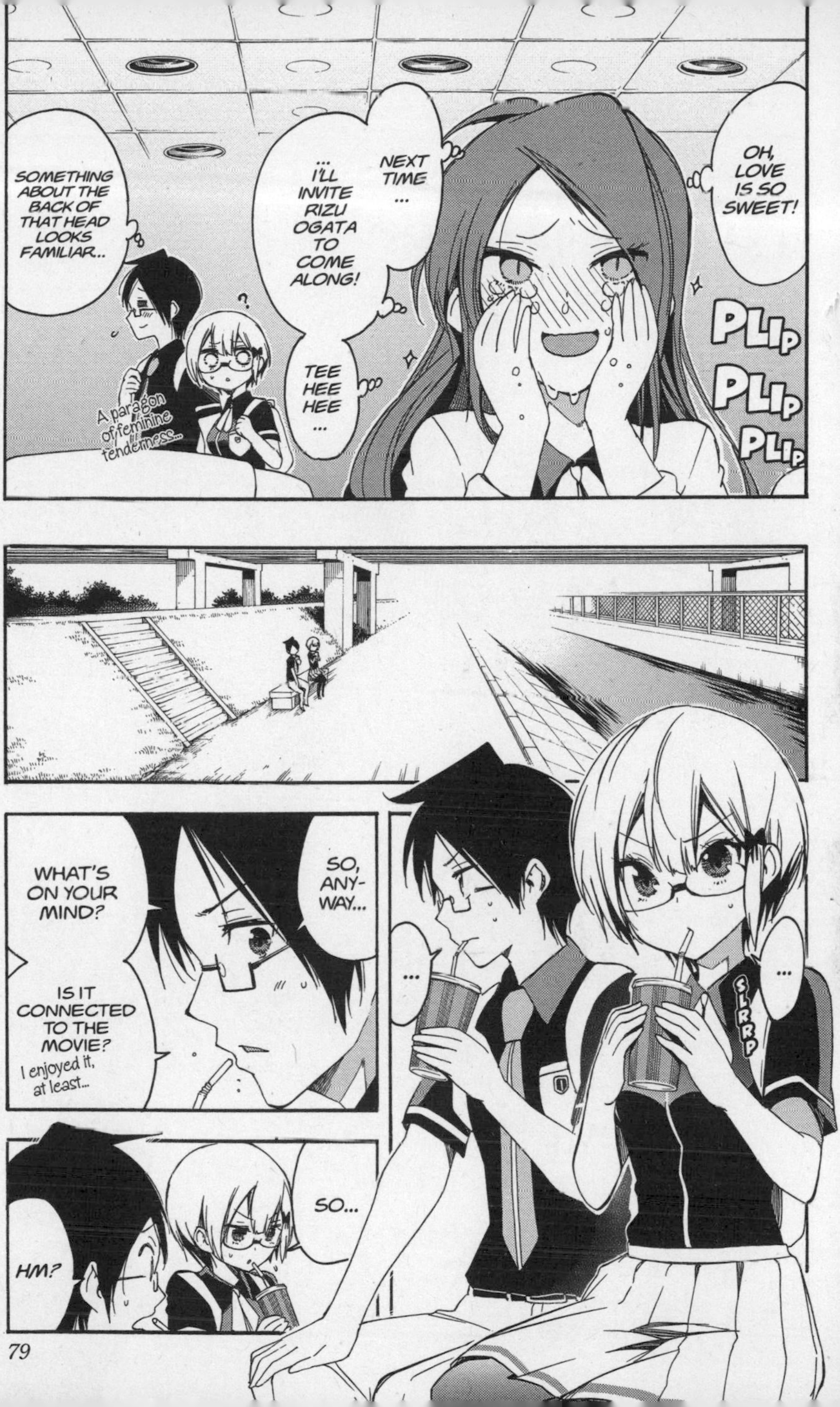
OH, LOVE IS SO SWEET!
PLIP PLIP PLIP
NEXT TIME ...
... I'LL INVITE RIZU OGATA TO COME ALONG!
TEE HEE HEE ...
SOMETHING ABOUT THE BACK OF THAT HEAD LOOKS FAMILIAR...
A paragon of feminine tenderness...
SO, ANYWAY...
...
SLRRP
...
WHAT'S ON YOUR MIND?
IS IT CONNECTED TO THE MOVIE?
I enjoyed it, at least...
SO...
HM?

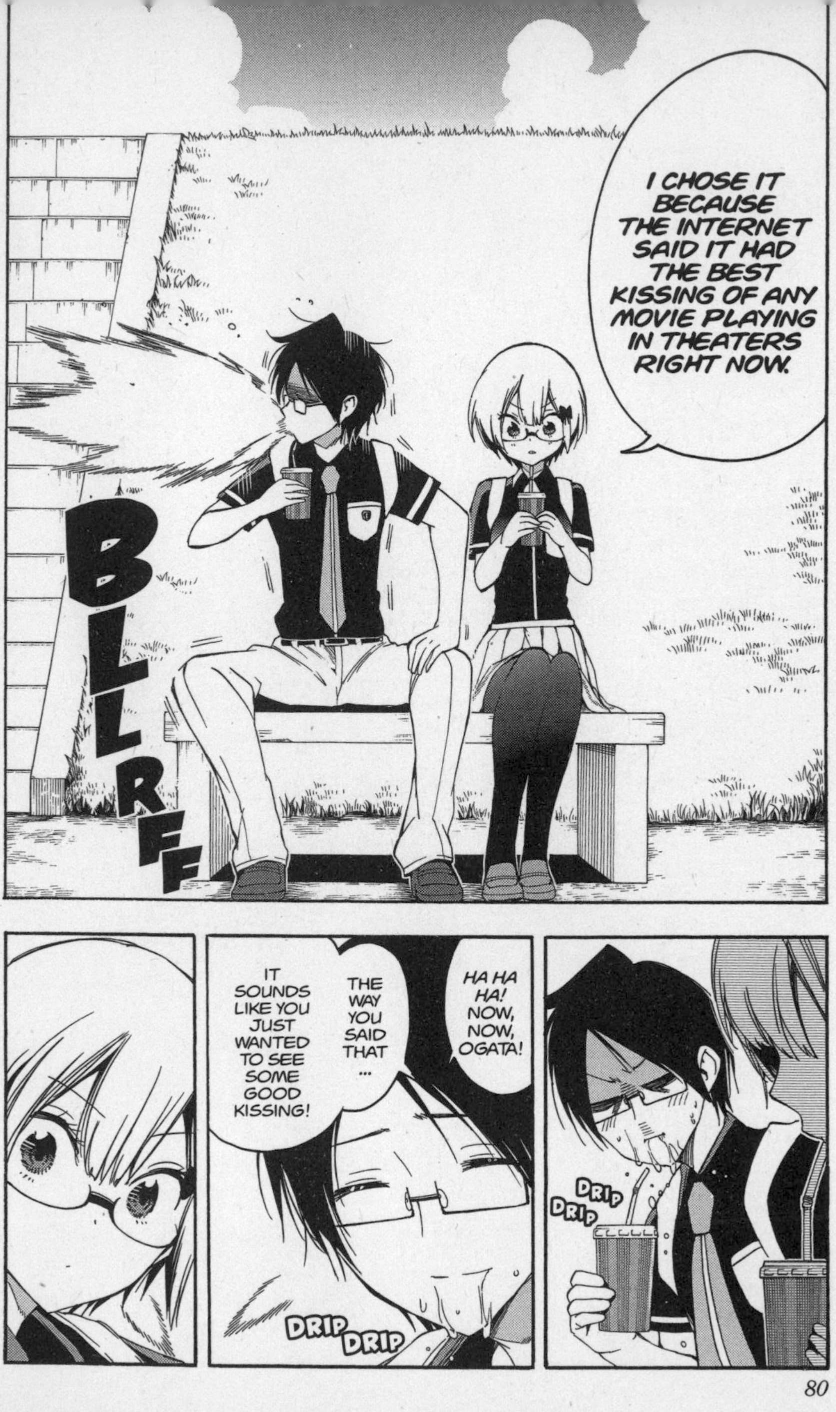
I CHOSE IT BECAUSE THE INTERNET SAID IT HAD THE BEST KISSING OF ANY MOVIE PLAYING IN THEATERS RIGHT NOW.
BLLRFF
DRIP DRIP
HA HA HA! NOW, NOW, OGATA!
THE WAY YOU SAID THAT ...
IT SOUNDS LIKE YOU JUST WANTED TO SEE SOME GOOD KISSING!
DRIP DRIP

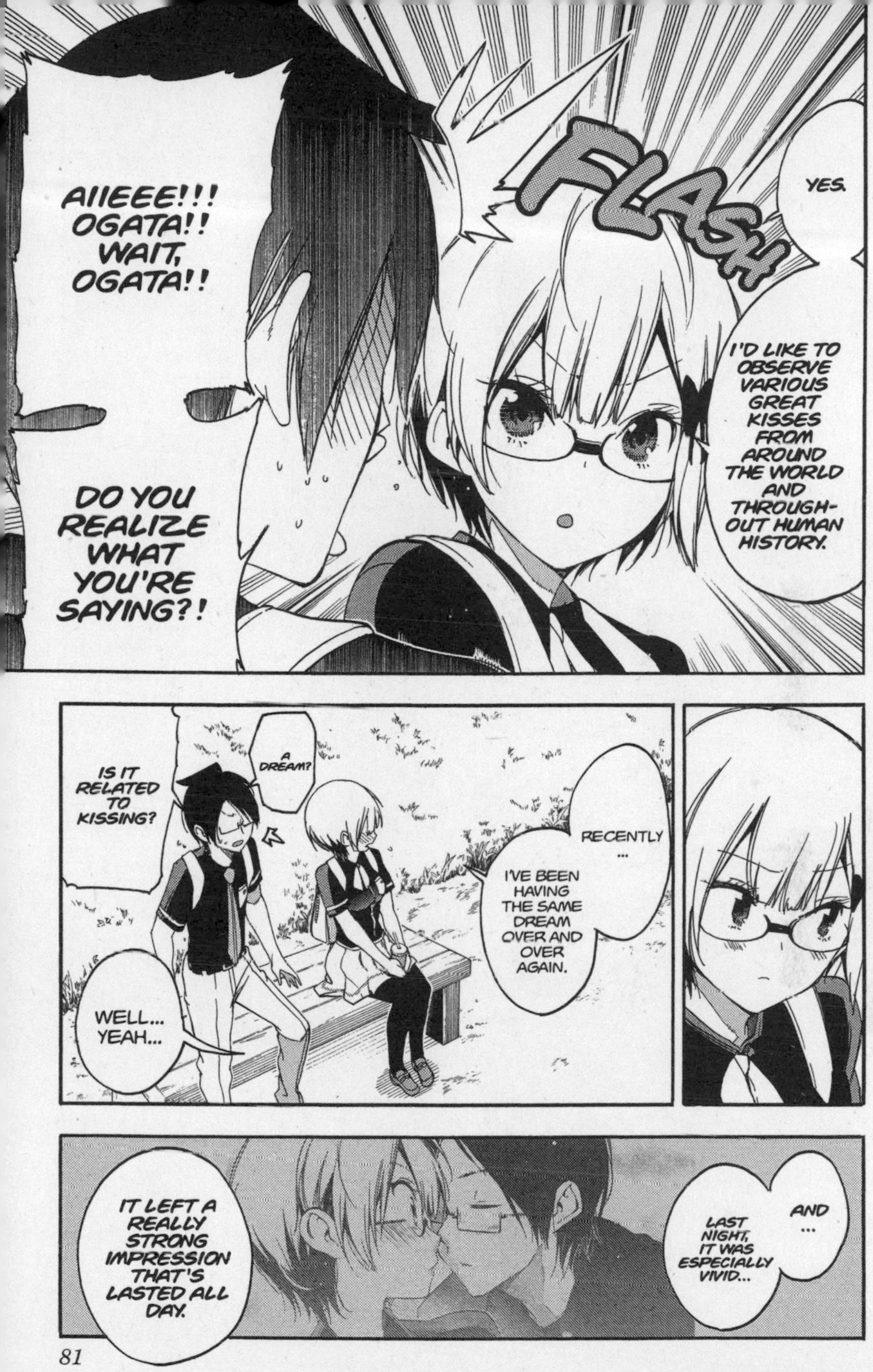
YES.
I'D LIKE TO OBSERVE VARIOUS GREAT KISSES FROM AROUND THE WORLD AND THROUGH-OUT HUMAN HISTORY.
FLASH
AIIEEE!!! OGATA!! WAIT, OGATA!!
DO YOU REALIZE WHAT YOU'RE SAYING?!
RECENTLY ...
I'VE BEEN HAVING THE SAME DREAM OVER AND OVER AGAIN.
A DREAM?
IS IT RELATED TO KISSING?
WELL... YEAH...
AND ...
LAST NIGHT, IT WAS ESPECIALLY VIVID...
IT LEFT A REALLY STRONG IMPRESSION THAT'S LASTED ALL DAY.

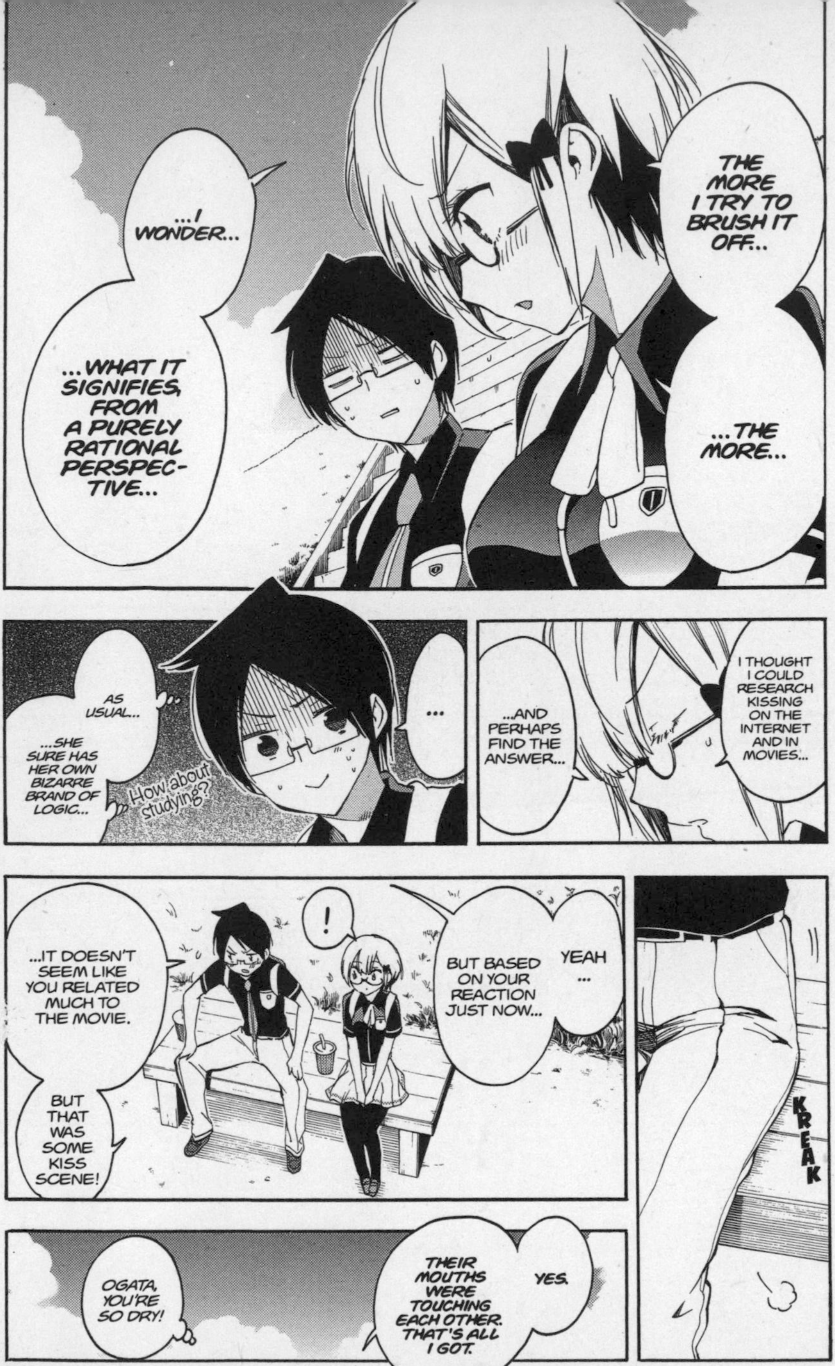
THE MORE I TRY TO BRUSH IT OFF...
...THE MORE...
...I WONDER...
...WHAT IT SIGNIFIES, FROM A PURELY RATIONAL PERSPECTIVE...
I THOUGHT I COULD RESEARCH KISSING ON THE INTERNET AND IN MOVIES...
...AND PERHAPS FIND THE ANSWER...
...
AS USUAL...
...SHE SURE HAS HER OWN BIZARRE BRAND OF LOGIC...
How about studying?
KREAK
YEAH ...
BUT BASED ON YOUR REACTION JUST NOW...
!
...IT DOESN'T SEEM LIKE YOU RELATED MUCH TO THE MOVIE.
BUT THAT WAS SOME KISS SCENE!
YES.
THEIR MOUTHS WERE TOUCHING EACH OTHER. THAT'S ALL I GOT.
OGATA, YOU'RE SO DRY!

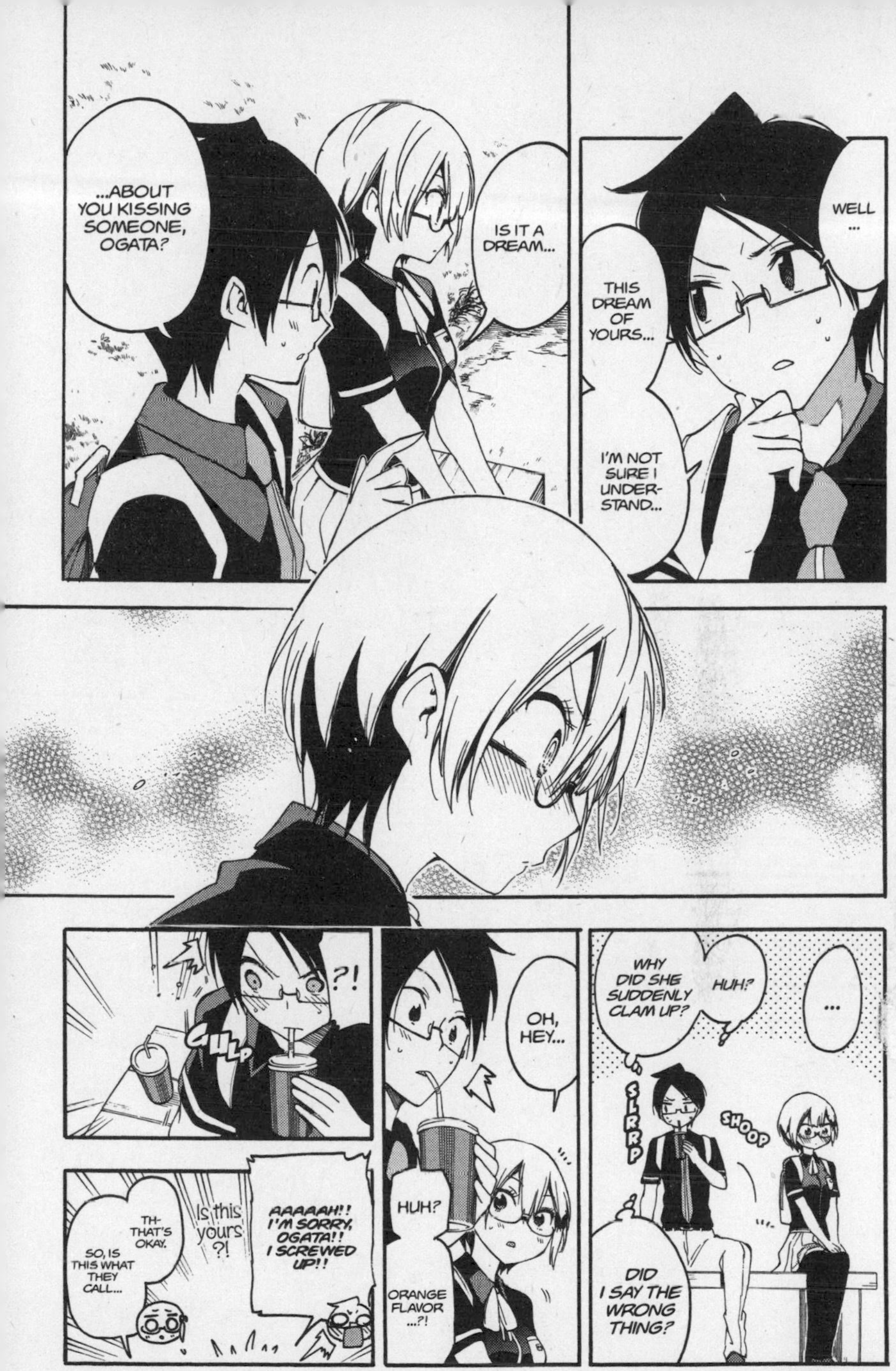
WELL ...
THIS DREAM OF YOURS...
I'M NOT SURE I UNDERSTAND...
IS IT A DREAM...
...ABOUT YOU KISSING SOMEONE, OGATA?
...
HUH?
WHY DID SHE SUDDENLY CLAM UP?
SHOOP
SLRRP
DID I SAY THE WRONG THING?
OH, HEY...
HUH?
ORANGE FLAVOR ...?!
?!
GULP
AAAAAH!! I'M SORRY, OGATA!! I SCREWED UP!!
Is this yours?!
TH-THAT'S OKAY.
SO, IS THIS WHAT THEY CALL...

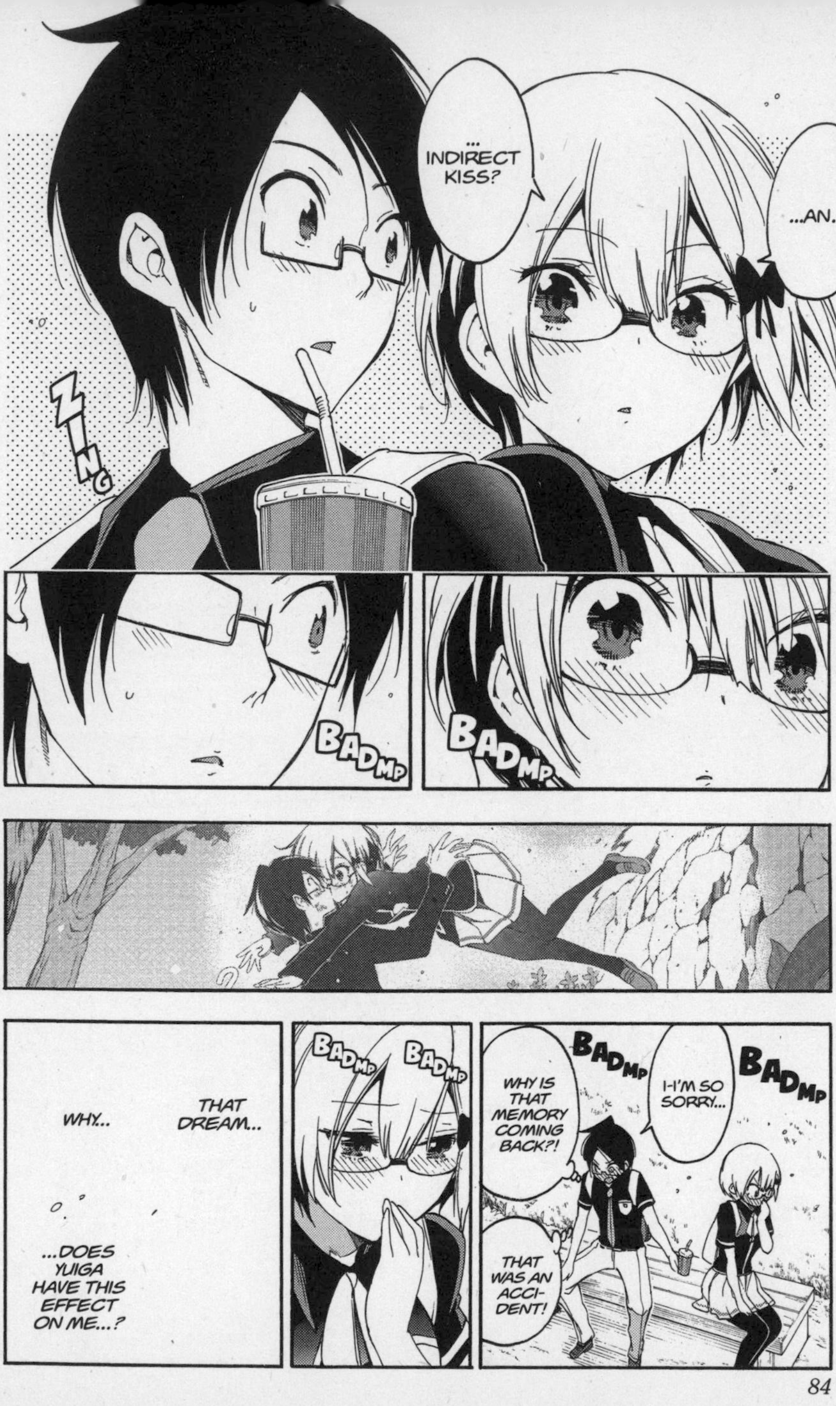
...AN...
... INDIRECT KISS?
ZING
BADMP
BADMP
BADMP
I-I'M SO SORRY...
BADMP
WHY IS THAT MEMORY COMING BACK?!
THAT WAS AN ACCI-DENT!
BADMP
BADMP
THAT DREAM...
WHY...
...DOES YUIGA HAVE THIS EFFECT ON ME...?

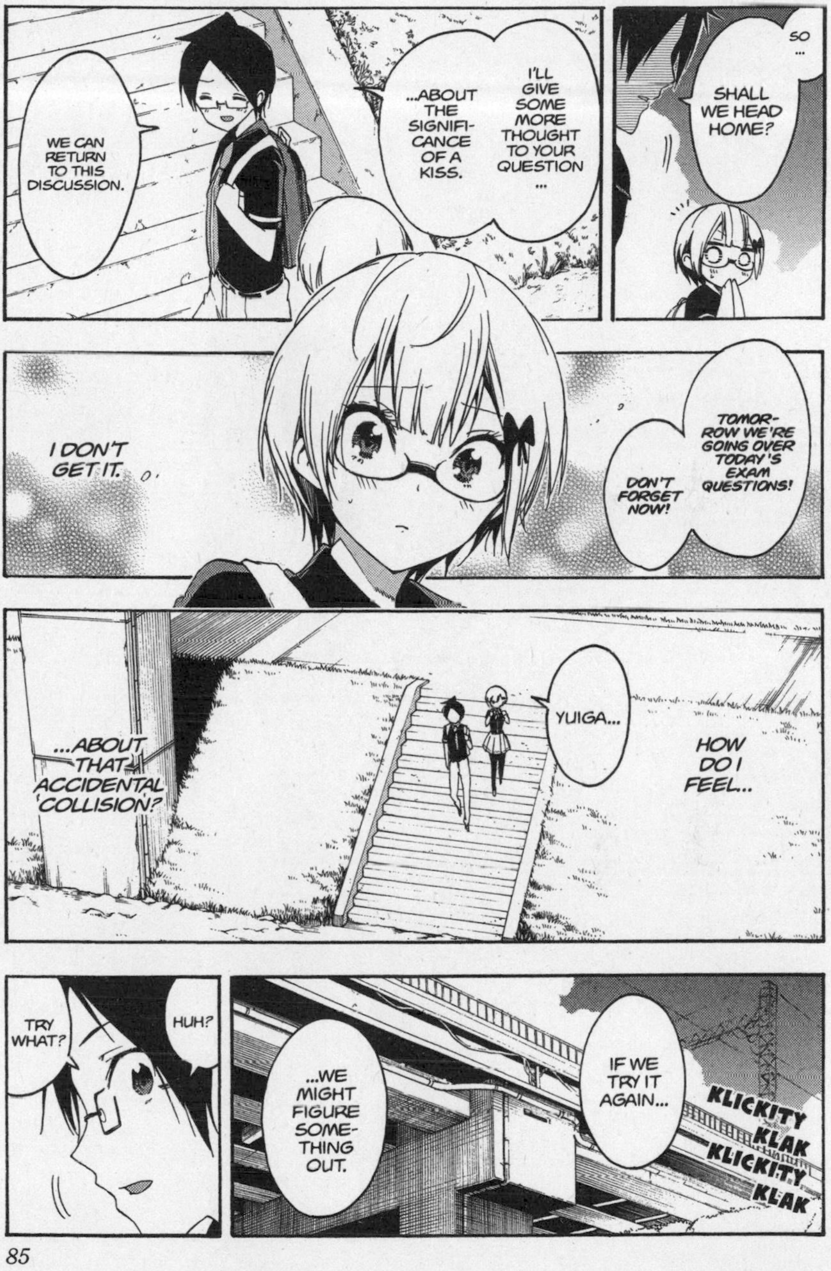
SO ...
SHALL WE HEAD HOME?
I'LL GIVE SOME MORE THOUGHT TO YOUR QUESTION ...
...ABOUT THE SIGNIFICANCE OF A KISS.
WE CAN RETURN TO THIS DISCUSSION.
TOMORROW WE'RE GOING OVER TODAY'S EXAM QUESTIONS!
DON'T FORGET NOW!
I DON'T GET IT.
YUIGA...
HOW DO I FEEL...
...ABOUT THAT ACCIDENTAL 'COLLISION'?
IF WE TRY IT AGAIN...
...WE MIGHT FIGURE SOMETHING OUT.
KLICKITY KLAK KLICKITY KLAK
HUH?
TRY WHAT?

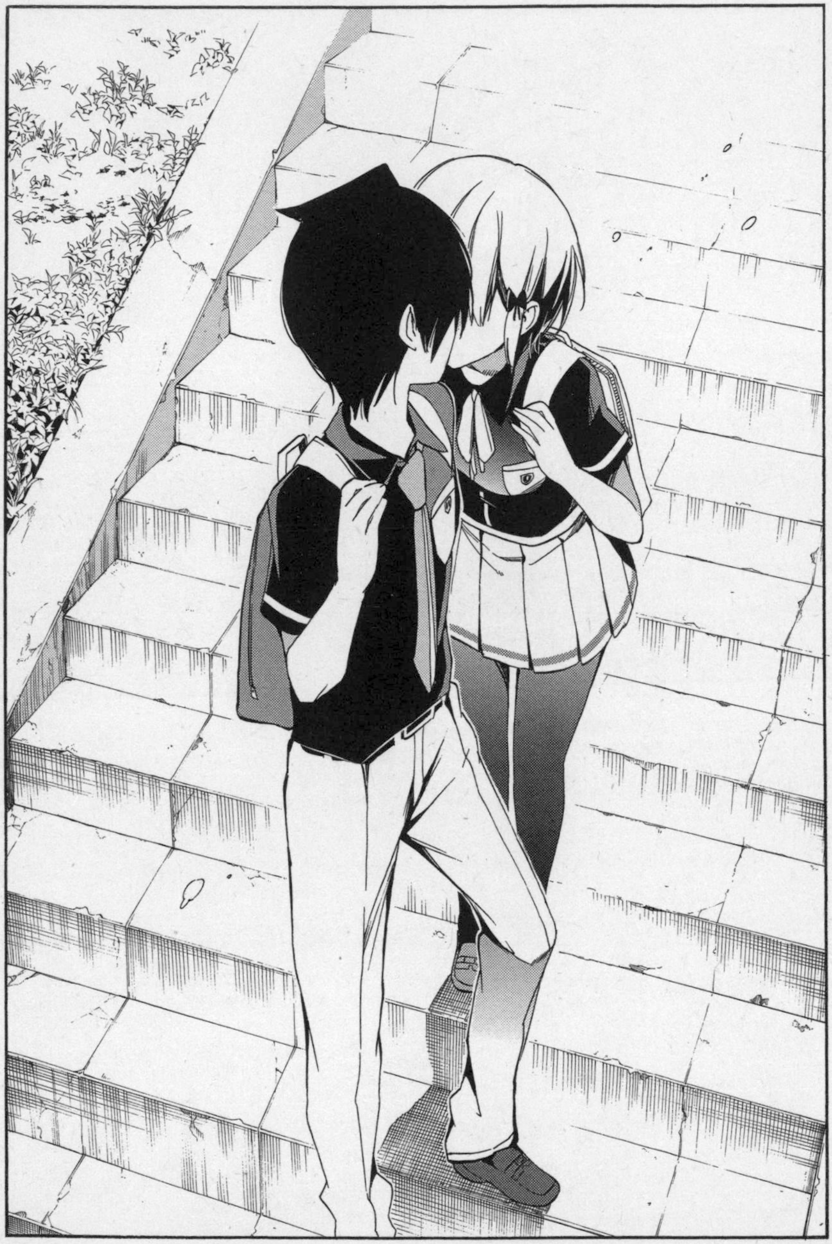

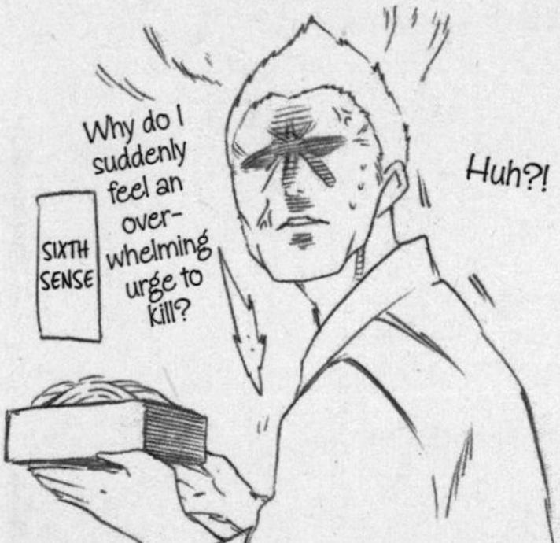
Huh?!
Why do I suddenly feel an over-whelming urge to kill?
SIXTH SENSE

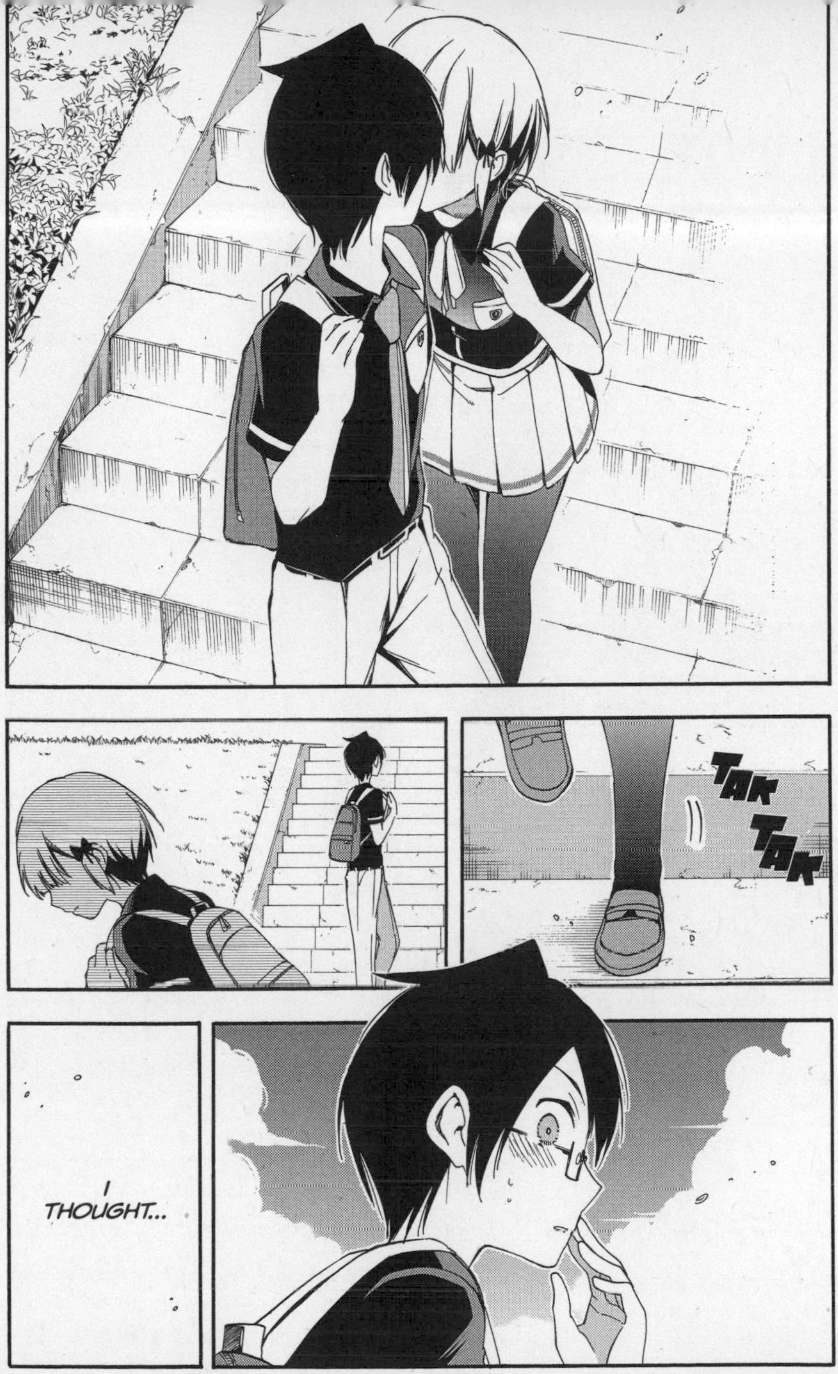
TAK TAK
I THOUGHT...

Question 30: A Genius Is Avidly Dedicated to the Investigation of [X]

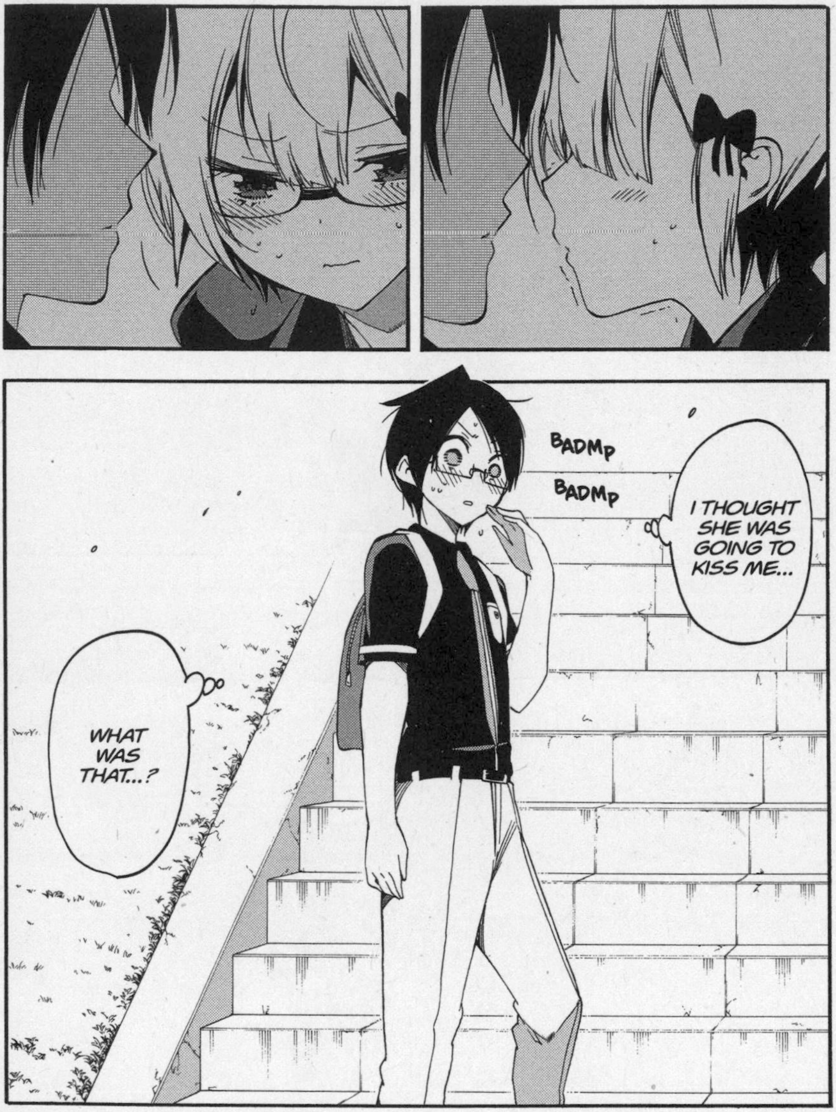
BADMP
BADMP
I THOUGHT SHE WAS GOING TO KISS ME...
WHAT WAS THAT...?

Question 30: A Genius Is Avidly Dedicated to the Investigation of [*X*]

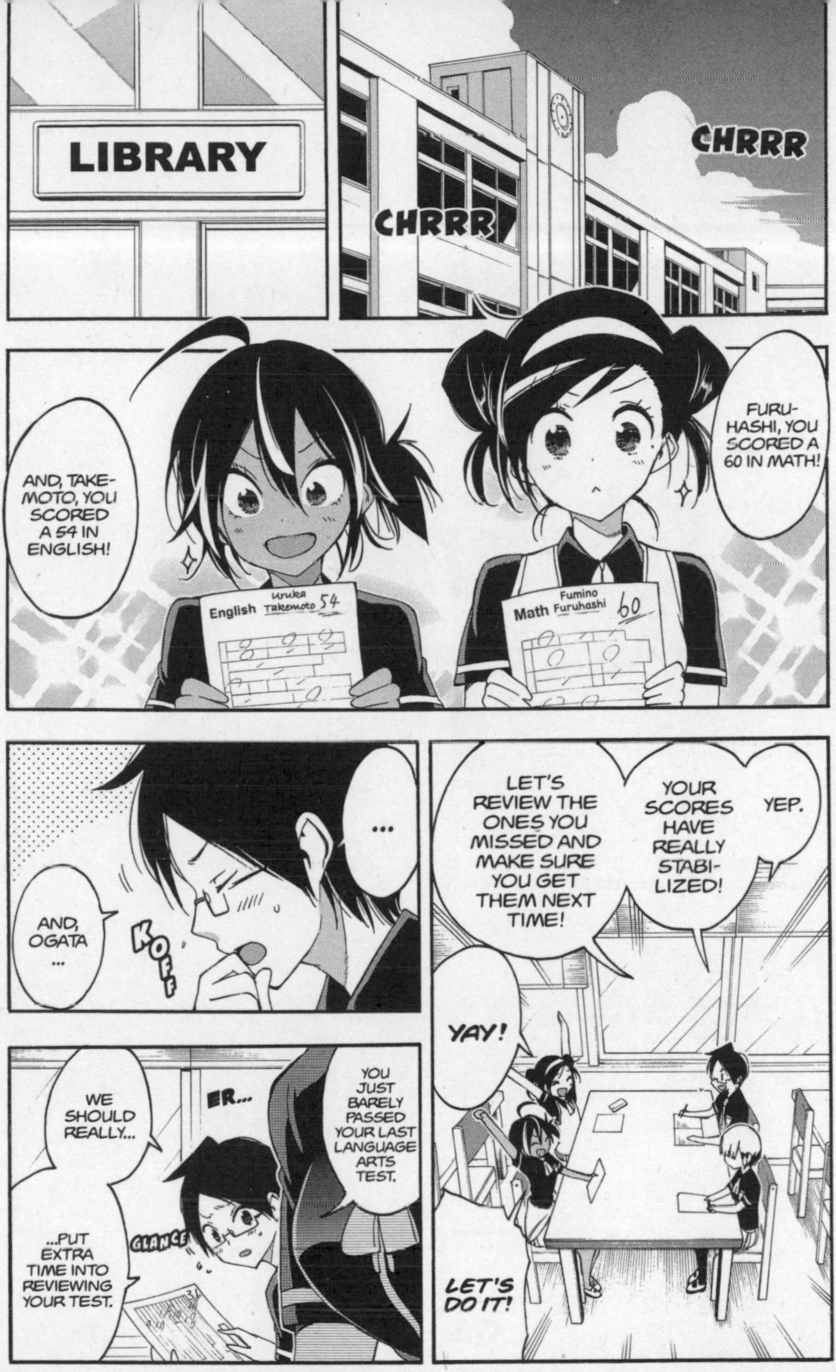

CHRRR
CHRRR
LIBRARY
FURU-HASHI, YOU SCORED A 60 IN MATH!
Math Fumino Furuhashi 60
AND, TAKE-MOTO, YOU SCORED A 54 IN ENGLISH!
English Uruka Takemoto 54
YEP.
YOUR SCORES HAVE REALLY STABI-LIZED!
LET'S REVIEW THE ONES YOU MISSED AND MAKE SURE YOU GET THEM NEXT TIME!
YAY!
LET'S DO IT!
...
AND, OGATA ...
KOFF
YOU JUST BARELY PASSED YOUR LAST LANGUAGE ARTS TEST.
ER...
WE SHOULD REALLY...
GLANCE
...PUT EXTRA TIME INTO REVIEWING YOUR TEST.

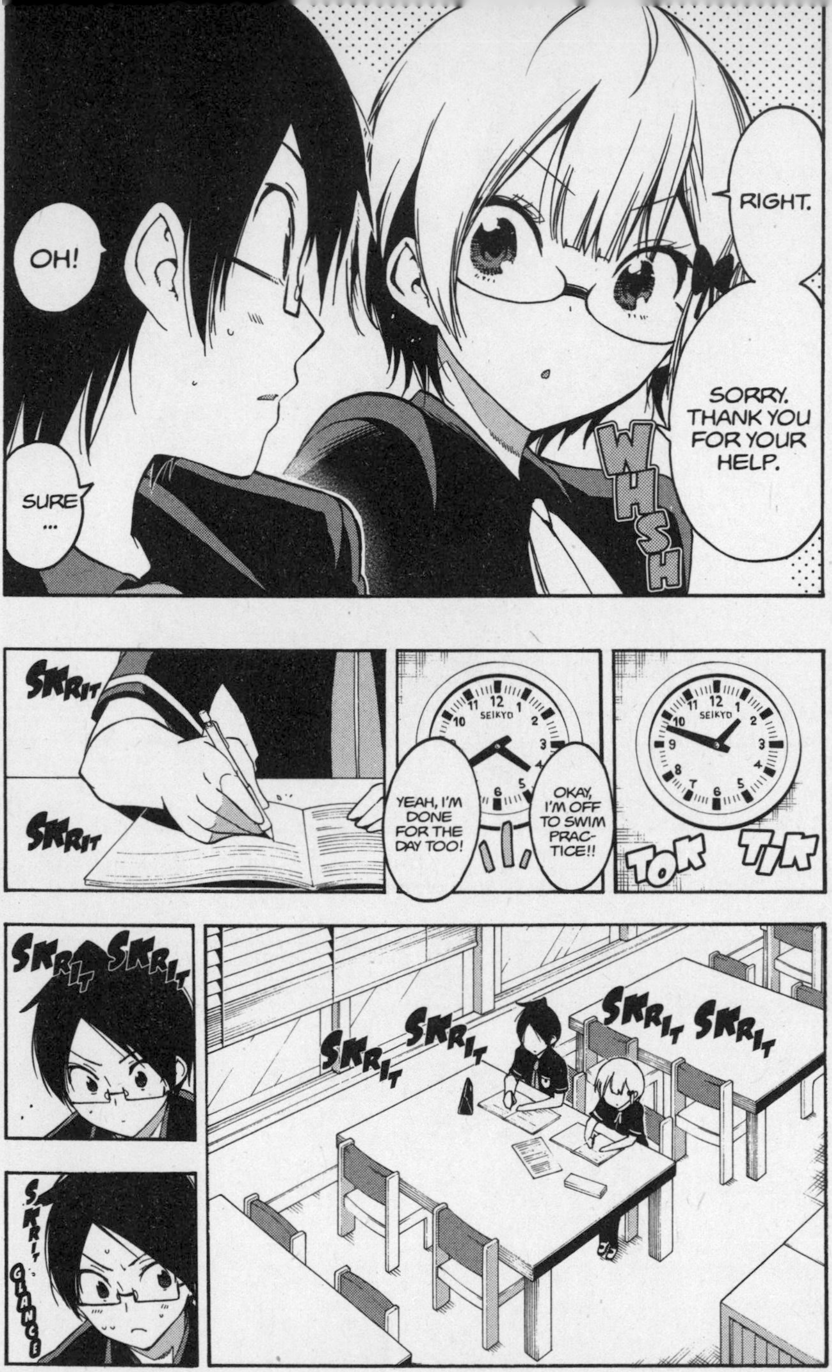

RIGHT.
OH!
SORRY. THANK YOU FOR YOUR HELP.
WHSH
SURE...
TIK
TOK
OKAY, I'M OFF TO SWIM PRAC-TICE!!
YEAH, I'M DONE FOR THE DAY TOO!
SKRIT
SKRIT
SKRIT SKRIT
SKRIT SKRIT
SKRIT SKRIT
SKRIT
GLANCE

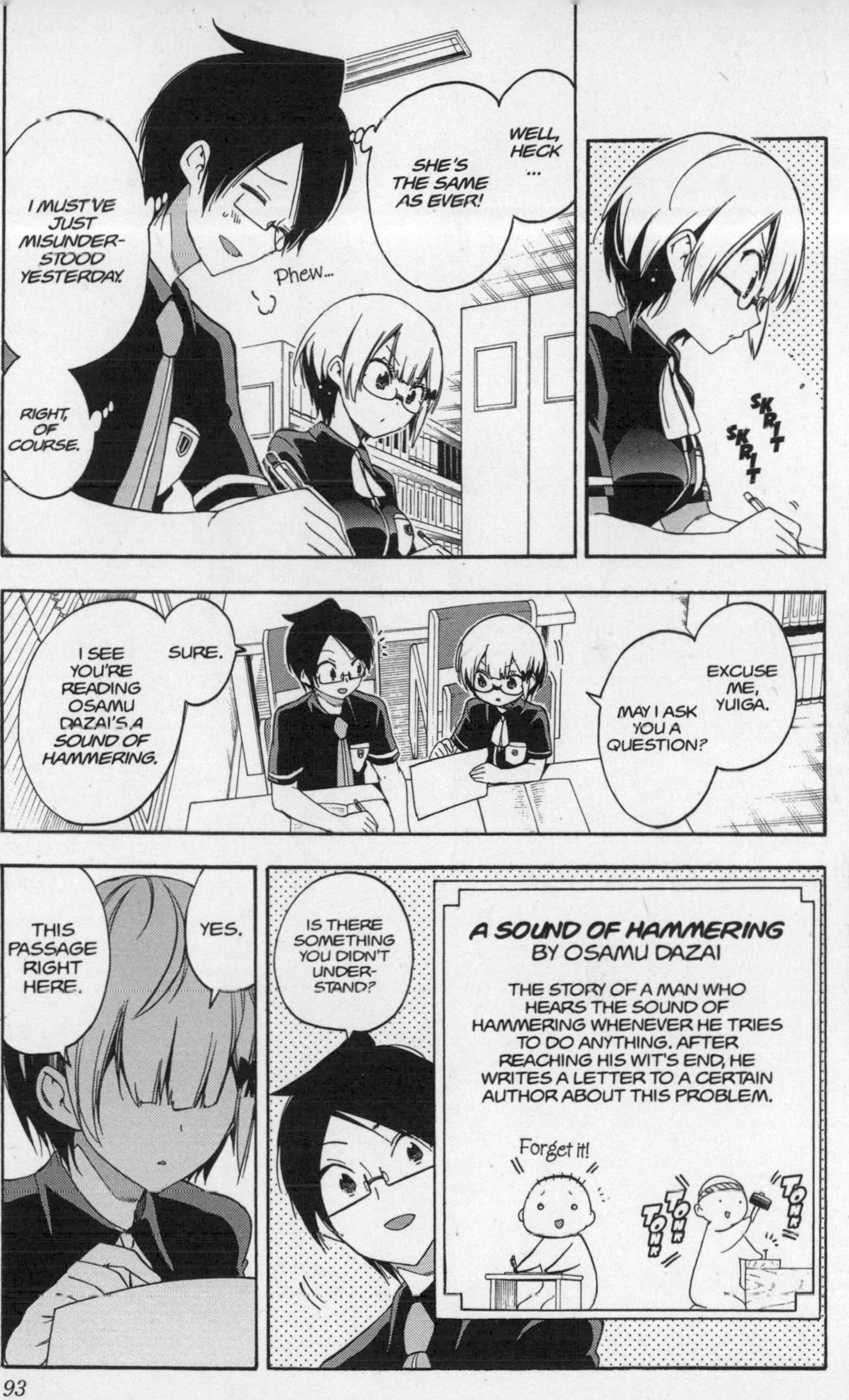
SKRIT
SKRIT
WELL, HECK ...
SHE'S THE SAME AS EVER!
Phew...
I MUST'VE JUST MISUNDER-STOOD YESTERDAY.
RIGHT, OF COURSE.
EXCUSE ME, YUIGA.
MAY I ASK YOU A QUESTION?
SURE.
I SEE YOU'RE READING OSAMU DAZAI'S A SOUND OF HAMMERING.
A SOUND OF HAMMERING
BY OSAMU DAZAI
THE STORY OF A MAN WHO HEARS THE SOUND OF HAMMERING WHENEVER HE TRIES TO DO ANYTHING. AFTER REACHING HIS WIT'S END, HE WRITES A LETTER TO A CERTAIN AUTHOR ABOUT THIS PROBLEM.
Forget it!
TONK
TONK
TONK
IS THERE SOMETHING YOU DIDN'T UNDER-STAND?
YES.
THIS PASSAGE RIGHT HERE.

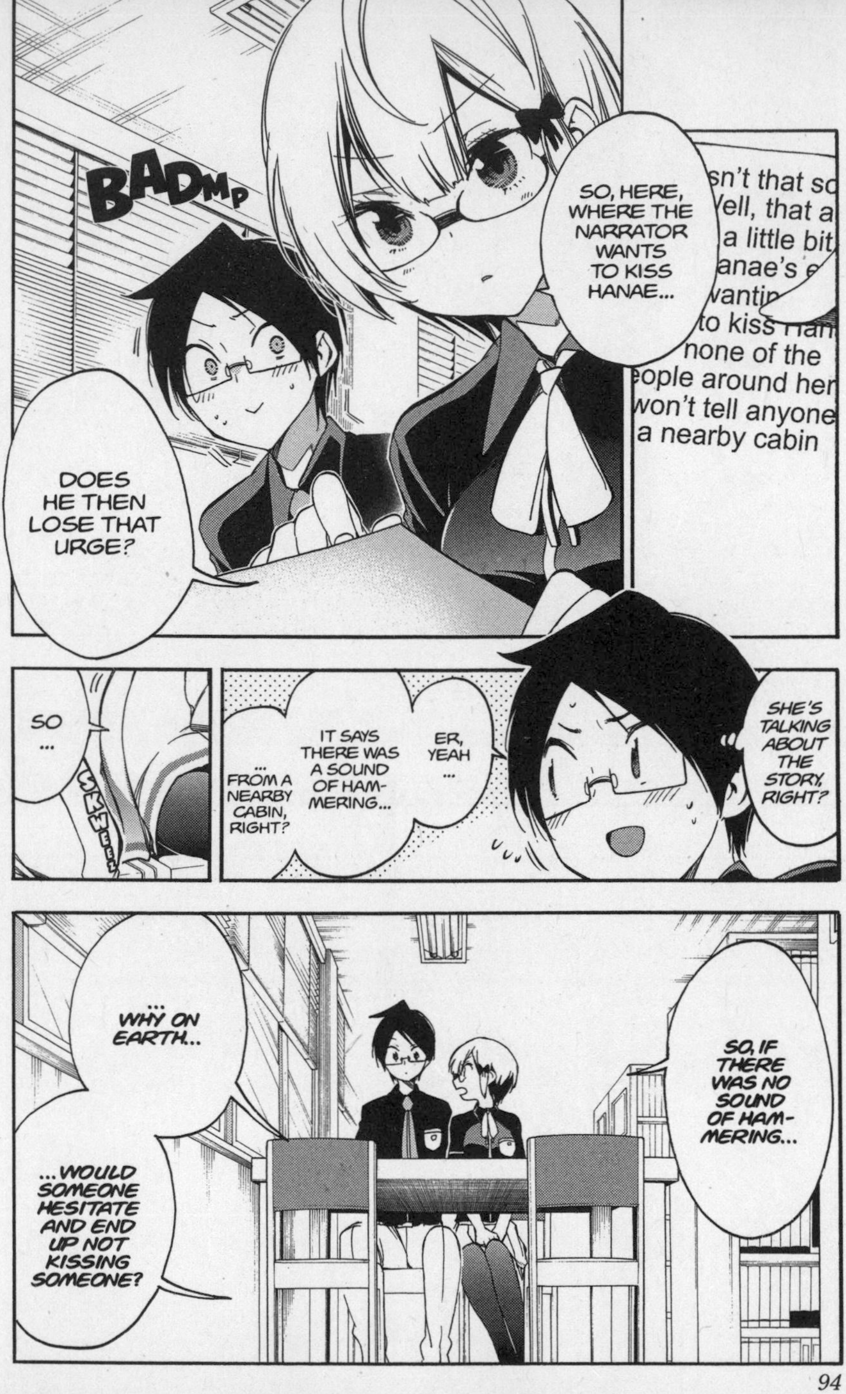
sn't that sc
Vell, that a
a little bit
lanae's e
vantin
to kiss Han
none of the
eople around her
won't tell anyone
a nearby cabin
SO, HERE, WHERE THE NARRATOR WANTS TO KISS HANAE...
BADMP
DOES HE THEN LOSE THAT URGE?
SHE'S TALKING ABOUT THE STORY, RIGHT?
ER, YEAH ...
IT SAYS THERE WAS A SOUND OF HAMMERING...
... FROM A NEARBY CABIN, RIGHT?
SO ...
SKWEEE
SO, IF THERE WAS NO SOUND OF HAMMERING...
... WHY ON EARTH...
...WOULD SOMEONE HESITATE AND END UP NOT KISSING SOMEONE?

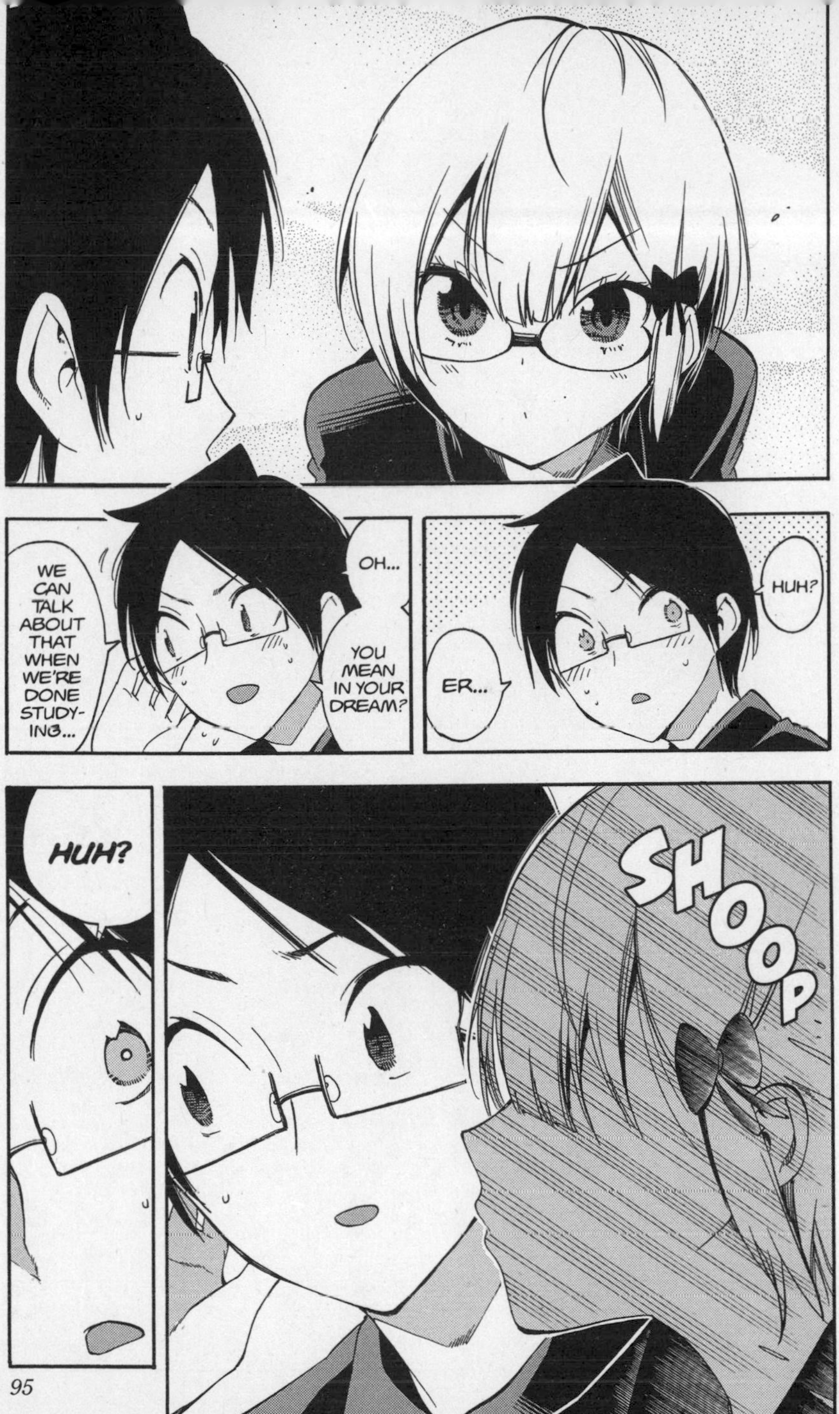
HUH?
ER...
OH...
YOU MEAN IN YOUR DREAM?
WE CAN TALK ABOUT THAT WHEN WE'RE DONE STUDYING...
SHOOP
HUH?

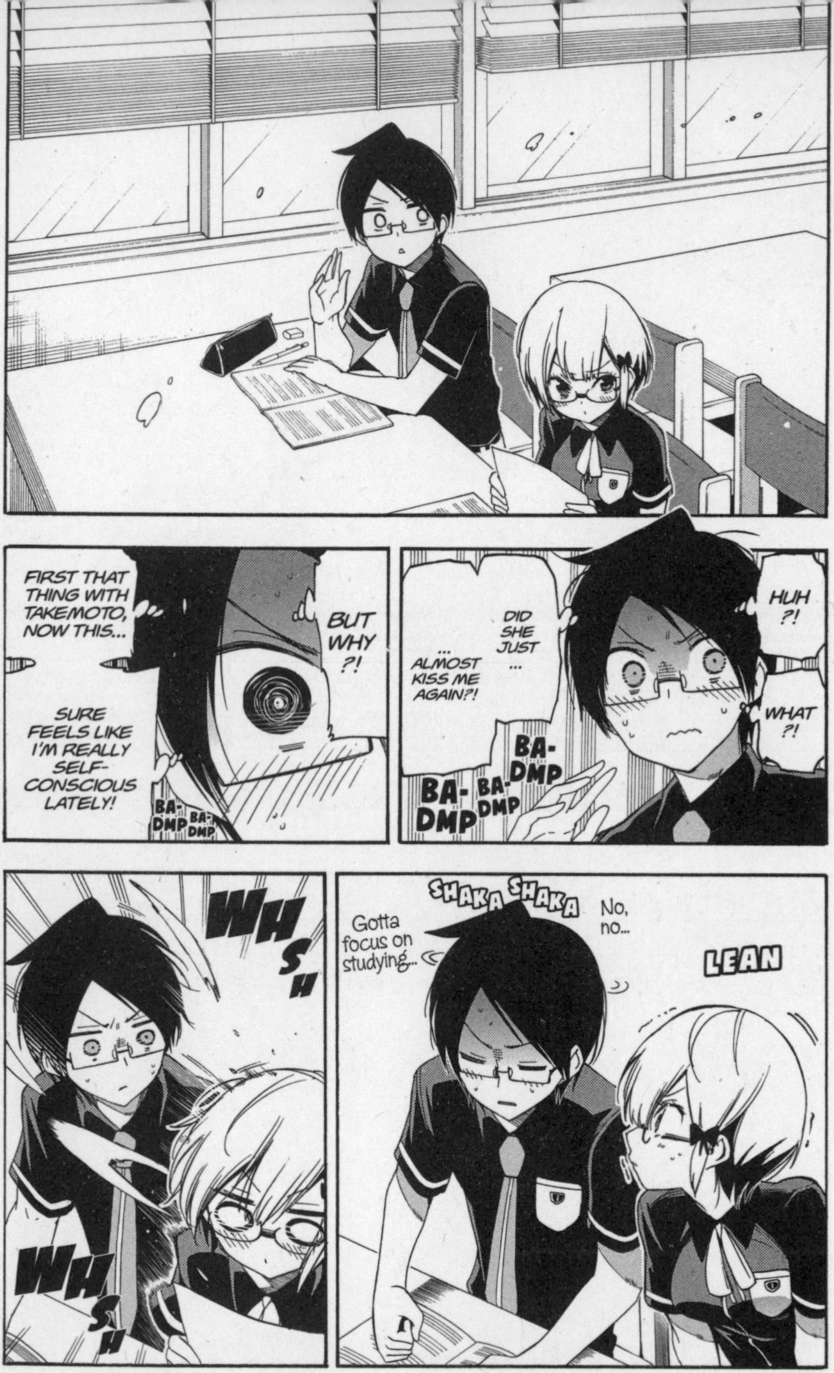
HUH?!
WHAT?!
DID SHE JUST ... ... ALMOST KISS ME AGAIN?!
BA-DMP
BA-DMP
BA-DMP
BUT WHY?!
FIRST THAT THING WITH TAKEMOTO, NOW THIS...
SURE FEELS LIKE I'M REALLY SELF-CONSCIOUS LATELY!
BA-DMP
BA-DMP
SHAKA SHAKA
No, no...
Gotta focus on studying...
LEAN
WHSH
WHSH

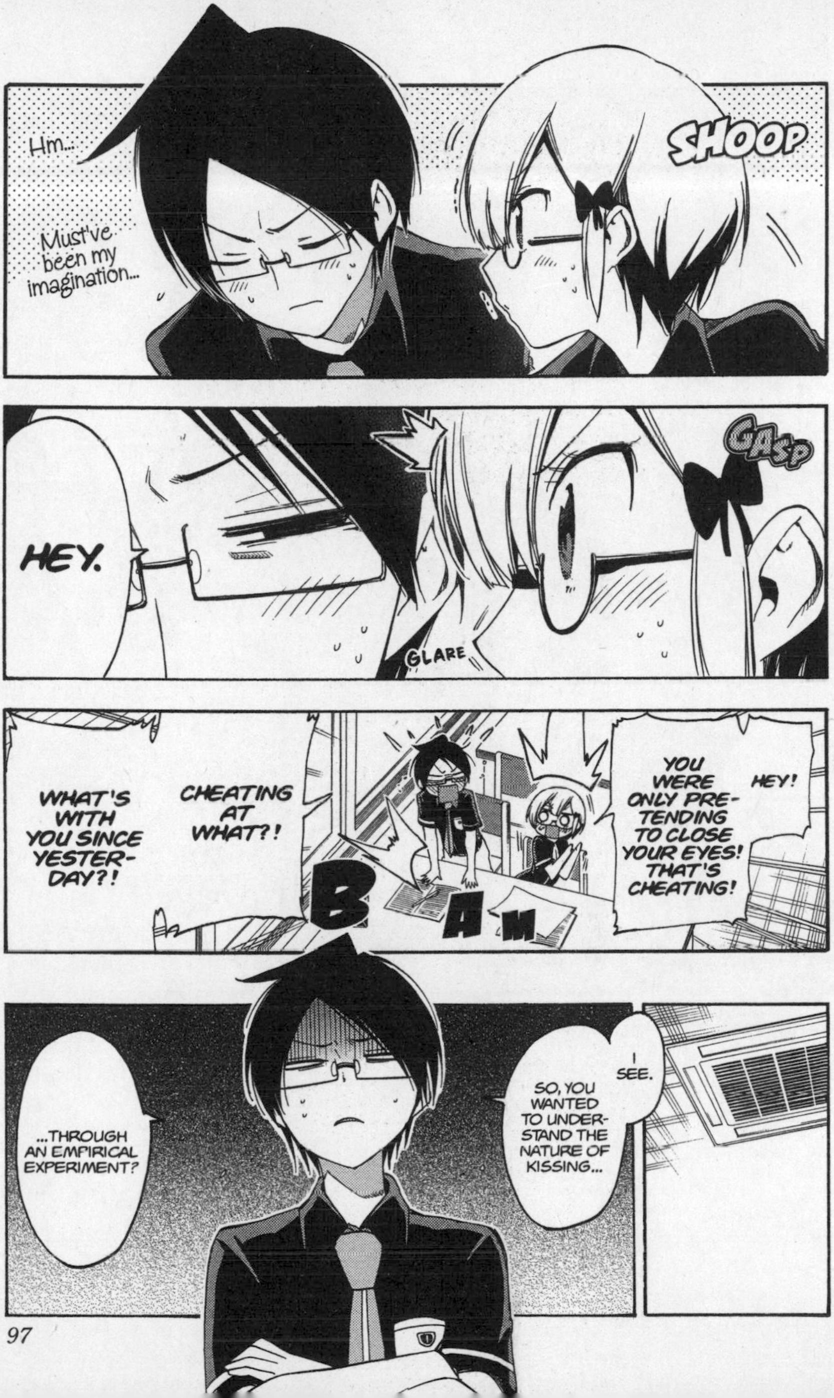
SHOOP
Hm...
Must've been my imagination...
GASP
HEY.
GLARE
HEY!
YOU WERE ONLY PRETENDING TO CLOSE YOUR EYES! THAT'S CHEATING!
BAM
CHEATING AT WHAT?!
WHAT'S WITH YOU SINCE YESTERDAY?!
I SEE.
SO, YOU WANTED TO UNDERSTAND THE NATURE OF KISSING...
...THROUGH AN EMPIRICAL EXPERIMENT?

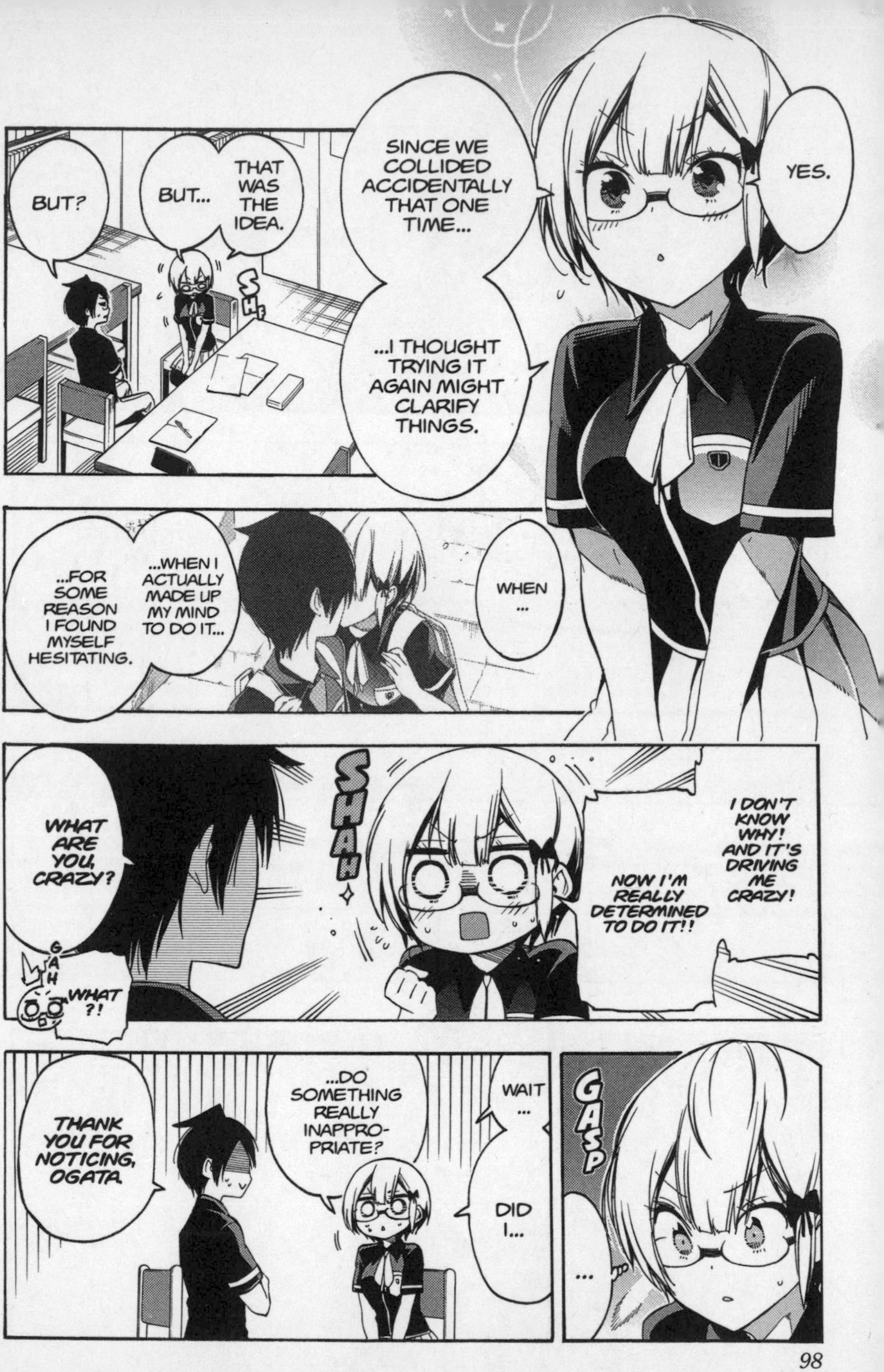

YES.
SINCE WE COLLIDED ACCIDENTALLY THAT ONE TIME...
...I THOUGHT TRYING IT AGAIN MIGHT CLARIFY THINGS.
THAT WAS THE IDEA.
BUT...
BUT?
SHF
WHEN ...
...WHEN I ACTUALLY MADE UP MY MIND TO DO IT...
...FOR SOME REASON I FOUND MYSELF HESITATING.
I DON'T KNOW WHY! AND IT'S DRIVING ME CRAZY!
NOW I'M REALLY DETERMINED TO DO IT!!
SHAH
WHAT ARE YOU, CRAZY?
GAH
WHAT ?!
GASP
...
DID I...
WAIT ...
...DO SOMETHING REALLY INAPPROPRIATE?
THANK YOU FOR NOTICING, OGATA.

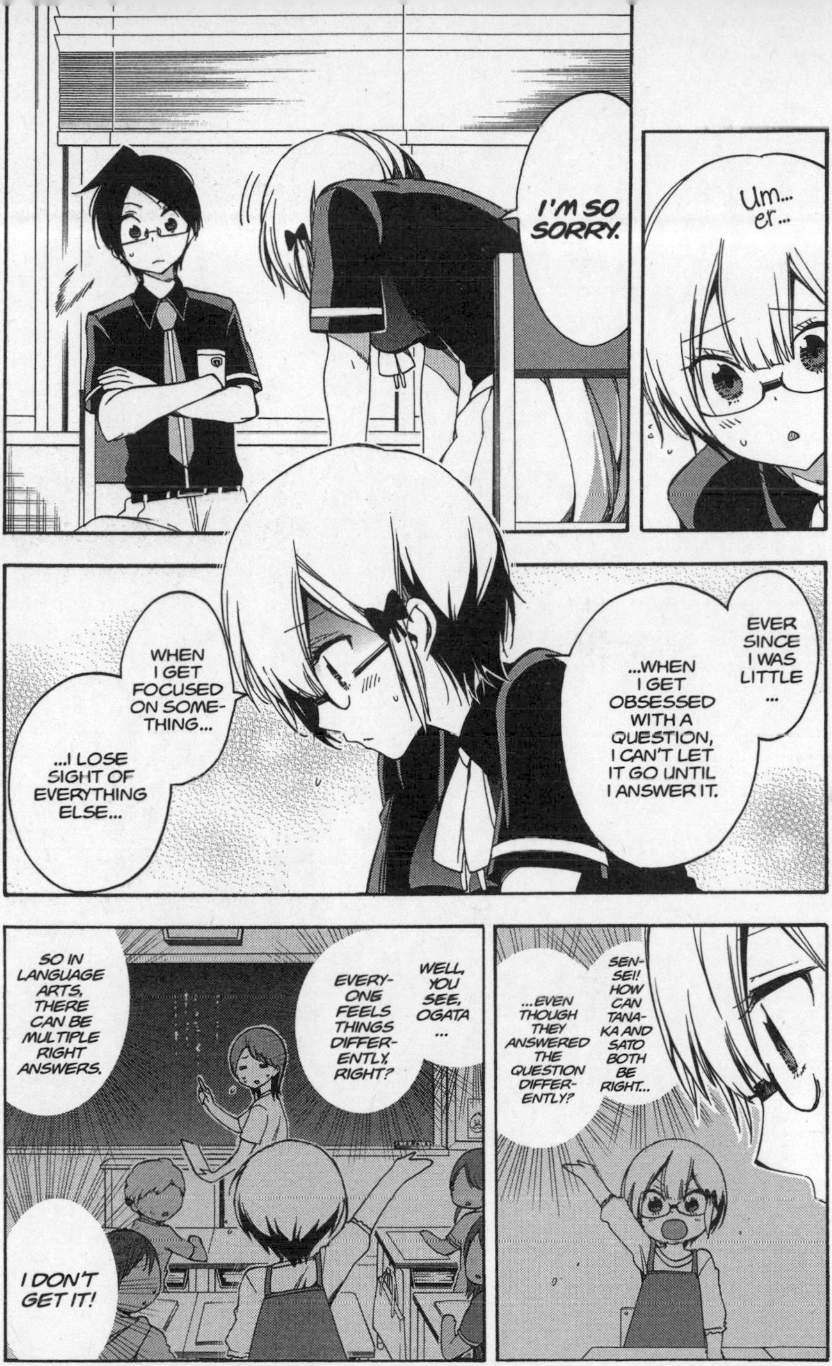
Um... er...
I'M SO SORRY.
EVER SINCE I WAS LITTLE ...
...WHEN I GET OBSESSED WITH A QUESTION, I CAN'T LET IT GO UNTIL I ANSWER IT.
WHEN I GET FOCUSED ON SOMETHING...
...I LOSE SIGHT OF EVERYTHING ELSE...
SENSEI! HOW CAN TANAKA AND SATO BOTH BE RIGHT...
...EVEN THOUGH THEY ANSWERED THE QUESTION DIFFERENTLY?
WELL, YOU SEE, OGATA ...
EVERYONE FEELS THINGS DIFFERENTLY, RIGHT?
SO IN LANGUAGE ARTS, THERE CAN BE MULTIPLE RIGHT ANSWERS.
I DON'T GET IT!

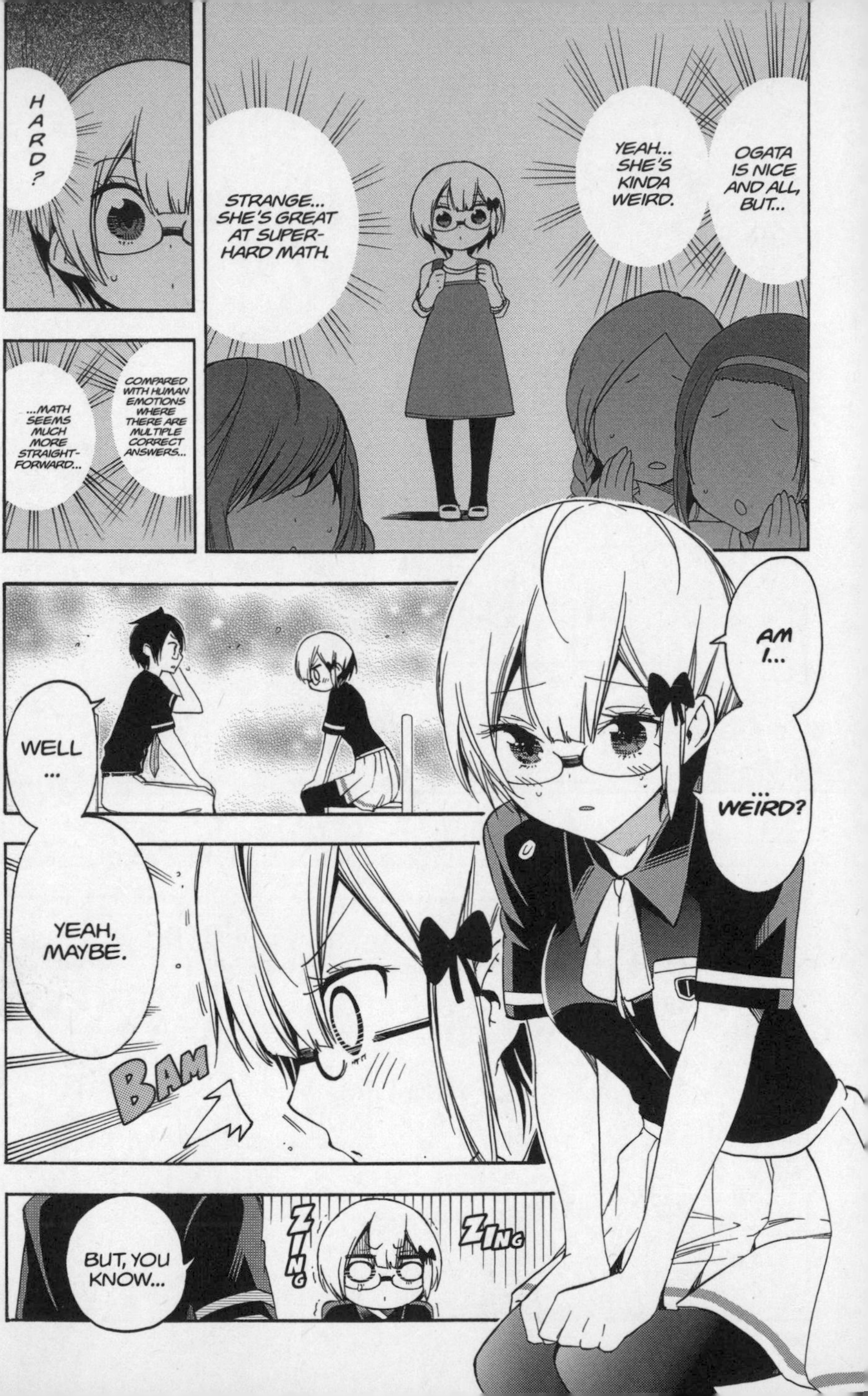
OGATA IS NICE AND ALL, BUT...
YEAH... SHE'S KINDA WEIRD.
STRANGE... SHE'S GREAT AT SUPER-HARD MATH.
HARD?
COMPARED WITH HUMAN EMOTIONS WHERE THERE ARE MULTIPLE CORRECT ANSWERS...
...MATH SEEMS MUCH MORE STRAIGHT-FORWARD...
AM I...
... WEIRD?
WELL ...
YEAH, MAYBE.
BAM
ZING
ZING
BUT, YOU KNOW...

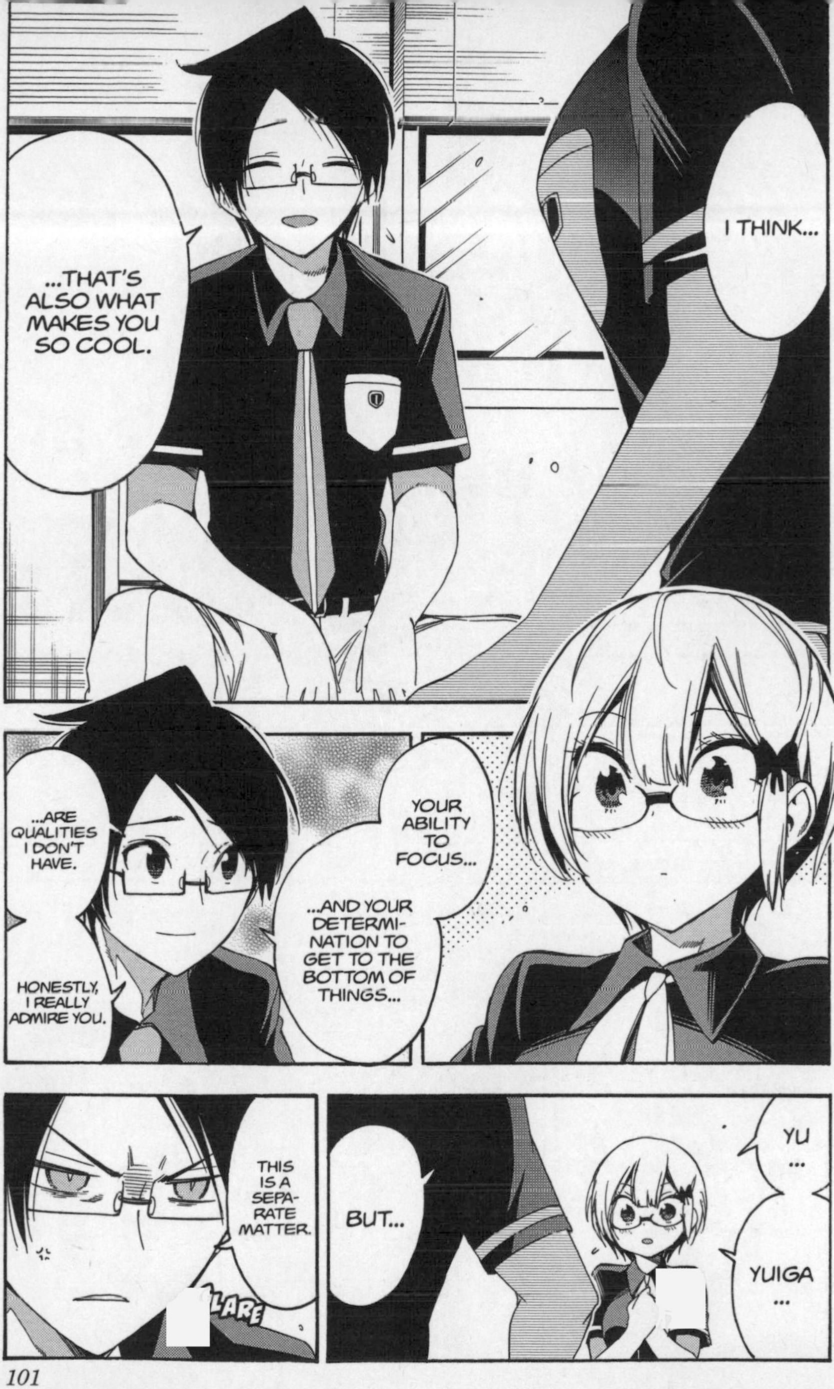
I THINK...
...THAT'S ALSO WHAT MAKES YOU SO COOL.
YOUR ABILITY TO FOCUS...
...AND YOUR DETERMINATION TO GET TO THE BOTTOM OF THINGS...
...ARE QUALITIES I DON'T HAVE.
HONESTLY, I REALLY ADMIRE YOU.
YU...
YUIGA...
BUT...
THIS IS A SEPARATE MATTER.
GLARE

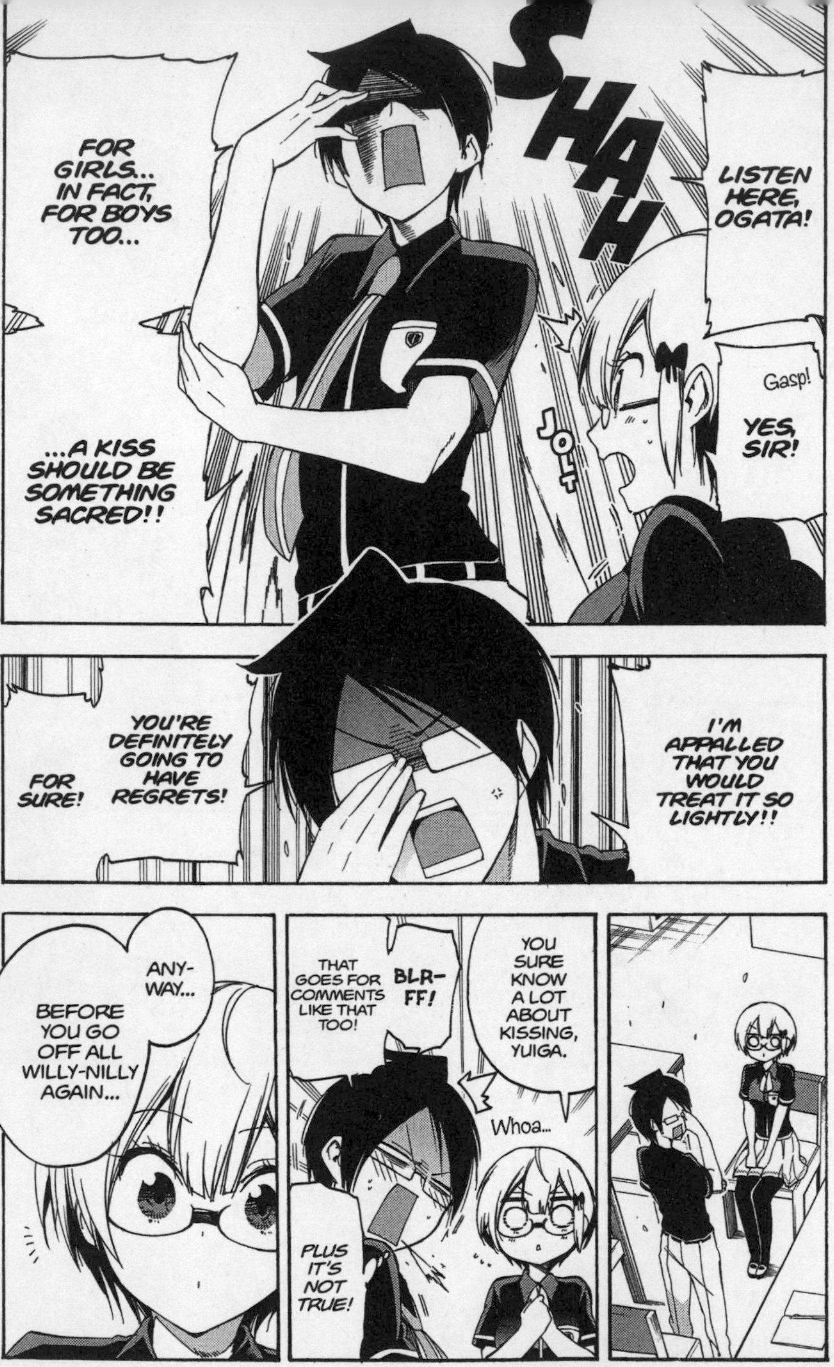
LISTEN HERE, OGATA!
SHAH
Gasp!
YES, SIR!
FOR GIRLS... IN FACT, FOR BOYS TOO...
JOLT
...A KISS SHOULD BE SOMETHING SACRED!!
I'M APPALLED THAT YOU WOULD TREAT IT SO LIGHTLY!!
YOU'RE DEFINITELY GOING TO HAVE REGRETS!
FOR SURE!
YOU SURE KNOW A LOT ABOUT KISSING, YUIGA.
BLR-FF!
THAT GOES FOR COMMENTS LIKE THAT TOO!
Whoa...
PLUS IT'S NOT TRUE!
ANY-WAY...
BEFORE YOU GO OFF ALL WILLY-NILLY AGAIN...

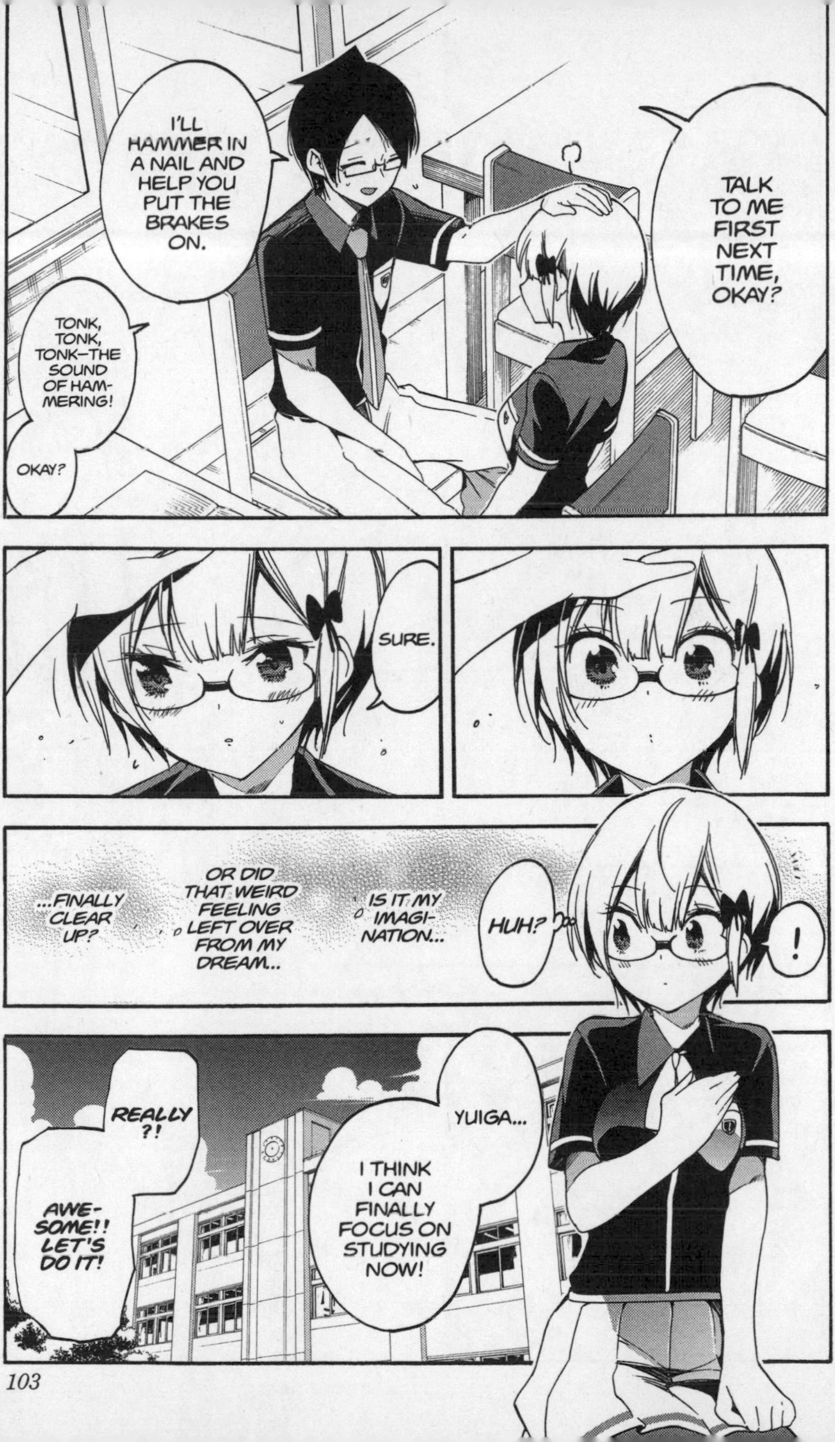
TALK TO ME FIRST NEXT TIME, OKAY?
I'LL HAMMER IN A NAIL AND HELP YOU PUT THE BRAKES ON.
TONK, TONK, TONK—THE SOUND OF HAMMERING!
OKAY?
SURE.
!
HUH?
IS IT MY IMAGINATION...
OR DID THAT WEIRD FEELING LEFT OVER FROM MY DREAM...
...FINALLY CLEAR UP?
YUIGA...
I THINK I CAN FINALLY FOCUS ON STUDYING NOW!
REALLY?!
AWE-SOME!! LET'S DO IT!

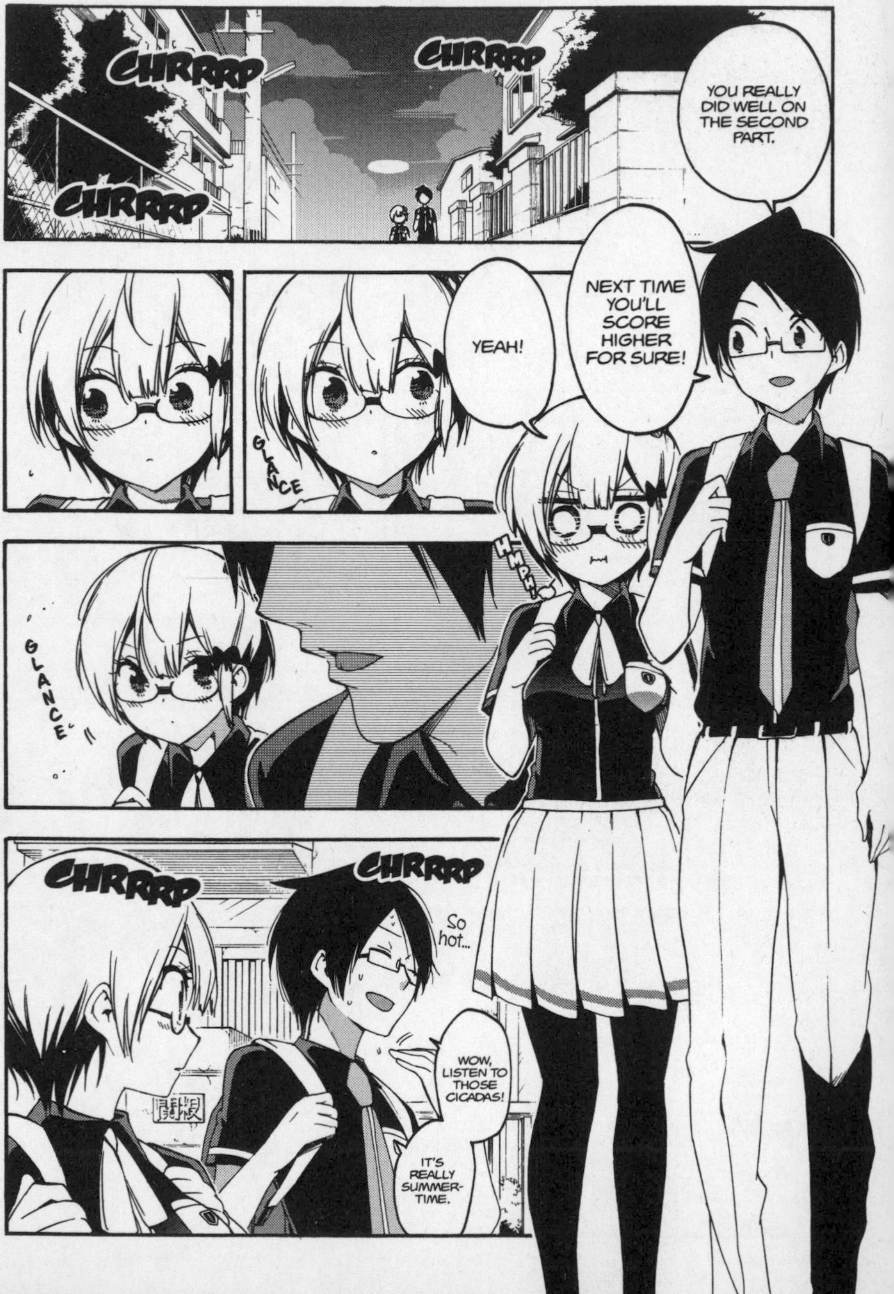
CHRRRP
CHRRRP
CHRRRP
YOU REALLY DID WELL ON THE SECOND PART.
NEXT TIME YOU'LL SCORE HIGHER FOR SURE!
YEAH!
HMPH!
GLANCE
GLANCE
CHRRRP
CHRRRP
So hot...
WOW, LISTEN TO THOSE CICADAS!
IT'S REALLY SUMMER-TIME.

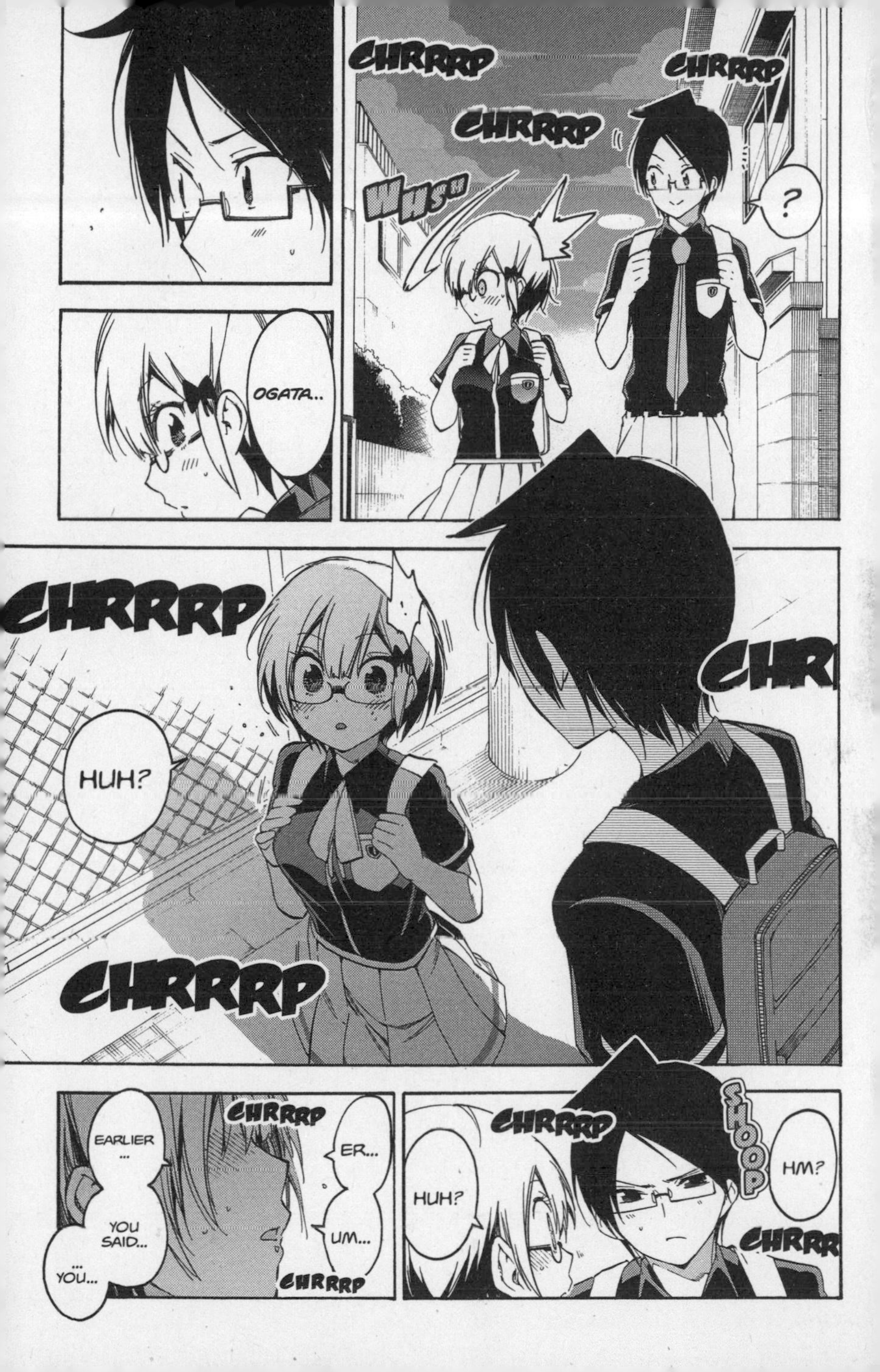
CHRRRP
?
CHRRRP
CHRRRP
OGATA...
CHR
CHRRRP
HUH?
CHRRRP
SHOOP
HM?
CHRRRP
CHRRR
HUH?
CHRRRP
ER...
UM...
CHRRRP
EARLIER...
YOU SAID...
...YOU...

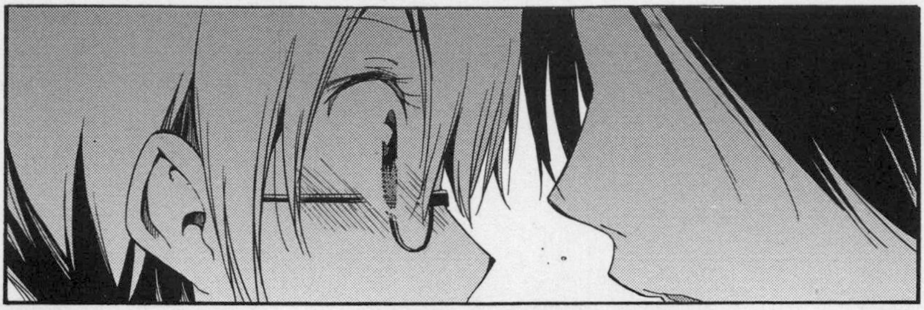

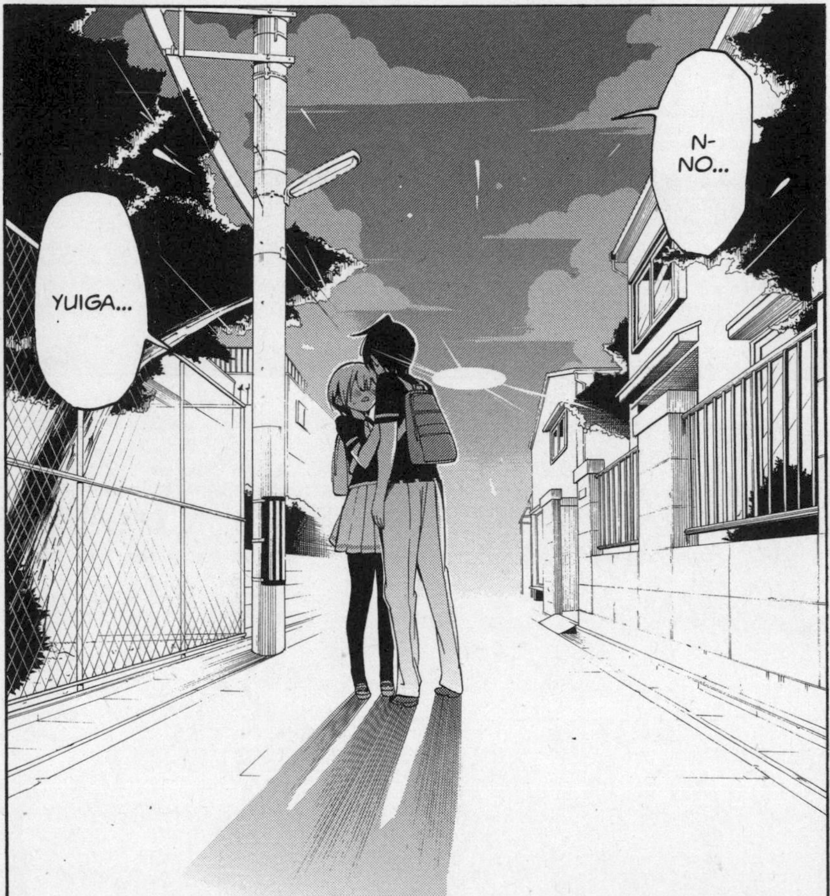
N- NO...
YUIGA...

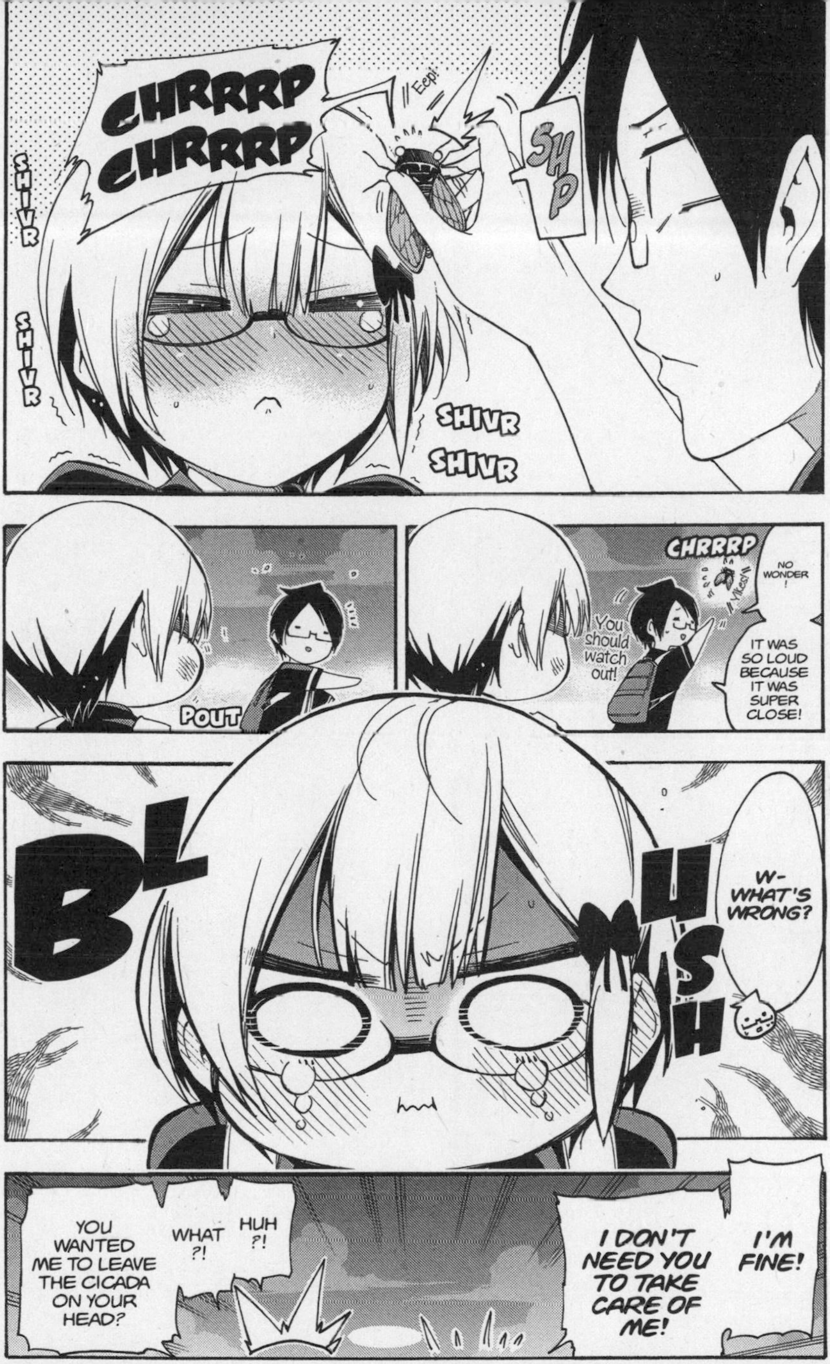
SHP
Eep!
CHRRRP CHRRRP
SHIVR SHIVR
SHIVR SHIVR
CHRRRP
NO WONDER!
IT WAS SO LOUD BECAUSE IT WAS SUPER CLOSE!
Yikes!
You should watch out!
POUT
W-WHAT'S WRONG?
BLUSH
I'M FINE!
I DON'T NEED YOU TO TAKE CARE OF ME!
HUH?!
WHAT?!
YOU WANTED ME TO LEAVE THE CICADA ON YOUR HEAD?

CHRRRP

Summer vacation-miiin!

Next time...

Question 31: A Lost Lamb in New Territory Encounters [X]

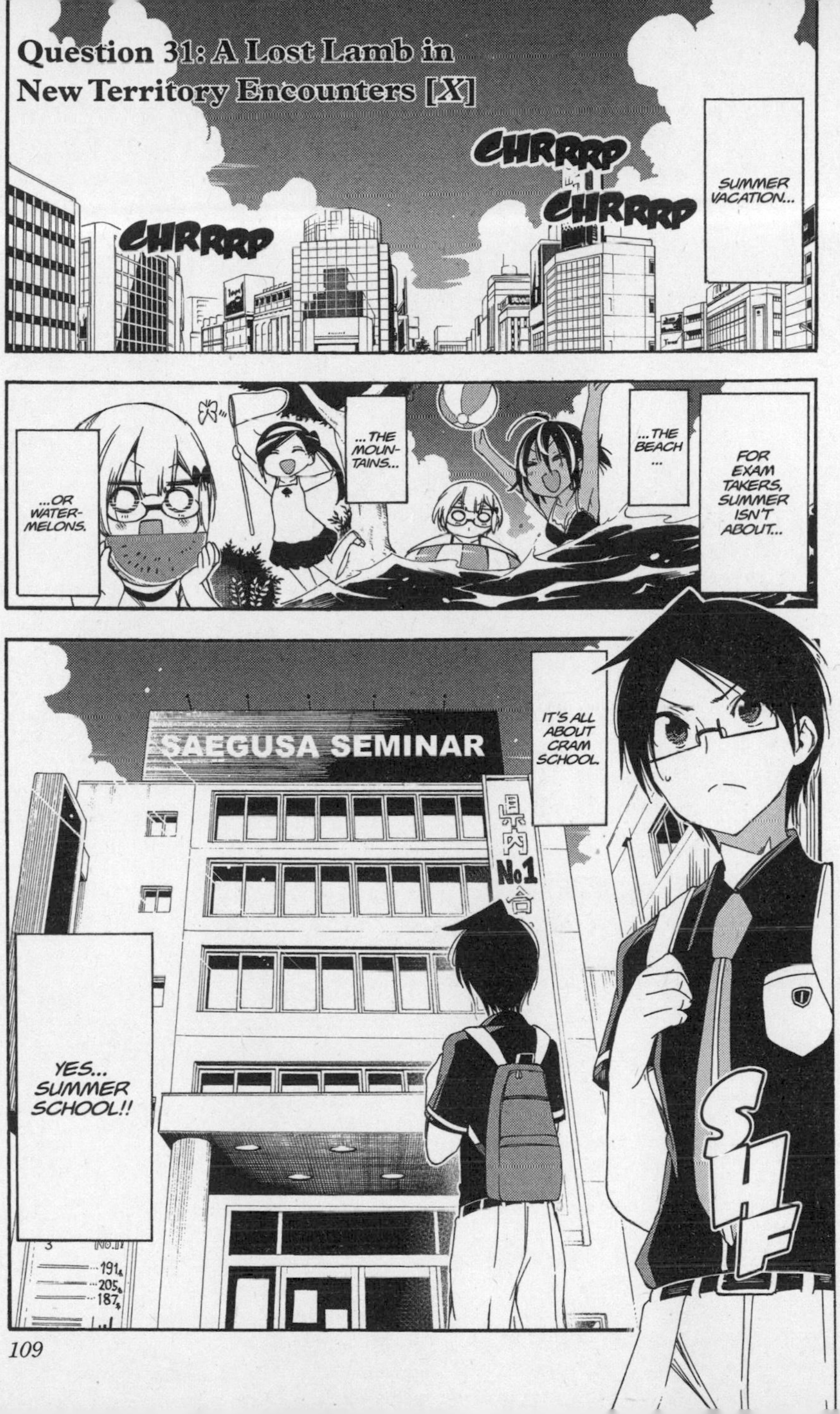
SUMMER VACATION...
CHRRRP
CHRRRP
CHRRRP
FOR EXAM TAKERS, SUMMER ISN'T ABOUT...
...THE BEACH...
...THE MOUN-TAINS...
...OR WATER-MELONS.
IT'S ALL ABOUT CRAM SCHOOL.
SAEGUSA SEMINAR
No1
YES... SUMMER SCHOOL!!

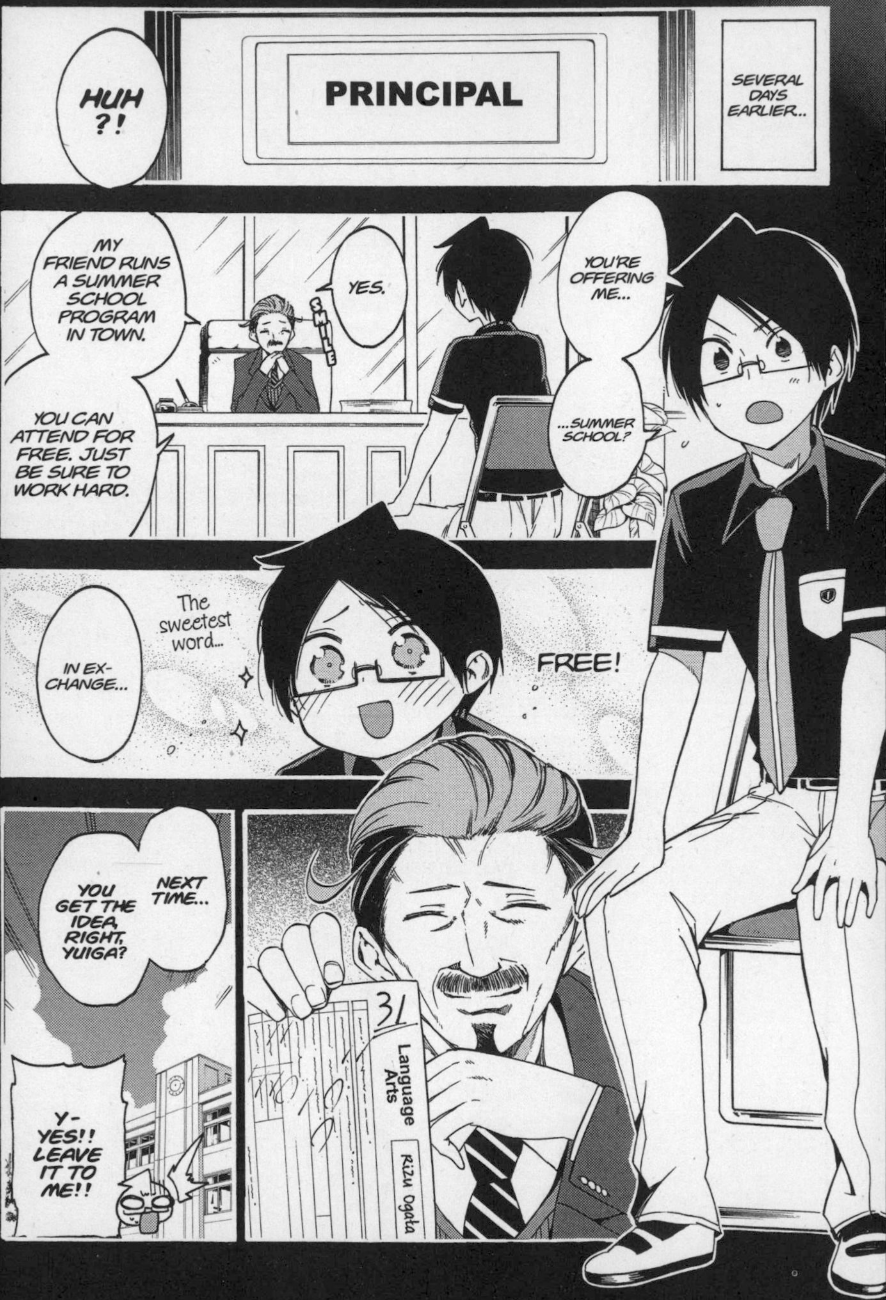
SEVERAL DAYS EARLIER..
PRINCIPAL
HUH?!
YOU'RE OFFERING ME...
...SUMMER SCHOOL?
YES.
SMILE
MY FRIEND RUNS A SUMMER SCHOOL PROGRAM IN TOWN.
YOU CAN ATTEND FOR FREE. JUST BE SURE TO WORK HARD.
FREE!
The sweetest word...
IN EX-CHANGE...
31
Language Arts
Rizu Ogata
NEXT TIME...
YOU GET THE IDEA, RIGHT, YUIGA?
Y-YES!! LEAVE IT TO ME!!

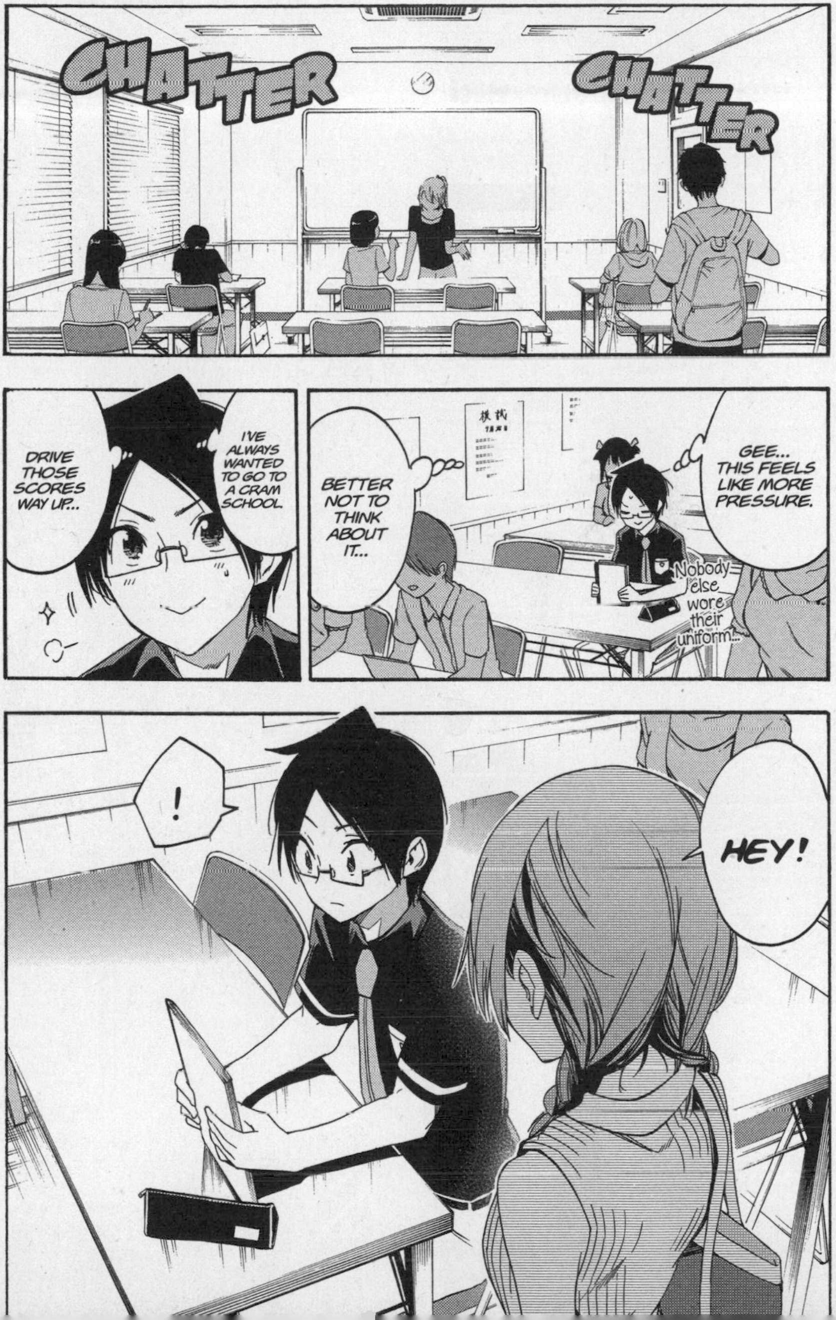
CHATTER
CHATTER
GEE... THIS FEELS LIKE MORE PRESSURE.
Nobody else wore their uniform...
BETTER NOT TO THINK ABOUT IT...
I'VE ALWAYS WANTED TO GO TO A CRAM SCHOOL.
DRIVE THOSE SCORES WAY UP...
HEY!
!

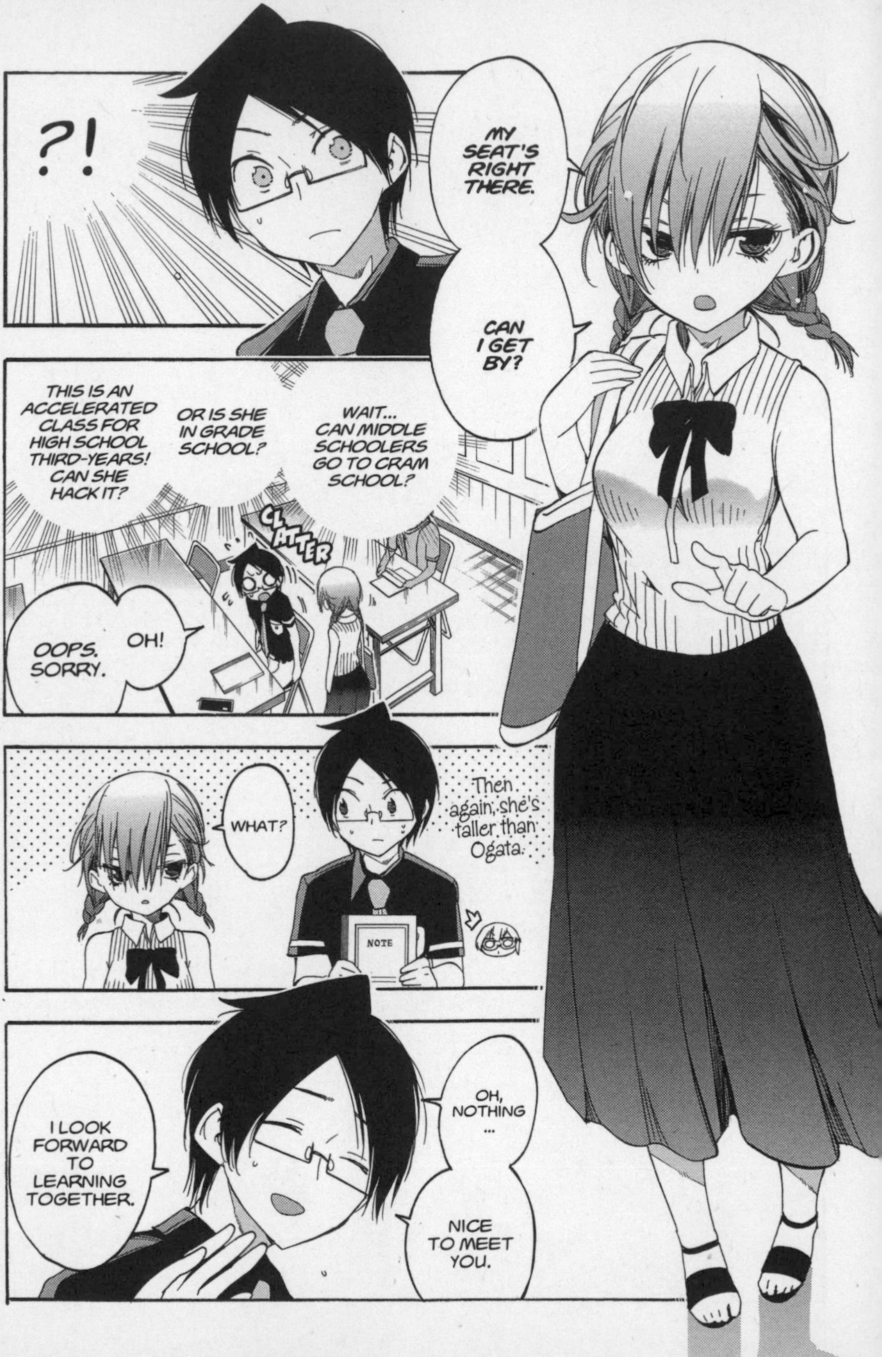
MY SEAT'S RIGHT THERE.
CAN I GET BY?
?!
WAIT... CAN MIDDLE SCHOOLERS GO TO CRAM SCHOOL?
OR IS SHE IN GRADE SCHOOL?
THIS IS AN ACCELERATED CLASS FOR HIGH SCHOOL THIRD-YEARS! CAN SHE HACK IT?
CLATTER
OH!
OOPS. SORRY.
Then again, she's taller than Ogata.
WHAT?
NOTE
OH, NOTHING ...
NICE TO MEET YOU.
I LOOK FORWARD TO LEARNING TOGETHER.

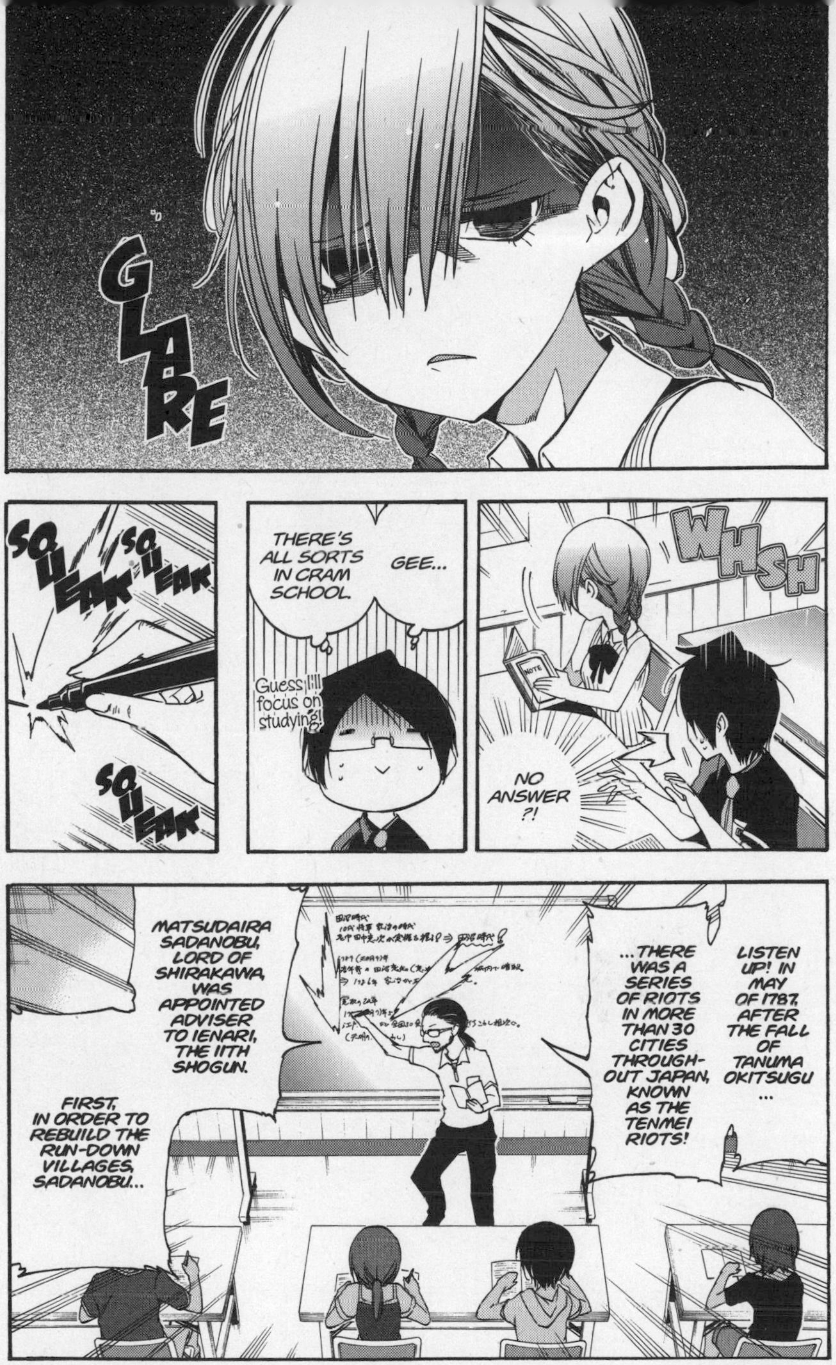
GLARE
WHSH
NO ANSWER ?!
GEE...
THERE'S ALL SORTS IN CRAM SCHOOL.
Guess I'll focus on studying!
SQUEAK
SQUEAK
SQUEAK
LISTEN UP! IN MAY OF 1787, AFTER THE FALL OF TANUMA OKITSUGU...
...THERE WAS A SERIES OF RIOTS IN MORE THAN 30 CITIES THROUGH-OUT JAPAN, KNOWN AS THE TENMEI RIOTS!
MATSUDAIRA SADANOBU, LORD OF SHIRAKAWA, WAS APPOINTED ADVISER TO IENARI, THE 11TH SHOGUN.
FIRST, IN ORDER TO REBUILD THE RUN-DOWN VILLAGES, SADANOBU...

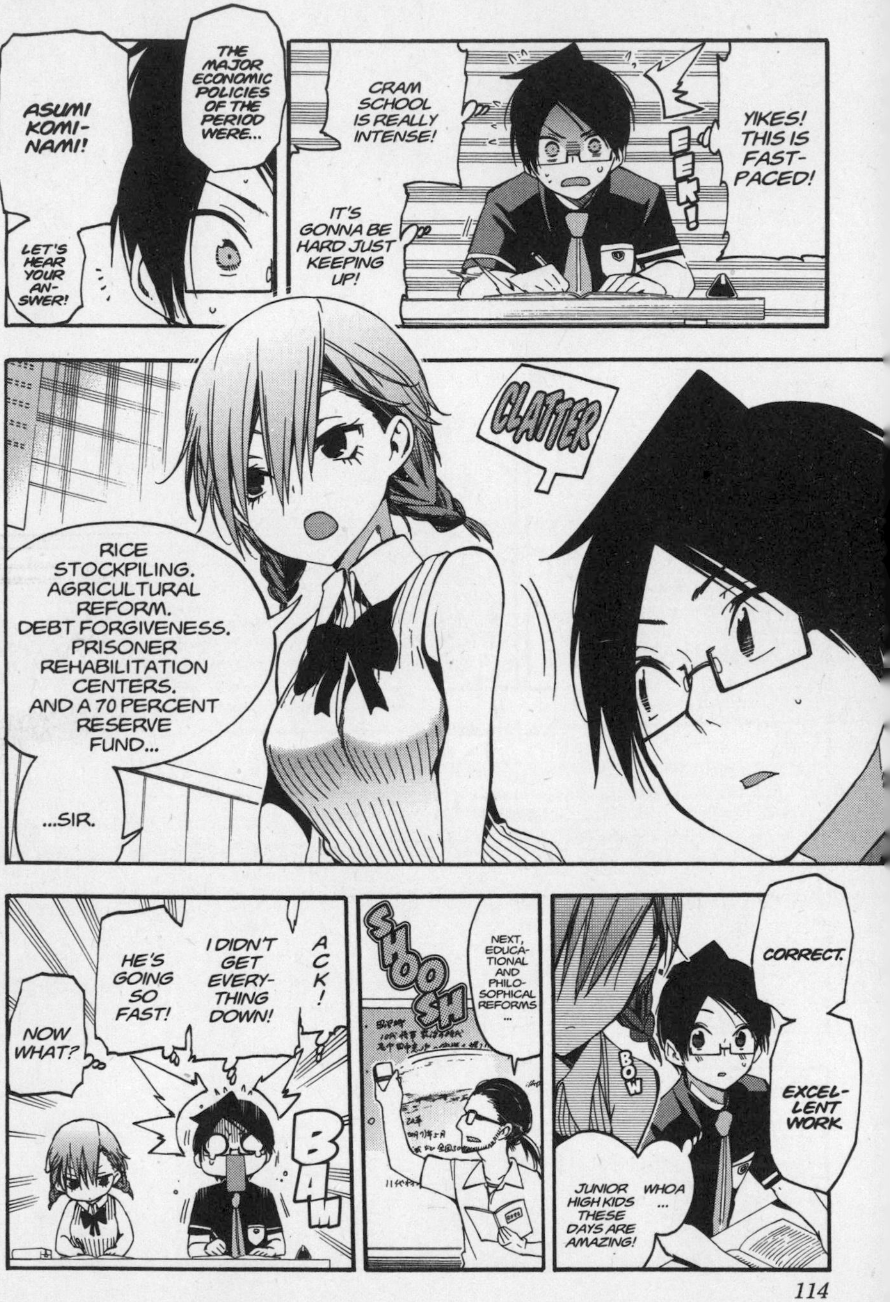
YIKES! THIS IS FAST-PACED!
EEEK!
CRAM SCHOOL IS REALLY INTENSE!
IT'S GONNA BE HARD JUST KEEPING UP!
THE MAJOR ECONOMIC POLICIES OF THE PERIOD WERE...
ASUMI KOMI-NAMI!
LET'S HEAR YOUR AN-SWER!
CLATTER
RICE STOCKPILING. AGRICULTURAL REFORM. DEBT FORGIVENESS. PRISONER REHABILITATION CENTERS. AND A 70 PERCENT RESERVE FUND...
...SIR.
CORRECT.
EXCEL-LENT WORK.
BOW
WHOA...
JUNIOR HIGH KIDS THESE DAYS ARE AMAZING!
SHOOSH
NEXT, EDUCA-TIONAL AND PHILO-SOPHICAL REFORMS...
ACK!
I DIDN'T GET EVERY-THING DOWN!
HE'S GOING SO FAST!
NOW WHAT?
BAM

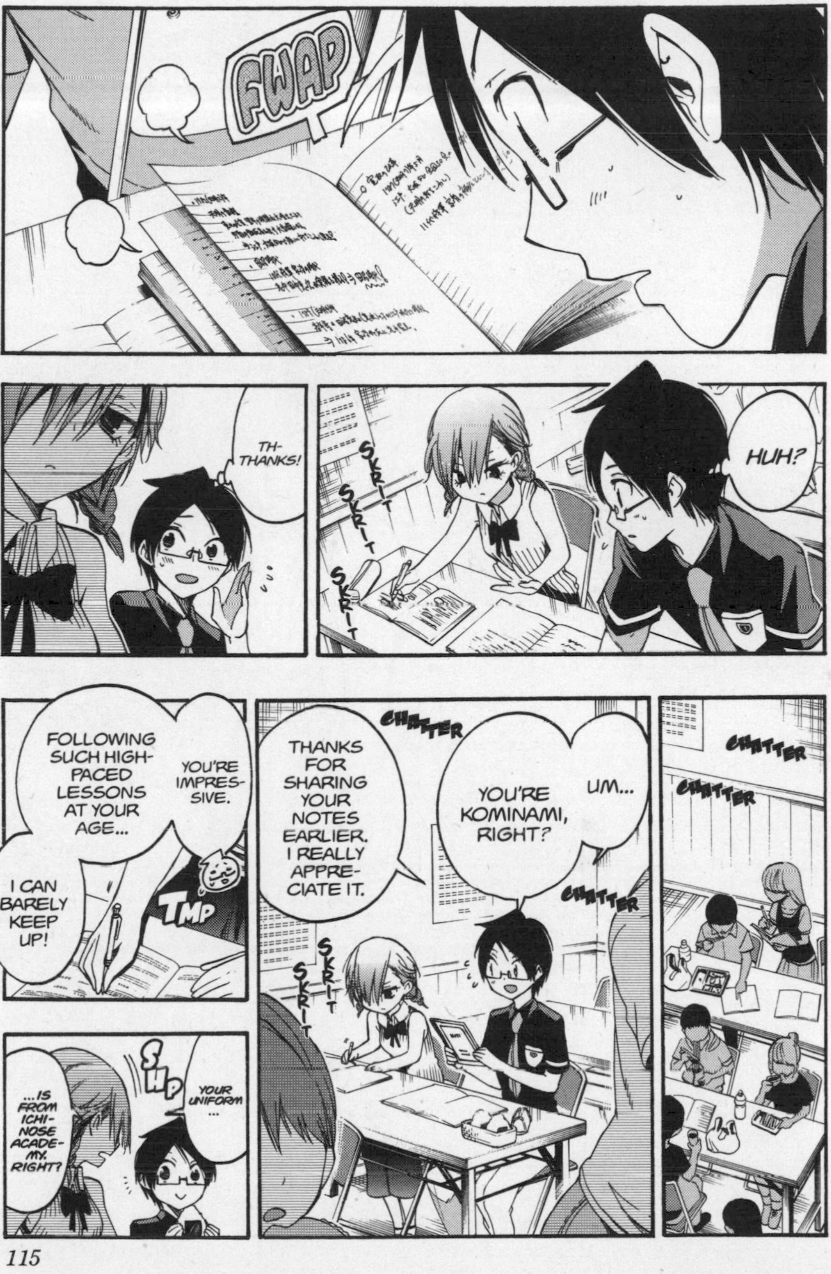
FWAP
HUH?
SKRIT
SKRIT
SKRIT
TH-THANKS!
CHATTER
CHATTER
CHATTER
UM... YOU'RE KOMINAMI, RIGHT?
THANKS FOR SHARING YOUR NOTES EARLIER. I REALLY APPRECIATE IT.
CHATTER
SKRIT
SKRIT
YOU'RE IMPRESSIVE.
FOLLOWING SUCH HIGH-PACED LESSONS AT YOUR AGE...
TMP
I CAN BARELY KEEP UP!
SHP
YOUR UNIFORM...
...IS FROM ICHINOSE ACADEMY. RIGHT?

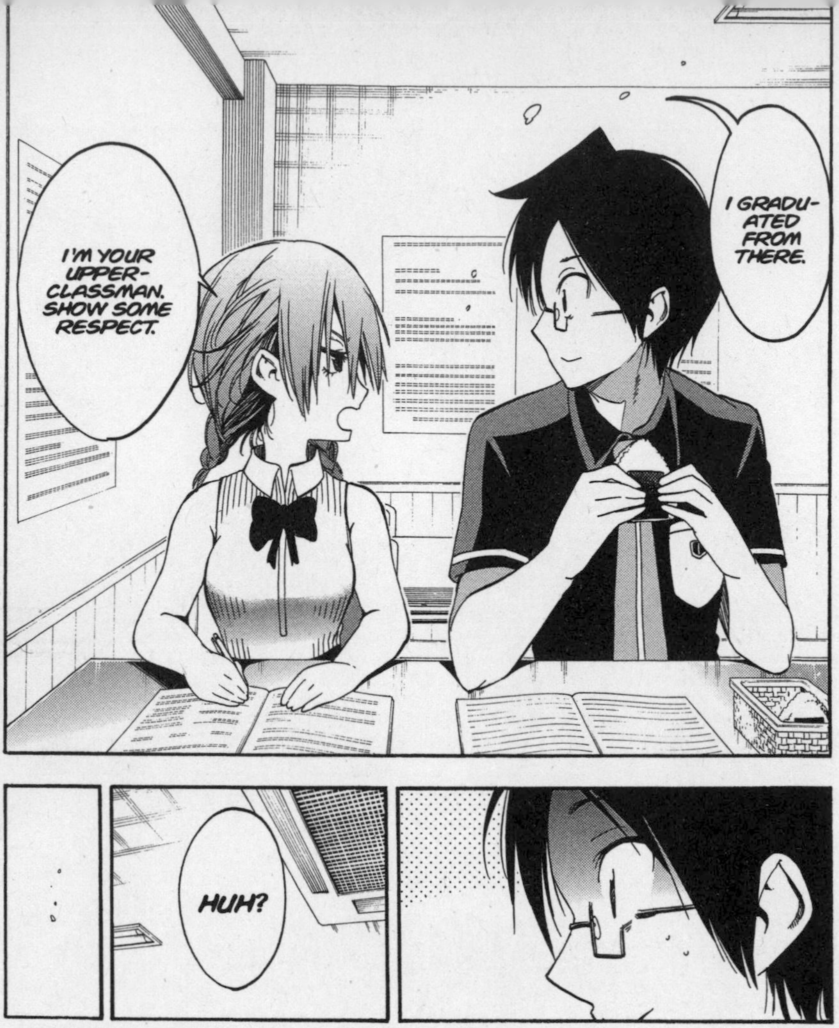
I GRADUATED FROM THERE.
I'M YOUR UPPERCLASSMAN. SHOW SOME RESPECT.
HUH?

*A RONIN IS A STUDENT WHO DIDN'T GET INTO THEIR COLLEGE OF CHOICE AND IS TAKING AN EXTRA YEAR TO STUDY AND RETAKE EXAMS.

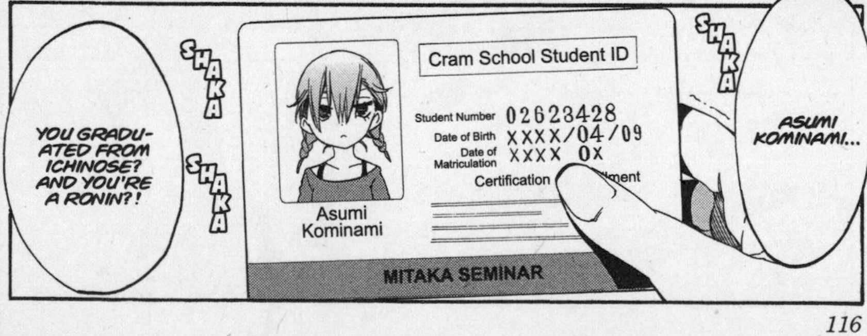
ASUMI KOMINAMI...
SHAKA
SHAKA
SHAKA
Cram School Student ID
Student Number 02623428
Date of Birth XXXX/04/09
Date of Matriculation XXXX 0X
Certification
Asumi Kominami
MITAKA SEMINAR
YOU GRADUATED FROM ICHINOSE? AND YOU'RE A RONIN?!

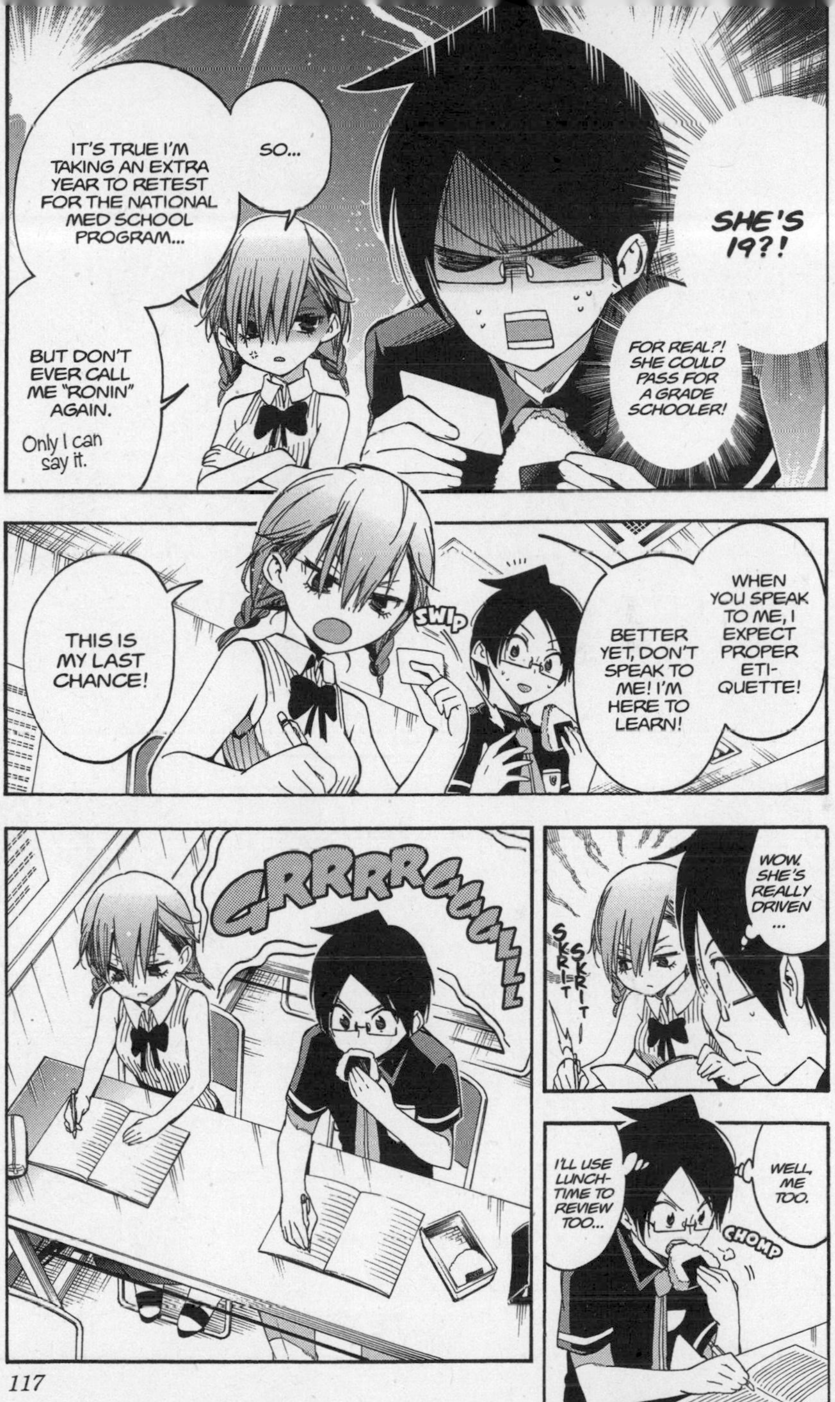
SHE'S 19?!
FOR REAL?! SHE COULD PASS FOR A GRADE SCHOOLER!
IT'S TRUE I'M TAKING AN EXTRA YEAR TO RETEST FOR THE NATIONAL MED SCHOOL PROGRAM...
SO...
BUT DON'T EVER CALL ME "RONIN" AGAIN.
Only I can say it.
WHEN YOU SPEAK TO ME, I EXPECT PROPER ETI-QUETTE!
BETTER YET, DON'T SPEAK TO ME! I'M HERE TO LEARN!
SWIP
THIS IS MY LAST CHANCE!
WOW. SHE'S REALLY DRIVEN ...
SKRIT SKRIT
WELL, ME TOO.
I'LL USE LUNCH-TIME TO REVIEW TOO...
CHOMP
GRRRRGUUULLL

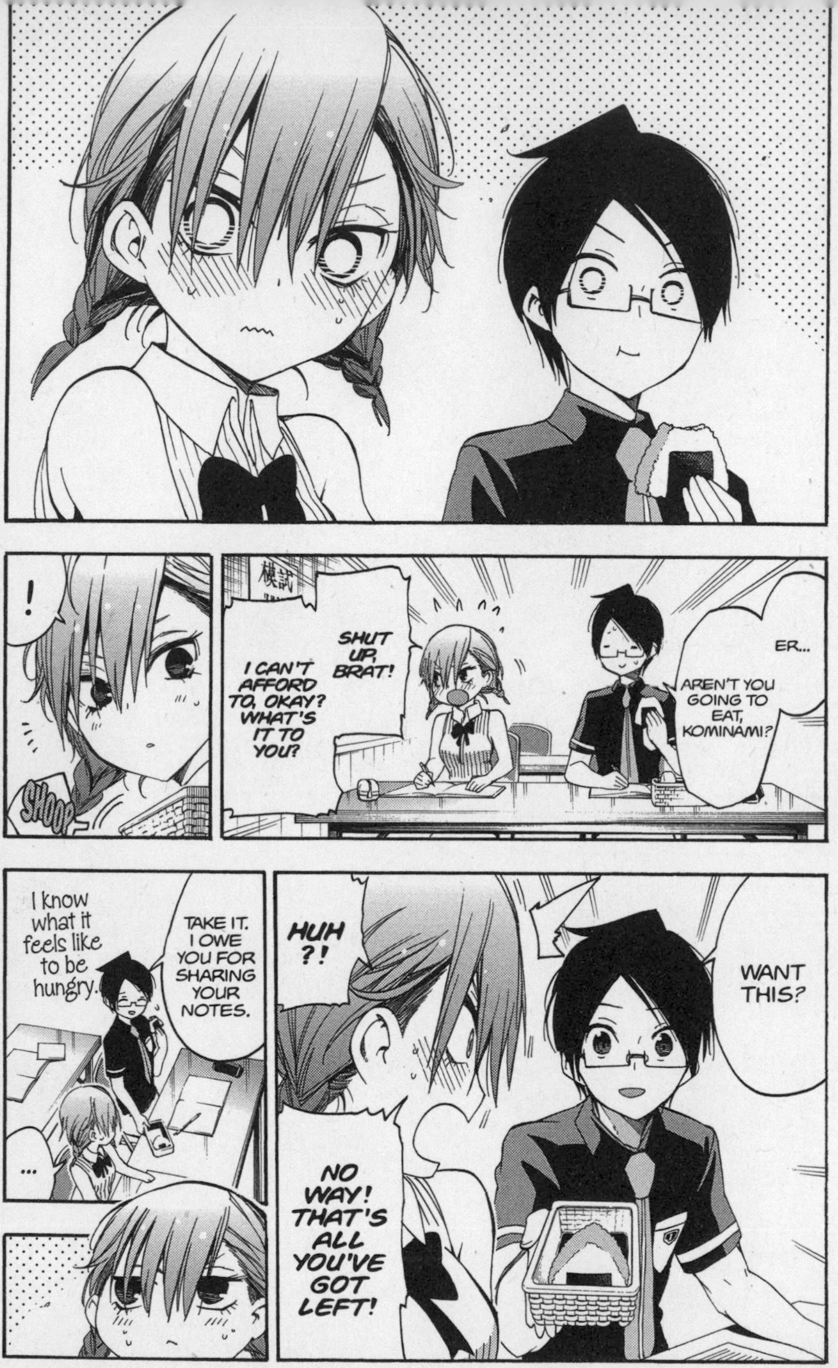

ER...
AREN'T YOU GOING TO EAT, KOMINAMI?
模試
SHUT UP, BRAT!
I CAN'T AFFORD TO, OKAY? WHAT'S IT TO YOU?
!
SHOOP
WANT THIS?
HUH?!
NO WAY! THAT'S ALL YOU'VE GOT LEFT!
TAKE IT. I OWE YOU FOR SHARING YOUR NOTES.
I know what it feels like to be hungry.
...

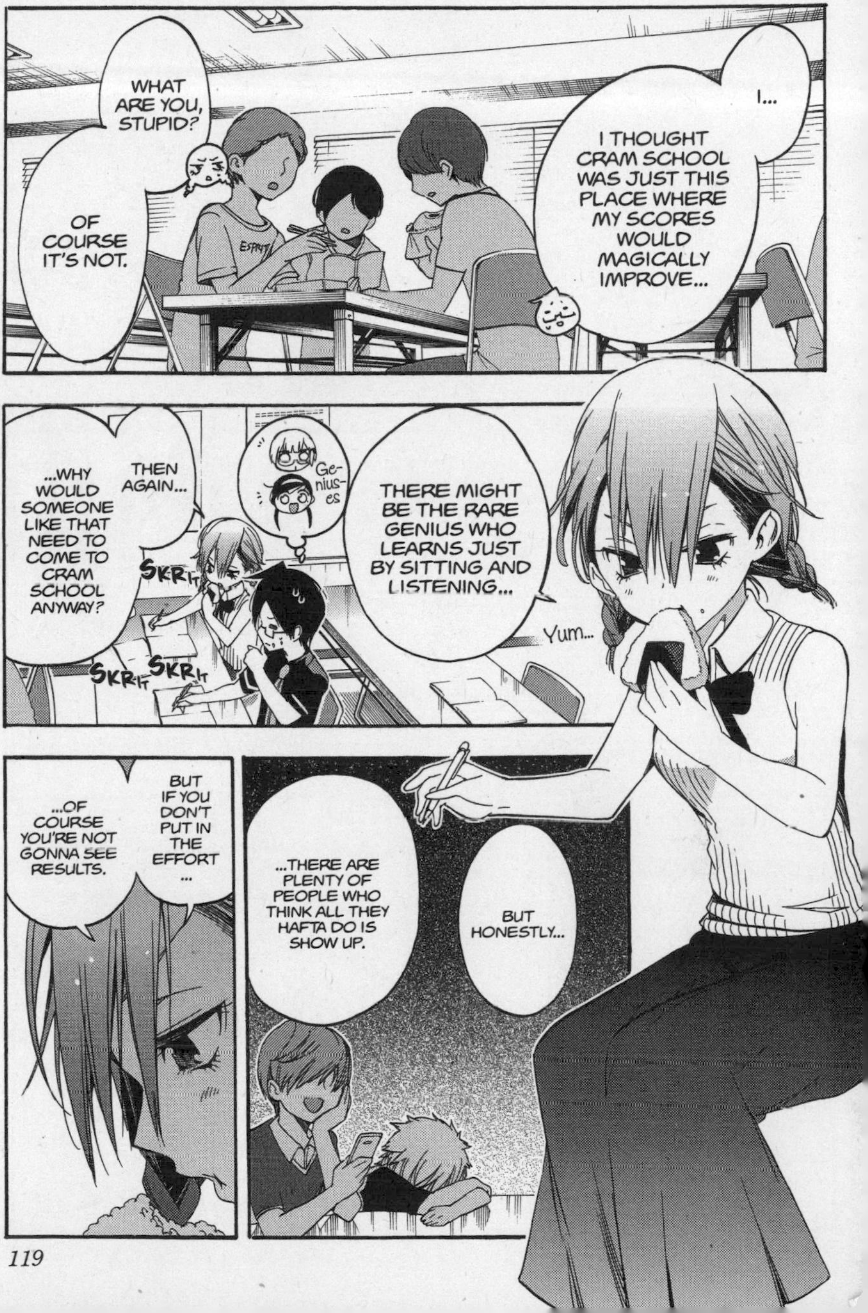
I...
I THOUGHT CRAM SCHOOL WAS JUST THIS PLACE WHERE MY SCORES WOULD MAGICALLY IMPROVE...
WHAT ARE YOU, STUPID?
OF COURSE IT'S NOT.
THERE MIGHT BE THE RARE GENIUS WHO LEARNS JUST BY SITTING AND LISTENING...
Yum...
Ge-nius-es
THEN AGAIN...
...WHY WOULD SOMEONE LIKE THAT NEED TO COME TO CRAM SCHOOL ANYWAY?
SKRIT
SKRIT SKRIT
BUT HONESTLY...
...THERE ARE PLENTY OF PEOPLE WHO THINK ALL THEY HAFTA DO IS SHOW UP.
BUT IF YOU DON'T PUT IN THE EFFORT ...
...OF COURSE YOU'RE NOT GONNA SEE RESULTS.

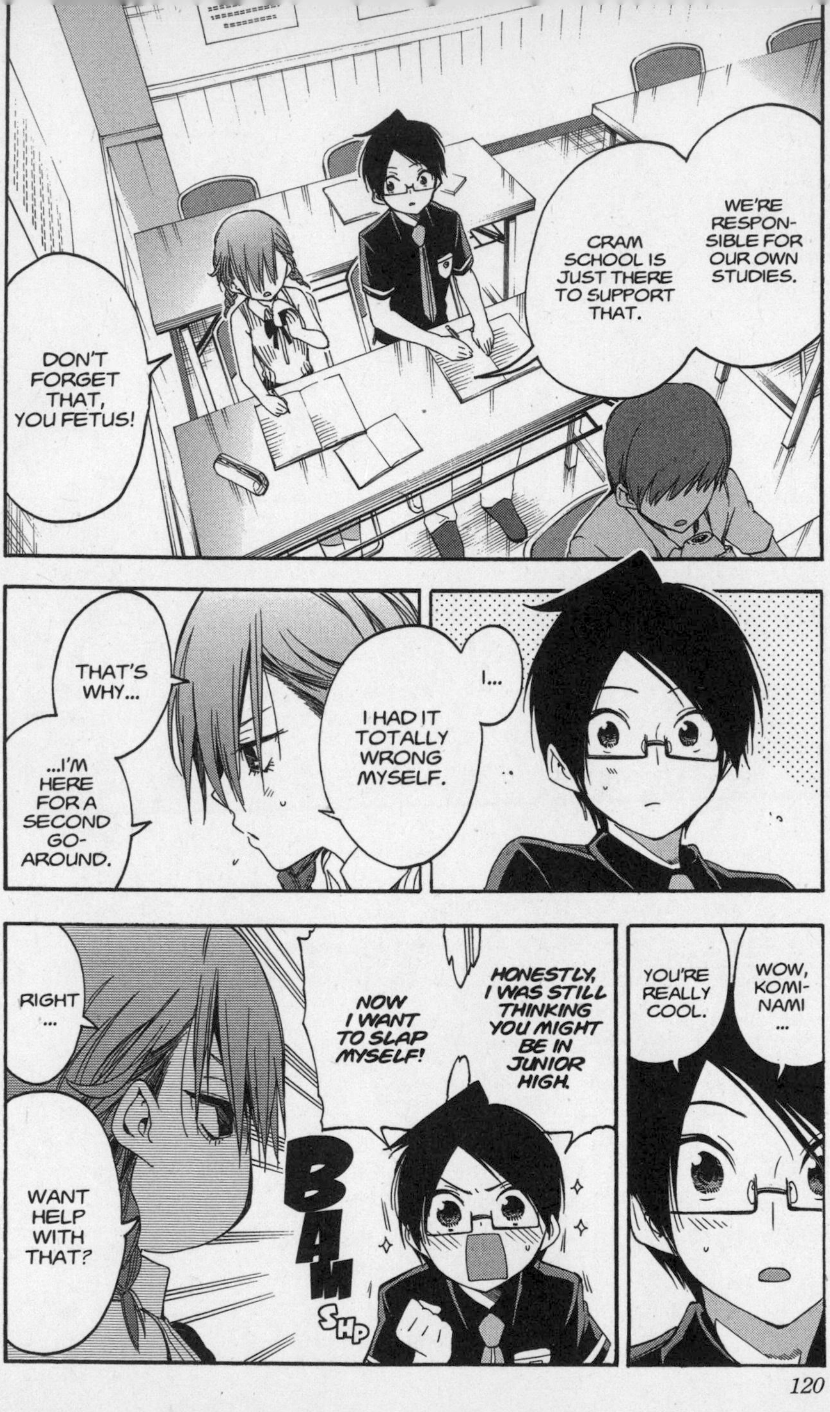
WE'RE RESPONSIBLE FOR OUR OWN STUDIES.
CRAM SCHOOL IS JUST THERE TO SUPPORT THAT.
DON'T FORGET THAT, YOU FETUS!
I...
I HAD IT TOTALLY WRONG MYSELF.
THAT'S WHY...
...I'M HERE FOR A SECOND GO-AROUND.
WOW, KOMINAMI...
YOU'RE REALLY COOL.
HONESTLY, I WAS STILL THINKING YOU MIGHT BE IN JUNIOR HIGH.
NOW I WANT TO SLAP MYSELF!
BAM
SHP
RIGHT...
WANT HELP WITH THAT?

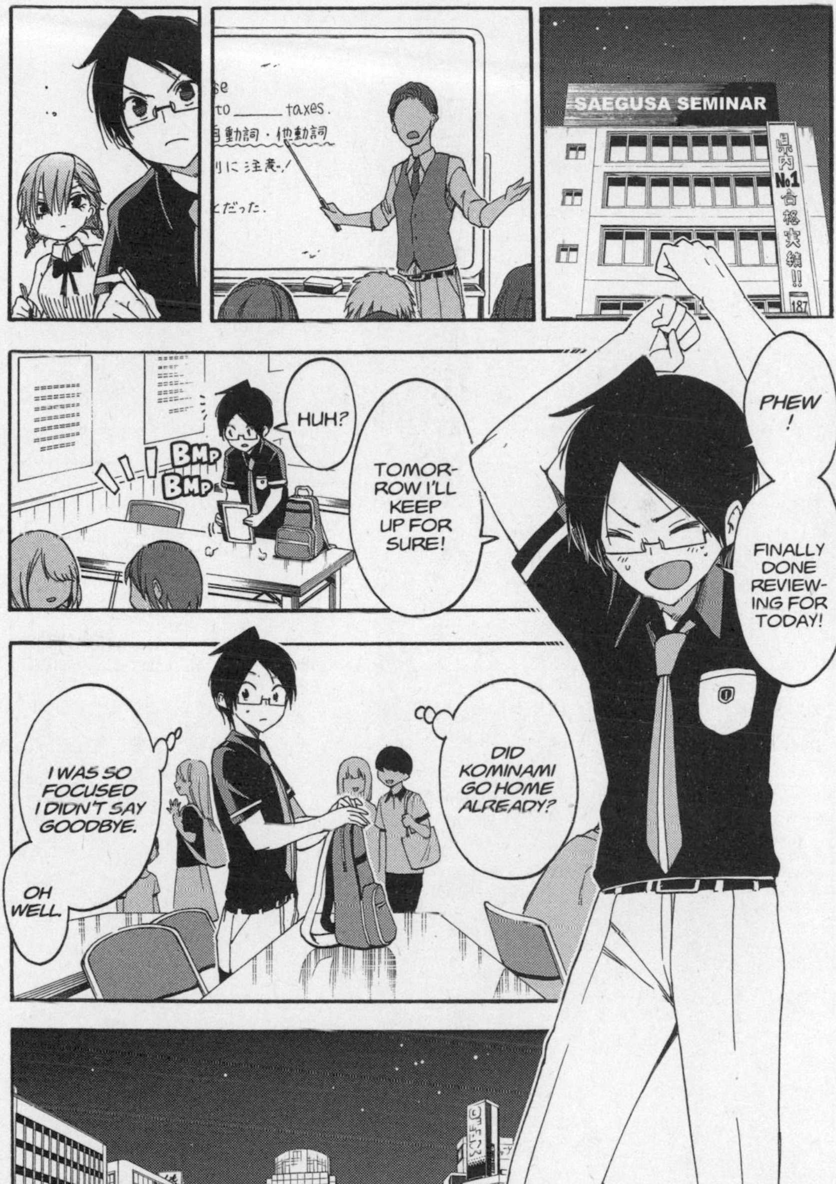
SAEGUSA SEMINAR
県内No.1合格実績!!
187
PHEW!
FINALLY DONE REVIEWING FOR TODAY!
TOMORROW I'LL KEEP UP FOR SURE!
HUH?
BMP BMP
DID KOMINAMI GO HOME ALREADY?
I WAS SO FOCUSED I DIDN'T SAY GOODBYE.
OH WELL.

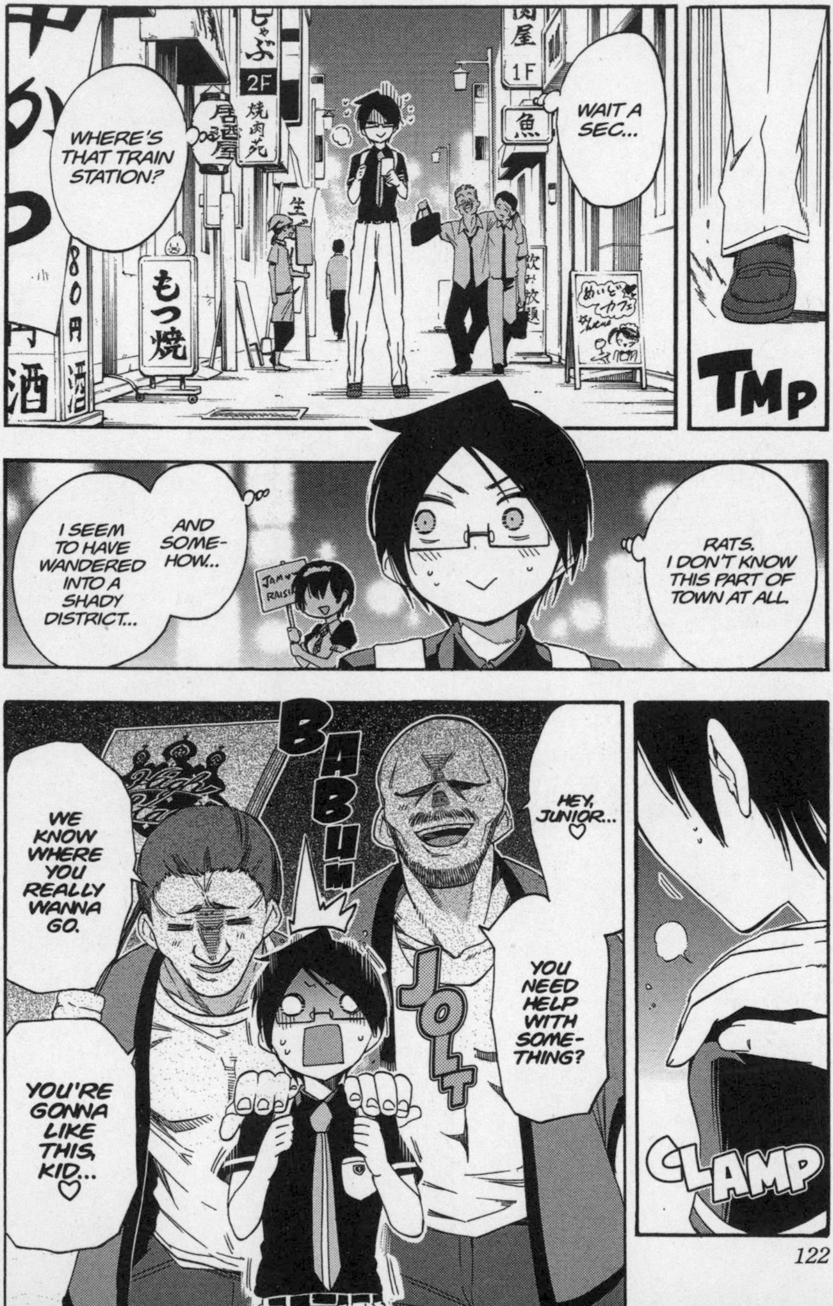
TMP
WAIT A SEC...
WHERE'S THAT TRAIN STATION?
RATS. I DON'T KNOW THIS PART OF TOWN AT ALL.
AND SOMEHOW...
I SEEM TO HAVE WANDERED INTO A SHADY DISTRICT...
CLAMP
HEY, JUNIOR...♡
BABUM
YOU NEED HELP WITH SOMETHING?
WE KNOW WHERE YOU REALLY WANNA GO.
JOLT
YOU'RE GONNA LIKE THIS, KID...♡

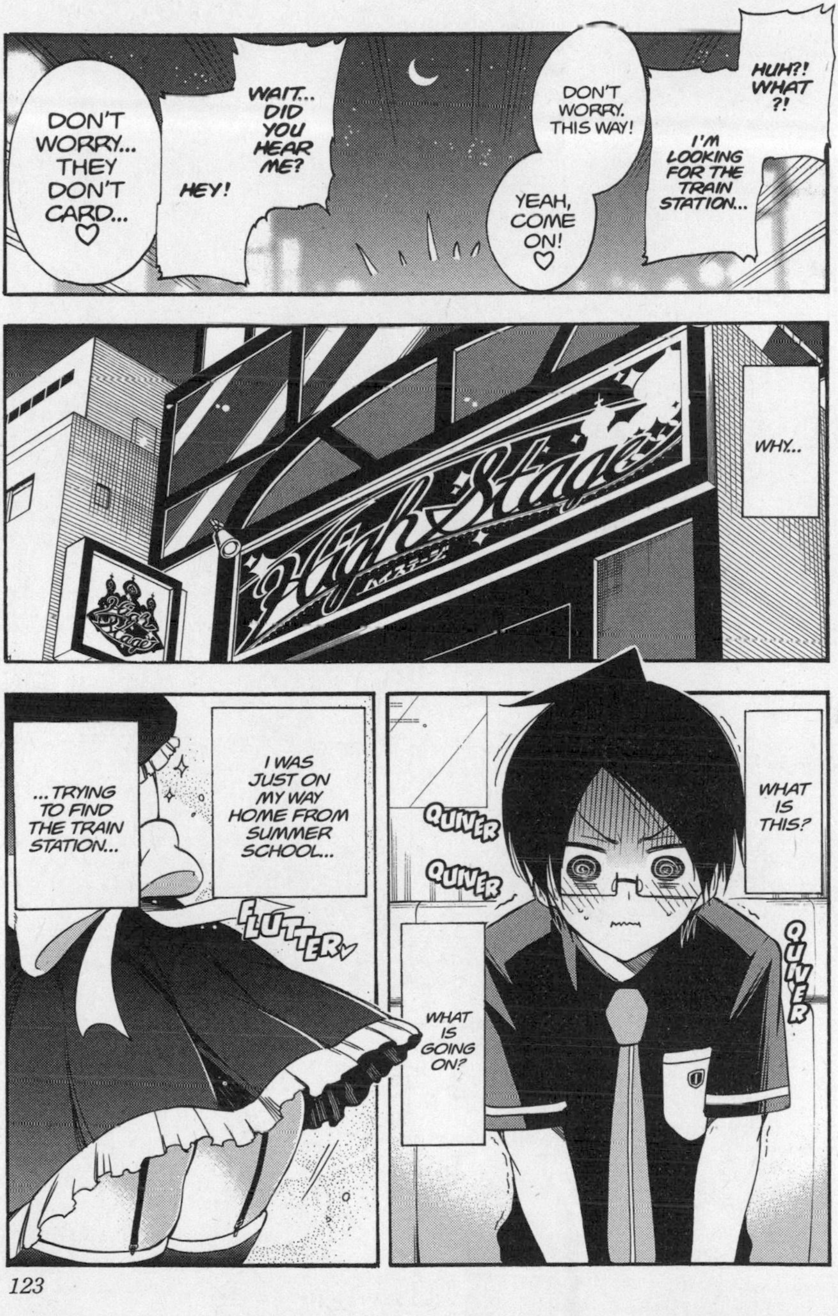
HUH?! WHAT?!
I'M LOOKING FOR THE TRAIN STATION...
DON'T WORRY. THIS WAY!
YEAH, COME ON! ♡
WAIT... DID YOU HEAR ME?
HEY!
DON'T WORRY... THEY DON'T CARD... ♡
WHY...
High Stage
WHAT IS THIS?
QUIVER
QUIVER
QUIVER
WHAT IS GOING ON?
I WAS JUST ON MY WAY HOME FROM SUMMER SCHOOL...
...TRYING TO FIND THE TRAIN STATION...
FLUTTER

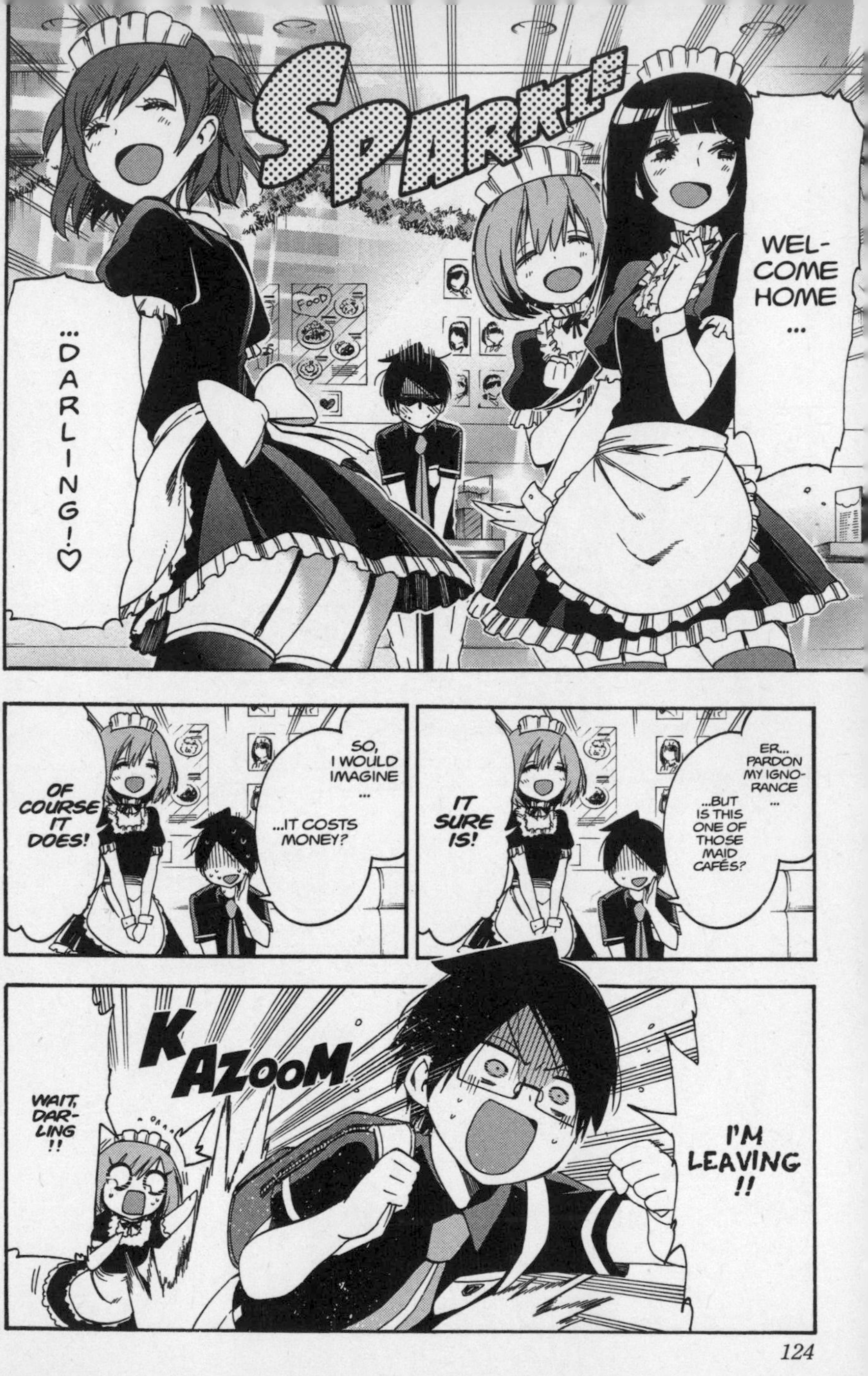
WELCOME HOME ...
SPARK!!
...DARLING!♡
ER... PARDON MY IGNORANCE ... ...BUT IS THIS ONE OF THOSE MAID CAFÉS?
IT SURE IS!
SO, I WOULD IMAGINE ... ...IT COSTS MONEY?
OF COURSE IT DOES!
I'M LEAVING !!
KAZOOM
WAIT, DARLING !!

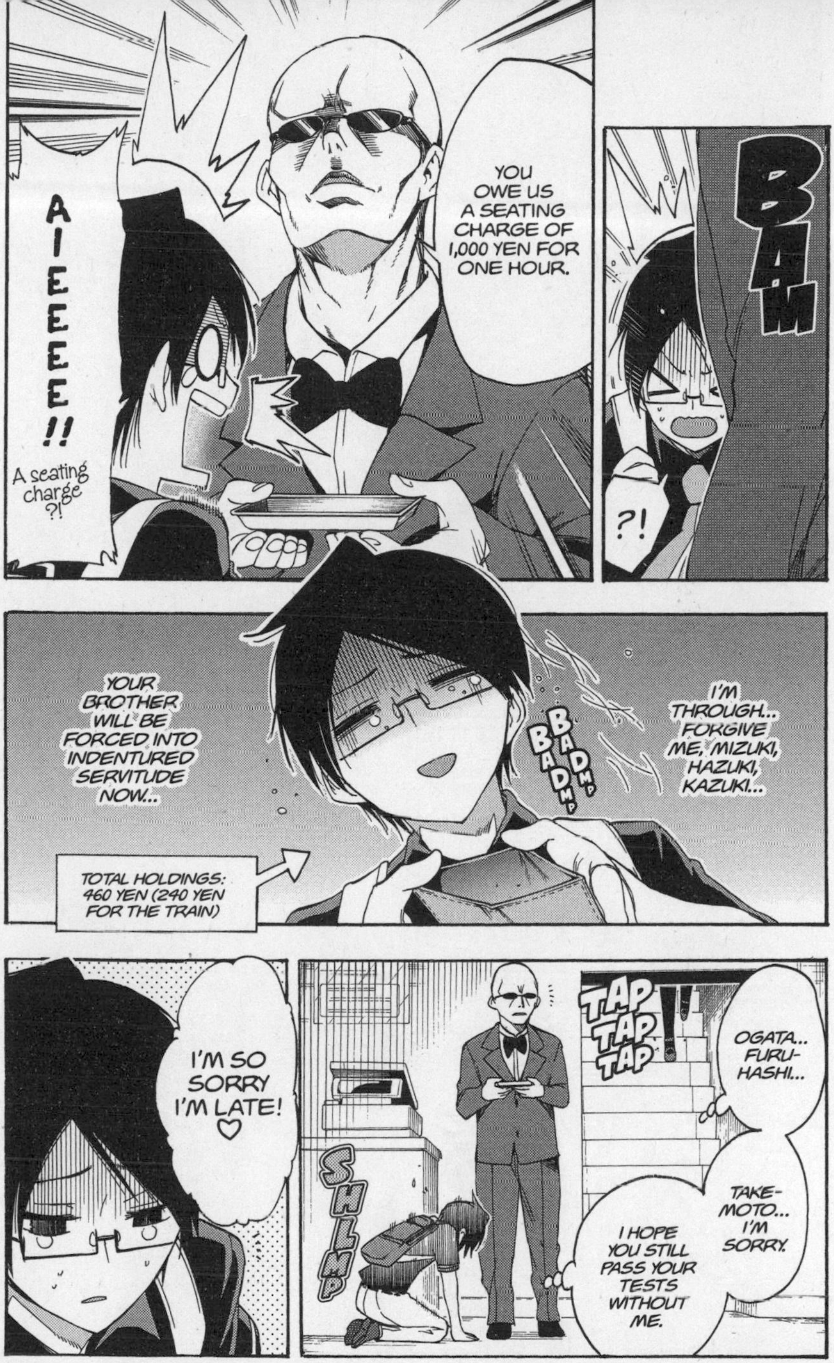
BAM
?!
YOU OWE US A SEATING CHARGE OF 1,000 YEN FOR ONE HOUR.
AIEEEE!!
A seating charge ?!
I'M THROUGH... FORGIVE ME, MIZUKI, HAZUKI, KAZUKI...
BADMP BADMP
YOUR BROTHER WILL BE FORCED INTO INDENTURED SERVITUDE NOW...
TOTAL HOLDINGS: 460 YEN (240 YEN FOR THE TRAIN)
OGATA... FURU-HASHI...
TAP TAP TAP
TAKE-MOTO... I'M SORRY.
I HOPE YOU STILL PASS YOUR TESTS WITHOUT ME.
SHLMP
I'M SO SORRY I'M LATE! ♡

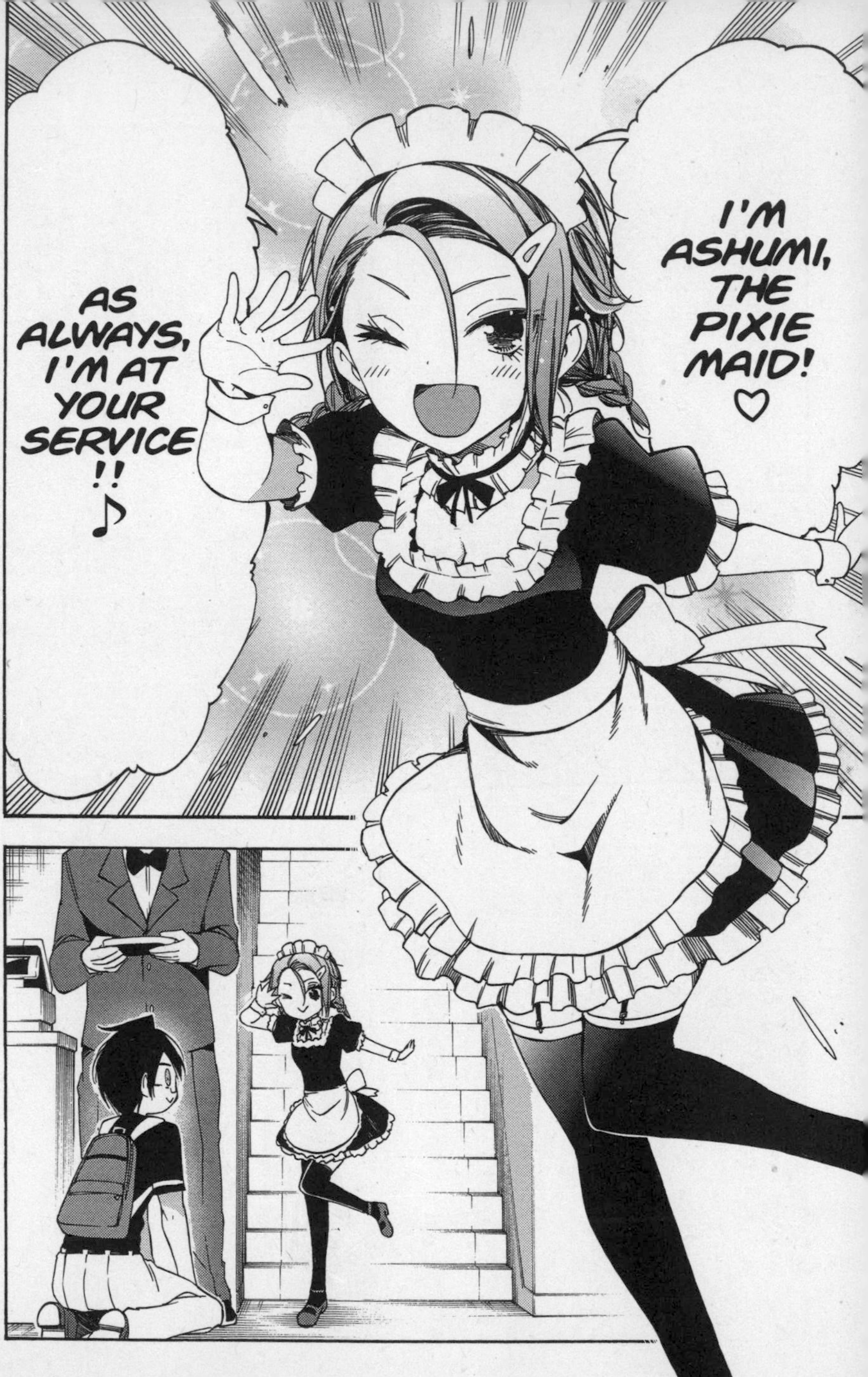
I'M ASHUMI, THE PIXIE MAID! ♡
AS ALWAYS, I'M AT YOUR SERVICE!! ♪

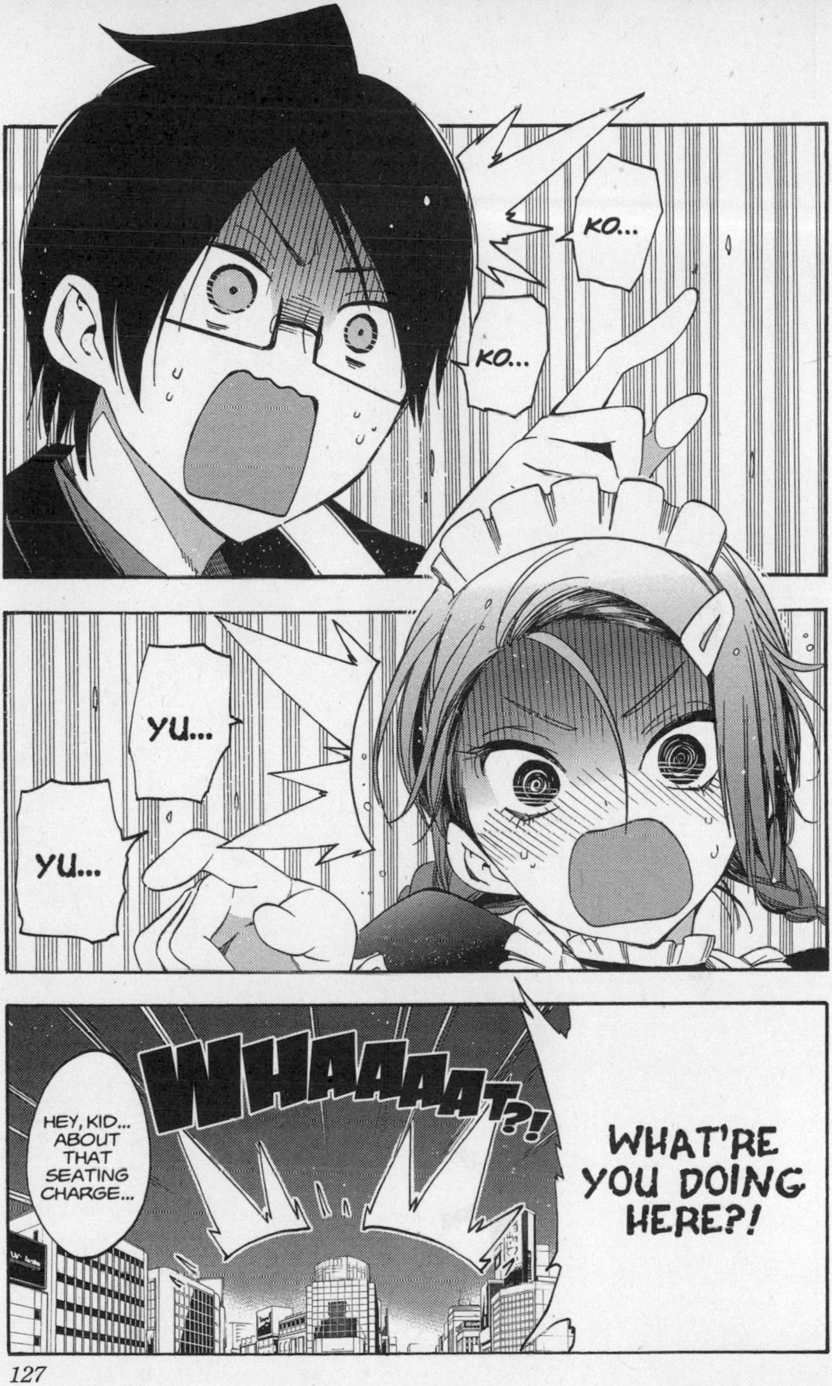
KO...
KO...
YU...
YU...
WHAT'RE YOU DOING HERE?!
WHAAAAAT?!
HEY, KID... ABOUT THAT SEATING CHARGE...

Machiko   Himura   Mikuni

Question 32: An Elder Sees an [X] Future with Naive Honesty

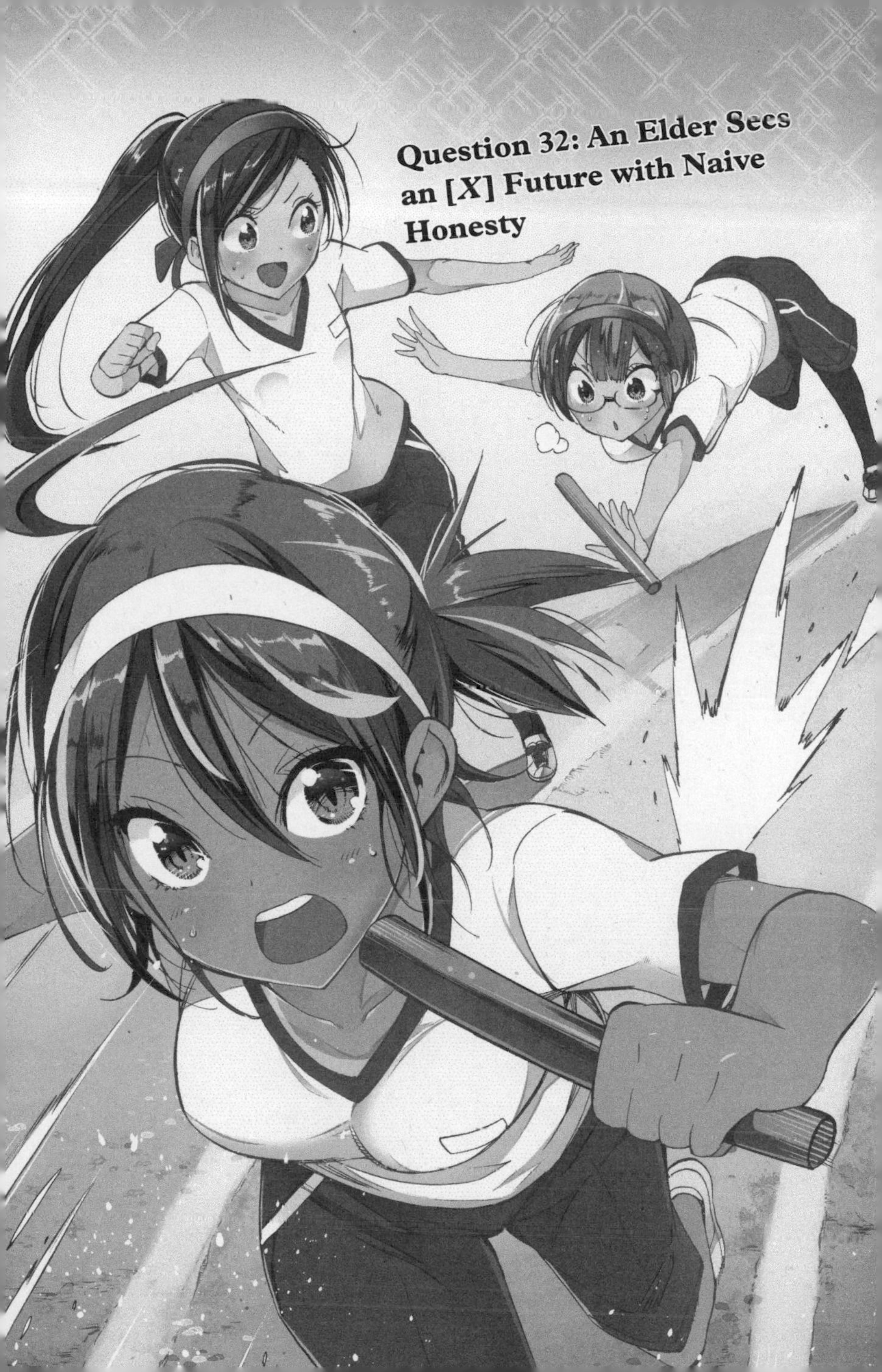

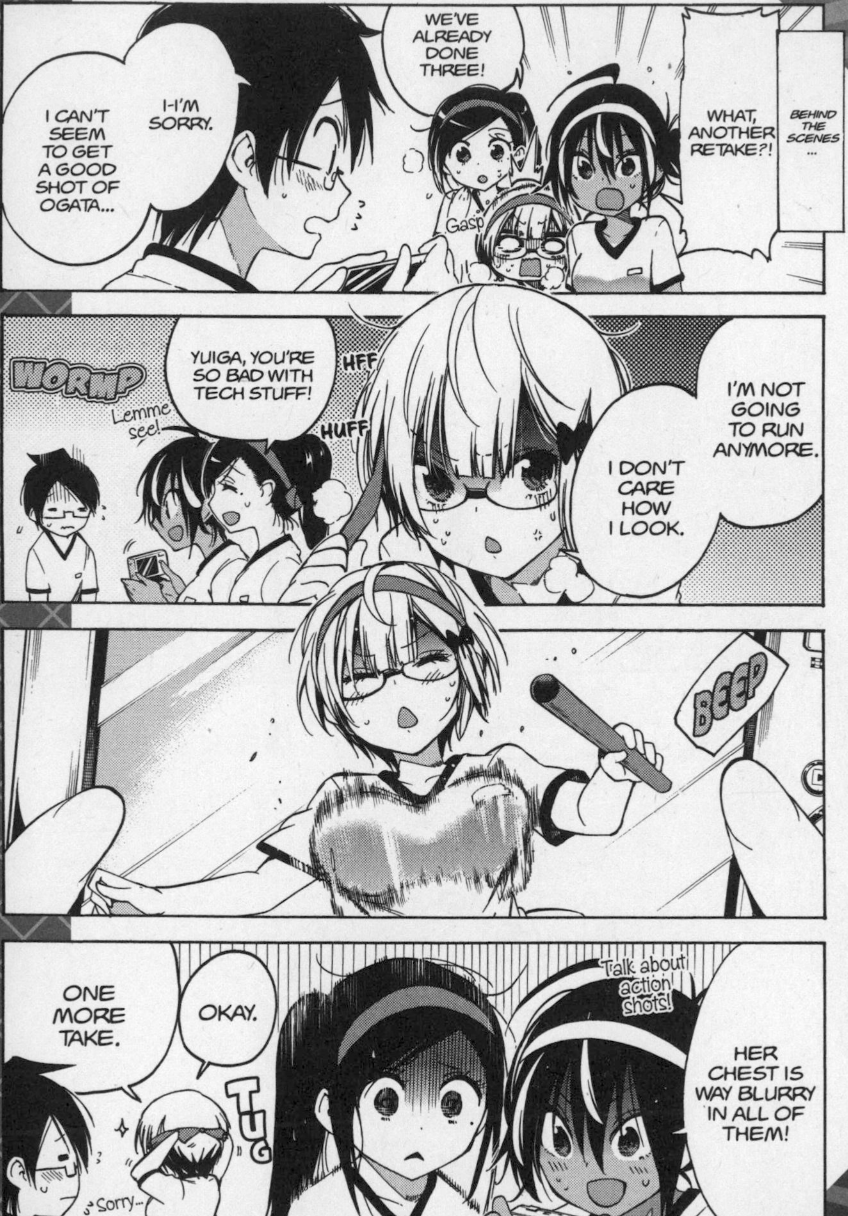
BEHIND THE SCENES...
WHAT, ANOTHER RETAKE?!
WE'VE ALREADY DONE THREE!
Gasp
I-I'M SORRY.
I CAN'T SEEM TO GET A GOOD SHOT OF OGATA...
I'M NOT GOING TO RUN ANYMORE.
I DON'T CARE HOW I LOOK.
HFF
HUFF
YUIGA, YOU'RE SO BAD WITH TECH STUFF!
Lemme see!
WORMP
BEEP
Talk about action shots!
HER CHEST IS WAY BLURRY IN ALL OF THEM!
TUG
OKAY.
ONE MORE TAKE.
Sorry...

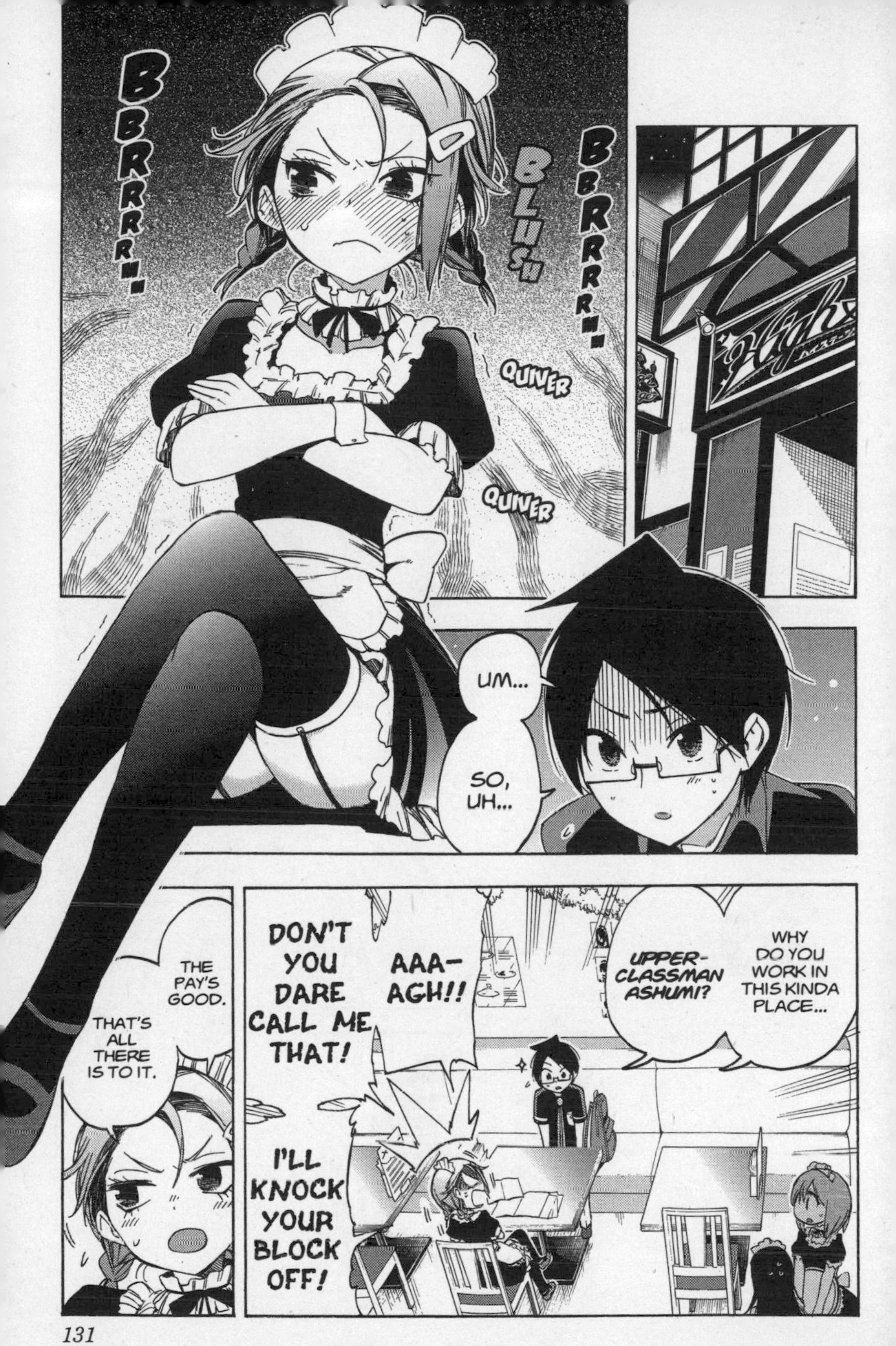
BBRRRRN
BLUSH
BBRRRRN
QUIVER
QUIVER
UM...
SO, UH...
UPPER-CLASSMAN ASHUMI? WHY DO YOU WORK IN THIS KINDA PLACE...
AAA-AGH!!
DON'T YOU DARE CALL ME THAT!
I'LL KNOCK YOUR BLOCK OFF!
THE PAY'S GOOD.
THAT'S ALL THERE IS TO IT.

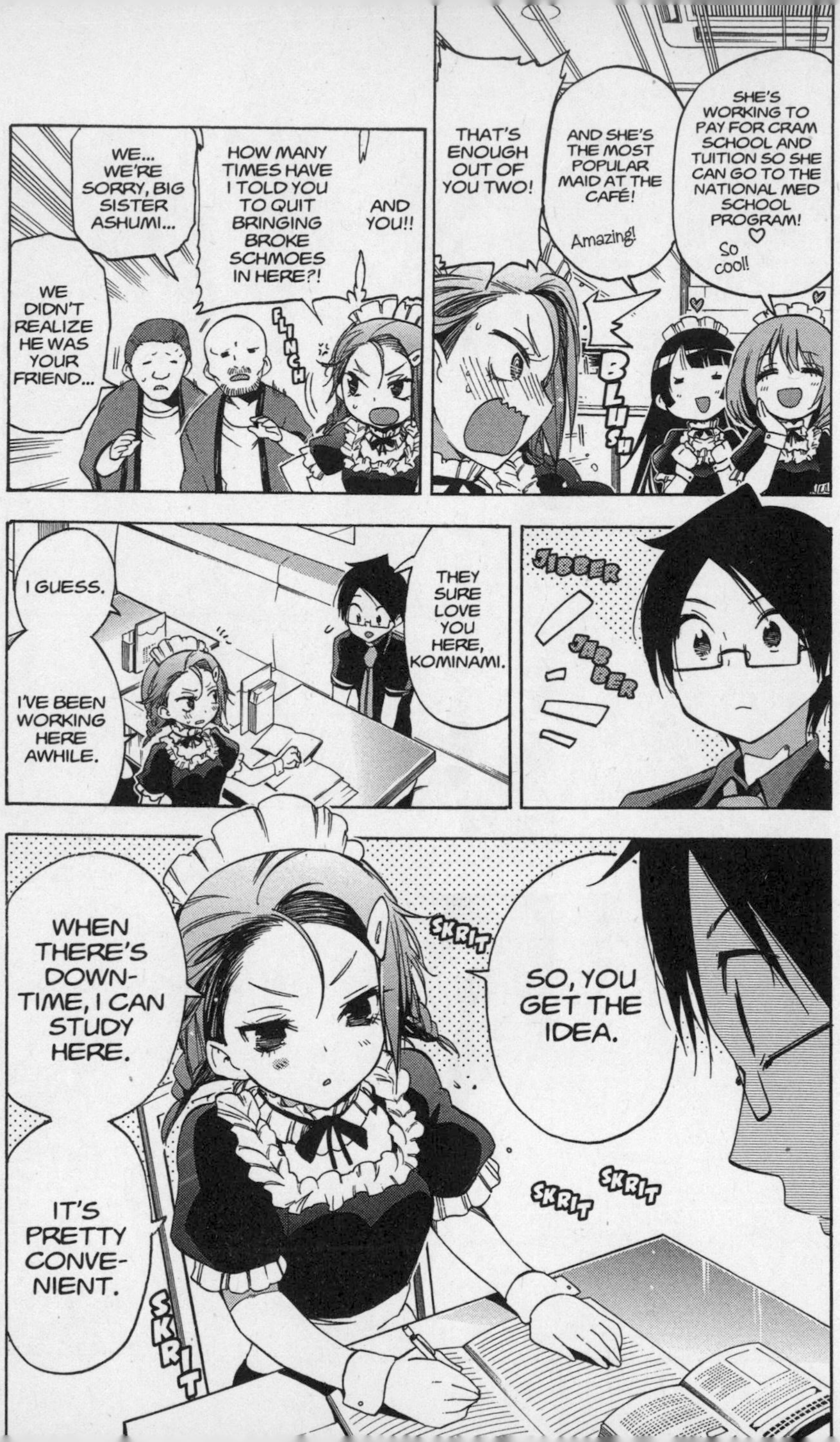
SHE'S WORKING TO PAY FOR CRAM SCHOOL AND TUITION SO SHE CAN GO TO THE NATIONAL MED SCHOOL PROGRAM! ♡
So cool!
AND SHE'S THE MOST POPULAR MAID AT THE CAFÉ!
Amazing!
BLUSH
THAT'S ENOUGH OUT OF YOU TWO!
AND YOU!!
HOW MANY TIMES HAVE I TOLD YOU TO QUIT BRINGING BROKE SCHMOES IN HERE?!
FLINCH
WE... WE'RE SORRY, BIG SISTER ASHUMI...
WE DIDN'T REALIZE HE WAS YOUR FRIEND...
JIBBER
JABBER
THEY SURE LOVE YOU HERE, KOMINAMI.
I GUESS.
I'VE BEEN WORKING HERE AWHILE.
SO, YOU GET THE IDEA.
SKRIT
WHEN THERE'S DOWN-TIME, I CAN STUDY HERE.
SKRIT
SKRIT
IT'S PRETTY CONVE-NIENT.
SKRIT

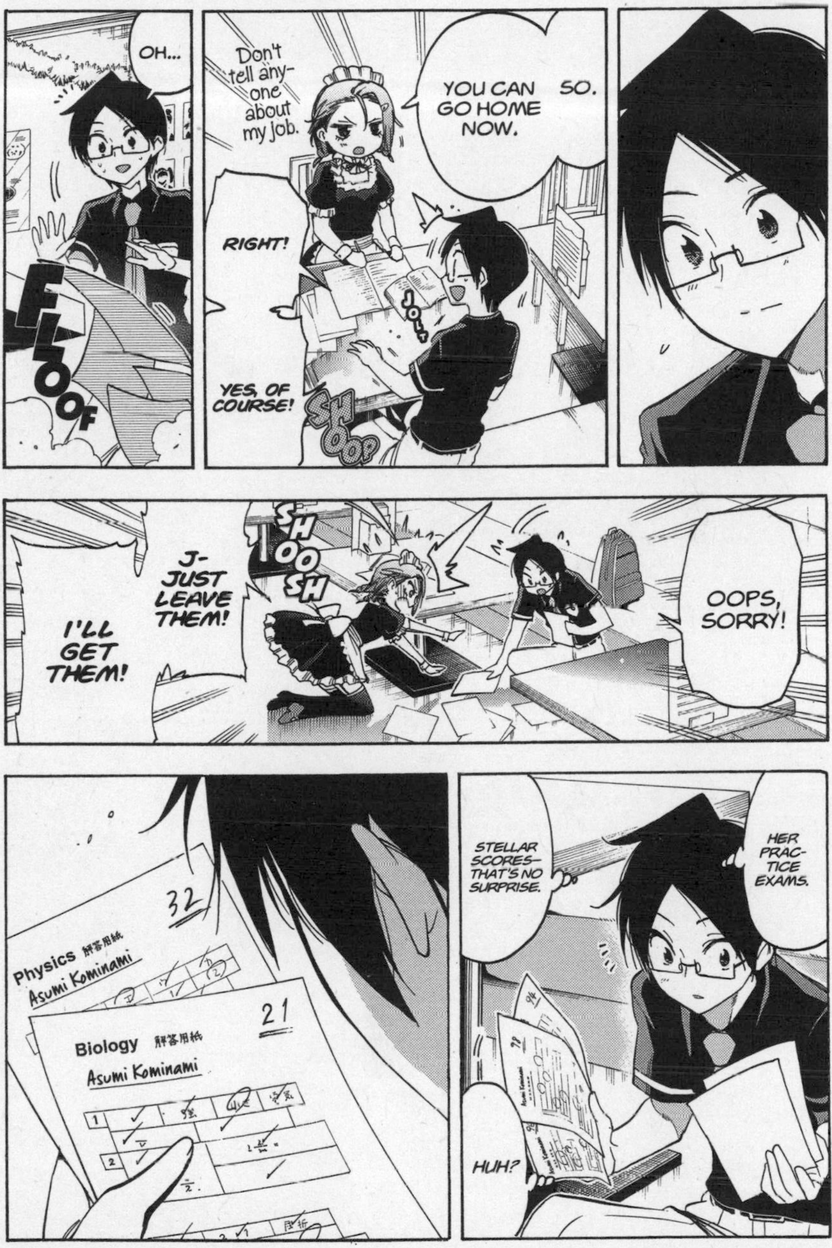
YOU CAN GO HOME NOW. SO.
Don't tell anyone about my job.
RIGHT!
JOLT
YES, OF COURSE!
SHOOP
OH...
FLOOF
OOPS, SORRY!
SHOOSH
J-JUST LEAVE THEM!
I'LL GET THEM!
HER PRACTICE EXAMS.
STELLAR SCORES—THAT'S NO SURPRISE.
HUH?
32
Physics 解答用紙
Asumi Kominami
21
Biology 解答用紙
Asumi Kominami

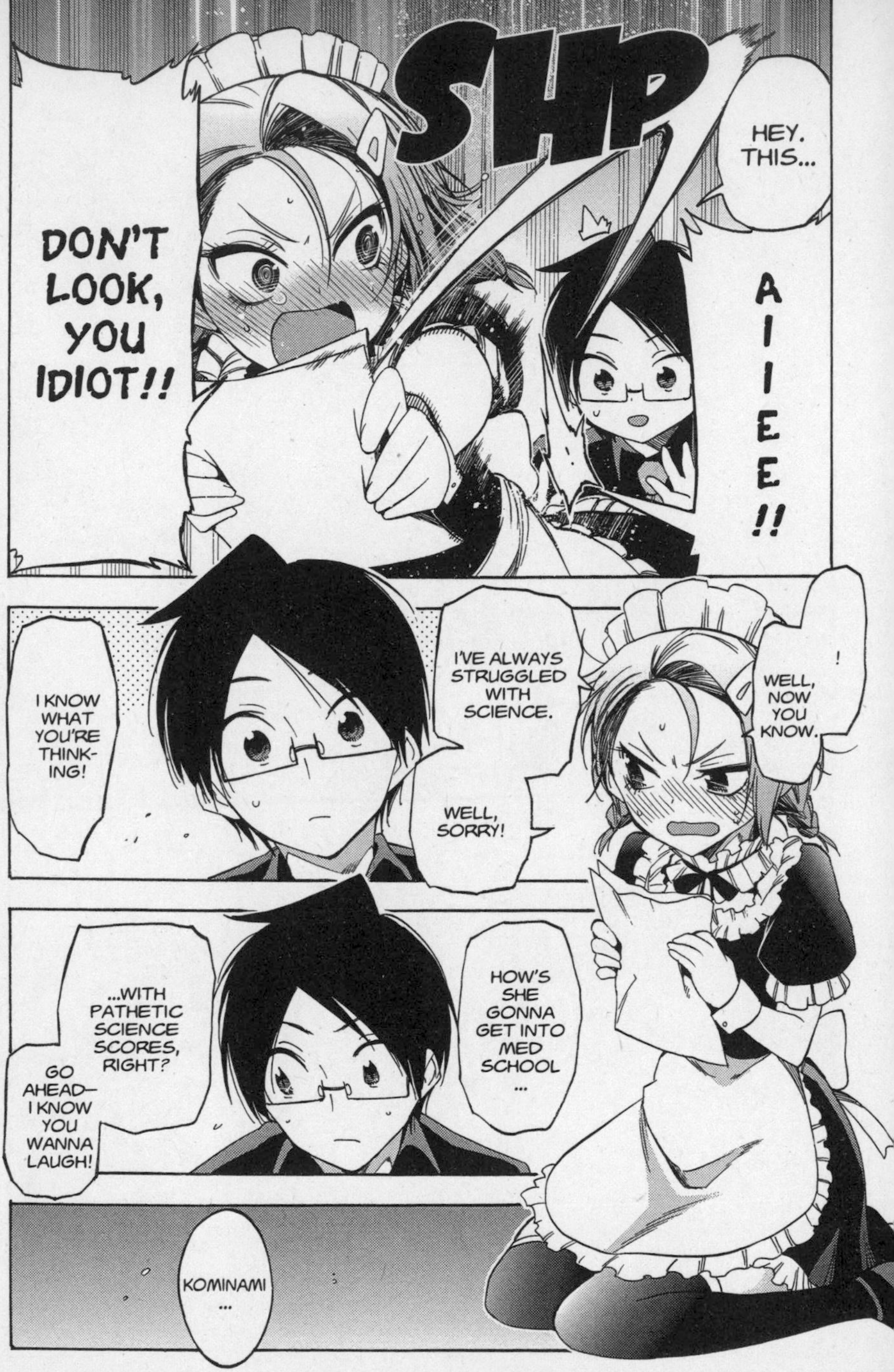
HEY. THIS...
SHP
AIIEE!!
DON'T LOOK, YOU IDIOT!!
!
WELL, NOW YOU KNOW.
I'VE ALWAYS STRUGGLED WITH SCIENCE.
WELL, SORRY!
I KNOW WHAT YOU'RE THINKING!
HOW'S SHE GONNA GET INTO MED SCHOOL...
...WITH PATHETIC SCIENCE SCORES, RIGHT?
GO AHEAD—I KNOW YOU WANNA LAUGH!
KOMINAMI...

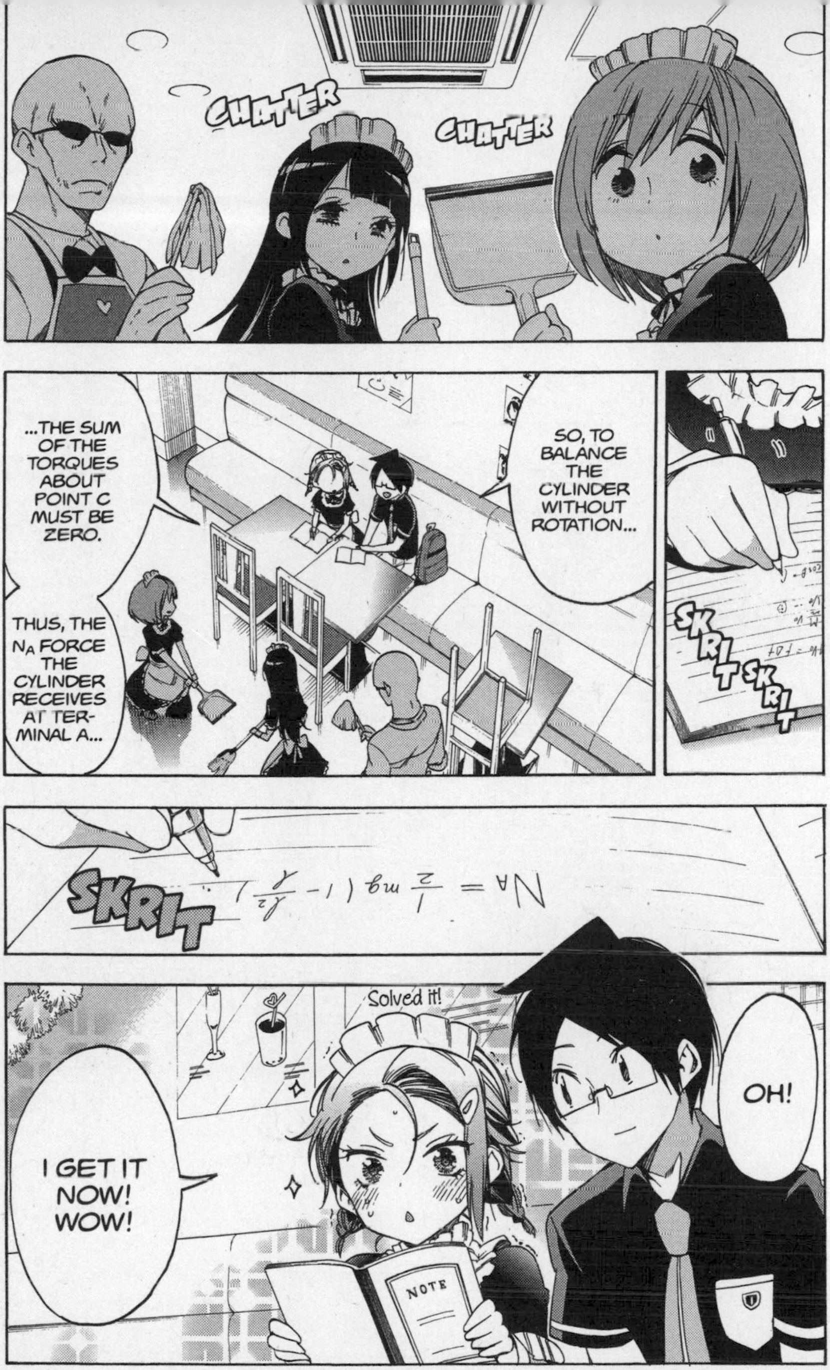
CHATTER
CHATTER
SKRIT SKRIT
SO, TO BALANCE THE CYLINDER WITHOUT ROTATION...
...THE SUM OF THE TORQUES ABOUT POINT C MUST BE ZERO.
THUS, THE N_A FORCE THE CYLINDER RECEIVES AT TERMINAL A...
SKRIT
OH!
Solved it!
I GET IT NOW! WOW!

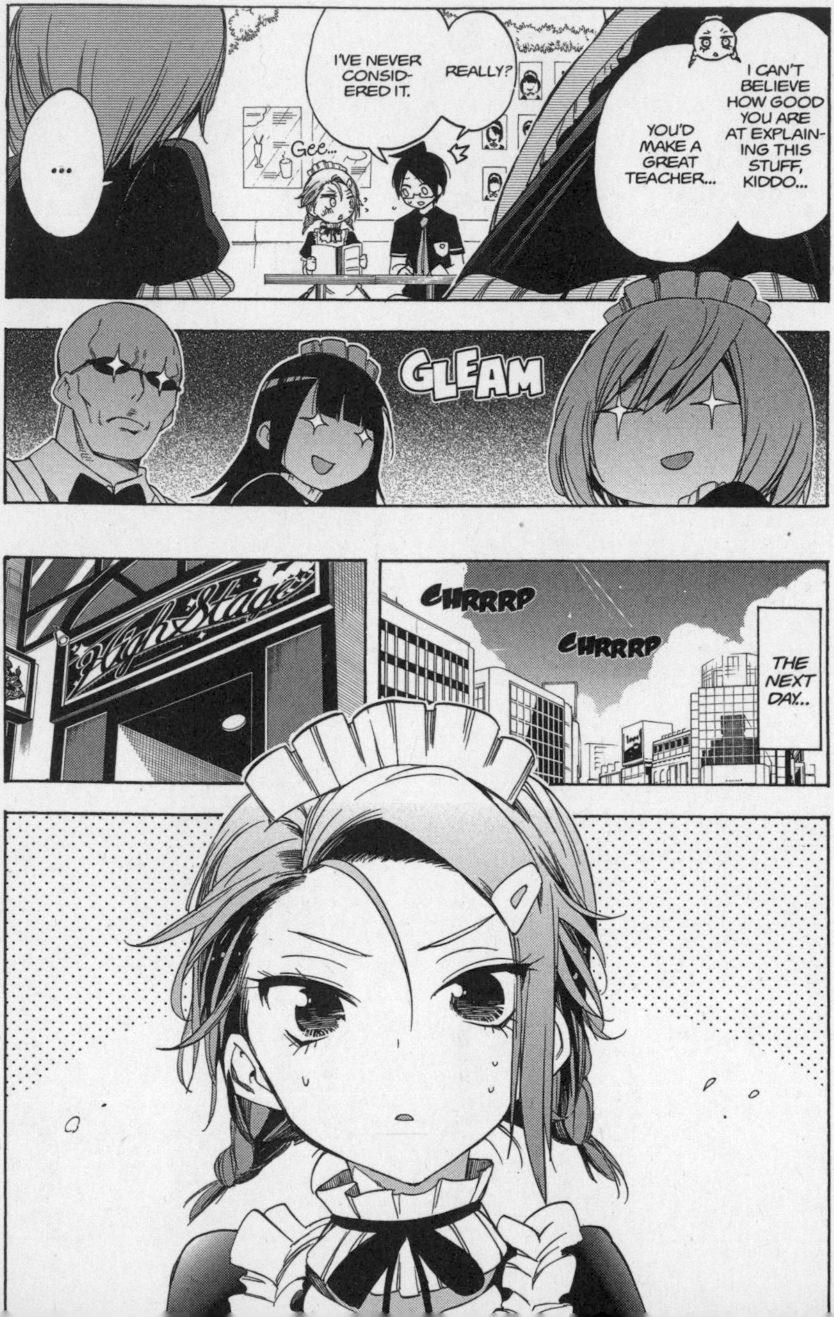
I CAN'T BELIEVE HOW GOOD YOU ARE AT EXPLAINING THIS STUFF, KIDDO...
YOU'D MAKE A GREAT TEACHER...
REALLY?
I'VE NEVER CONSIDERED IT.
Gee...
...
GLEAM
THE NEXT DAY...
CHRRRP
CHRRRP
High Stage

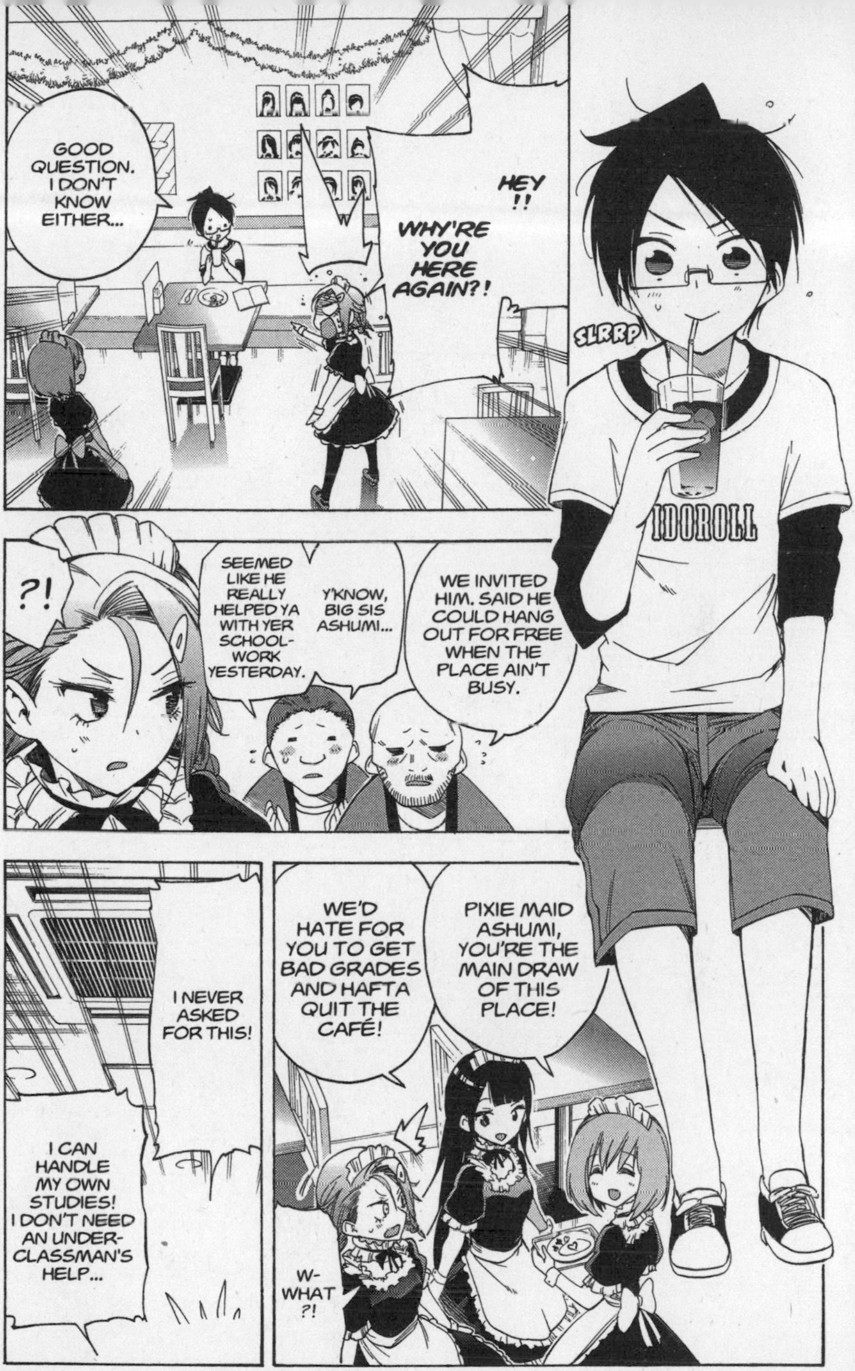
SLRRP
HEY!!
WHY'RE YOU HERE AGAIN?!
GOOD QUESTION. I DON'T KNOW EITHER...
WE INVITED HIM. SAID HE COULD HANG OUT FOR FREE WHEN THE PLACE AIN'T BUSY.
Y'KNOW, BIG SIS ASHUMI...
SEEMED LIKE HE REALLY HELPED YA WITH YER SCHOOL-WORK YESTERDAY.
?!
PIXIE MAID ASHUMI, YOU'RE THE MAIN DRAW OF THIS PLACE!
WE'D HATE FOR YOU TO GET BAD GRADES AND HAFTA QUIT THE CAFÉ!
W-WHAT?!
I NEVER ASKED FOR THIS!
I CAN HANDLE MY OWN STUDIES! I DON'T NEED AN UNDER-CLASSMAN'S HELP...
IDOROLL

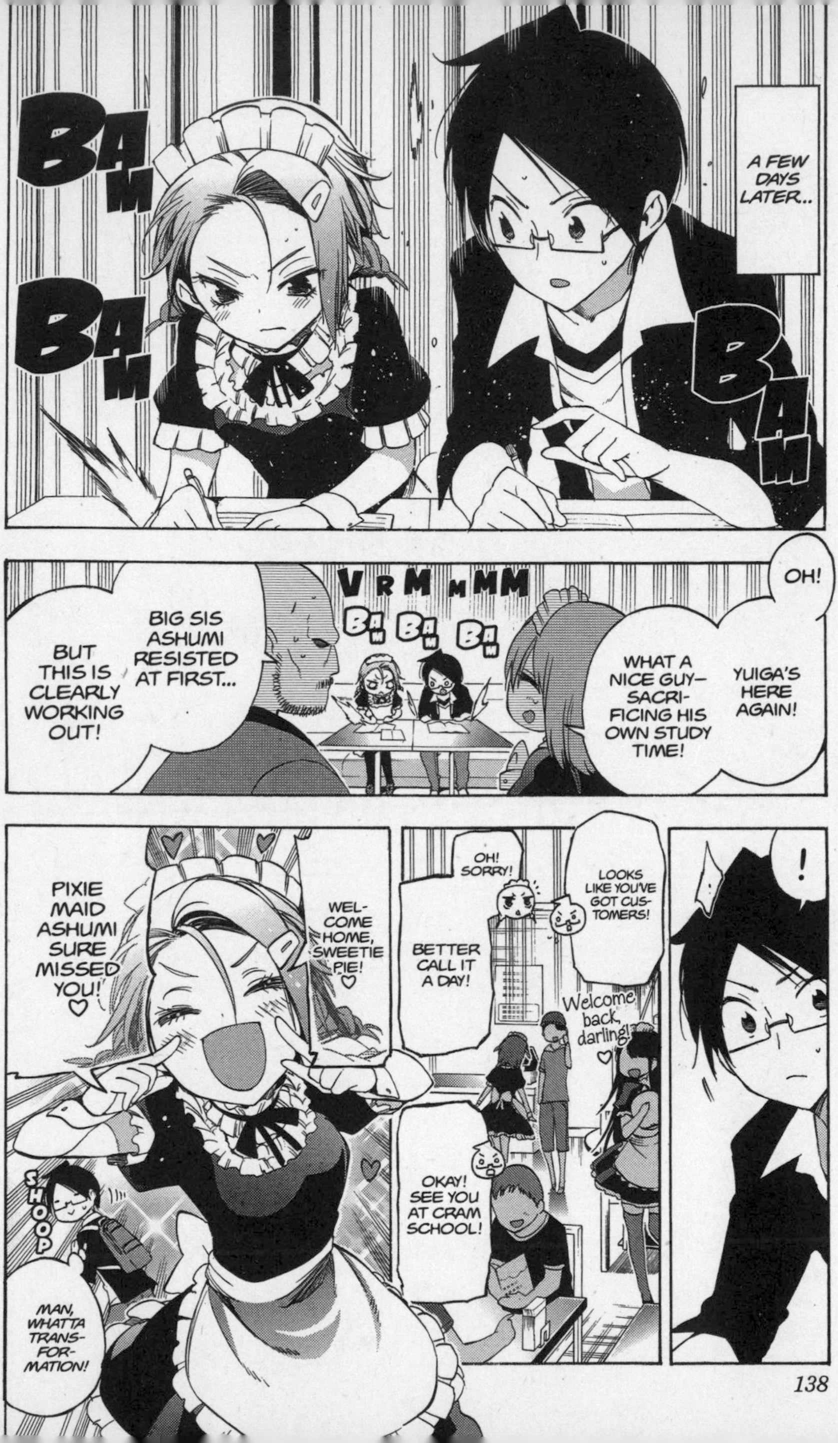
A FEW DAYS LATER...
BAM
BAM
BAM
OH!
YUIGA'S HERE AGAIN!
WHAT A NICE GUY—SACRIFICING HIS OWN STUDY TIME!
VRMMMMM
BAM BAM BAM
BIG SIS ASHUMI RESISTED AT FIRST...
BUT THIS IS CLEARLY WORKING OUT!
!
LOOKS LIKE YOU'VE GOT CUSTOMERS!
OH! SORRY!
BETTER CALL IT A DAY!
Welcome back, darling! ♡
OKAY! SEE YOU AT CRAM SCHOOL!
WELCOME HOME, SWEETIE PIE! ♡
PIXIE MAID ASHUMI SURE MISSED YOU! ♡
SHOOP
MAN, WHATTA TRANSFORMATION!

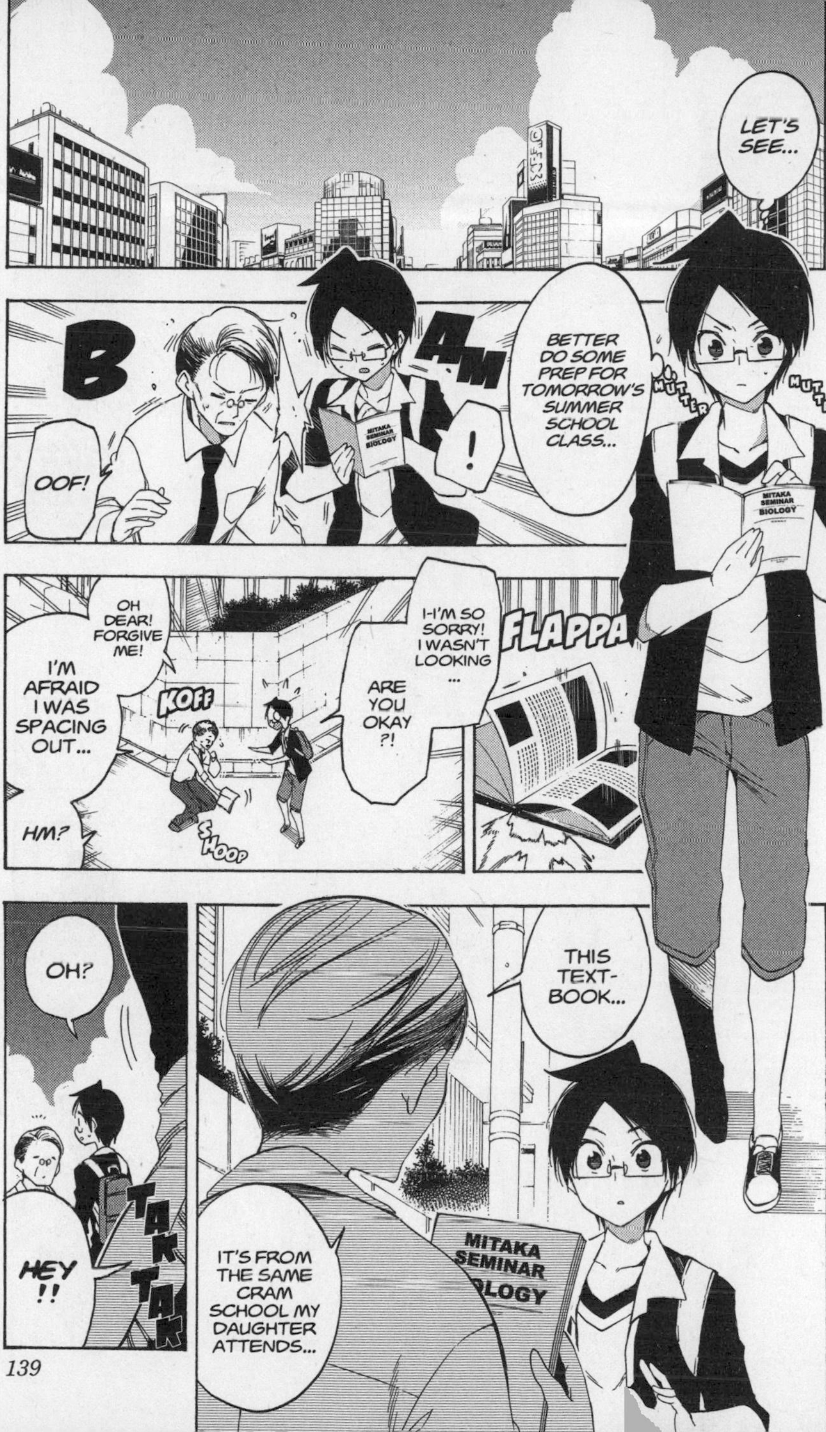
LET'S SEE...
BETTER DO SOME PREP FOR TOMORROW'S SUMMER SCHOOL CLASS...
MUTTER
MUTTER
BAM
!
OOF!
FLAPPA
I-I'M SO SORRY! I WASN'T LOOKING...
ARE YOU OKAY?!
OH DEAR! FORGIVE ME!
I'M AFRAID I WAS SPACING OUT...
KOFF
SHOOP
HM?
THIS TEXT-BOOK...
MITAKA SEMINAR
IT'S FROM THE SAME CRAM SCHOOL MY DAUGHTER ATTENDS...
OH?
TAK TAK
HEY!!

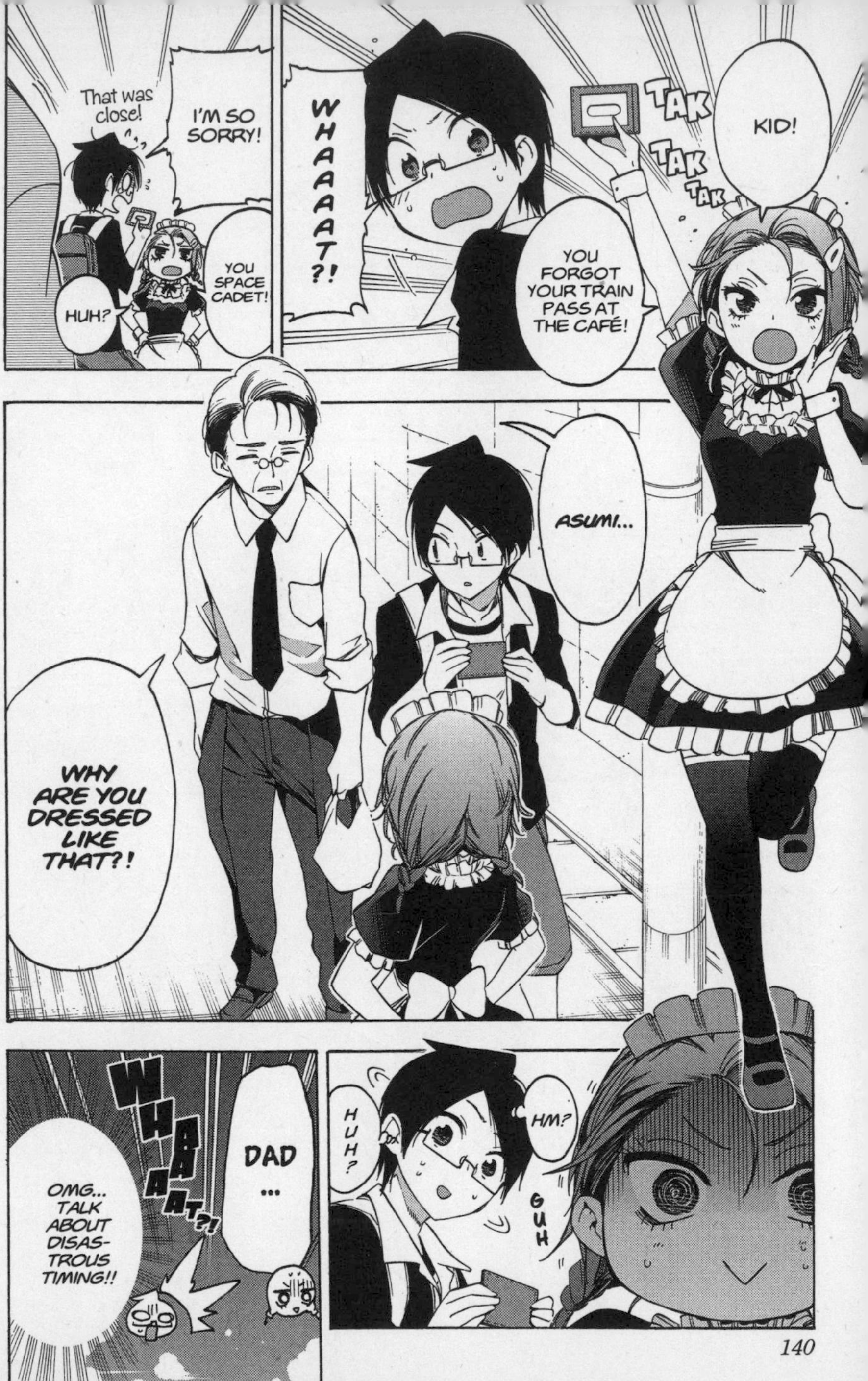
KID!
TAK TAK TAK
YOU FORGOT YOUR TRAIN PASS AT THE CAFÉ!
WHAAAAAT?!
I'M SO SORRY!
That was close!
YOU SPACE CADET!
HUH?
ASUMI...
WHY ARE YOU DRESSED LIKE THAT?!
HM?
HUH?
GUH
DAD ...
WHAAAT?!
OMG... TALK ABOUT DISAS-TROUS TIMING!!

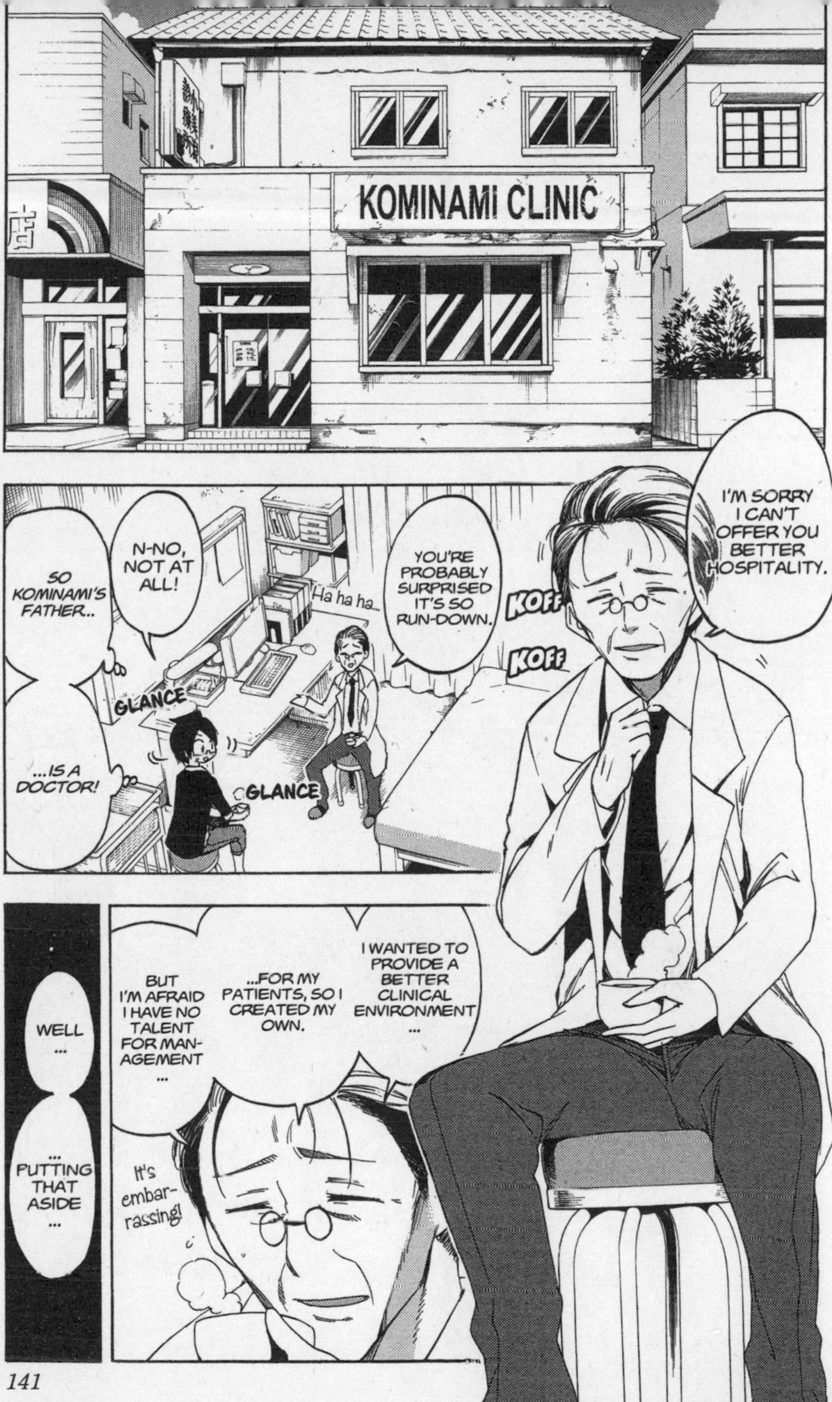
KOMINAMI CLINIC
I'M SORRY I CAN'T OFFER YOU BETTER HOSPITALITY.
KOFF
KOFF
YOU'RE PROBABLY SURPRISED IT'S SO RUN-DOWN.
Ha ha ha...
N-NO, NOT AT ALL!
GLANCE
GLANCE
SO KOMINAMI'S FATHER...
...IS A DOCTOR!
I WANTED TO PROVIDE A BETTER CLINICAL ENVIRONMENT...
...FOR MY PATIENTS, SO I CREATED MY OWN.
BUT I'M AFRAID I HAVE NO TALENT FOR MANAGEMENT...
It's embarrassing!
WELL...
...PUTTING THAT ASIDE...

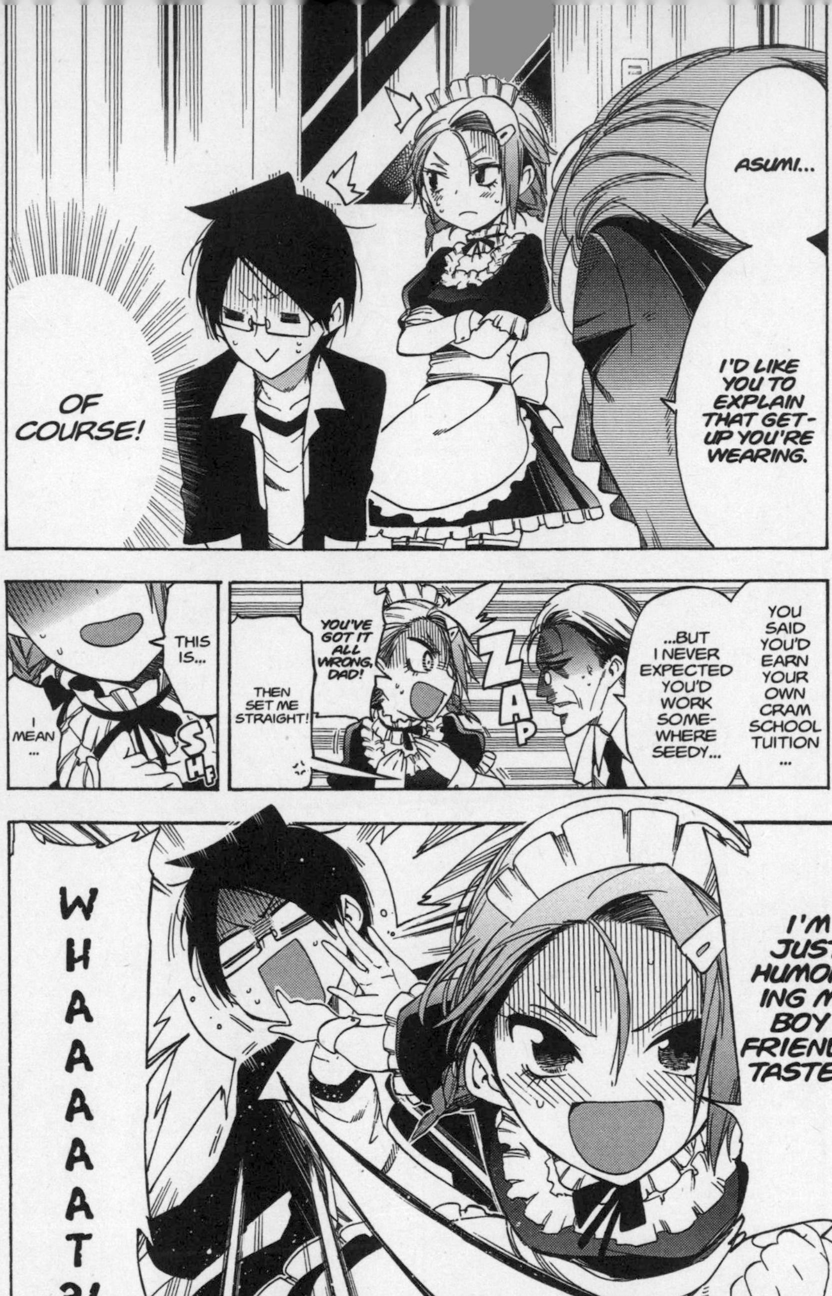
ASUMI...
I'D LIKE YOU TO EXPLAIN THAT GET-UP YOU'RE WEARING.
OF COURSE!
YOU SAID YOU'D EARN YOUR OWN CRAM SCHOOL TUITION...
...BUT I NEVER EXPECTED YOU'D WORK SOME-WHERE SEEDY...
ZAP
YOU'VE GOT IT ALL WRONG, DAD!
THEN SET ME STRAIGHT!
THIS IS...
I MEAN...
SHF
I'M JUST HUMOR-ING MY BOY-FRIEND'S TASTES!
WHAAAAAT?!

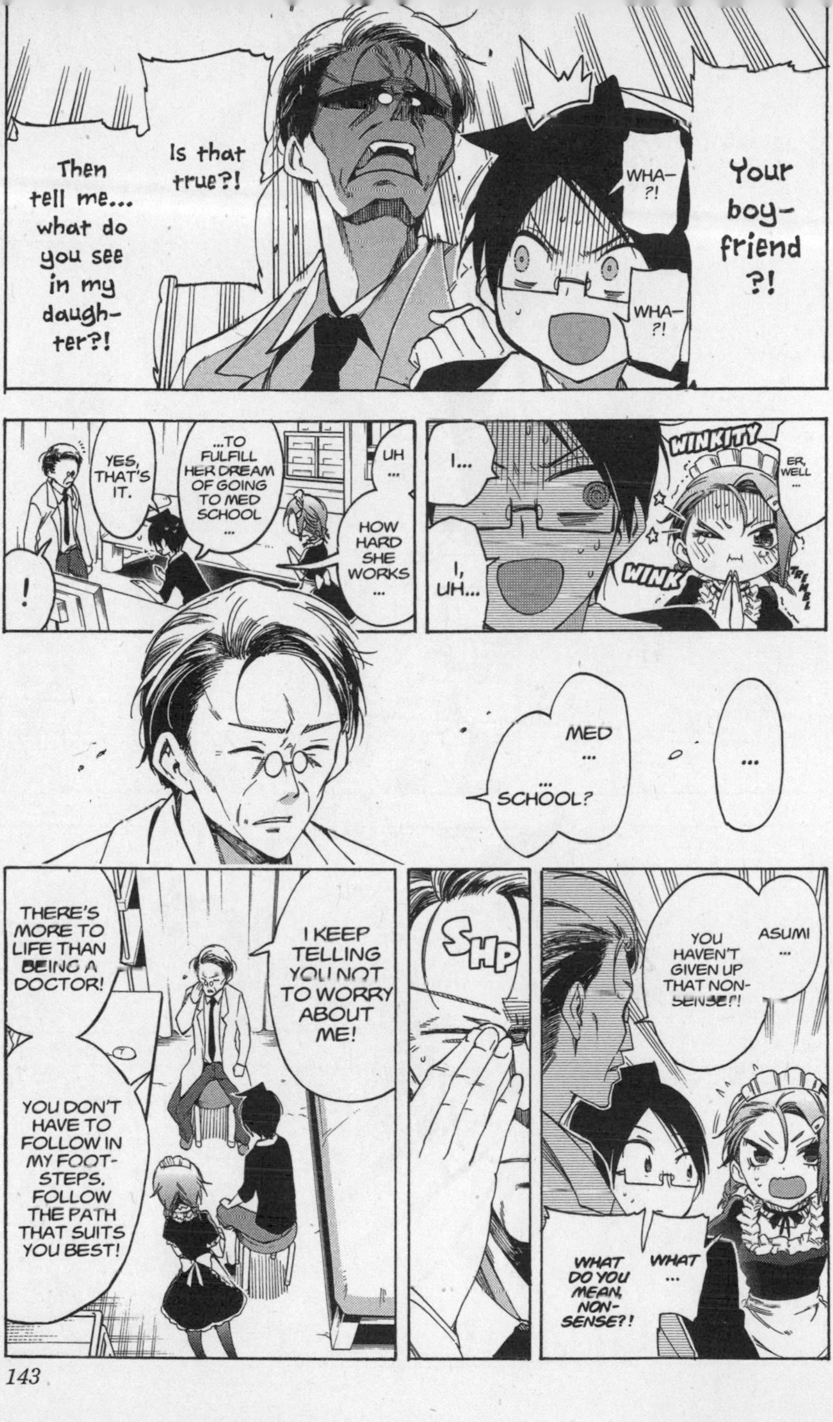
Your boy-friend?!
WHA-?!
WHA-?!
Is that true?!
Then tell me... what do you see in my daughter?!
ER, WELL ...
WINKITY
WINK
TREMBL
I...
I, UH...
UH ... HOW HARD SHE WORKS ...
...TO FULFILL HER DREAM OF GOING TO MED SCHOOL ...
YES, THAT'S IT.
!
...
MED ... ... SCHOOL?
ASUMI ...
YOU HAVEN'T GIVEN UP THAT NON-SENSE?!
WHAT ...
WHAT DO YOU MEAN, NON-SENSE?!
SHP
I KEEP TELLING YOU NOT TO WORRY ABOUT ME!
THERE'S MORE TO LIFE THAN BEING A DOCTOR!
YOU DON'T HAVE TO FOLLOW IN MY FOOT-STEPS. FOLLOW THE PATH THAT SUITS YOU BEST!

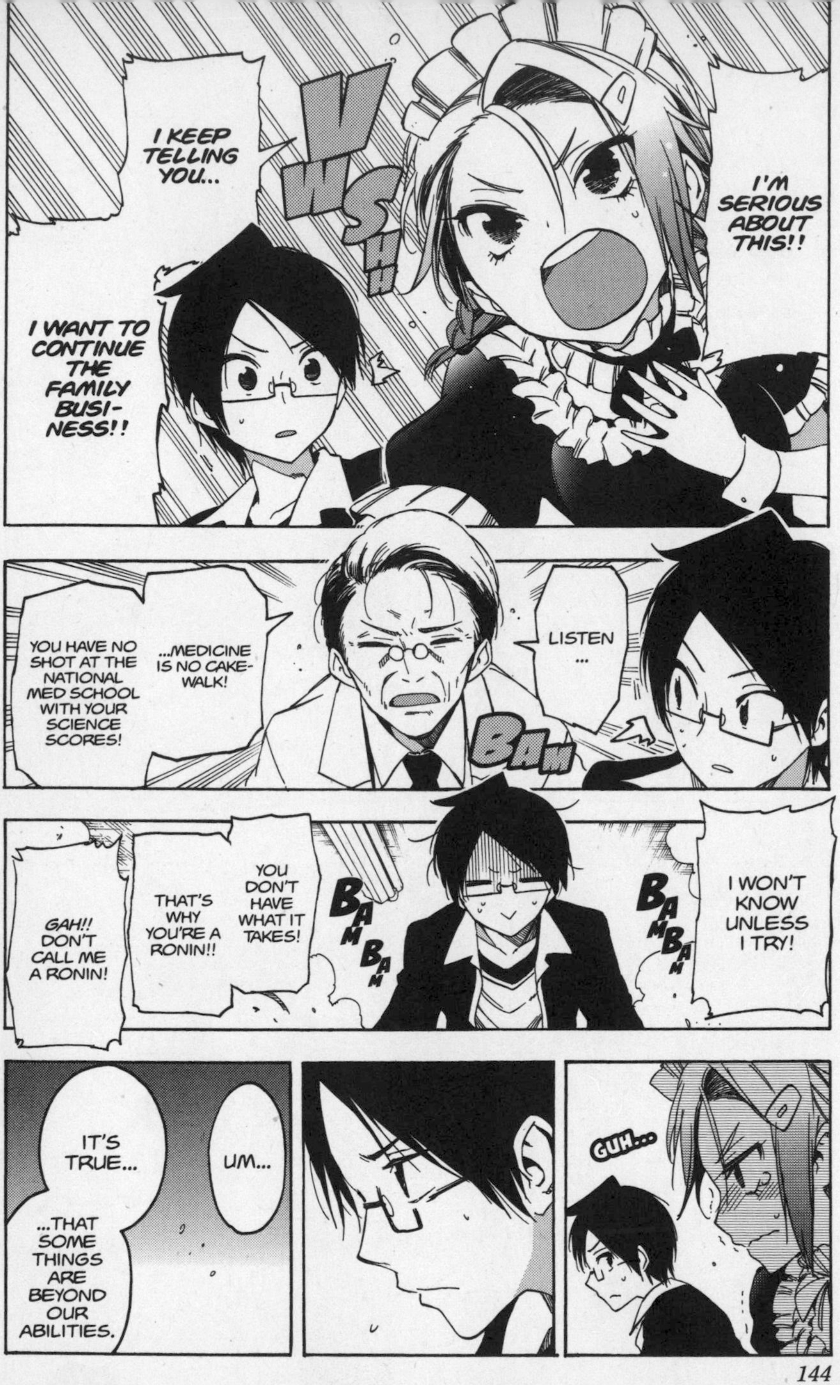
I'M SERIOUS ABOUT THIS!!
VWSH
I KEEP TELLING YOU...
I WANT TO CONTINUE THE FAMILY BUSINESS!!
LISTEN...
BAM
...MEDICINE IS NO CAKEWALK!
YOU HAVE NO SHOT AT THE NATIONAL MED SCHOOL WITH YOUR SCIENCE SCORES!
I WON'T KNOW UNLESS I TRY!
BAM BAM
BAM BAM
YOU DON'T HAVE WHAT IT TAKES!
THAT'S WHY YOU'RE A RONIN!!
GAH!! DON'T CALL ME A RONIN!
GUH...
UM...
IT'S TRUE...
...THAT SOME THINGS ARE BEYOND OUR ABILITIES.

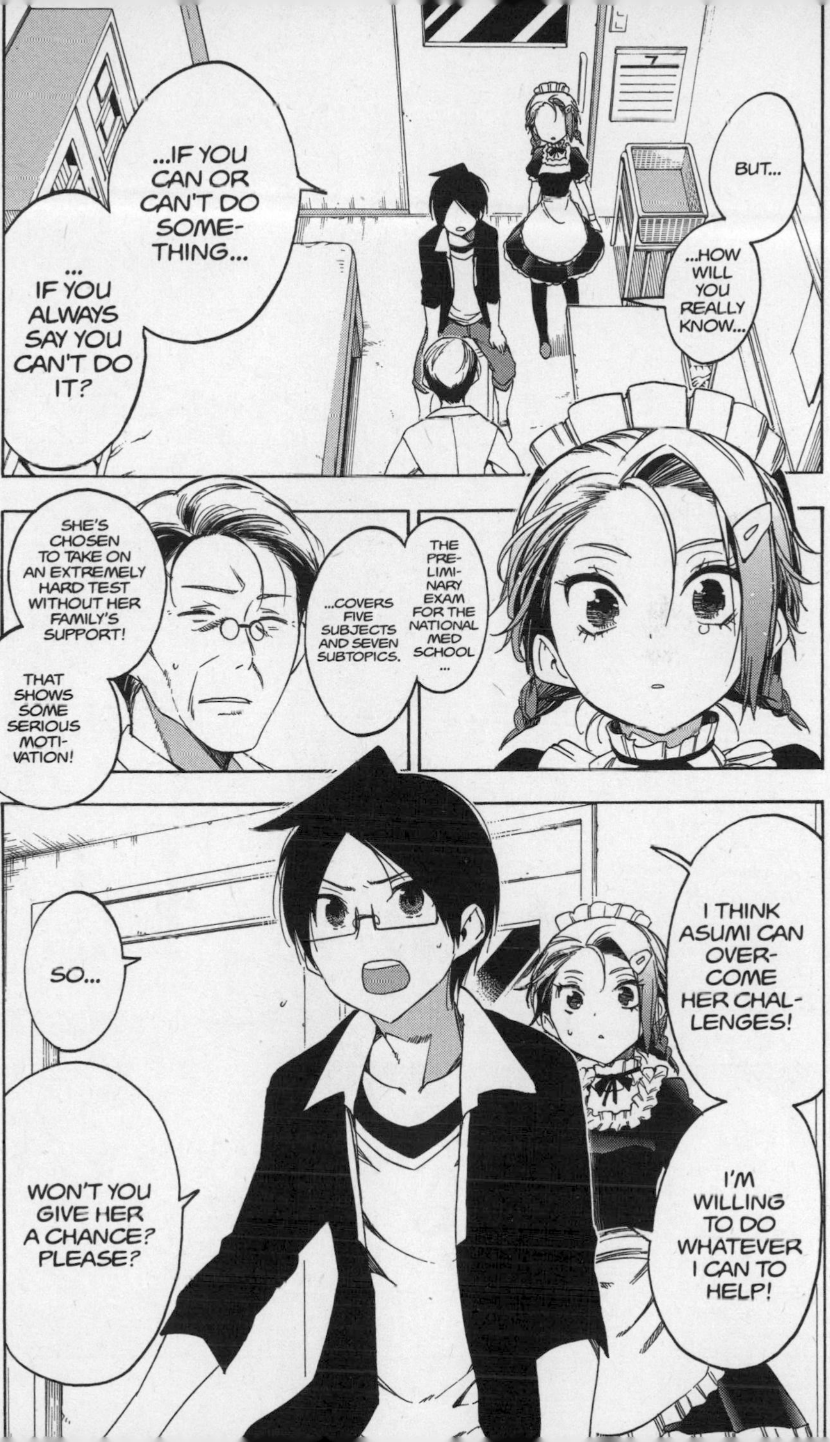
BUT...
...HOW WILL YOU REALLY KNOW...
...IF YOU CAN OR CAN'T DO SOME-THING...
... IF YOU ALWAYS SAY YOU CAN'T DO IT?
THE PRE-LIMI-NARY EXAM FOR THE NATIONAL MED SCHOOL ...
...COVERS FIVE SUBJECTS AND SEVEN SUBTOPICS.
SHE'S CHOSEN TO TAKE ON AN EXTREMELY HARD TEST WITHOUT HER FAMILY'S SUPPORT!
THAT SHOWS SOME SERIOUS MOTI-VATION!
I THINK ASUMI CAN OVER-COME HER CHAL-LENGES!
I'M WILLING TO DO WHATEVER I CAN TO HELP!
SO...
WON'T YOU GIVE HER A CHANCE? PLEASE?

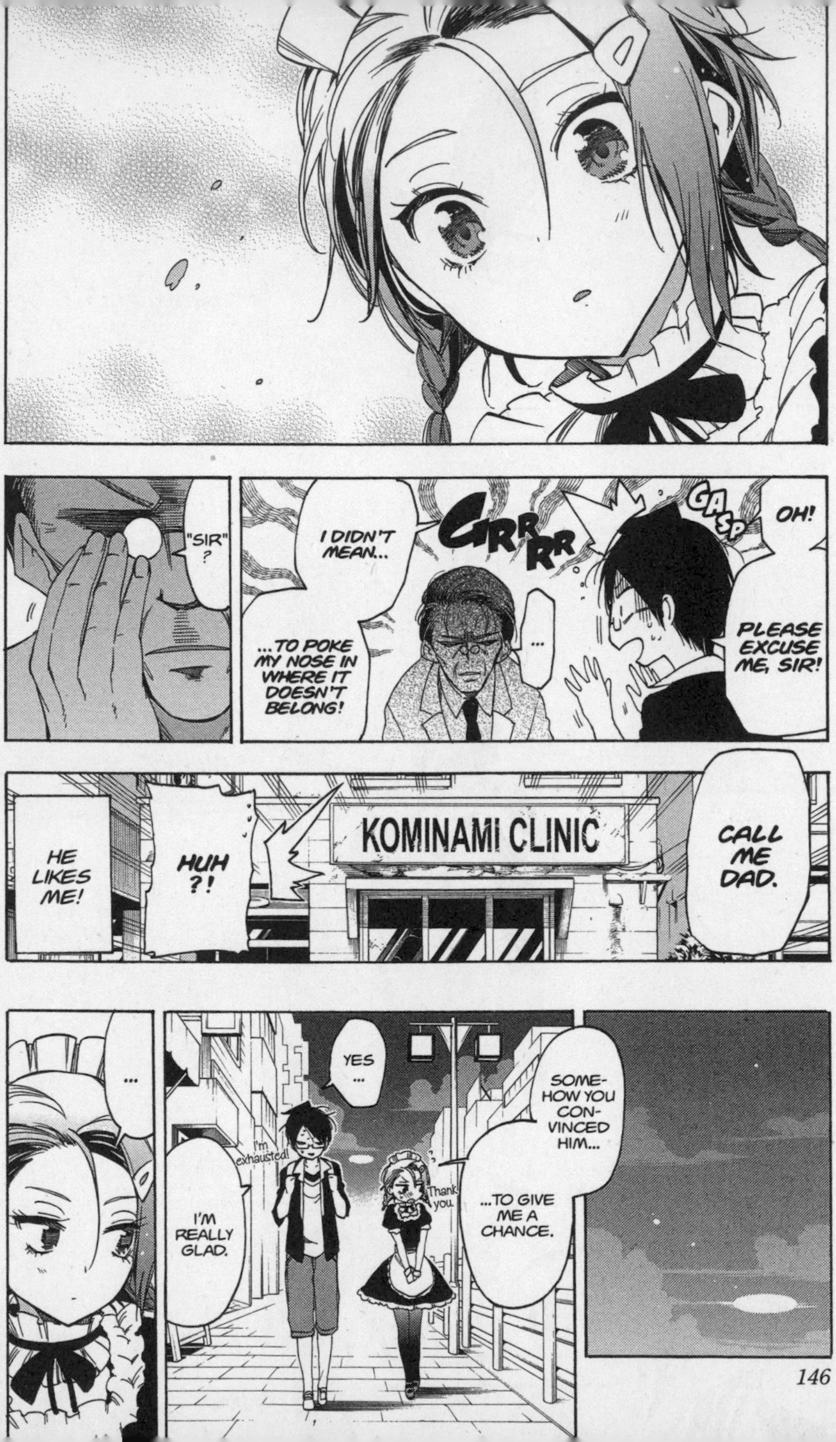
GASP
OH!
PLEASE EXCUSE ME, SIR!
GRRRR
...
I DIDN'T MEAN...
...TO POKE MY NOSE IN WHERE IT DOESN'T BELONG!
"SIR"?
CALL ME DAD.
KOMINAMI CLINIC
HUH?!
HE LIKES ME!
SOME-HOW YOU CON-VINCED HIM...
...TO GIVE ME A CHANCE.
YES...
Thank you.
I'm exhausted!
I'M REALLY GLAD.
...

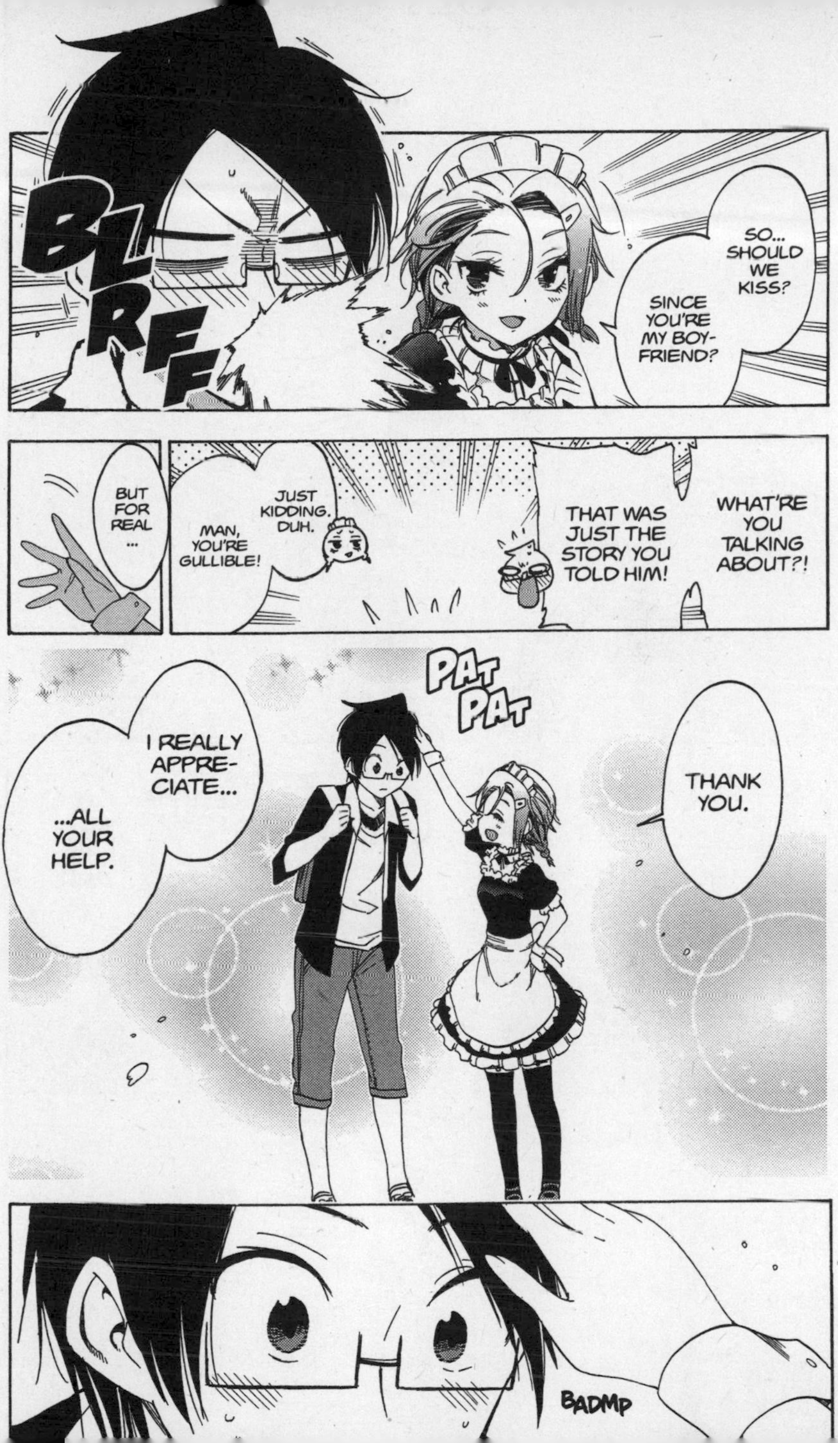
SO... SHOULD WE KISS?
SINCE YOU'RE MY BOY-FRIEND?
BLRFF
WHAT'RE YOU TALKING ABOUT?!
THAT WAS JUST THE STORY YOU TOLD HIM!
JUST KIDDING. DUH.
MAN, YOU'RE GULLIBLE!
BUT FOR REAL ...
PAT PAT
THANK YOU.
I REALLY APPRE-CIATE...
...ALL YOUR HELP.
BADMP

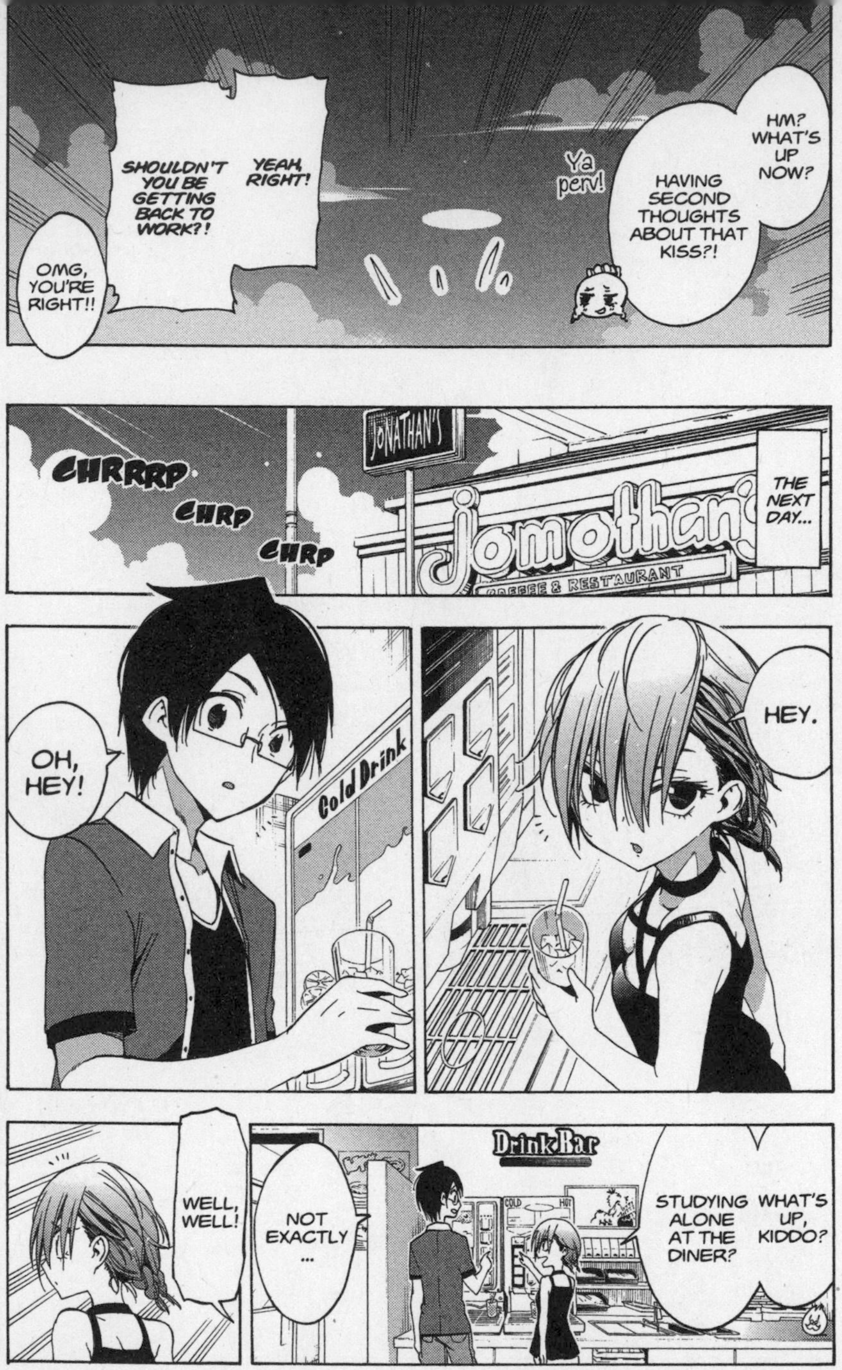
HM? WHAT'S UP NOW?
HAVING SECOND THOUGHTS ABOUT THAT KISS?!
Ya perv!
YEAH, RIGHT!
SHOULDN'T YOU BE GETTING BACK TO WORK?!
OMG, YOU'RE RIGHT!!
THE NEXT DAY...
JONATHAN'S
jomothan's
COFFEE & RESTAURANT
CHRRRP
CHRP
CHRP
HEY.
OH, HEY!
Cold Drink
WHAT'S UP, KIDDO?
STUDYING ALONE AT THE DINER?
Drink Bar
COLD
HOT
NOT EXACTLY ...
WELL, WELL!

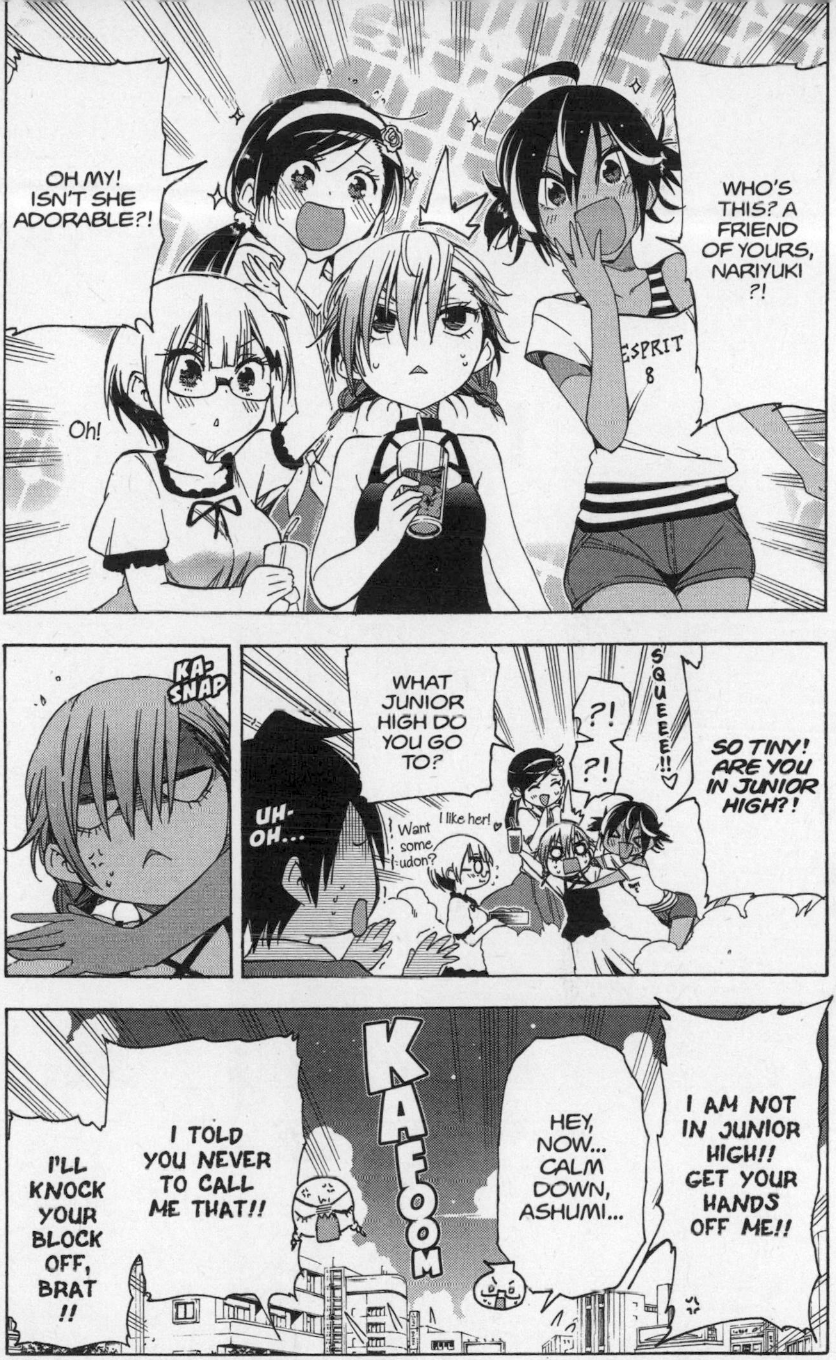
WHO'S THIS? A FRIEND OF YOURS, NARIYUKI ?!
OH MY! ISN'T SHE ADORABLE?!
Oh!
SO TINY! ARE YOU IN JUNIOR HIGH?!
SQUEEEE!!♡
?!
?!
WHAT JUNIOR HIGH DO YOU GO TO?
I like her!
Want some udon?
UH-OH...
KA-SNAP
I AM NOT IN JUNIOR HIGH!! GET YOUR HANDS OFF ME!!
HEY, NOW... CALM DOWN, ASHUMI...
KAFOOM
I TOLD YOU NEVER TO CALL ME THAT!!
I'LL KNOCK YOUR BLOCK OFF, BRAT !!

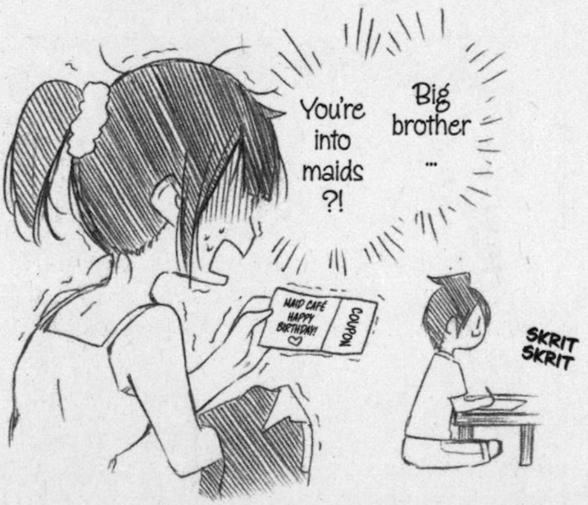
Big brother …
You're into maids ?!
SKRIT SKRIT
MAID CAFÉ HAPPY BIRTHDAY!
COUPON

Question 33: Geniuses and a Predecessor Cause Mental Anguish for [X]

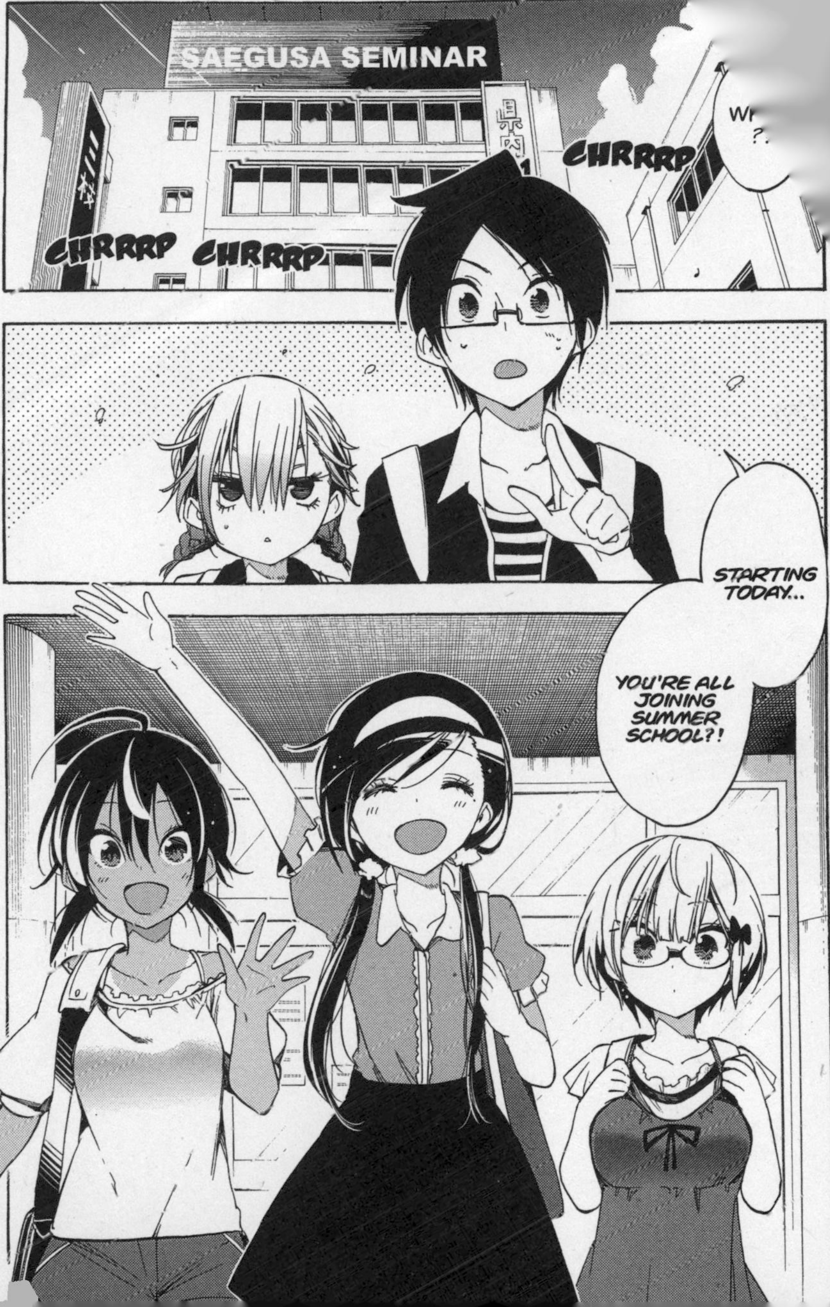
CHRRRP
SAEGUSA SEMINAR
CHRRRP
CHRRRP
STARTING TODAY...
YOU'RE ALL JOINING SUMMER SCHOOL?!

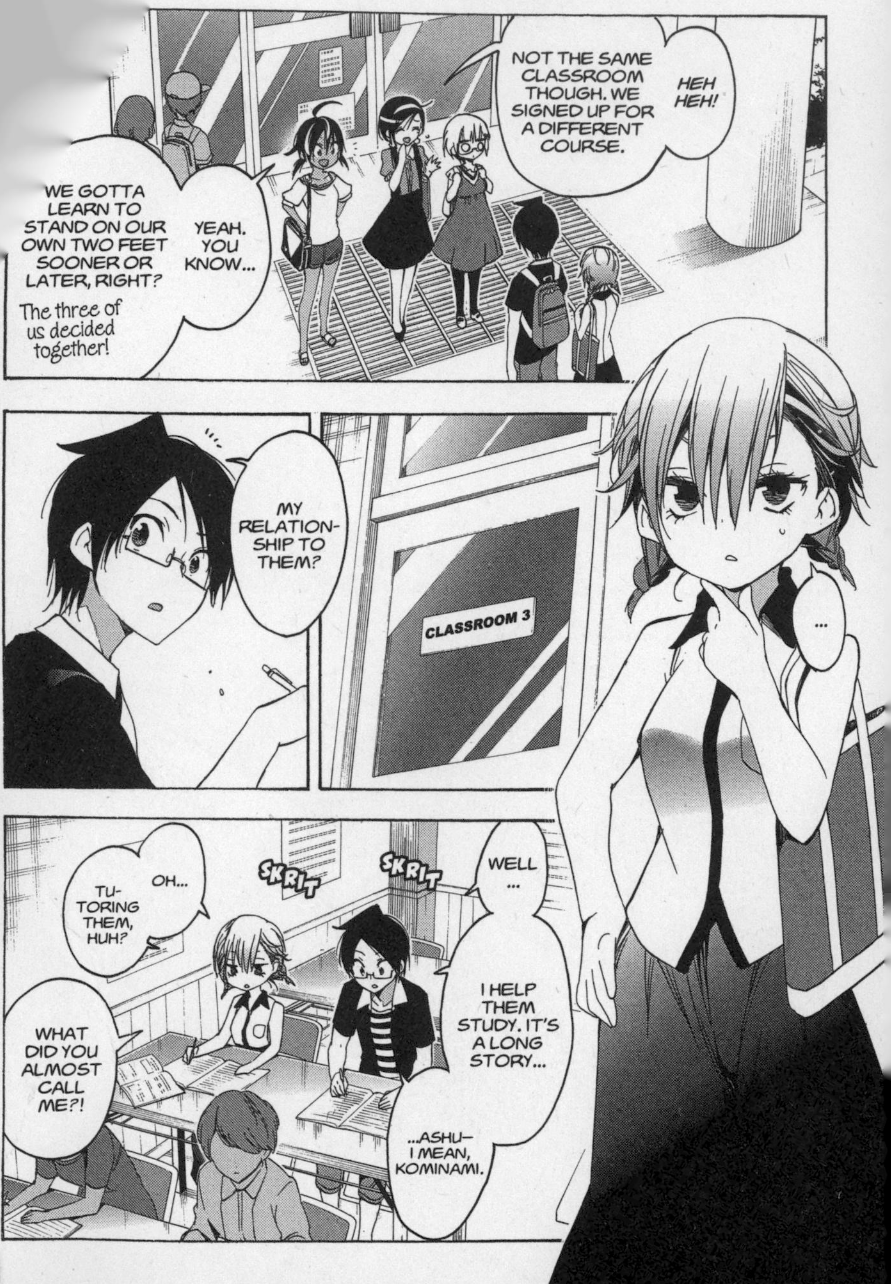
NOT THE SAME CLASSROOM THOUGH. WE SIGNED UP FOR A DIFFERENT COURSE.
HEH HEH!
YEAH. YOU KNOW...
WE GOTTA LEARN TO STAND ON OUR OWN TWO FEET SOONER OR LATER, RIGHT?
The three of us decided together!
...
CLASSROOM 3
MY RELATION-SHIP TO THEM?
WELL ...
SKRIT
SKRIT
I HELP THEM STUDY. IT'S A LONG STORY...
OH...
TU-TORING THEM, HUH?
...ASHU- I MEAN, KOMINAMI.
WHAT DID YOU ALMOST CALL ME?!

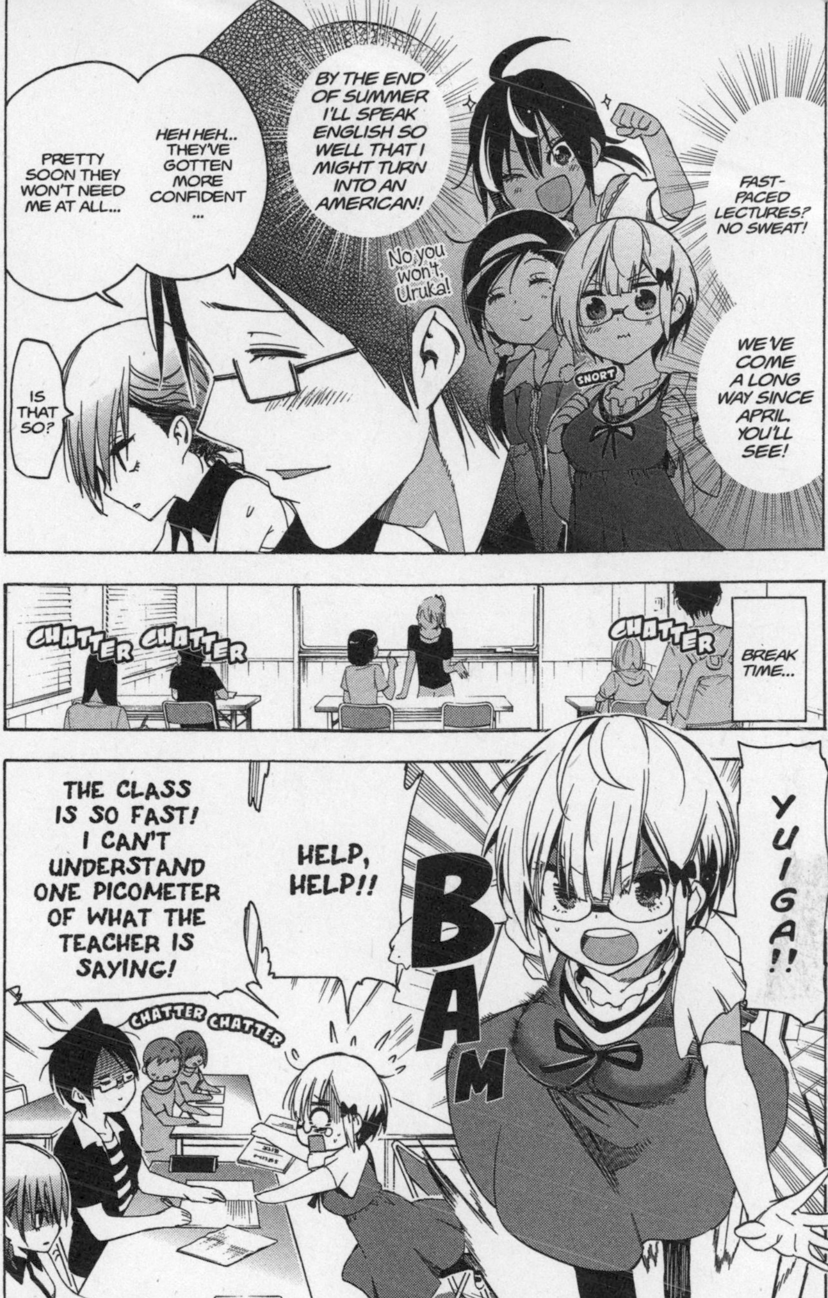
FAST-PACED LECTURES? NO SWEAT!
BY THE END OF SUMMER I'LL SPEAK ENGLISH SO WELL THAT I MIGHT TURN INTO AN AMERICAN!
No you won't, Uruka!
WE'VE COME A LONG WAY SINCE APRIL. YOU'LL SEE!
SNORT
HEH HEH... THEY'VE GOTTEN MORE CONFIDENT ...
PRETTY SOON THEY WON'T NEED ME AT ALL...
IS THAT SO?
BREAK TIME...
CHATTER
CHATTER CHATTER
YUIGA!!
BAM
HELP, HELP!!
THE CLASS IS SO FAST! I CAN'T UNDERSTAND ONE PICOMETER OF WHAT THE TEACHER IS SAYING!
CHATTER CHATTER

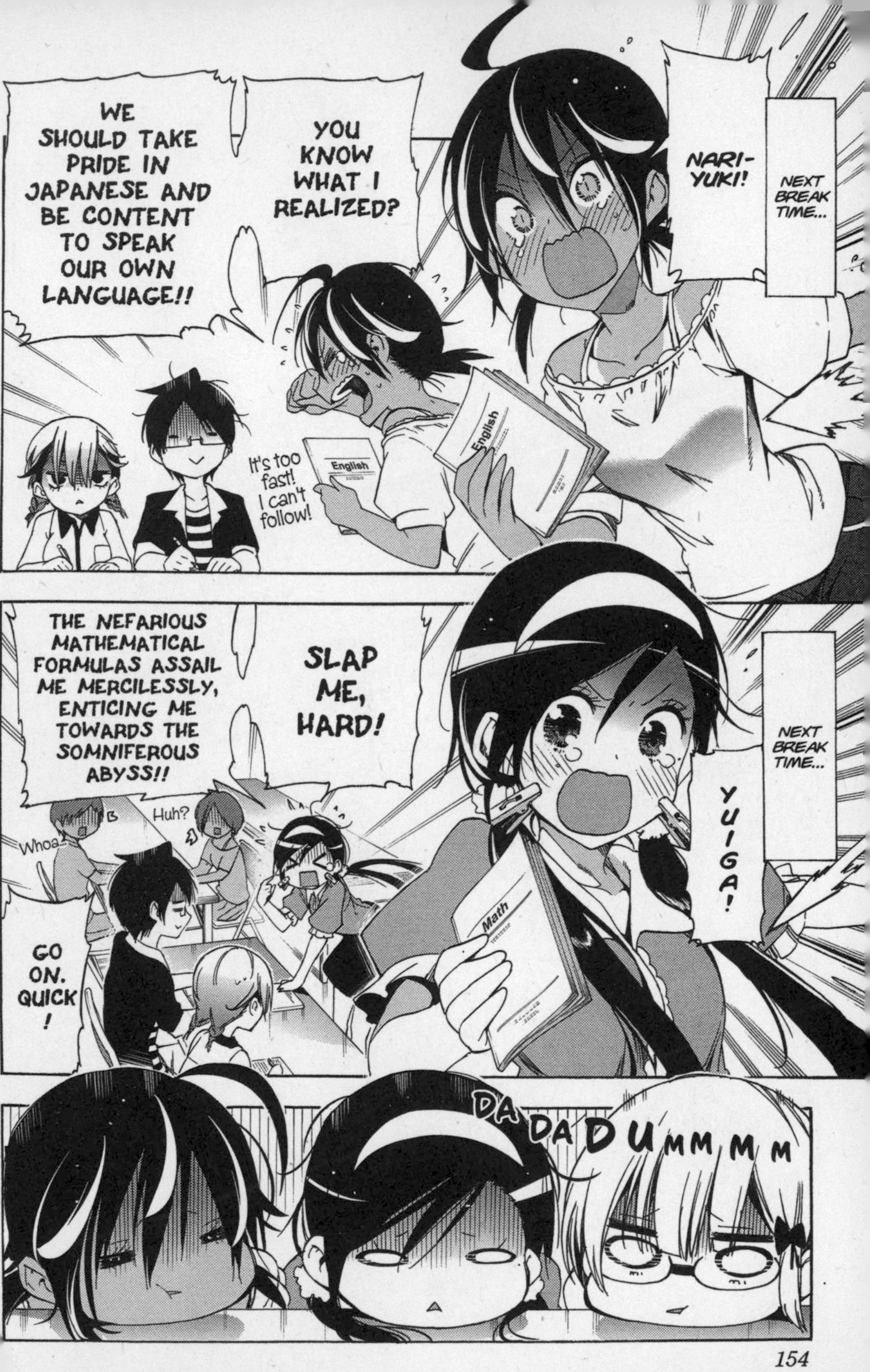
NEXT BREAK TIME...
NARI-YUKI!
YOU KNOW WHAT I REALIZED?
WE SHOULD TAKE PRIDE IN JAPANESE AND BE CONTENT TO SPEAK OUR OWN LANGUAGE!!
English
English
It's too fast! I can't follow!
NEXT BREAK TIME...
YUIGA!
SLAP ME, HARD!
THE NEFARIOUS MATHEMATICAL FORMULAS ASSAIL ME MERCILESSLY, ENTICING ME TOWARDS THE SOMNIFEROUS ABYSS!!
Math
Huh?
Whoa...
GO ON. QUICK!
DA DA DUMMMMM

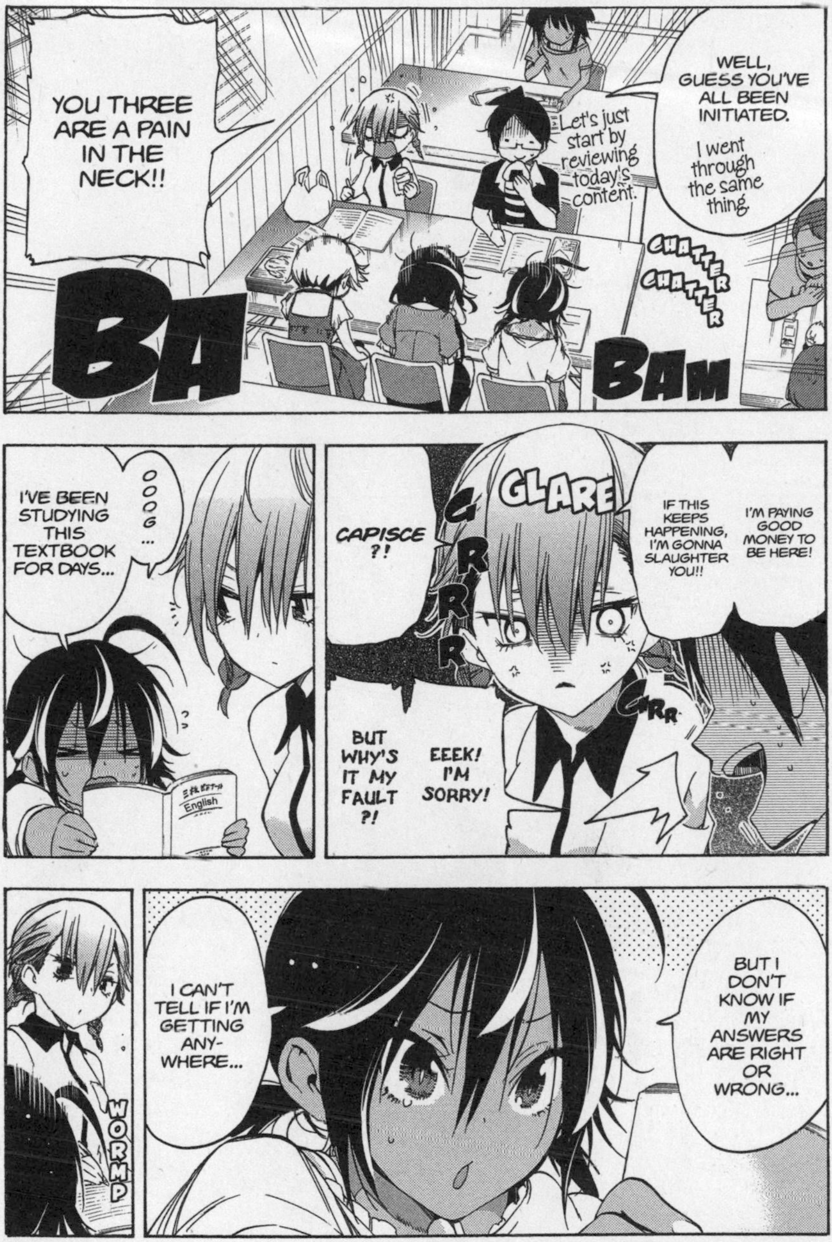
WELL, GUESS YOU'VE ALL BEEN INITIATED.
I went through the same thing.
Let's just start by reviewing today's content.
CHATTER CHATTER
BAM
YOU THREE ARE A PAIN IN THE NECK!!
BA
I'M PAYING GOOD MONEY TO BE HERE!
IF THIS KEEPS HAPPENING, I'M GONNA SLAUGHTER YOU!!
GLARE
CAPISCE?!
GRRRR
GRRR
EEEK! I'M SORRY!
BUT WHY'S IT MY FAULT?!
OOOG...
I'VE BEEN STUDYING THIS TEXTBOOK FOR DAYS...
English
BUT I DON'T KNOW IF MY ANSWERS ARE RIGHT OR WRONG...
I CAN'T TELL IF I'M GETTING ANY-WHERE...
WORMP

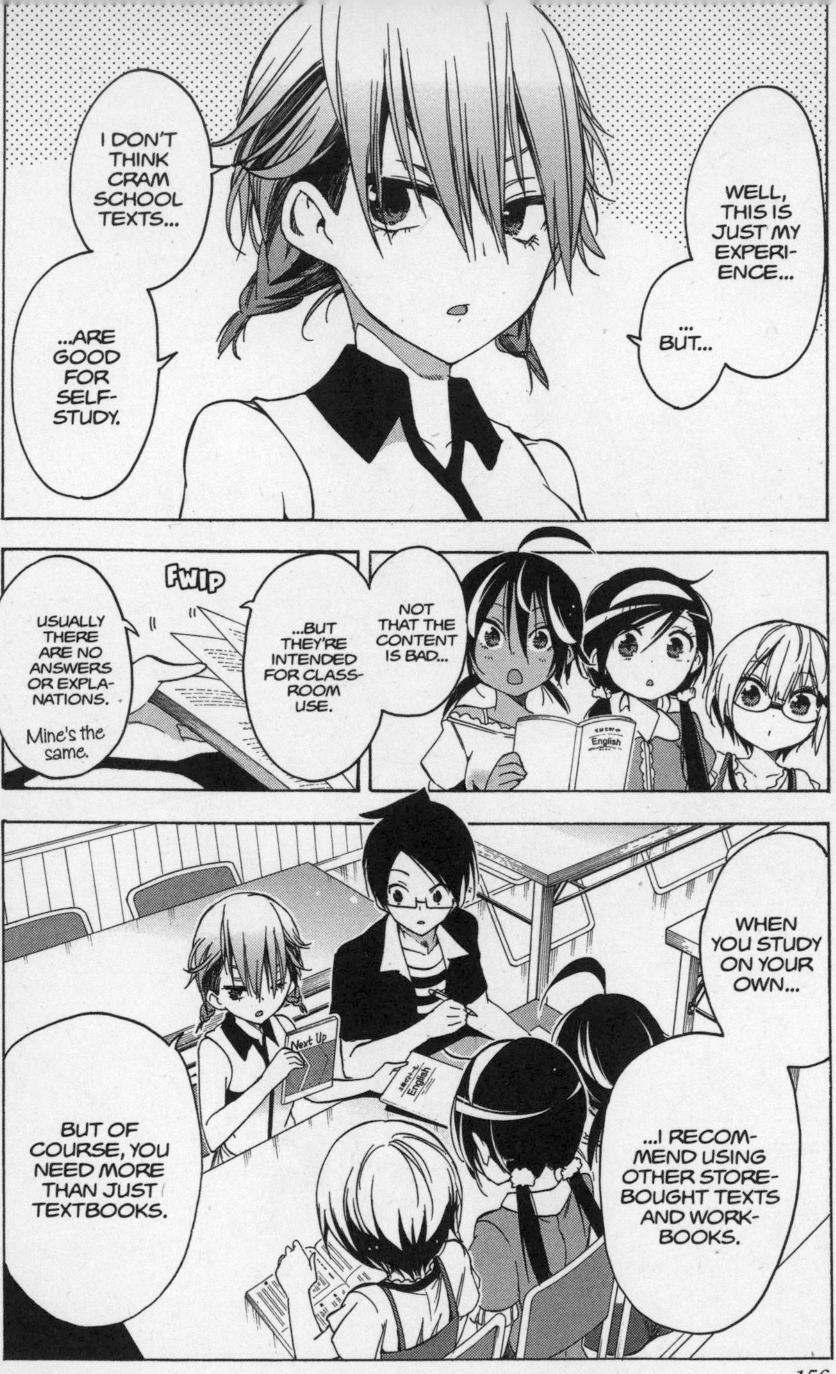
WELL, THIS IS JUST MY EXPERIENCE...
... BUT...
I DON'T THINK CRAM SCHOOL TEXTS...
...ARE GOOD FOR SELF-STUDY.
NOT THAT THE CONTENT IS BAD...
...BUT THEY'RE INTENDED FOR CLASSROOM USE.
English
FWIP
USUALLY THERE ARE NO ANSWERS OR EXPLANATIONS.
Mine's the same.
WHEN YOU STUDY ON YOUR OWN...
...I RECOMMEND USING OTHER STORE-BOUGHT TEXTS AND WORKBOOKS.
English
Next Up
BUT OF COURSE, YOU NEED MORE THAN JUST TEXTBOOKS.

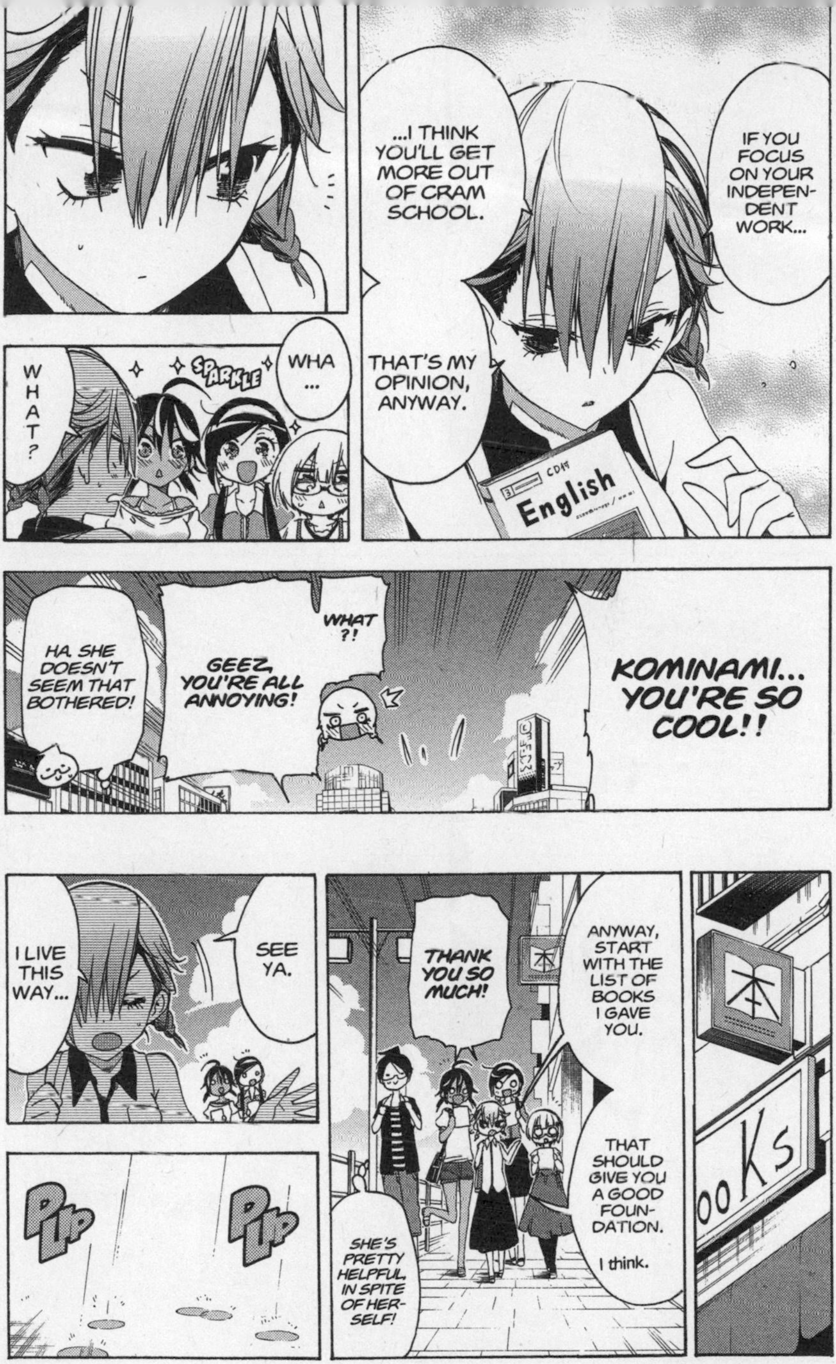
IF YOU FOCUS ON YOUR INDEPENDENT WORK...
...I THINK YOU'LL GET MORE OUT OF CRAM SCHOOL.
THAT'S MY OPINION, ANYWAY.
English
WHA...
SPARKLE
WHAT?
KOMINAMI... YOU'RE SO COOL!!
WHAT?!
GEEZ, YOU'RE ALL ANNOYING!
HA. SHE DOESN'T SEEM THAT BOTHERED!
ANYWAY, START WITH THE LIST OF BOOKS I GAVE YOU.
THAT SHOULD GIVE YOU A GOOD FOUNDATION.
I think.
THANK YOU SO MUCH!
SHE'S PRETTY HELPFUL, IN SPITE OF HERSELF!
SEE YA.
I LIVE THIS WAY...
PLIP
PLIP

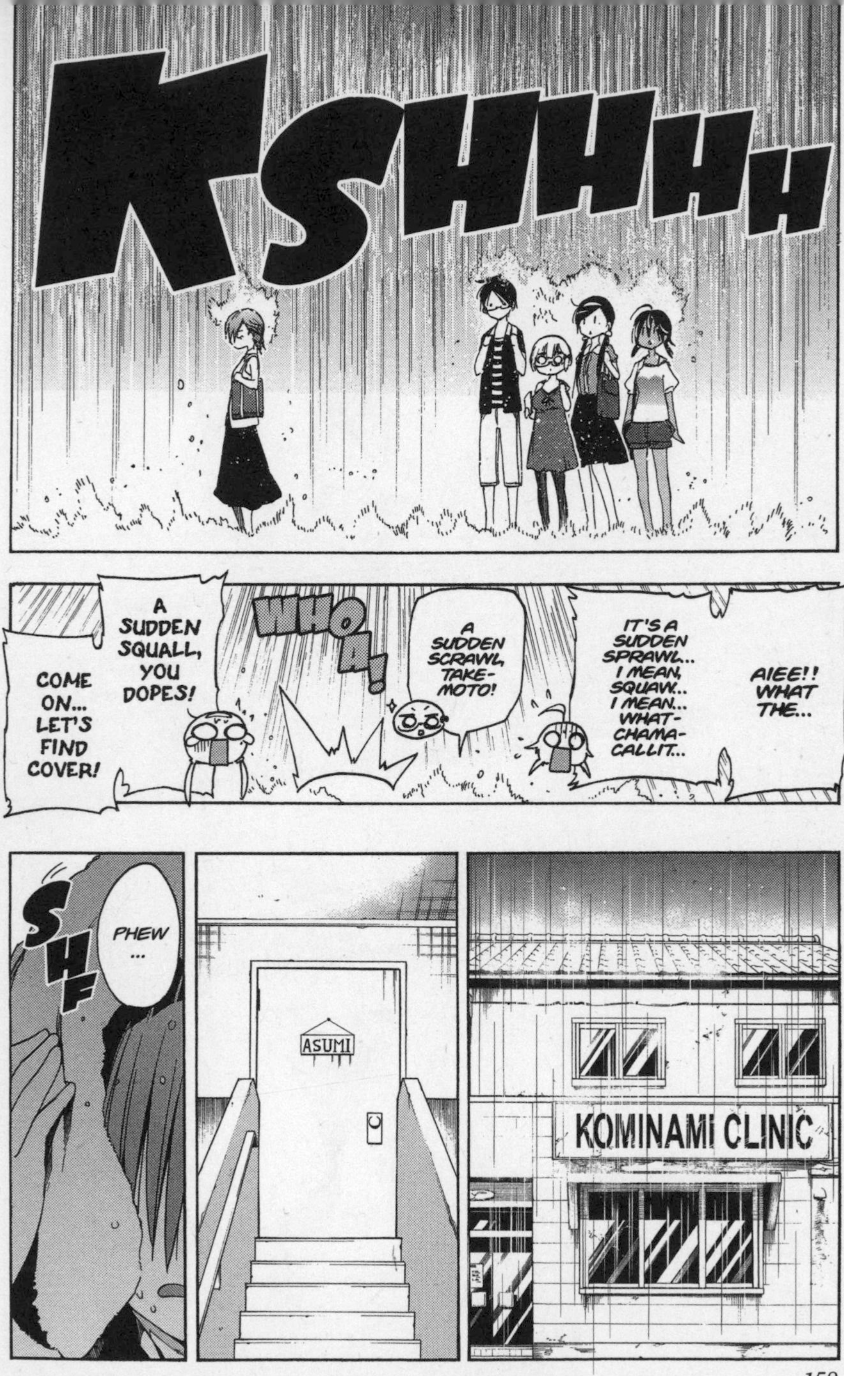
KSHHHHH
AIEE!! WHAT THE...
IT'S A SUDDEN SPRAWL... I MEAN, SQUAW... I MEAN... WHAT-CHAMA-CALLIT...
A SUDDEN SCRAWL, TAKE-MOTO!
WHOA!
A SUDDEN SQUALL, YOU DOPES!
COME ON... LET'S FIND COVER!
KOMINAMI CLINIC
ASUMI
SHF
PHEW...

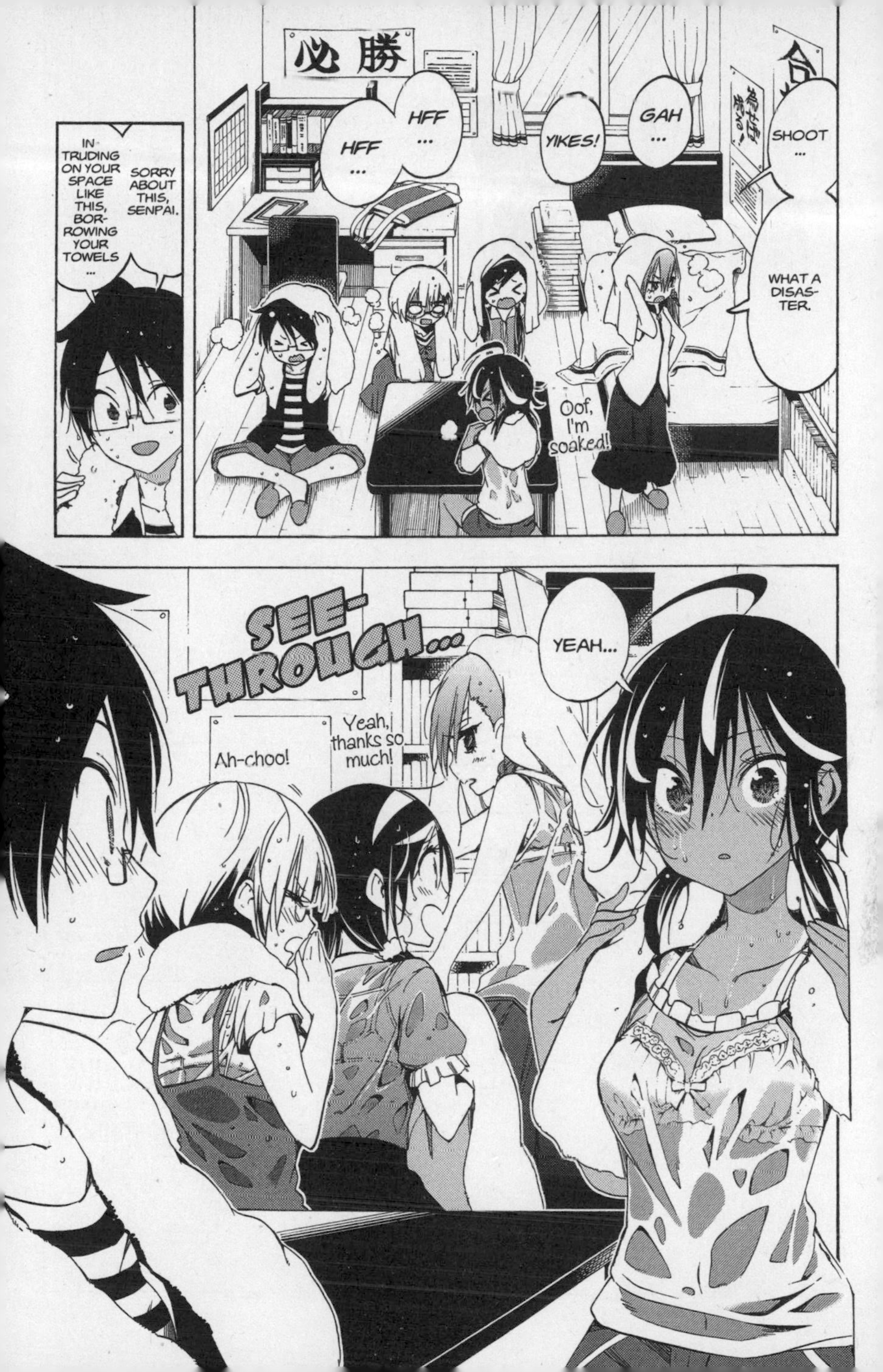
必勝
SHOOT ...
WHAT A DISASTER.
GAH ...
YIKES!
HFF ...
HFF ...
Oof, I'm soaked!
SORRY ABOUT THIS, SENPAI.
INTRUDING ON YOUR SPACE LIKE THIS, BORROWING YOUR TOWELS ...
YEAH...
SEE-THROUGH...
Yeah, thanks so much!
Ah-choo!

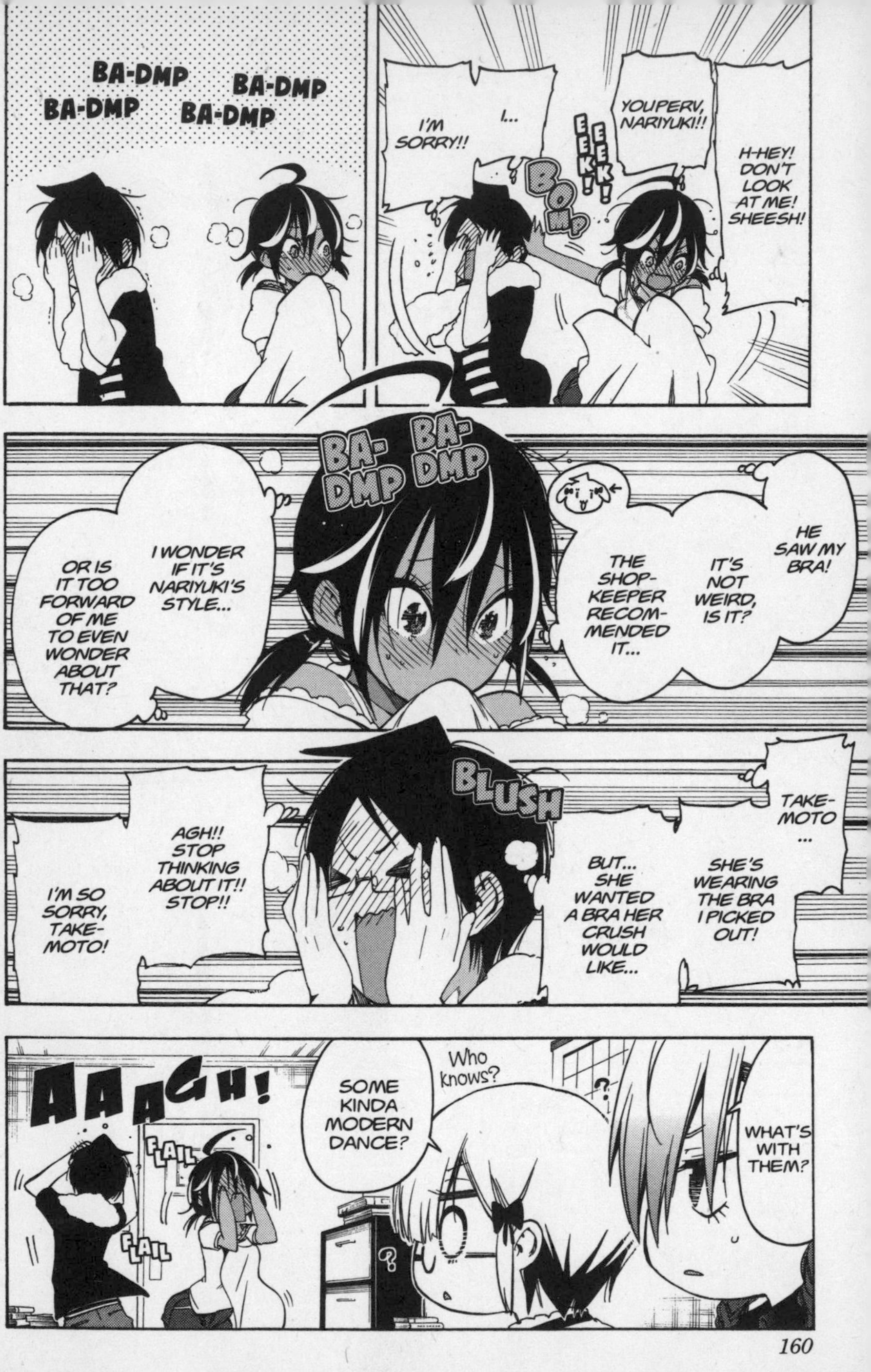
H-HEY! DON'T LOOK AT ME! SHEESH!
YOU PERV, NARIYUKI!!
EEK! EEK!
BOMP
I...
I'M SORRY!!
BA-DMP BA-DMP
BA-DMP BA-DMP
HE SAW MY BRA!
IT'S NOT WEIRD, IS IT?
THE SHOP-KEEPER RECOM-MENDED IT...
BA-DMP BA-DMP
I WONDER IF IT'S NARIYUKI'S STYLE...
OR IS IT TOO FORWARD OF ME TO EVEN WONDER ABOUT THAT?
TAKE-MOTO ...
SHE'S WEARING THE BRA I PICKED OUT!
BUT... SHE WANTED A BRA HER CRUSH WOULD LIKE...
BLUSH
AGH!! STOP THINKING ABOUT IT!! STOP!!
I'M SO SORRY, TAKE-MOTO!
WHAT'S WITH THEM?
Who knows?
SOME KINDA MODERN DANCE?
AAAGH!
FLAIL
FLAIL

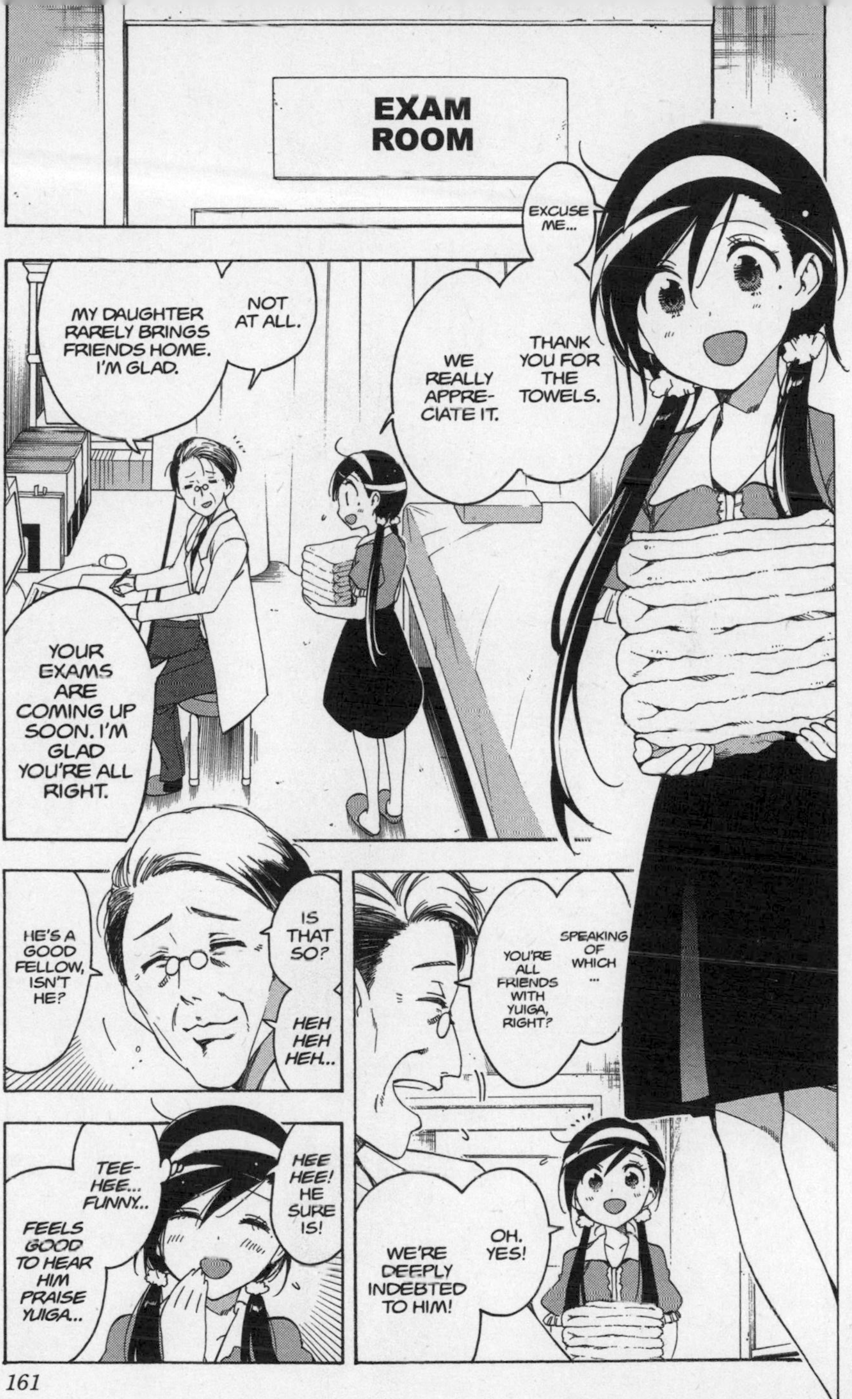
EXAM ROOM
EXCUSE ME...
THANK YOU FOR THE TOWELS.
WE REALLY APPRE-CIATE IT.
NOT AT ALL.
MY DAUGHTER RARELY BRINGS FRIENDS HOME. I'M GLAD.
YOUR EXAMS ARE COMING UP SOON. I'M GLAD YOU'RE ALL RIGHT.
SPEAKING OF WHICH ...
YOU'RE ALL FRIENDS WITH YUIGA, RIGHT?
IS THAT SO?
HE'S A GOOD FELLOW, ISN'T HE?
HEH HEH HEH...
OH. YES!
WE'RE DEEPLY INDEBTED TO HIM!
HEE HEE! HE SURE IS!
TEE-HEE... FUNNY...
FEELS GOOD TO HEAR HIM PRAISE YUIGA...

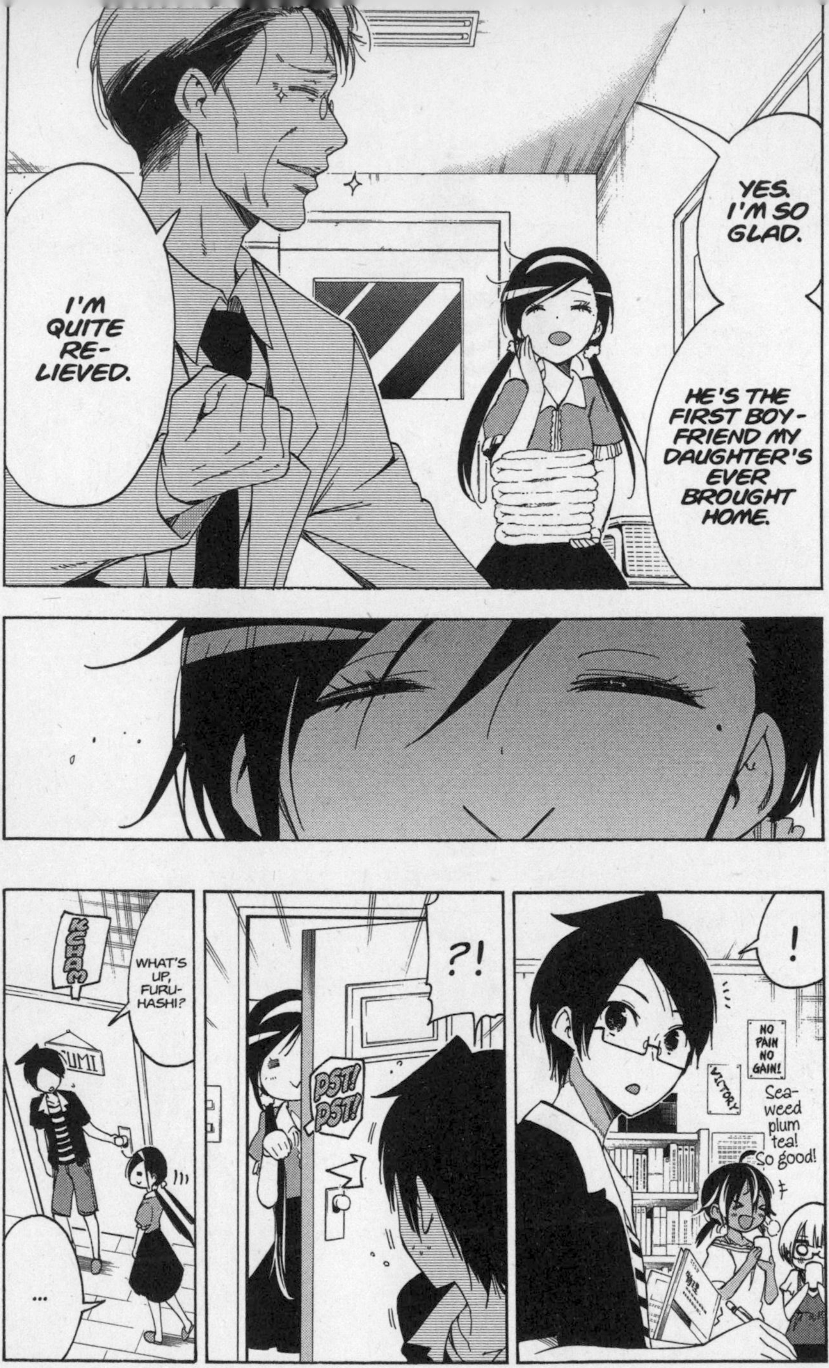
YES. I'M SO GLAD.
HE'S THE FIRST BOY-FRIEND MY DAUGHTER'S EVER BROUGHT HOME.
I'M QUITE RE-LIEVED.
!
NO PAIN NO GAIN!
VICTORY
Sea-weed plum tea! So good!
?!
PST! PST!
KCHAM
WHAT'S UP, FURU-HASHI?
...

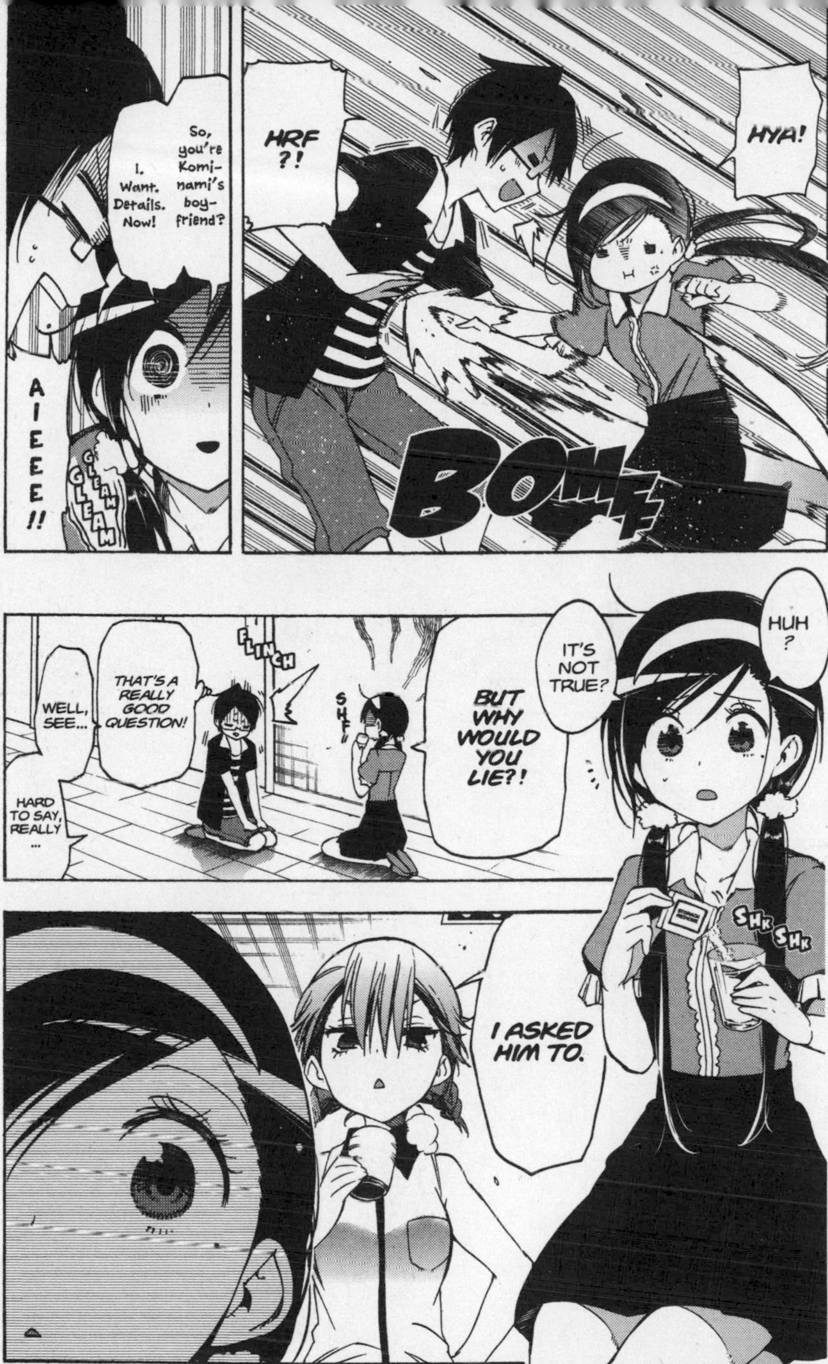
HYA!
HRF ?!
BOMF
So, you're Komi-nami's boy-friend?
I. Want. Details. Now!
AIEEE!!
GLEAM GLEAM
HUH?
IT'S NOT TRUE?
SHK SHK
BUT WHY WOULD YOU LIE?!
SHF
FLINCH
THAT'S A REALLY GOOD QUESTION!
WELL, SEE...
HARD TO SAY, REALLY ...
I ASKED HIM TO.

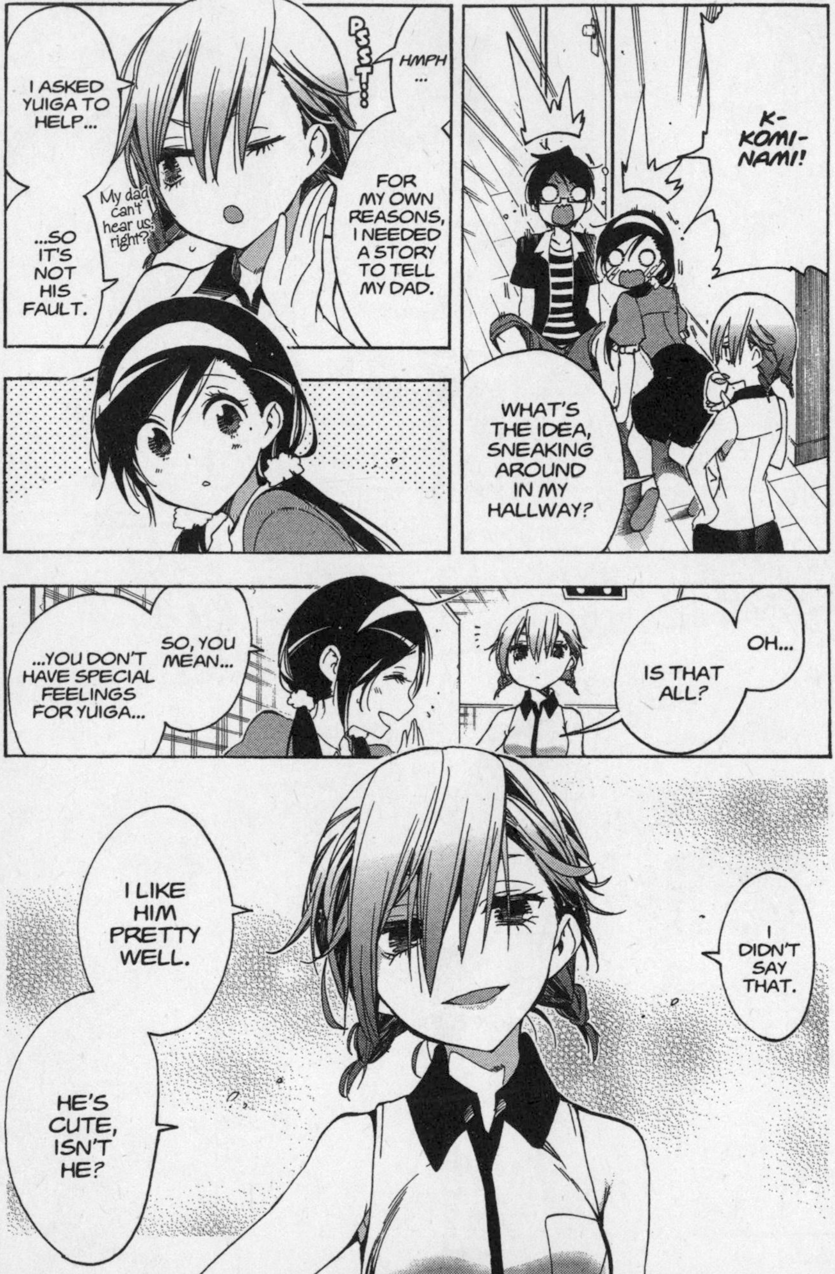
K-KOMINAMI!
WHAT'S THE IDEA, SNEAKING AROUND IN MY HALLWAY?
PSSST...
HMPH ...
FOR MY OWN REASONS, I NEEDED A STORY TO TELL MY DAD.
My dad can't hear us, right?
I ASKED YUIGA TO HELP...
...SO IT'S NOT HIS FAULT.
OH...
IS THAT ALL?
SO, YOU MEAN...
...YOU DON'T HAVE SPECIAL FEELINGS FOR YUIGA...
I DIDN'T SAY THAT.
I LIKE HIM PRETTY WELL.
HE'S CUTE, ISN'T HE?

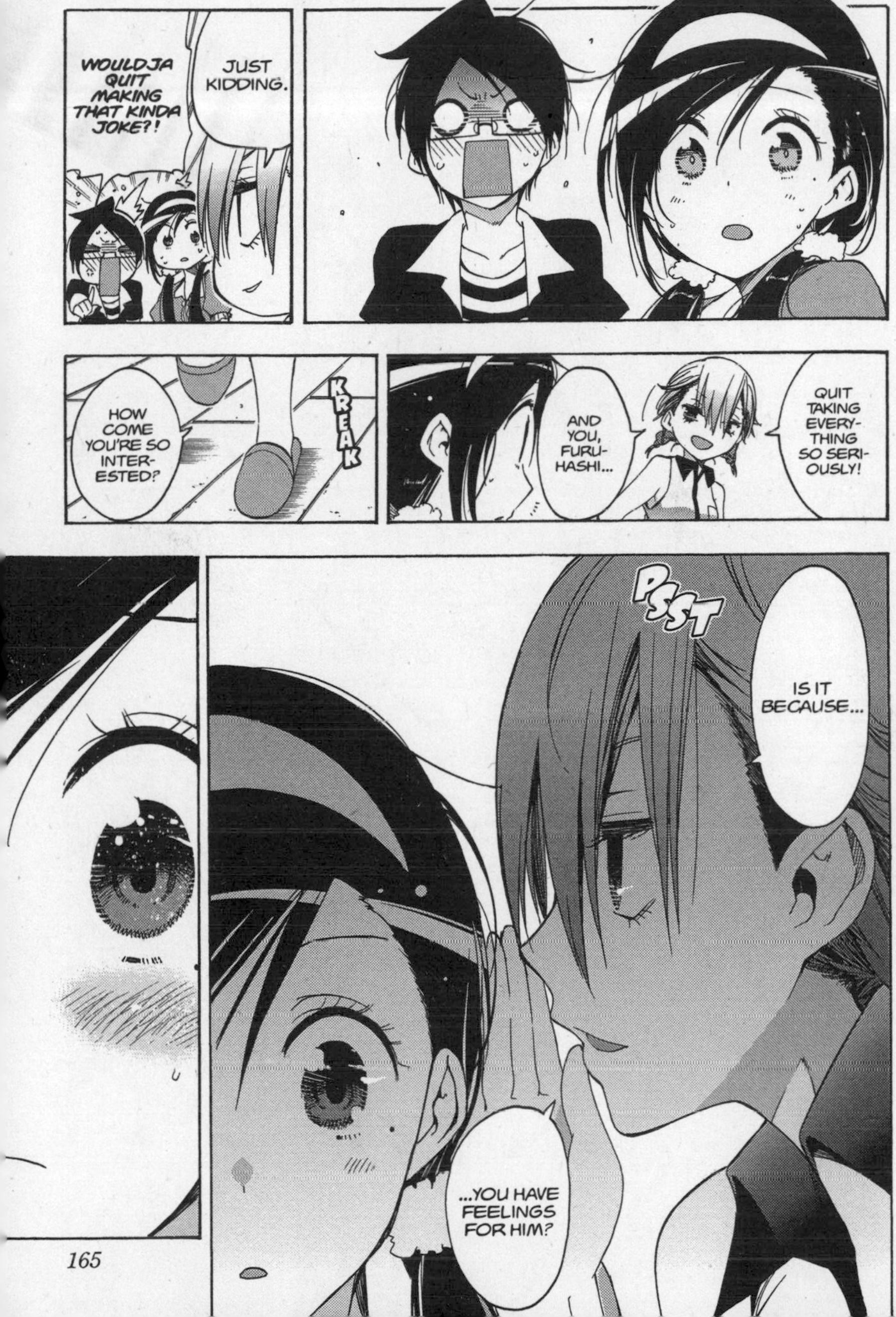
JUST KIDDING.
WOULDJA QUIT MAKING THAT KINDA JOKE?!
QUIT TAKING EVERY-THING SO SERI-OUSLY!
AND YOU, FURU-HASHI...
KREAK
HOW COME YOU'RE SO INTER-ESTED?
PSST
IS IT BECAUSE...
...YOU HAVE FEELINGS FOR HIM?

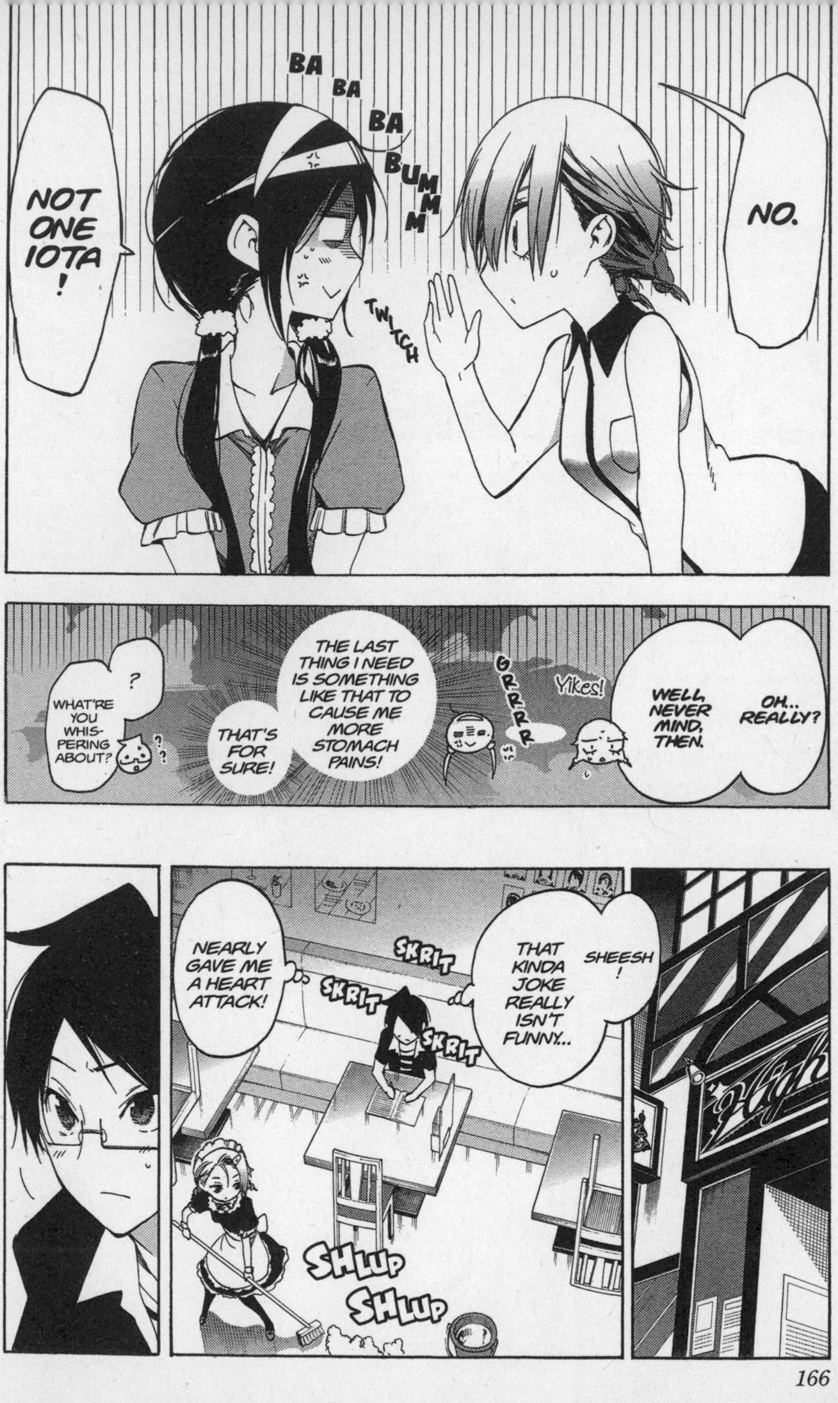
NO.
BA BA BA BUMMM
NOT ONE IOTA!
TWITCH
OH... REALLY?
WELL, NEVER MIND, THEN.
Yikes!
GRRRR
THE LAST THING I NEED IS SOMETHING LIKE THAT TO CAUSE ME MORE STOMACH PAINS!
THAT'S FOR SURE!
?
WHAT'RE YOU WHISPERING ABOUT?
SHEESH!
THAT KINDA JOKE REALLY ISN'T FUNNY...
SKRIT
SKRIT
SKRIT
NEARLY GAVE ME A HEART ATTACK!
SHLUP
SHLUP

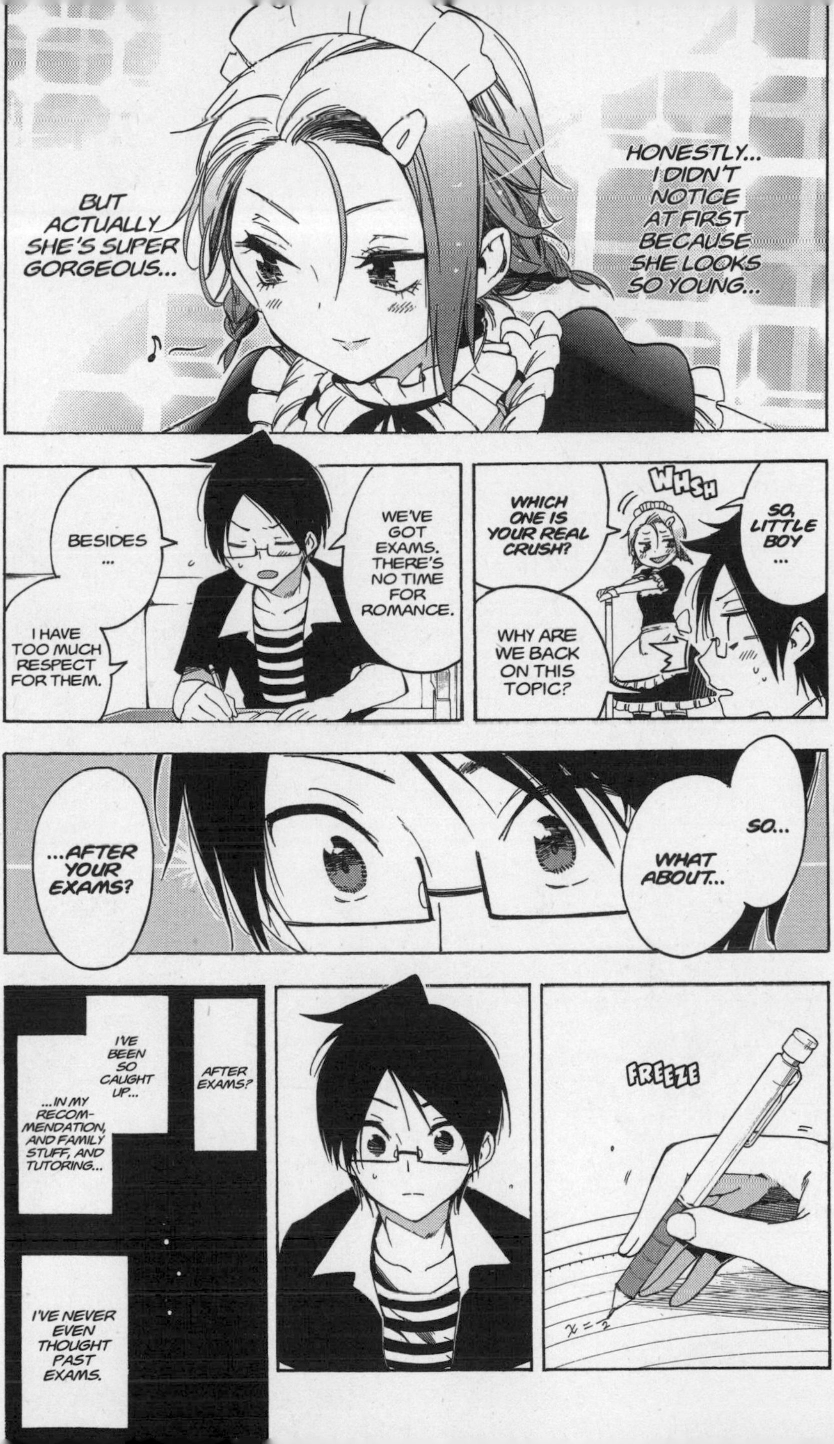
HONESTLY... I DIDN'T NOTICE AT FIRST BECAUSE SHE LOOKS SO YOUNG...
BUT ACTUALLY SHE'S SUPER GORGEOUS...
SO, LITTLE BOY ...
WHSH
WHICH ONE IS YOUR REAL CRUSH?
WHY ARE WE BACK ON THIS TOPIC?
WE'VE GOT EXAMS. THERE'S NO TIME FOR ROMANCE.
BESIDES ...
I HAVE TOO MUCH RESPECT FOR THEM.
SO...
WHAT ABOUT...
...AFTER YOUR EXAMS?
FREEZE
AFTER EXAMS?
I'VE BEEN SO CAUGHT UP...
...IN MY RECOM-MENDATION, AND FAMILY STUFF, AND TUTORING...
I'VE NEVER EVEN THOUGHT PAST EXAMS.

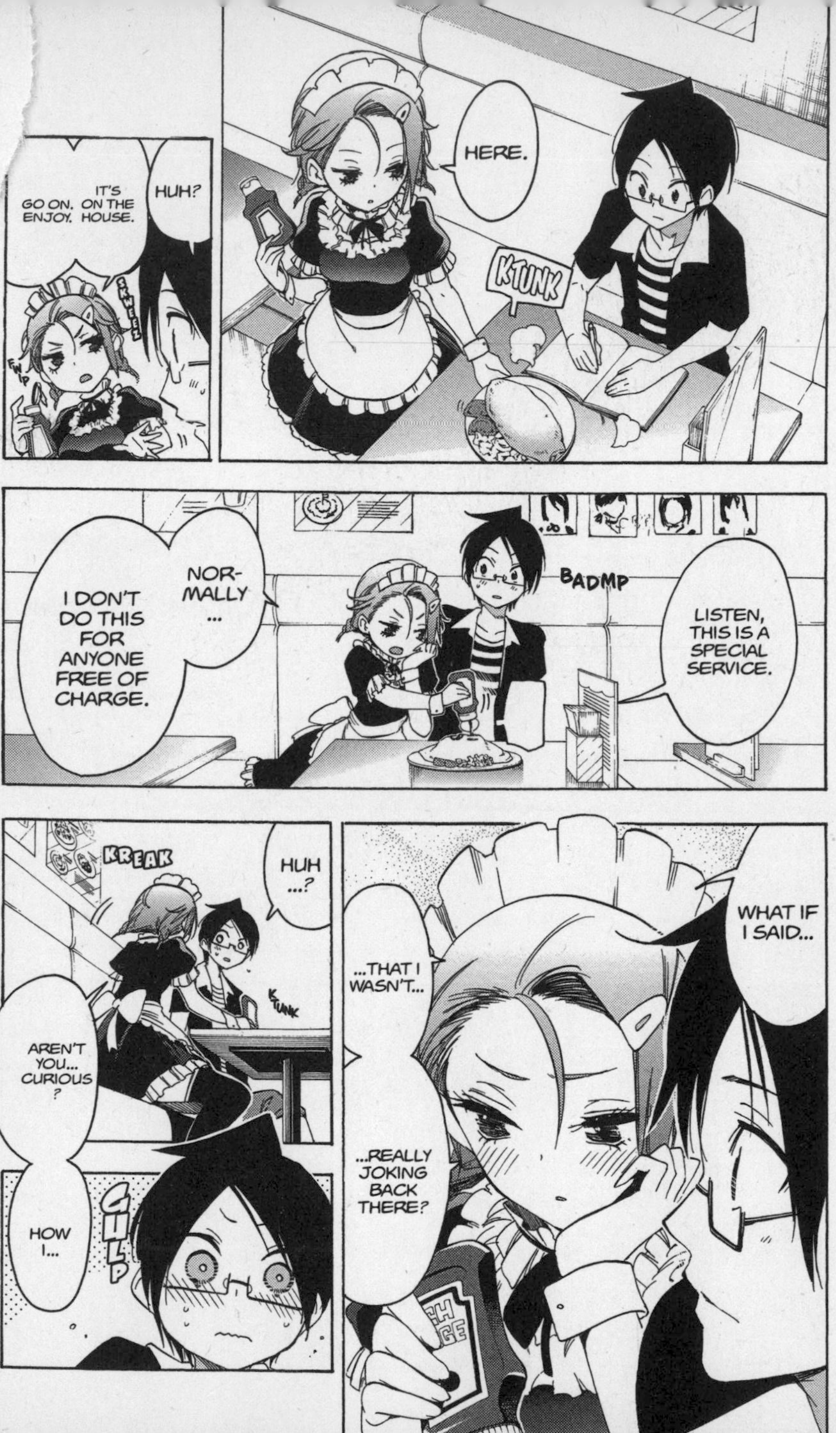
HERE.
KTUNK
HUH?
IT'S ON THE HOUSE.
GO ON. ENJOY.
SKWEEZ
FWIP
LISTEN, THIS IS A SPECIAL SERVICE.
BADMP
NOR-MALLY...
I DON'T DO THIS FOR ANYONE FREE OF CHARGE.
WHAT IF I SAID...
...THAT I WASN'T...
...REALLY JOKING BACK THERE?
HUH...?
KREAK
K-TUNK
AREN'T YOU... CURIOUS?
HOW I...
GULP

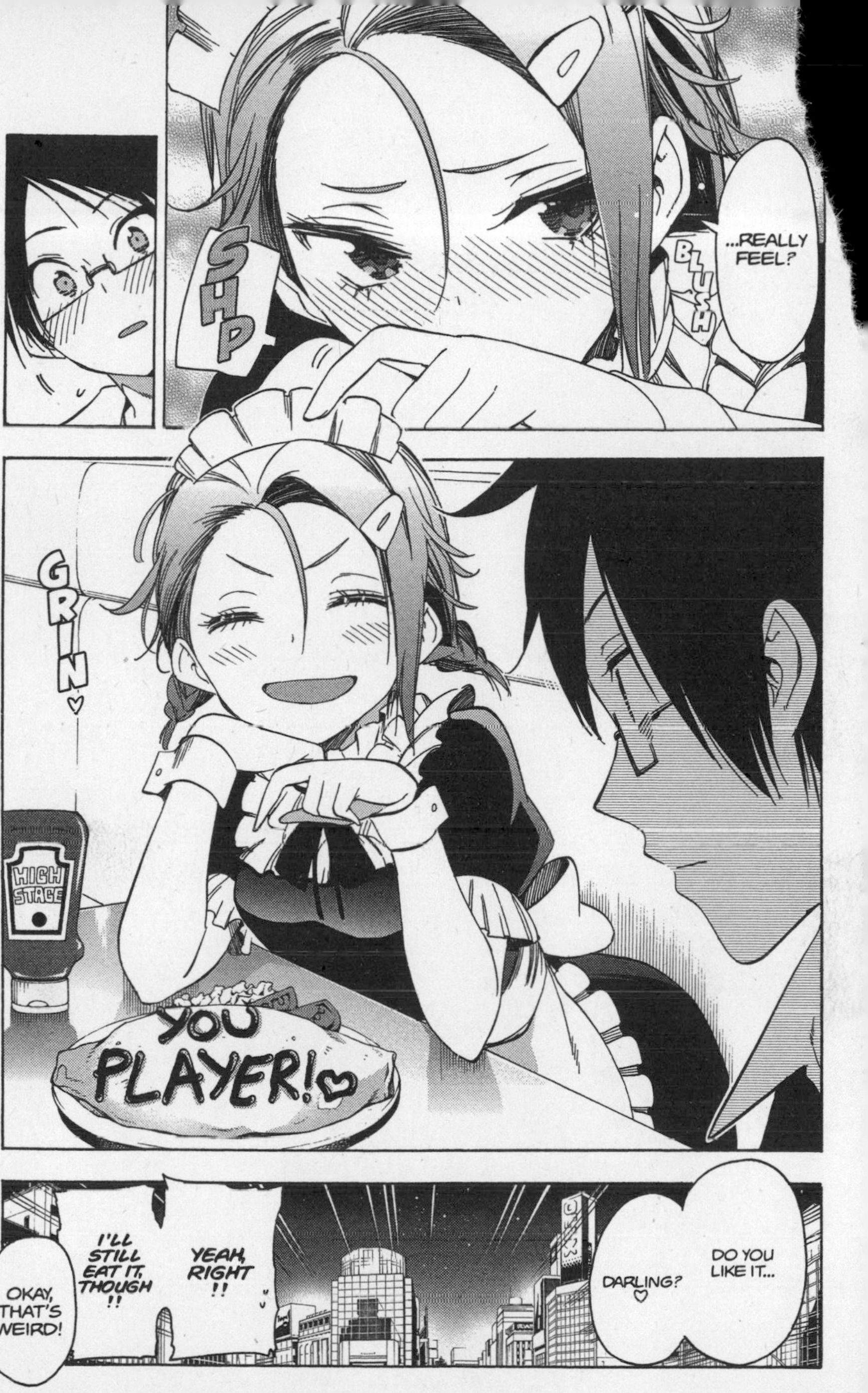
...REALLY FEEL?
BLUSH
SHP
GRIN♡
HIGH STAGE
YOU PLAYER!♡
DO YOU LIKE IT...
DARLING?♡
YEAH, RIGHT!!
I'LL STILL EAT IT, THOUGH!!
OKAY, THAT'S WEIRD!

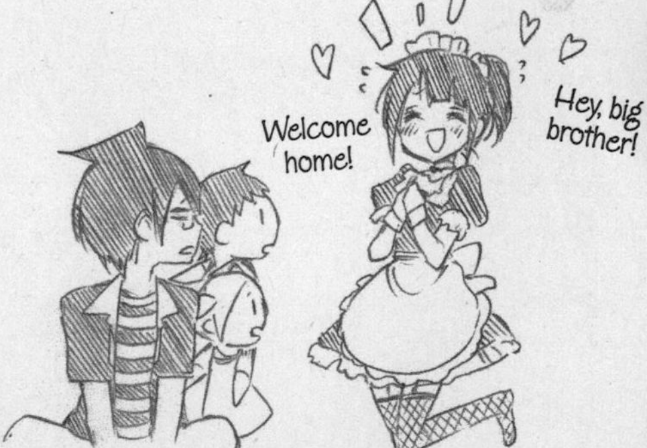
Hey, big brother!
Welcome home!

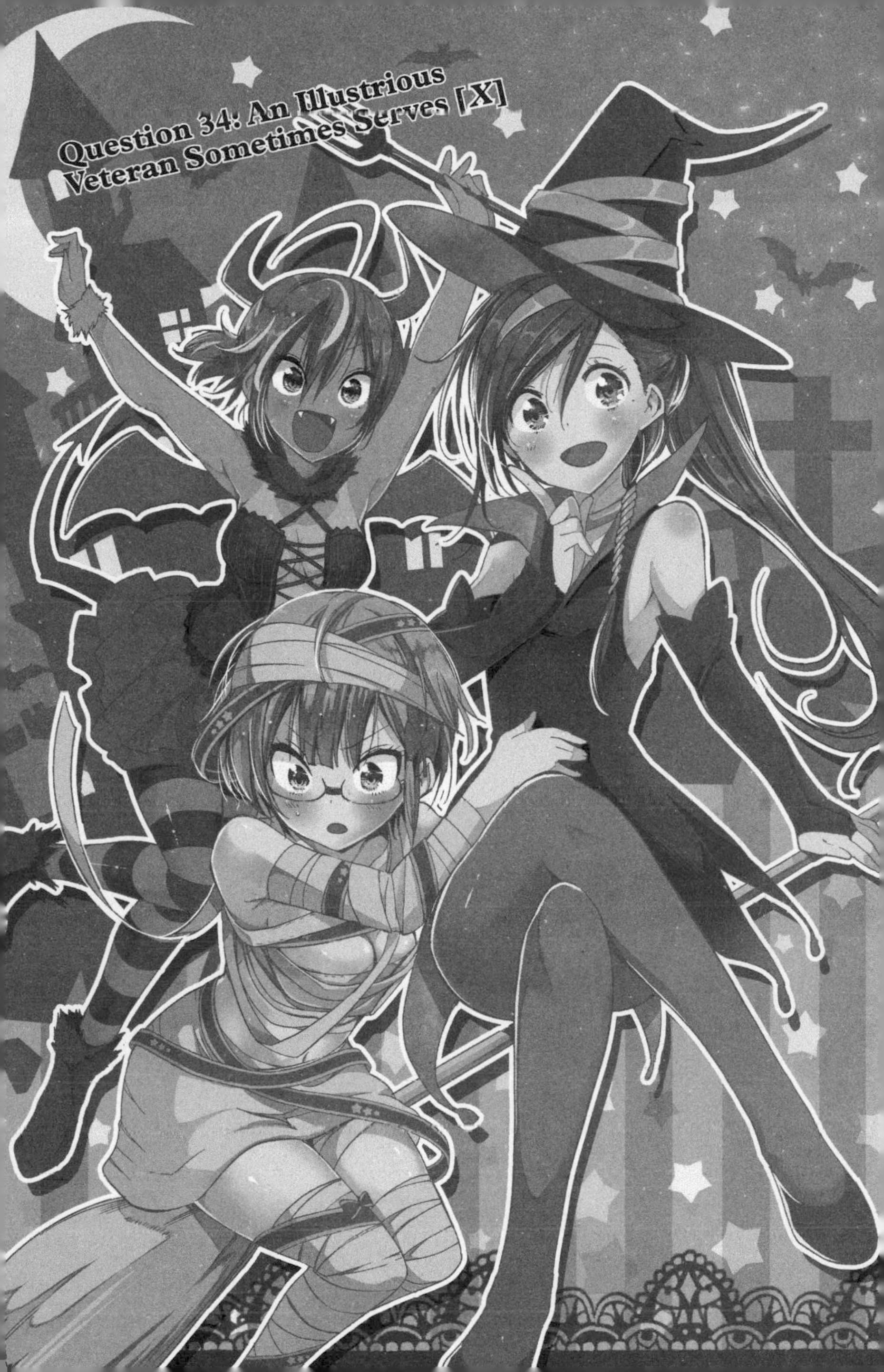
Question 34: An Illustrious Veteran Sometimes Serves [X]

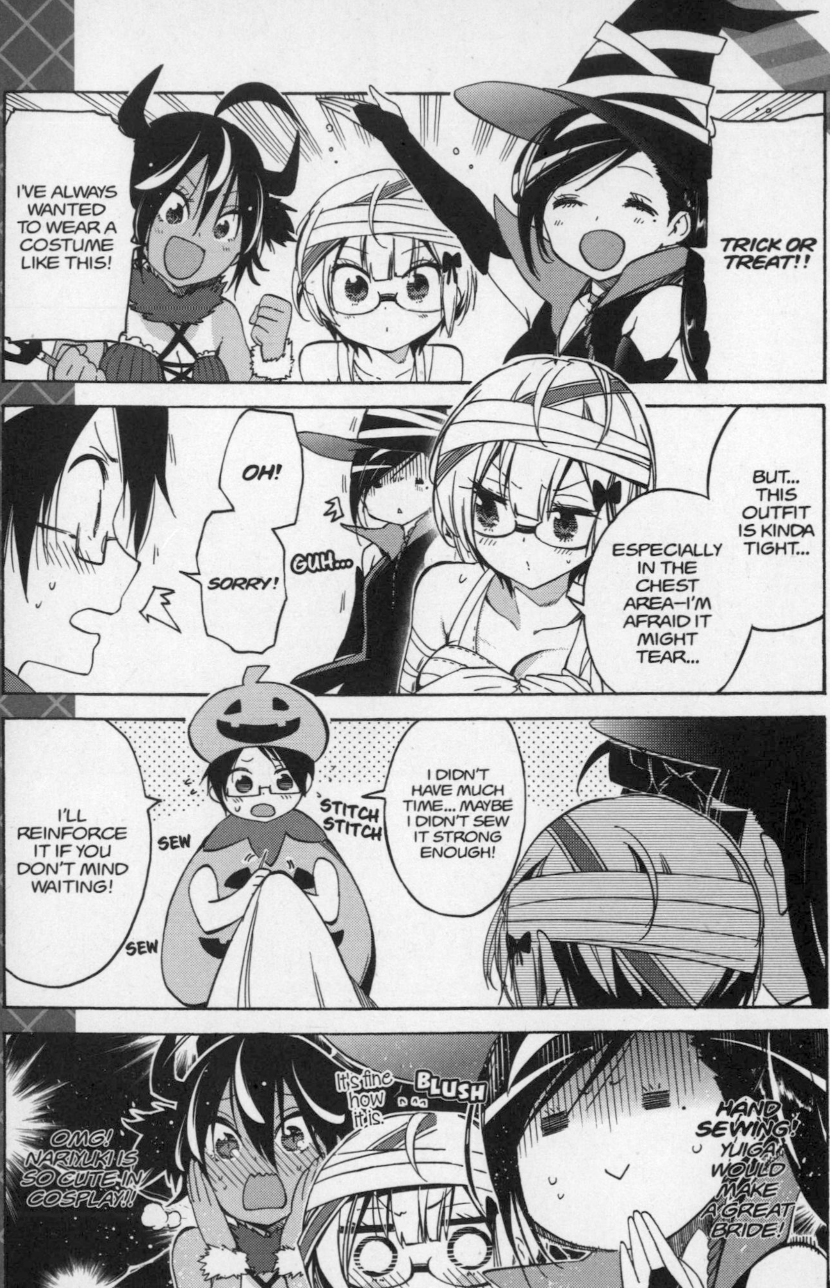
TRICK OR TREAT!!
I'VE ALWAYS WANTED TO WEAR A COSTUME LIKE THIS!
BUT... THIS OUTFIT IS KINDA TIGHT...
ESPECIALLY IN THE CHEST AREA—I'M AFRAID IT MIGHT TEAR...
GUH...
OH!
SORRY!
I DIDN'T HAVE MUCH TIME... MAYBE I DIDN'T SEW IT STRONG ENOUGH!
STITCH STITCH
SEW
I'LL REINFORCE IT IF YOU DON'T MIND WAITING!
SEW
HAND SEWING! YUIGA WOULD MAKE A GREAT BRIDE!
BLUSH
It's fine how it is.
OMG! NARIYUKI IS SO CUTE IN COSPLAY!!

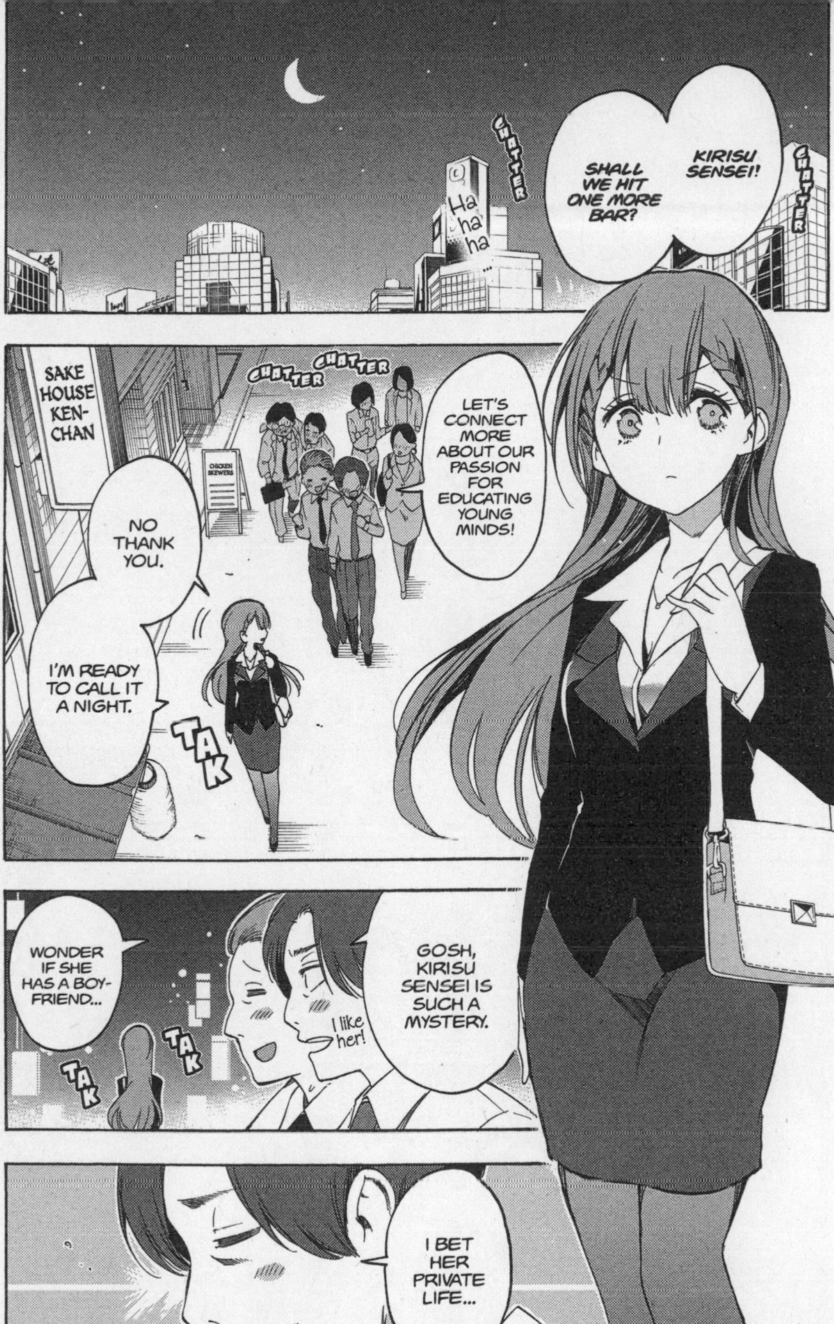
KIRISU SENSEI!
SHALL WE HIT ONE MORE BAR?
CHATTER
Ha ha ha
CHATTER
LET'S CONNECT MORE ABOUT OUR PASSION FOR EDUCATING YOUNG MINDS!
CHATTER CHATTER
SAKE HOUSE KEN-CHAN
CHICKEN SKEWERS
NO THANK YOU.
I'M READY TO CALL IT A NIGHT.
TAK
GOSH, KIRISU SENSEI IS SUCH A MYSTERY.
I like her!
WONDER IF SHE HAS A BOY-FRIEND...
TAK
TAK
I BET HER PRIVATE LIFE...

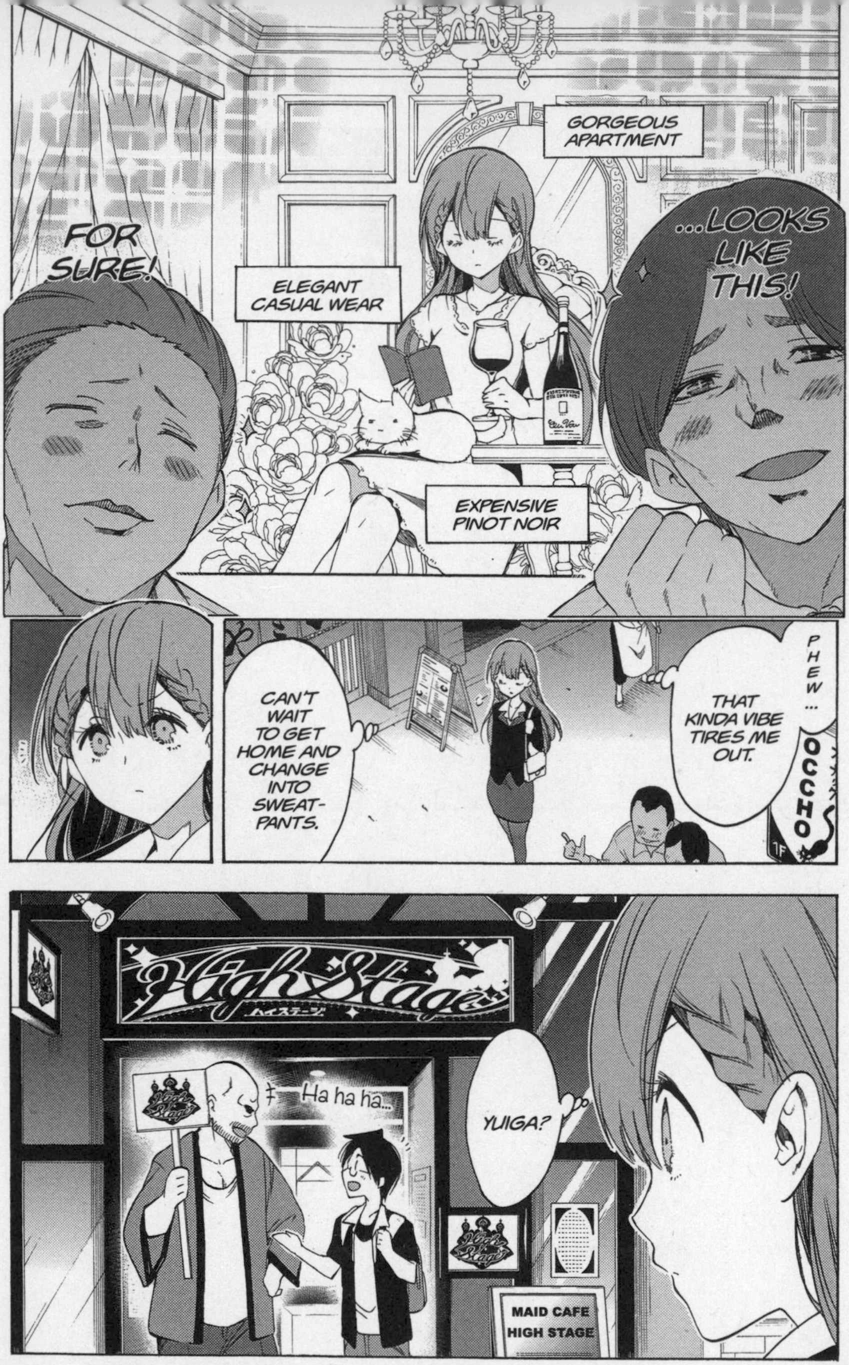
...LOOKS LIKE THIS!
GORGEOUS APARTMENT
ELEGANT CASUAL WEAR
EXPENSIVE PINOT NOIR
FOR SURE!
PHEW...
THAT KINDA VIBE TIRES ME OUT.
OCCHO
CAN'T WAIT TO GET HOME AND CHANGE INTO SWEAT-PANTS.
High Stage
ハイステージ
YUIGA?
Ha ha ha...
MAID CAFE HIGH STAGE

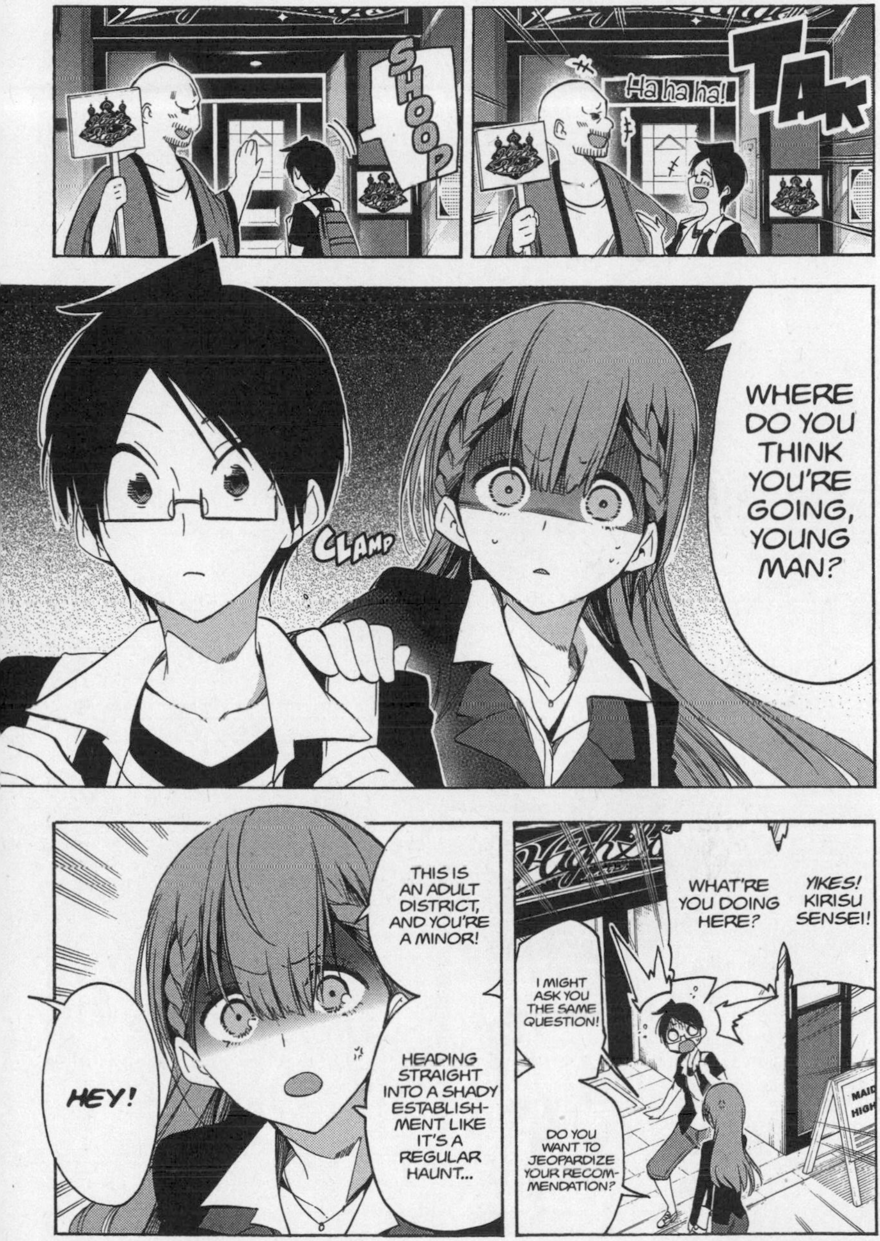

TAK
Ha ha ha!
SHOOP
WHERE DO YOU THINK YOU'RE GOING, YOUNG MAN?
CLAMP
YIKES! KIRISU SENSEI!
WHAT'RE YOU DOING HERE?
I MIGHT ASK YOU THE SAME QUESTION!
DO YOU WANT TO JEOPARDIZE YOUR RECOMMENDATION?
THIS IS AN ADULT DISTRICT, AND YOU'RE A MINOR!
HEADING STRAIGHT INTO A SHADY ESTABLISHMENT LIKE IT'S A REGULAR HAUNT...
HEY!

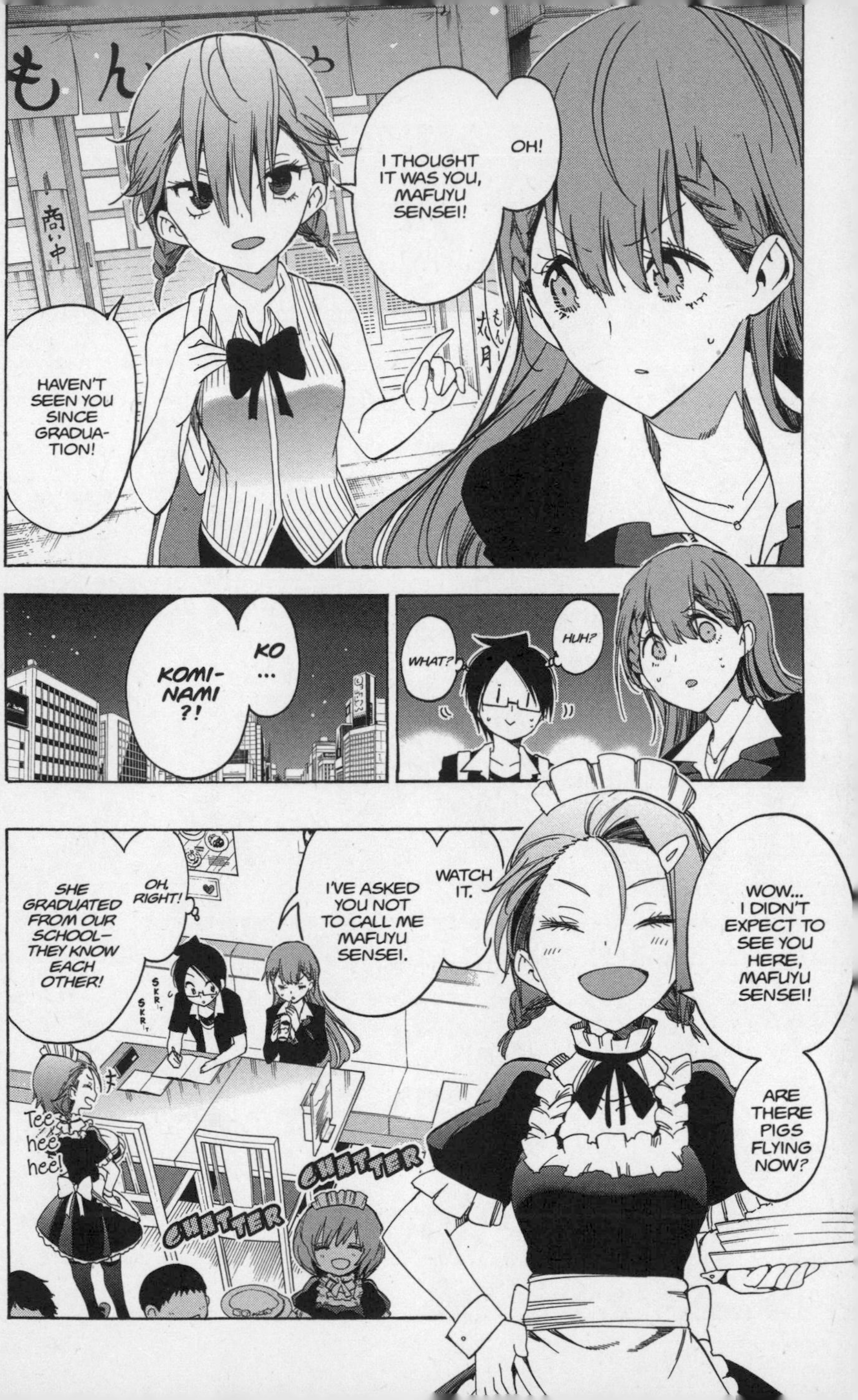
商い中
OH!
I THOUGHT IT WAS YOU, MAFUYU SENSEI!
HAVEN'T SEEN YOU SINCE GRADUATION!
HUH?
WHAT?
KO...
KOMINAMI?!
WOW... I DIDN'T EXPECT TO SEE YOU HERE, MAFUYU SENSEI!
ARE THERE PIGS FLYING NOW?
WATCH IT.
I'VE ASKED YOU NOT TO CALL ME MAFUYU SENSEI.
OH, RIGHT!
SHE GRADUATED FROM OUR SCHOOL—THEY KNOW EACH OTHER!
SKRIT SKRIT
CHITTER CHITTER
Tee hee hee!

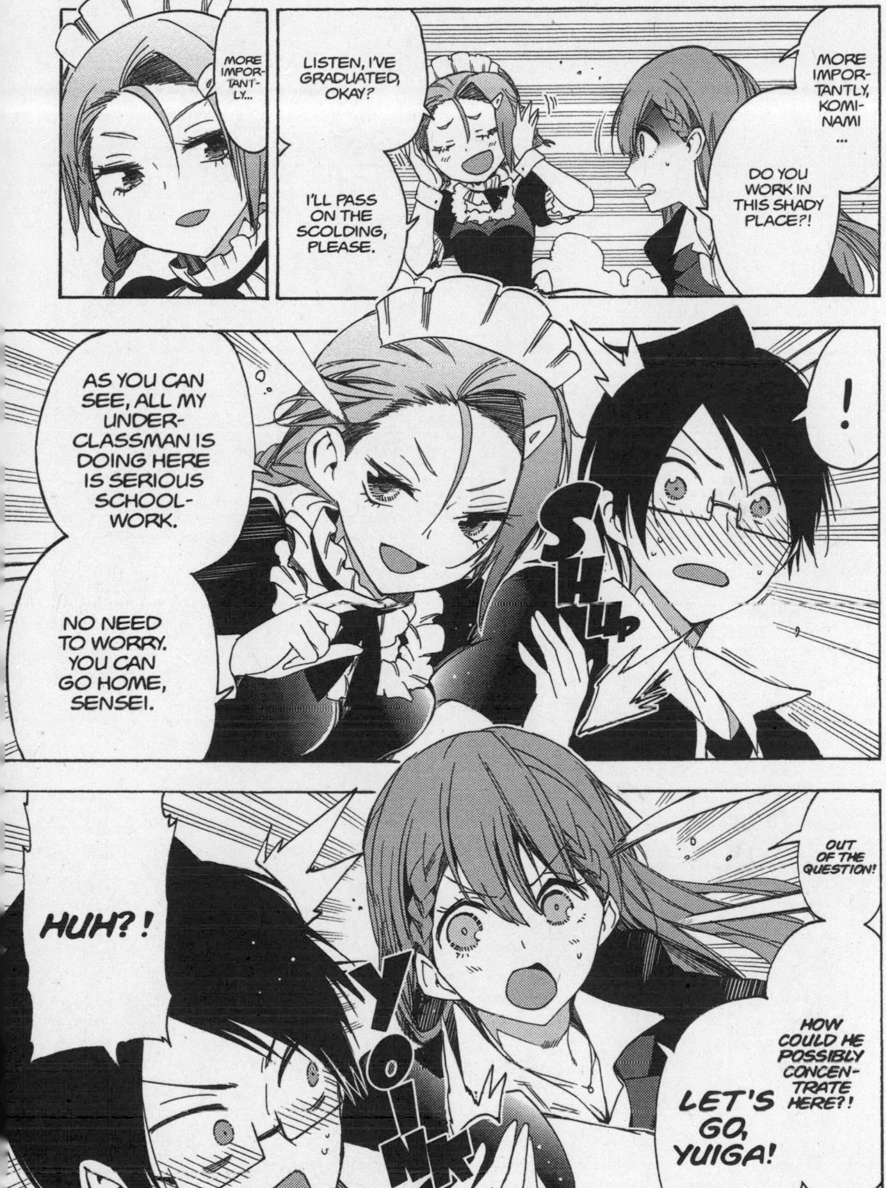
MORE IMPORTANTLY, KOMINAMI...
DO YOU WORK IN THIS SHADY PLACE?!
LISTEN, I'VE GRADUATED, OKAY?
I'LL PASS ON THE SCOLDING, PLEASE.
MORE IMPORTANTLY...
!
SHUP
AS YOU CAN SEE, ALL MY UNDERCLASSMAN IS DOING HERE IS SERIOUS SCHOOLWORK.
NO NEED TO WORRY. YOU CAN GO HOME, SENSEI.
OUT OF THE QUESTION!
HOW COULD HE POSSIBLY CONCENTRATE HERE?!
LET'S GO, YUIGA!
YOINK
HUH?!

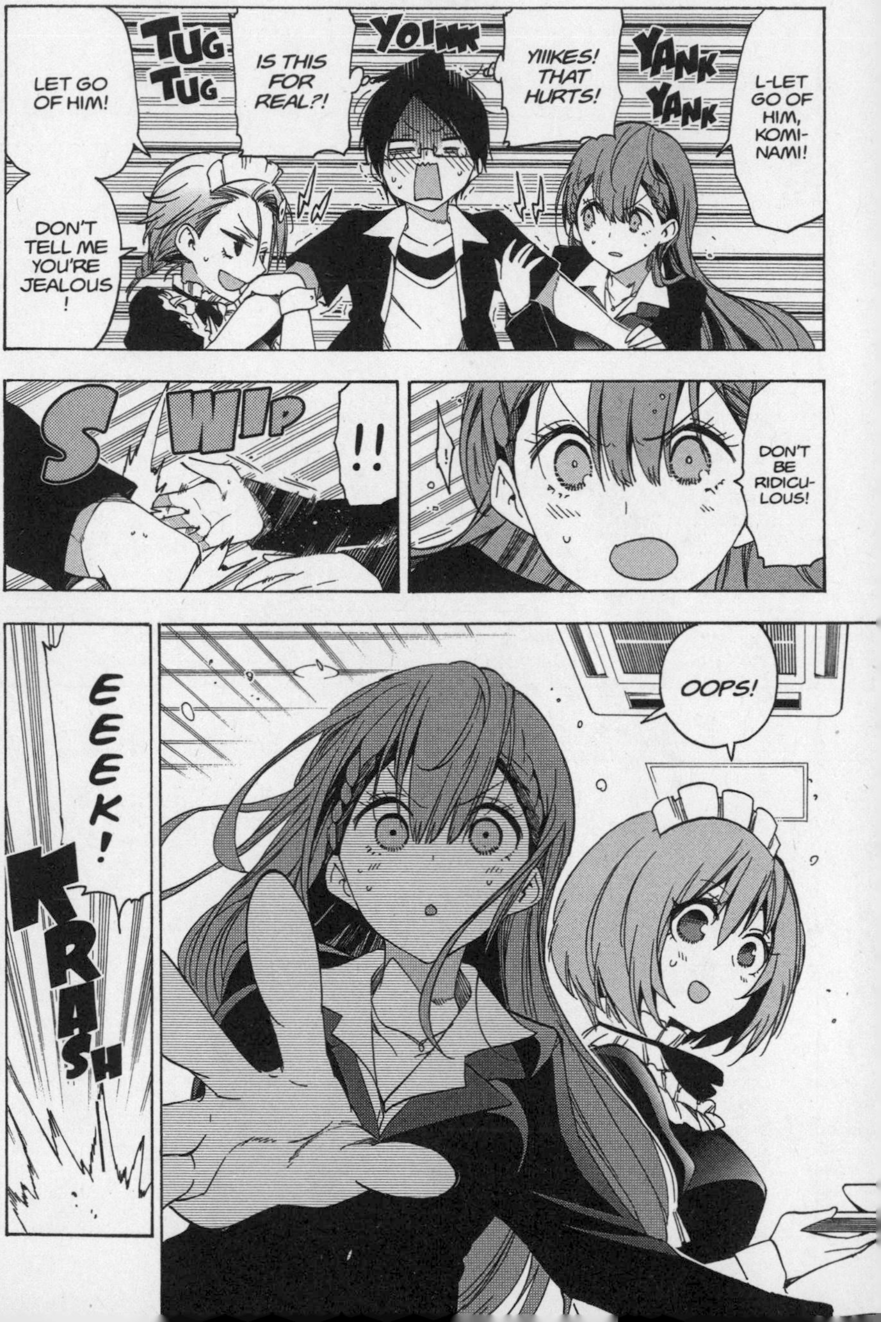
L-LET GO OF HIM, KOMI-NAMI!
YANK YANK
YIIIKES! THAT HURTS!
YOINK
IS THIS FOR REAL?!
TUG TUG
LET GO OF HIM!
DON'T TELL ME YOU'RE JEALOUS!
DON'T BE RIDICULOUS!
!!
SWIP
OOPS!
EEEK!
KRASH

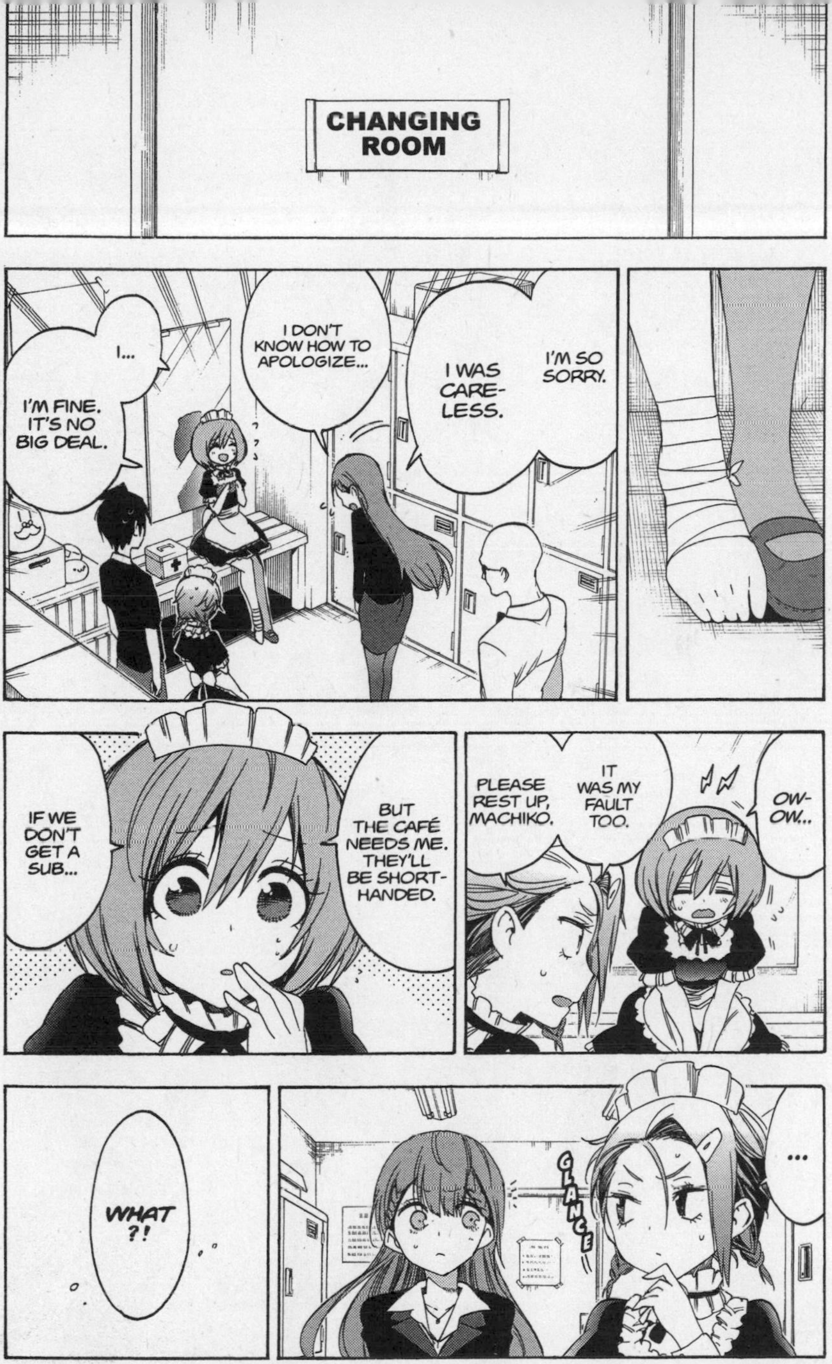
CHANGING ROOM
I'M SO SORRY.
I WAS CARELESS.
I DON'T KNOW HOW TO APOLOGIZE...
I...
I'M FINE. IT'S NO BIG DEAL.
OW-OW...
IT WAS MY FAULT TOO.
PLEASE REST UP, MACHIKO.
BUT THE CAFÉ NEEDS ME. THEY'LL BE SHORT-HANDED.
IF WE DON'T GET A SUB...
...
GLANCE
WHAT?!

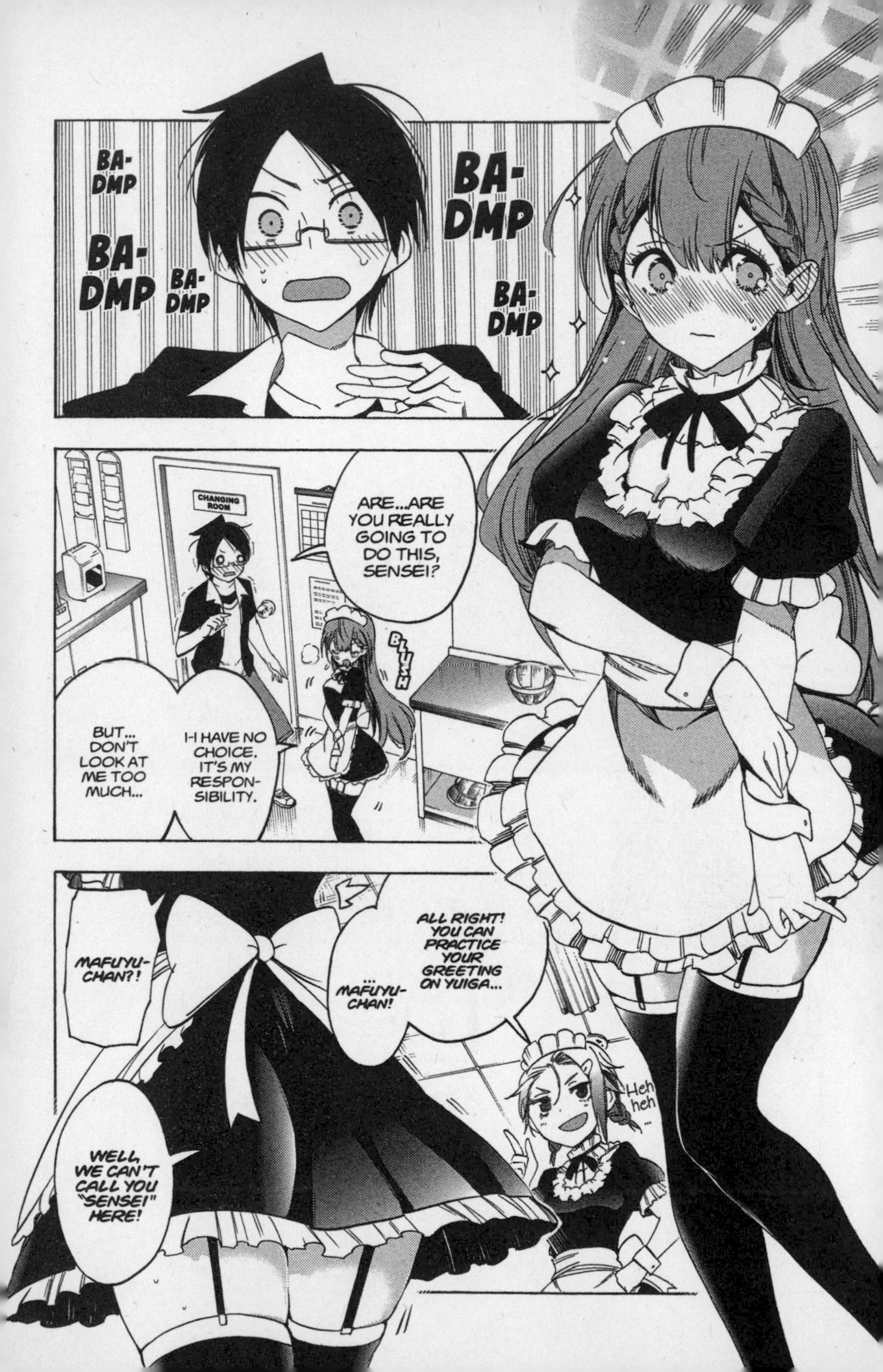
BA-DMP
BA-DMP
BA-DMP
BA-DMP
BA-DMP
ARE...ARE YOU REALLY GOING TO DO THIS, SENSEI?
CHANGING ROOM
BLUSH
I-I HAVE NO CHOICE. IT'S MY RESPONSIBILITY.
BUT... DON'T LOOK AT ME TOO MUCH...
ALL RIGHT! YOU CAN PRACTICE YOUR GREETING ON YUIGA...
...MAFUYU-CHAN!
Heh heh ...
MAFUYU-CHAN?!
WELL, WE CAN'T CALL YOU "SENSEI" HERE!

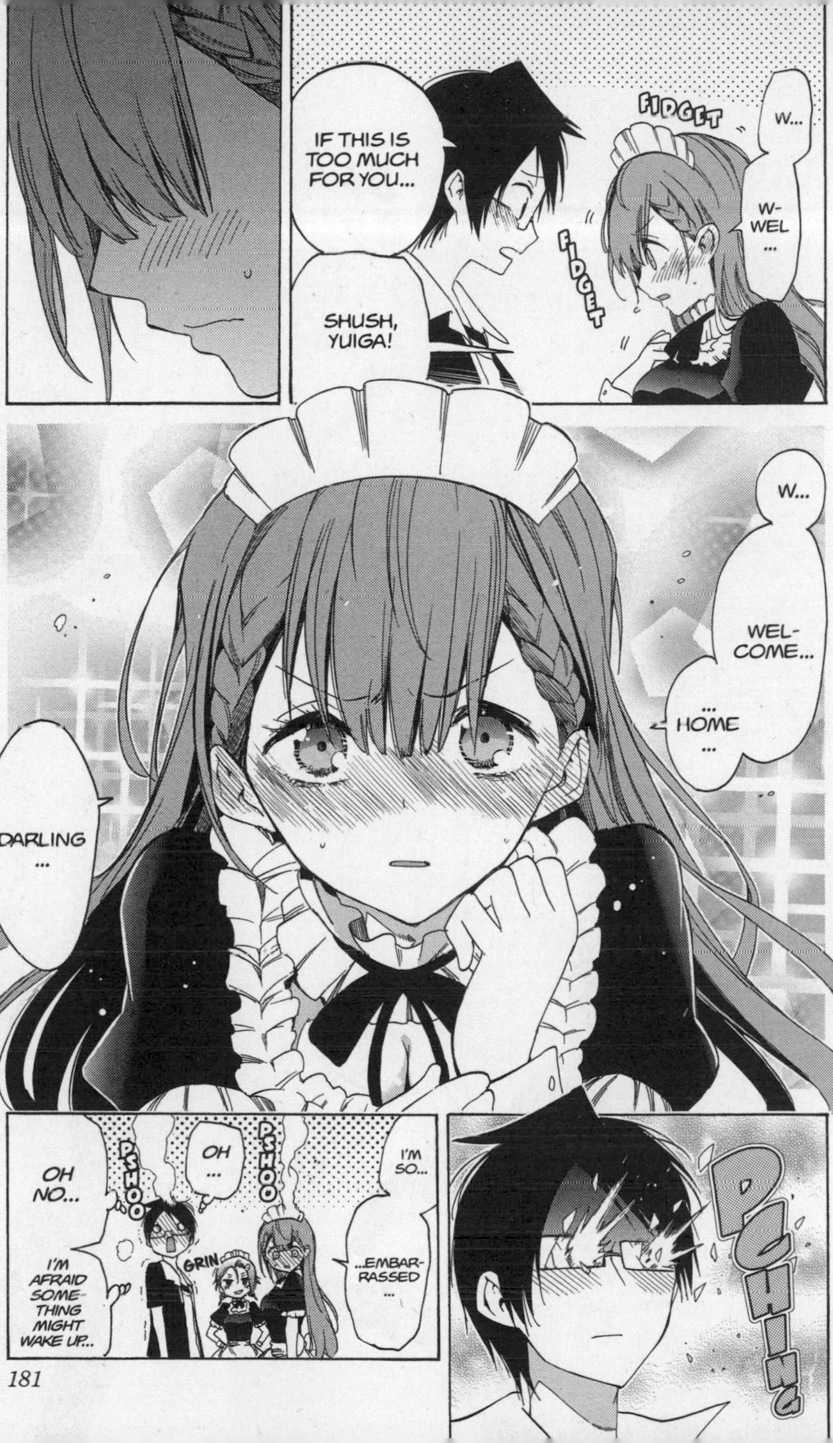
FIDGET
W...
W-WEL...
FIDGET
IF THIS IS TOO MUCH FOR YOU...
SHUSH, YUIGA!
W...
WEL-COME...
...HOME...
DARLING...
I'M SO...
...EMBARRASSED...
PSHOO
OH...
PSHOO
OH NO...
I'M AFRAID SOMETHING MIGHT WAKE UP...
GRIN

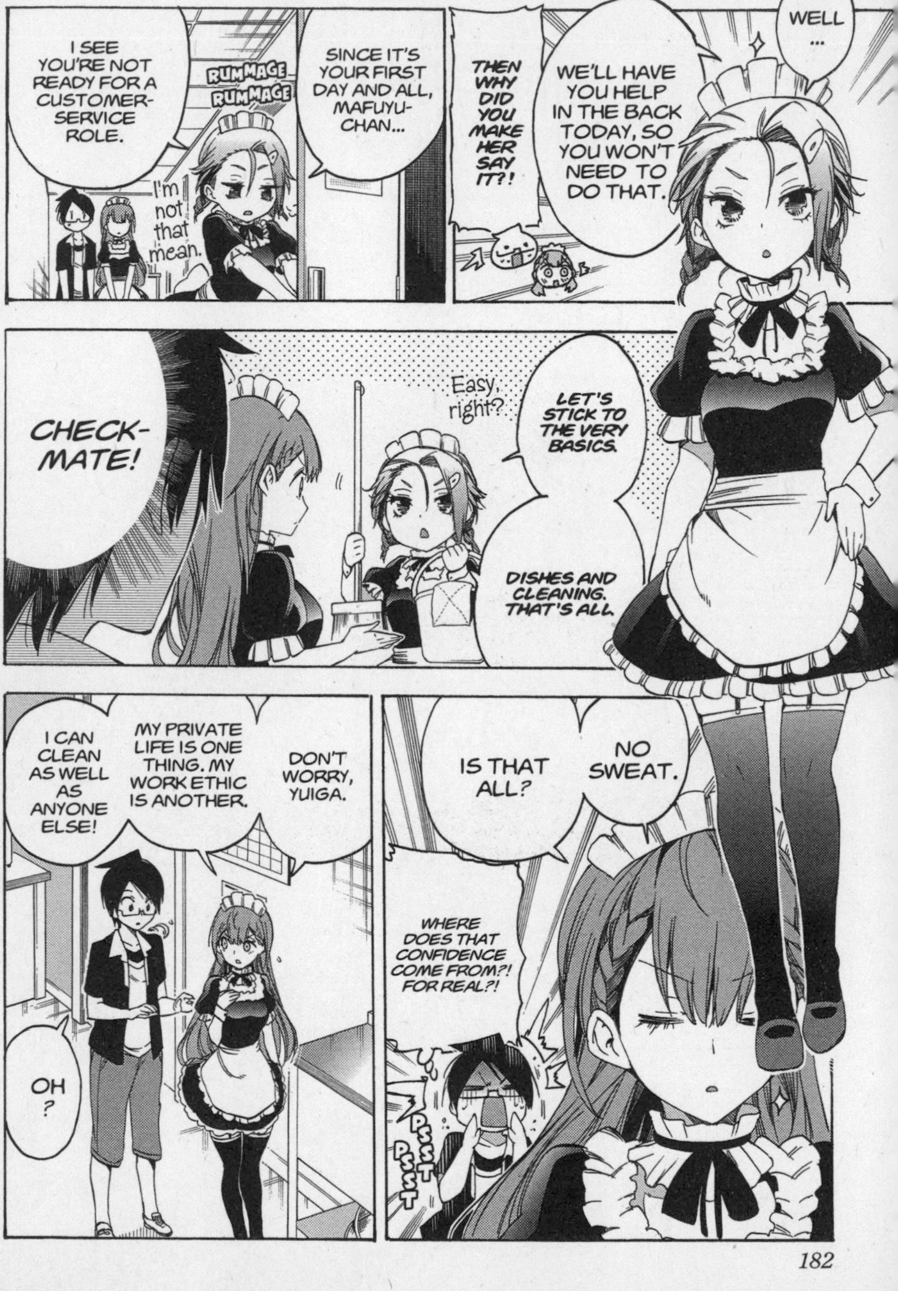
WELL ...
WE'LL HAVE YOU HELP IN THE BACK TODAY, SO YOU WON'T NEED TO DO THAT.
THEN WHY DID YOU MAKE HER SAY IT?!
SINCE IT'S YOUR FIRST DAY AND ALL, MAFUYU-CHAN...
RUMMAGE RUMMAGE
I SEE YOU'RE NOT READY FOR A CUSTOMER-SERVICE ROLE.
I'm not that mean.
LET'S STICK TO THE VERY BASICS.
DISHES AND CLEANING. THAT'S ALL.
Easy, right?
CHECK-MATE!
NO SWEAT.
IS THAT ALL?
WHERE DOES THAT CONFIDENCE COME FROM?! FOR REAL?!
PSST PSST
DON'T WORRY, YUIGA.
MY PRIVATE LIFE IS ONE THING. MY WORK ETHIC IS ANOTHER.
I CAN CLEAN AS WELL AS ANYONE ELSE!
OH ?

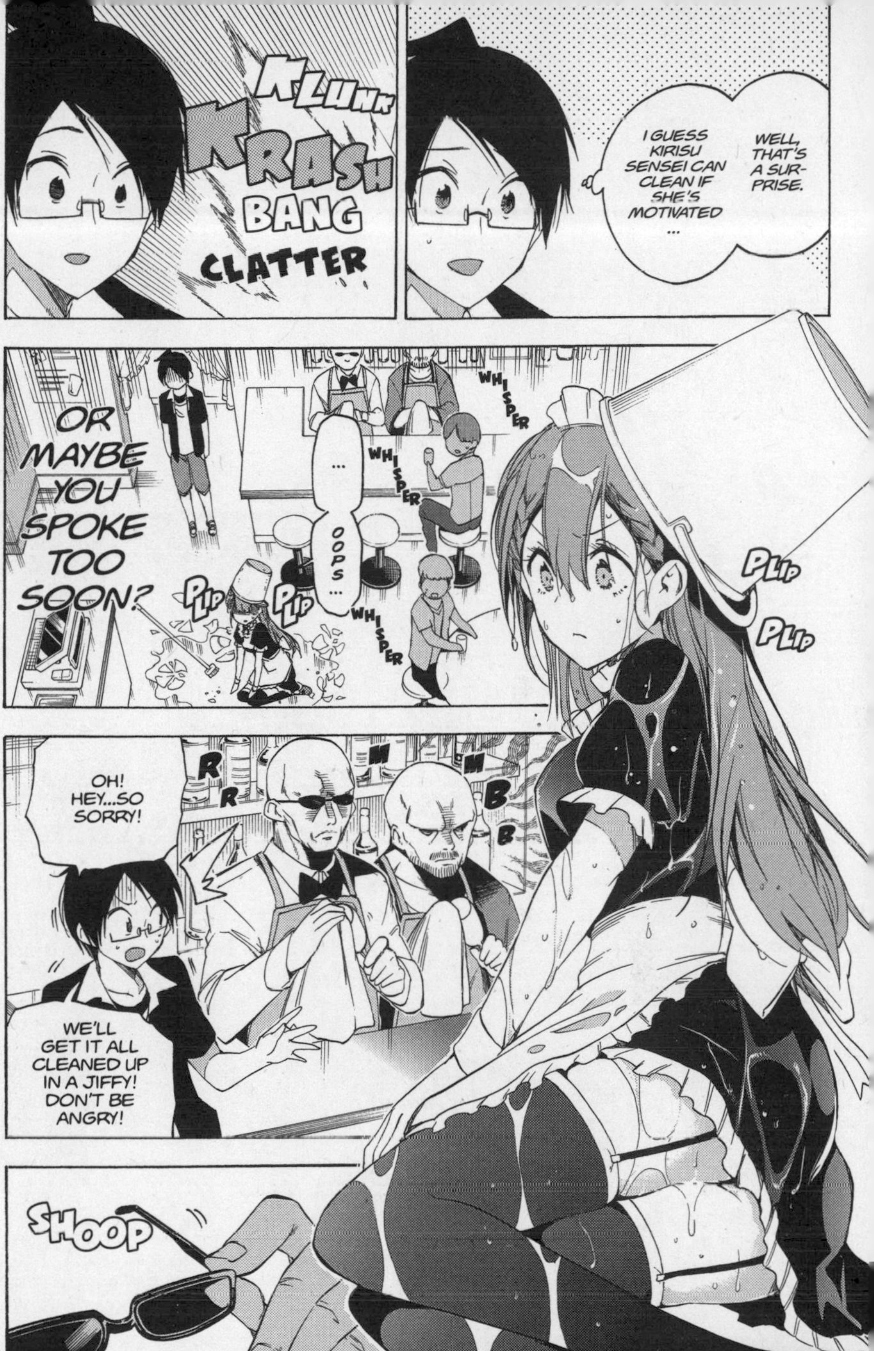
WELL, THAT'S A SURPRISE.
I GUESS KIRISU SENSEI CAN CLEAN IF SHE'S MOTIVATED ...
KLUNK
KRASH
BANG
CLATTER
PLIP
PLIP
OR MAYBE YOU SPOKE TOO SOON?
WHISPER
WHISPER
...
OOPS ...
WHISPER
PLIP
PLIP
RRR
MMM
BB
OH! HEY...SO SORRY!
WE'LL GET IT ALL CLEANED UP IN A JIFFY! DON'T BE ANGRY!
SHOOP

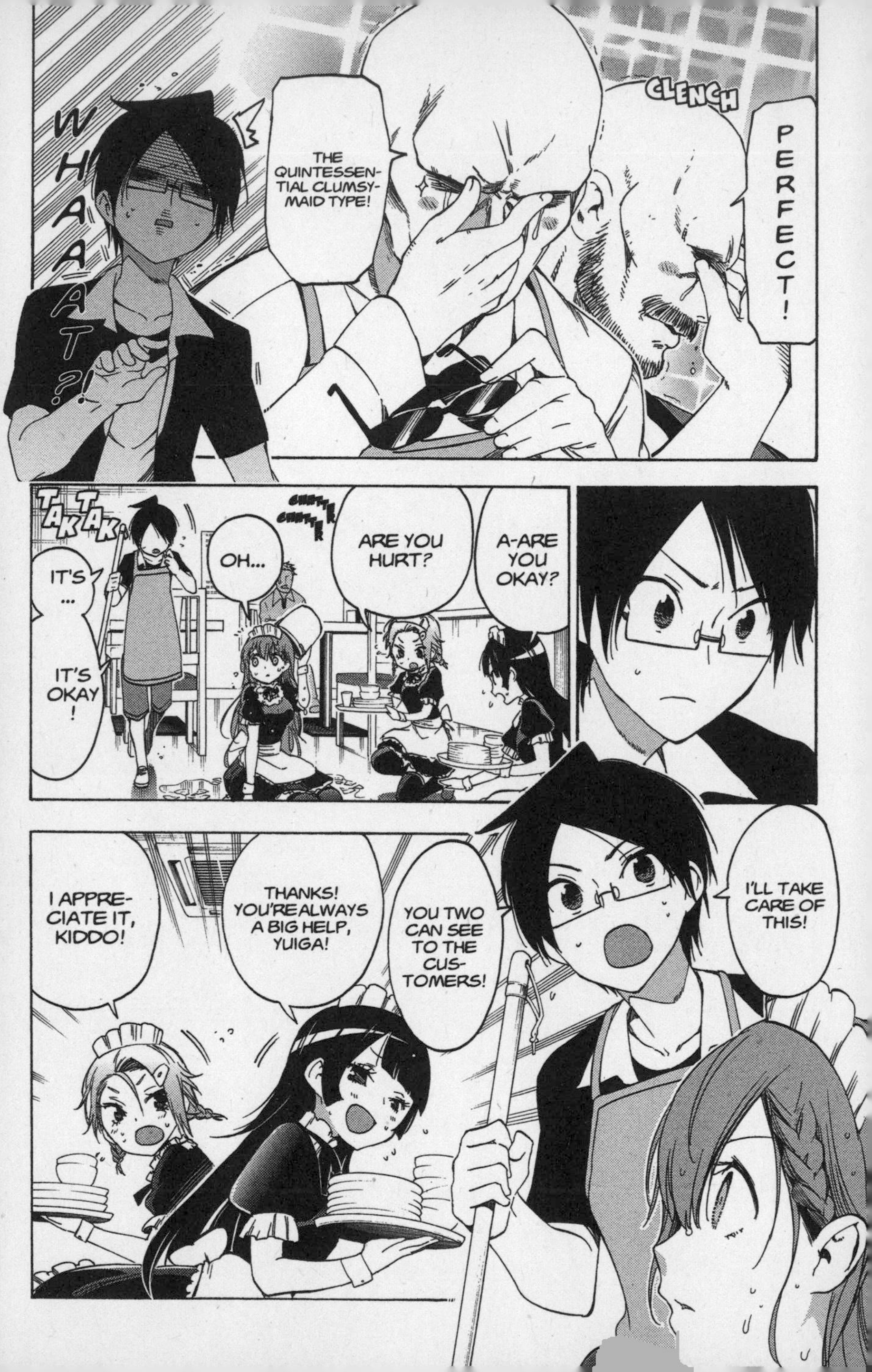
CLENCH
PERFECT!
THE QUINTESSENTIAL CLUMSY-MAID TYPE!
WHAAAT?!
A-ARE YOU OKAY?
ARE YOU HURT?
CHITTER CHITTER
OH...
TAK TAK
IT'S... IT'S OKAY!
I'LL TAKE CARE OF THIS!
YOU TWO CAN SEE TO THE CUSTOMERS!
THANKS! YOU'RE ALWAYS A BIG HELP, YUIGA!
I APPRECIATE IT, KIDDO!

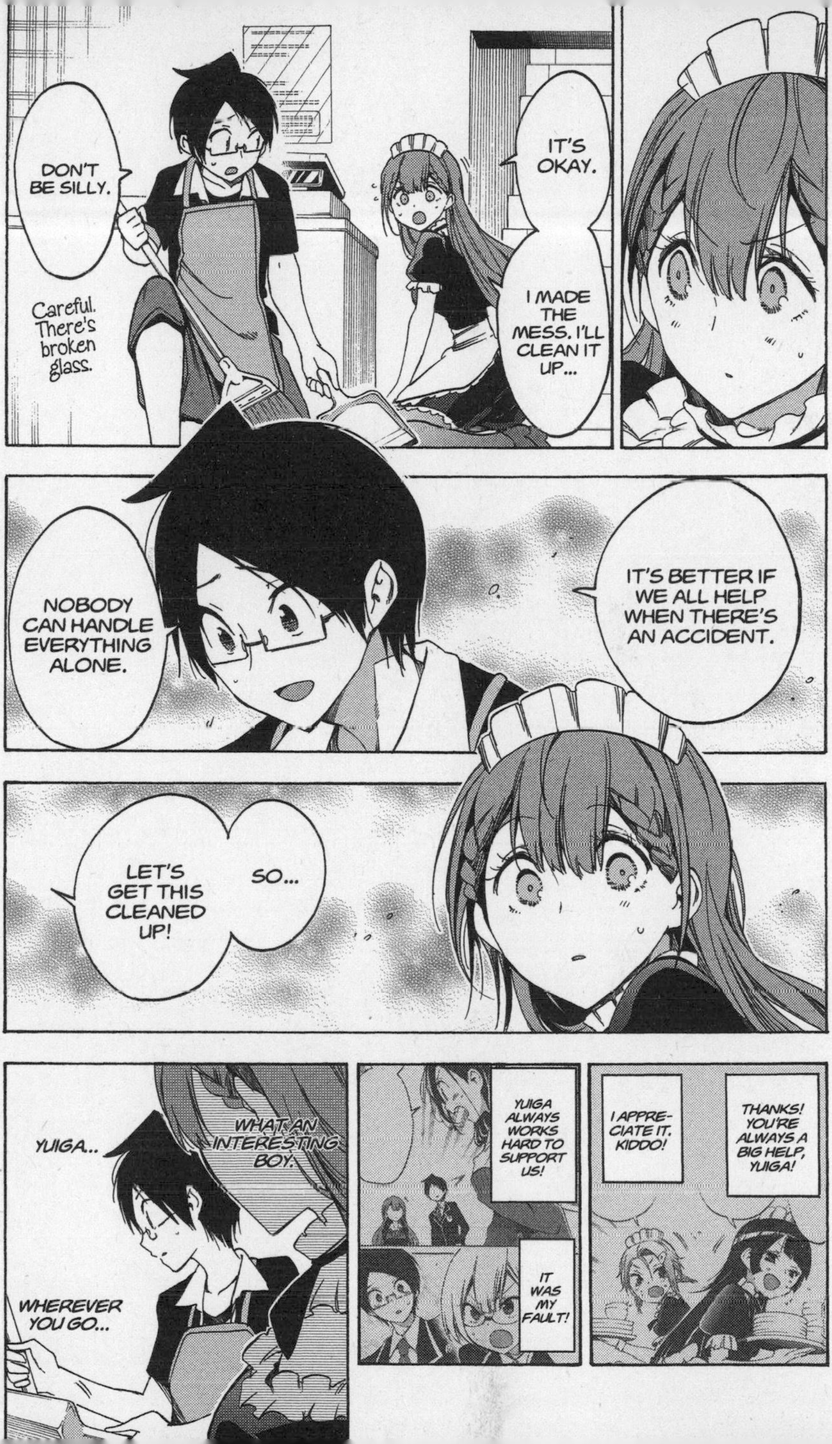
IT'S OKAY.
I MADE THE MESS. I'LL CLEAN IT UP...
DON'T BE SILLY.
Careful. There's broken glass.
IT'S BETTER IF WE ALL HELP WHEN THERE'S AN ACCIDENT.
NOBODY CAN HANDLE EVERYTHING ALONE.
SO...
LET'S GET THIS CLEANED UP!
THANKS! YOU'RE ALWAYS A BIG HELP, YUIGA!
I APPRECIATE IT. KIDDO!
YUIGA ALWAYS WORKS HARD TO SUPPORT US!
IT WAS MY FAULT!
WHAT AN INTERESTING BOY.
YUIGA...
WHEREVER YOU GO...

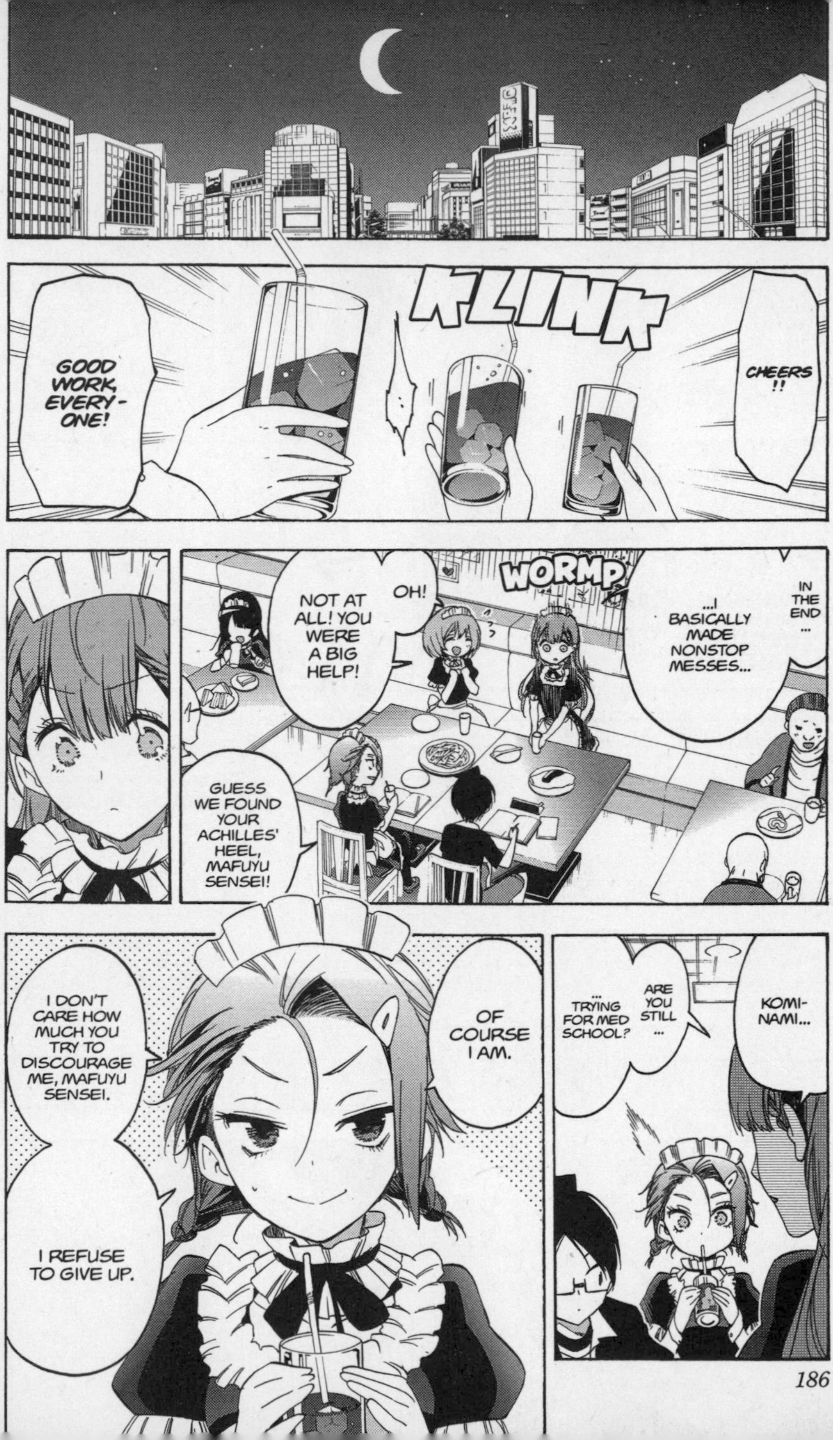
CHEERS!!
KLINK
GOOD WORK, EVERYONE!
IN THE END...
...I BASICALLY MADE NONSTOP MESSES...
WORMP
OH!
NOT AT ALL! YOU WERE A BIG HELP!
GUESS WE FOUND YOUR ACHILLES' HEEL, MAFUYU SENSEI!
KOMINAMI...
ARE YOU STILL...
...TRYING FOR MED SCHOOL?
OF COURSE I AM.
I DON'T CARE HOW MUCH YOU TRY TO DISCOURAGE ME, MAFUYU SENSEI.
I REFUSE TO GIVE UP.

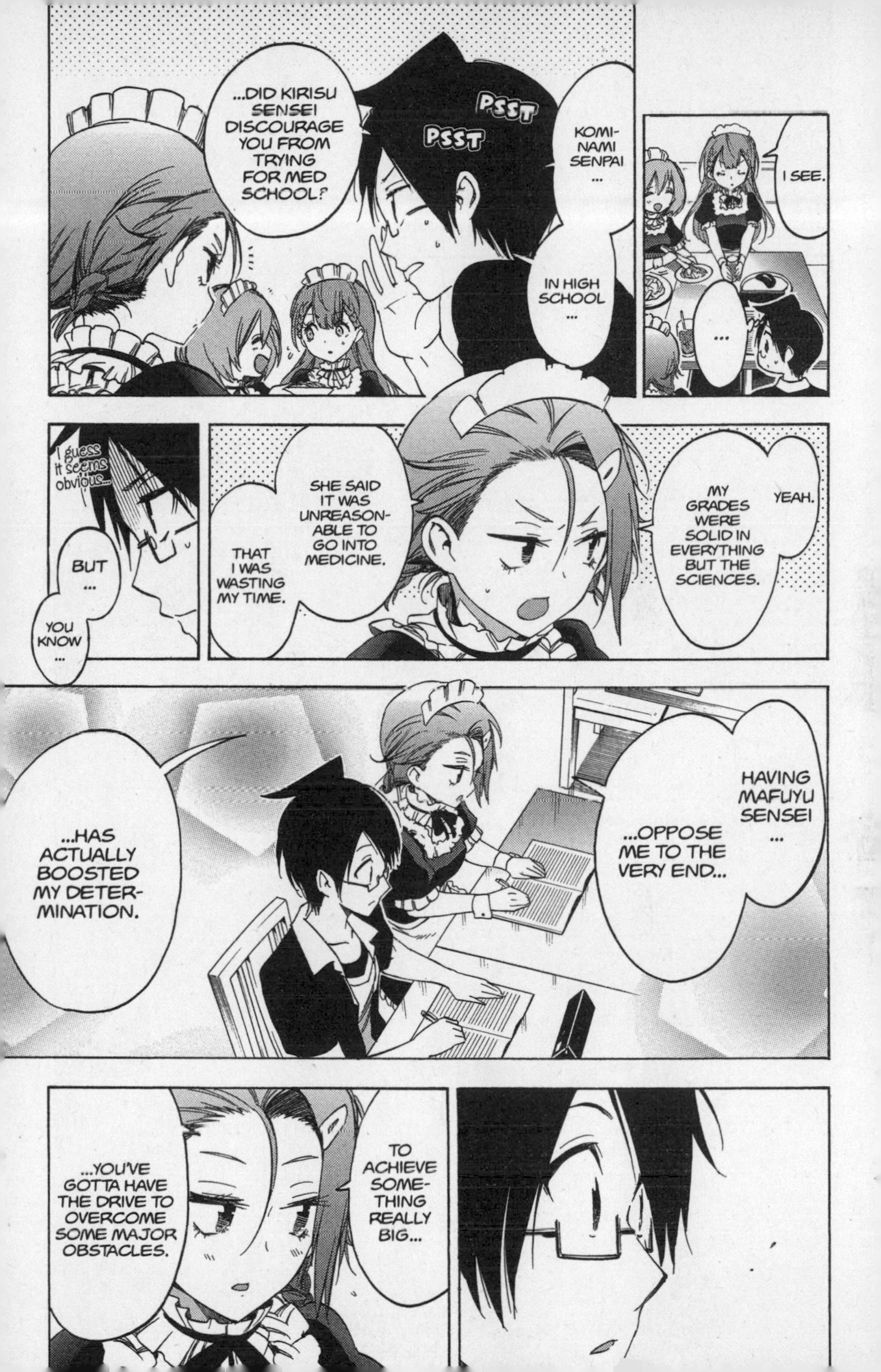
I SEE.
...
PSST
PSST
KOMI-NAMI SENPAI ...
IN HIGH SCHOOL ...
...DID KIRISU SENSEI DISCOURAGE YOU FROM TRYING FOR MED SCHOOL?
YEAH.
MY GRADES WERE SOLID IN EVERYTHING BUT THE SCIENCES.
SHE SAID IT WAS UNREASON-ABLE TO GO INTO MEDICINE.
THAT I WAS WASTING MY TIME.
I guess it seems obvious...
BUT ...
YOU KNOW ...
HAVING MAFUYU SENSEI ...
...OPPOSE ME TO THE VERY END...
...HAS ACTUALLY BOOSTED MY DETER-MINATION.
TO ACHIEVE SOME-THING REALLY BIG...
...YOU'VE GOTTA HAVE THE DRIVE TO OVERCOME SOME MAJOR OBSTACLES.

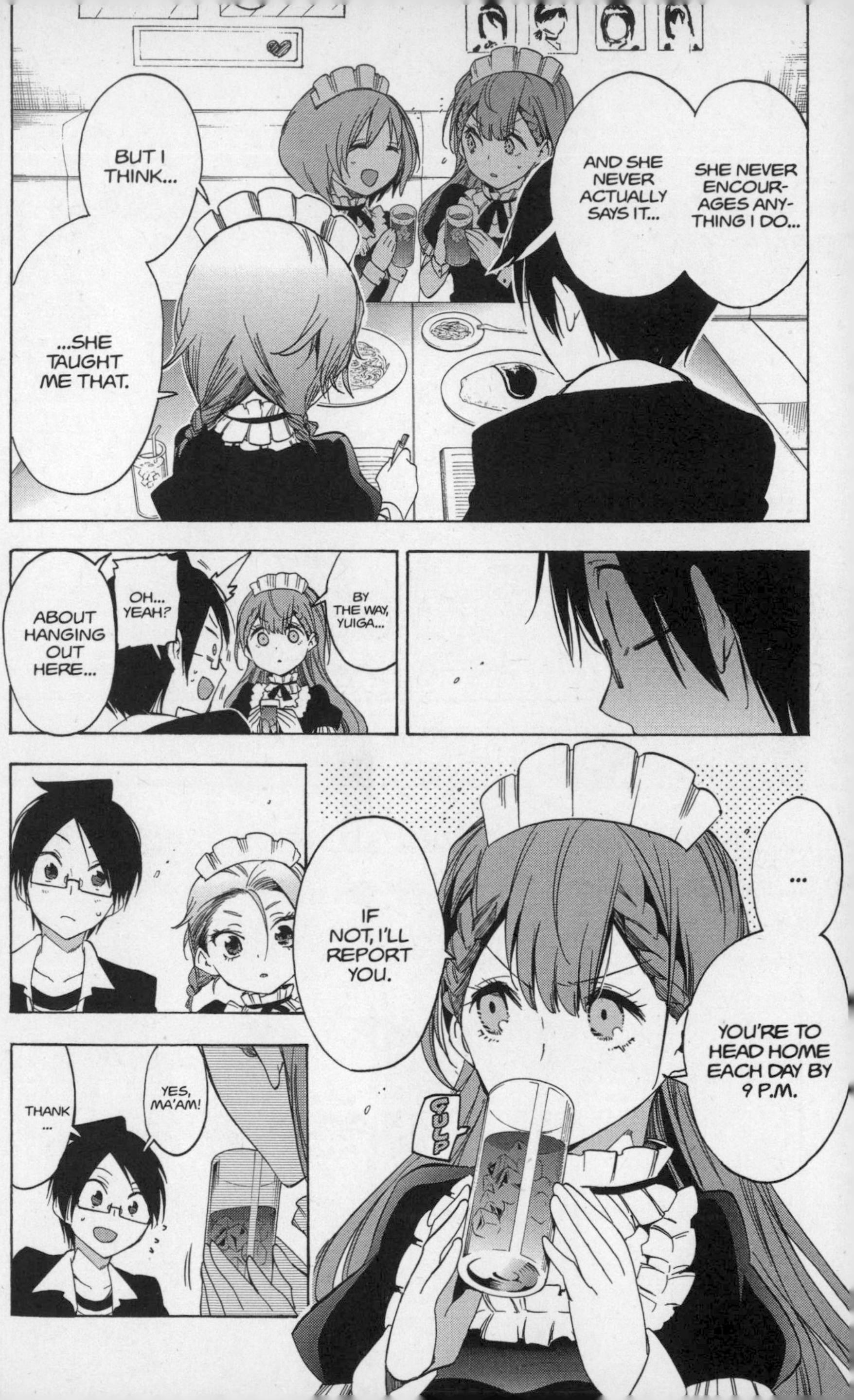
SHE NEVER ENCOURAGES ANYTHING I DO...
AND SHE NEVER ACTUALLY SAYS IT...
BUT I THINK...
...SHE TAUGHT ME THAT.
BY THE WAY, YUIGA...
OH... YEAH?
ABOUT HANGING OUT HERE...
...
YOU'RE TO HEAD HOME EACH DAY BY 9 P.M.
IF NOT, I'LL REPORT YOU.
GULP
YES, MA'AM!
THANK ...

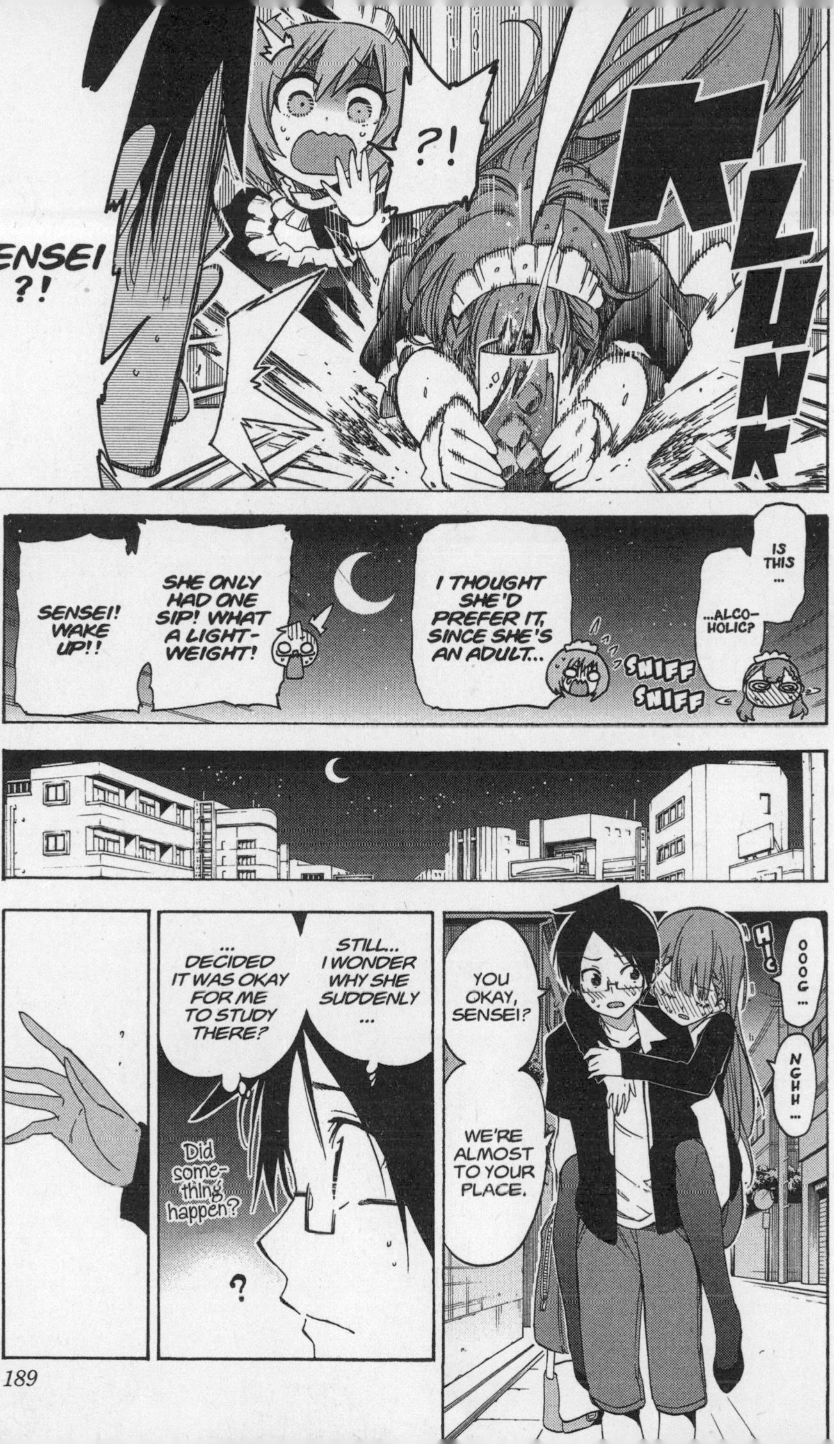
KLUNK
?!
SENSEI ?!
IS THIS ...
...ALCO-HOLIC?
SNIFF SNIFF
I THOUGHT SHE'D PREFER IT, SINCE SHE'S AN ADULT...
SHE ONLY HAD ONE SIP! WHAT A LIGHT-WEIGHT!
SENSEI! WAKE UP!!
HIC
OOOG ...
NGHH ...
YOU OKAY, SENSEI?
WE'RE ALMOST TO YOUR PLACE.
STILL... I WONDER WHY SHE SUDDENLY ...
... DECIDED IT WAS OKAY FOR ME TO STUDY THERE?
Did some-thing happen?
?

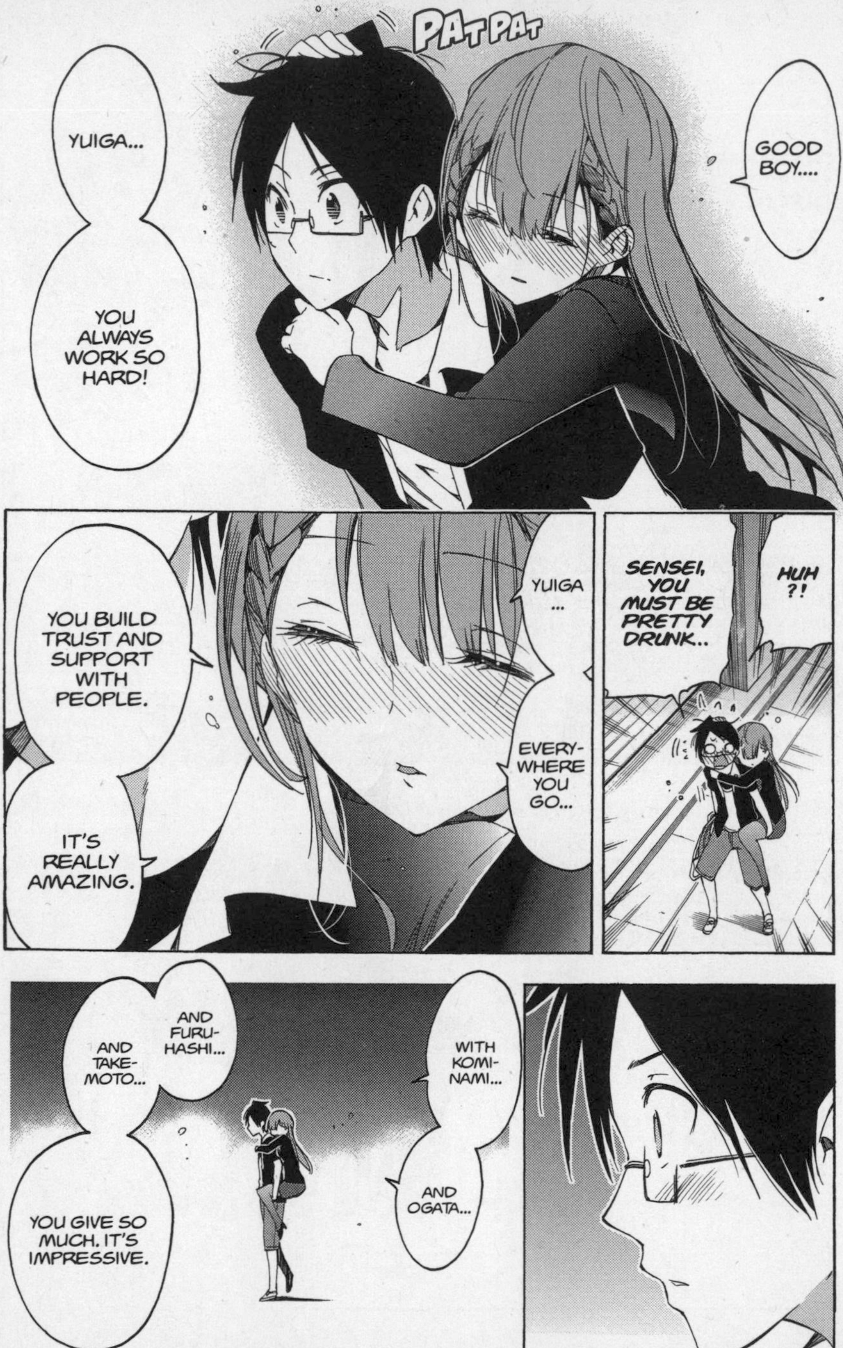
PAT PAT
GOOD BOY....
YUIGA...
YOU ALWAYS WORK SO HARD!
HUH ?!
SENSEI, YOU MUST BE PRETTY DRUNK..
YUIGA ...
EVERY-WHERE YOU GO...
YOU BUILD TRUST AND SUPPORT WITH PEOPLE.
IT'S REALLY AMAZING.
WITH KOMI-NAMI...
AND OGATA...
AND FURU-HASHI...
AND TAKE-MOTO...
YOU GIVE SO MUCH. IT'S IMPRESSIVE.

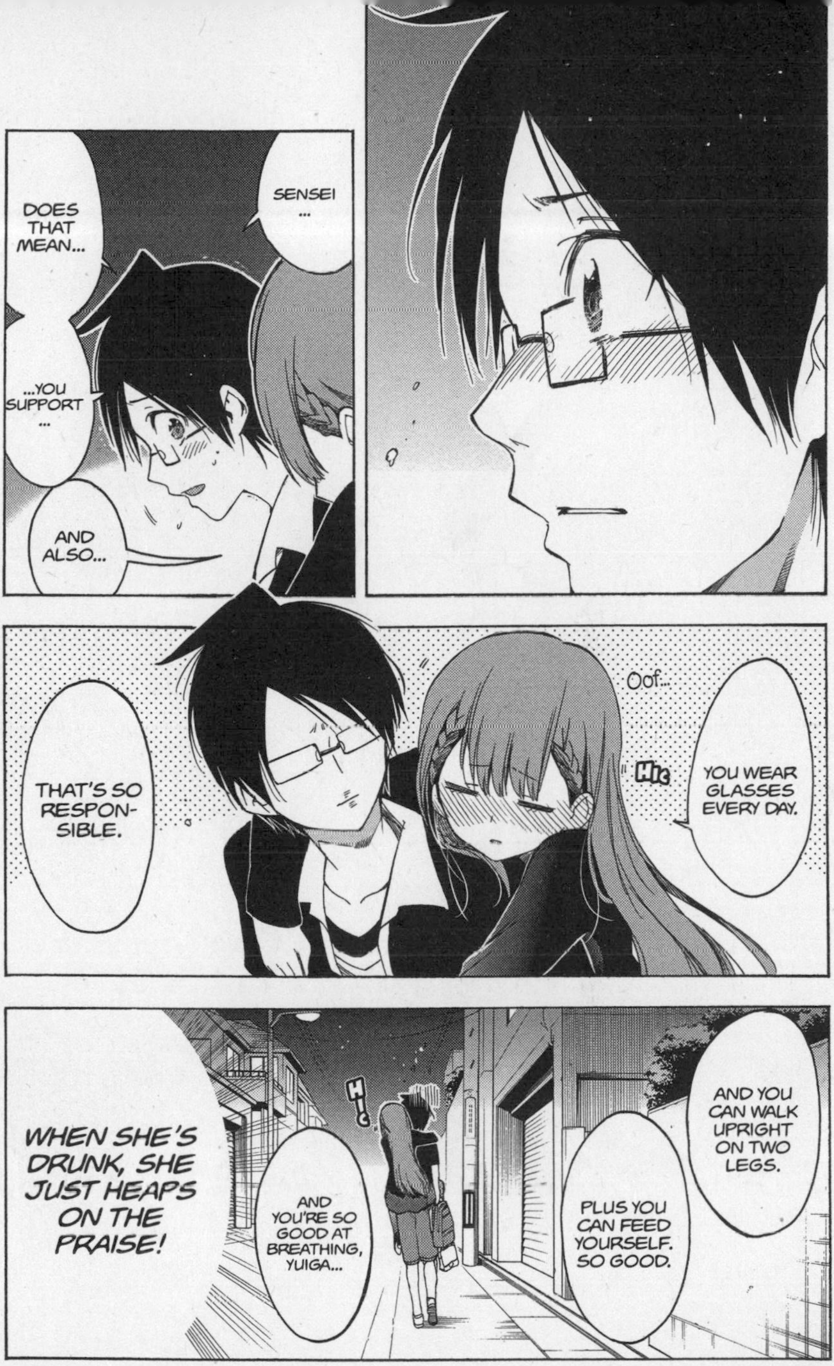
SENSEI ...
DOES THAT MEAN...
...YOU SUPPORT ...
AND ALSO...
Oof...
HIC
YOU WEAR GLASSES EVERY DAY.
THAT'S SO RESPONSIBLE.
AND YOU CAN WALK UPRIGHT ON TWO LEGS.
PLUS YOU CAN FEED YOURSELF. SO GOOD.
HIC
AND YOU'RE SO GOOD AT BREATHING, YUIGA...
WHEN SHE'S DRUNK, SHE JUST HEAPS ON THE PRAISE!

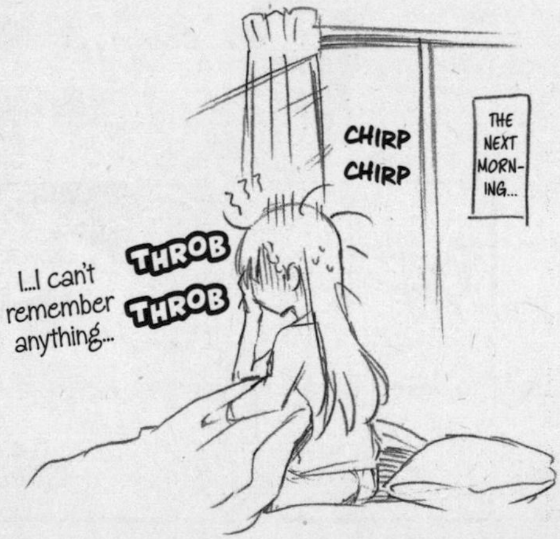
THE NEXT MORN-ING...
CHIRP CHIRP
THROB THROB
I...I can't remember anything...

[X] CHILDREN 2

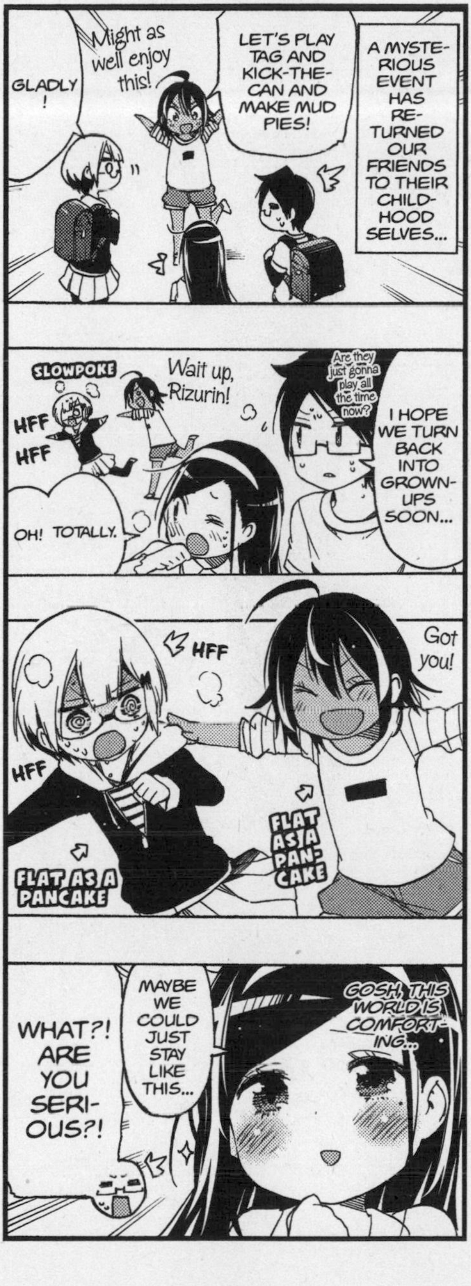
A MYSTERIOUS EVENT HAS RETURNED OUR FRIENDS TO THEIR CHILDHOOD SELVES...
LET'S PLAY TAG AND KICK-THE-CAN AND MAKE MUD PIES!
Might as well enjoy this!
GLADLY!
Are they just gonna play all the time now?
I HOPE WE TURN BACK INTO GROWN-UPS SOON...
Wait up, Rizurin!
SLOWPOKE
HFF HFF
OH! TOTALLY.
Got you!
HFF
FLAT AS A PANCAKE
HFF
FLAT AS A PANCAKE
GOSH, THIS WORLD IS COMFORTING...
MAYBE WE COULD JUST STAY LIKE THIS...
WHAT?! ARE YOU SERIOUS?!

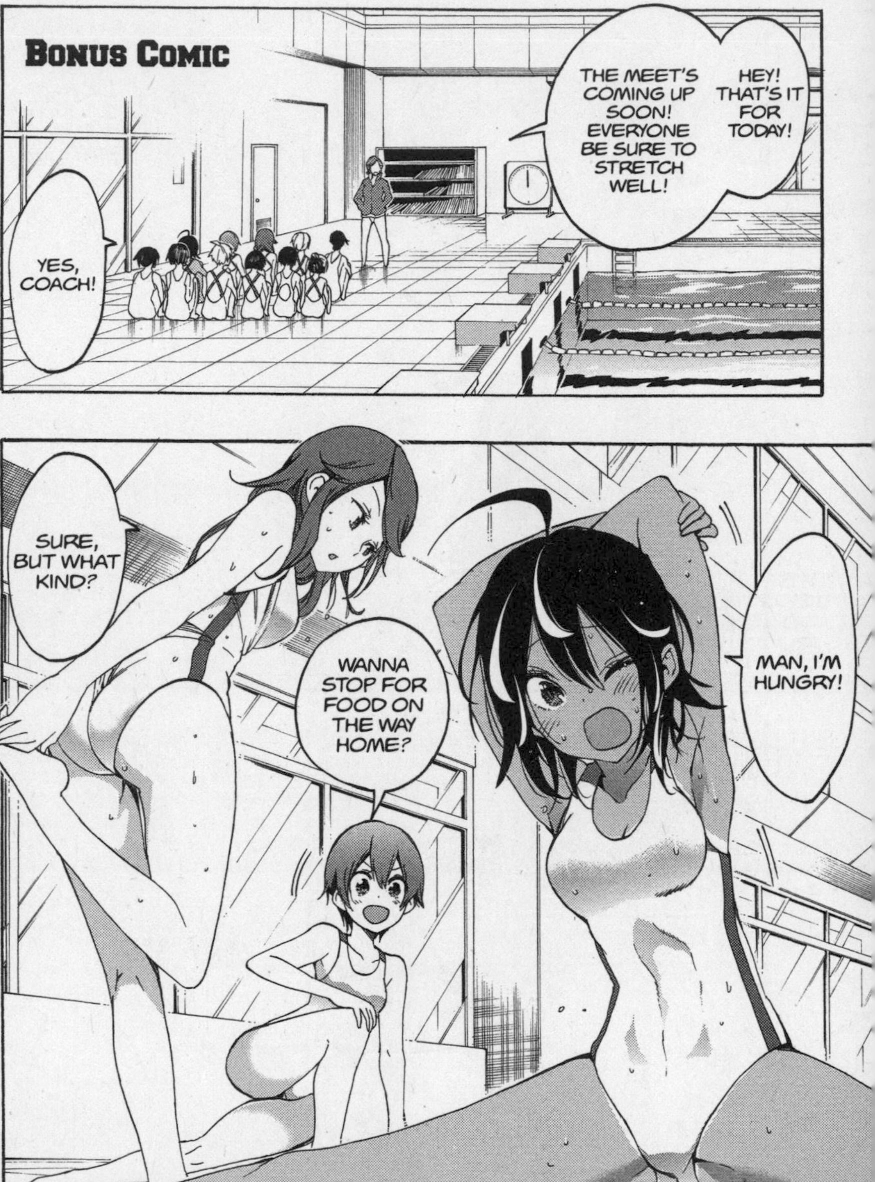
BONUS COMIC
HEY! THAT'S IT FOR TODAY!
THE MEET'S COMING UP SOON! EVERYONE BE SURE TO STRETCH WELL!
YES, COACH!
MAN, I'M HUNGRY!
WANNA STOP FOR FOOD ON THE WAY HOME?
SURE, BUT WHAT KIND?

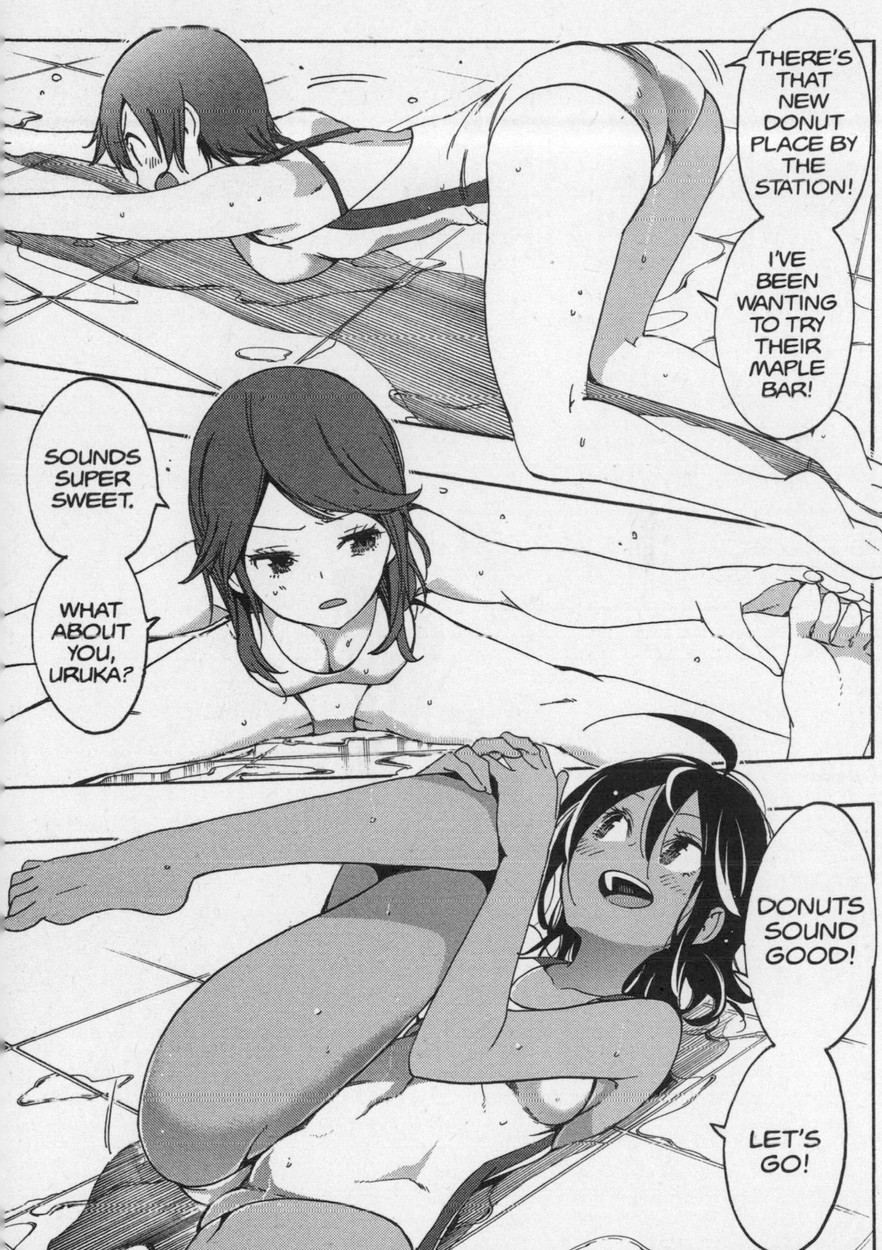
THERE'S THAT NEW DONUT PLACE BY THE STATION!
I'VE BEEN WANTING TO TRY THEIR MAPLE BAR!
SOUNDS SUPER SWEET.
WHAT ABOUT YOU, URUKA?
DONUTS SOUND GOOD!
LET'S GO!

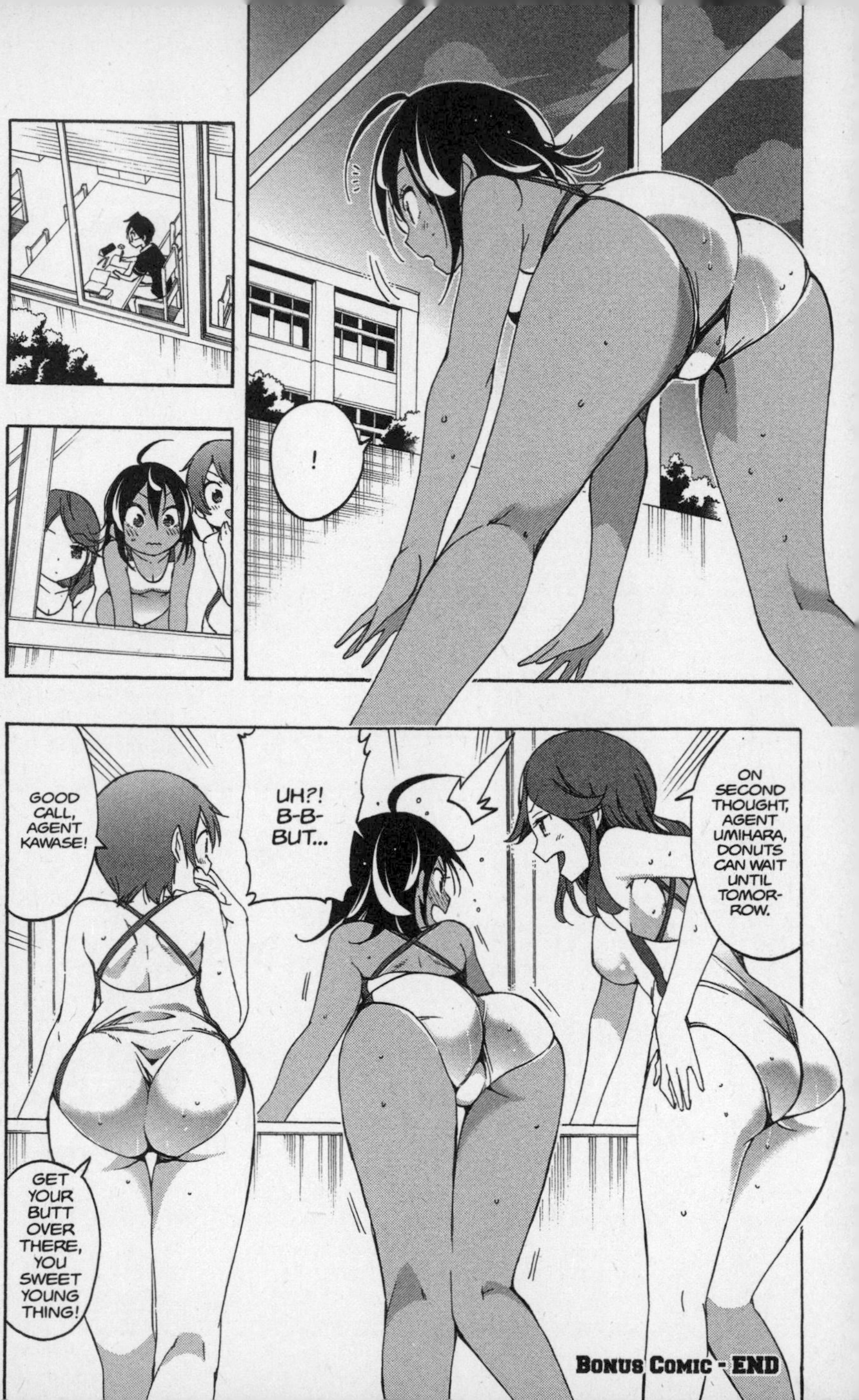
!
ON SECOND THOUGHT, AGENT UMIHARA, DONUTS CAN WAIT UNTIL TOMOR-ROW.
UH?! B-B-BUT...
GOOD CALL, AGENT KAWASE!
GET YOUR BUTT OVER THERE, YOU SWEET YOUNG THING!
BONUS COMIC - END

We Never Learn 4

STAFF

Taishi Tsutsui ....

....

Yu Kato ....

Naoki Ochiai ....

Sachiko ....

Yukki ....

HELP

Paripoi ....

Shinobu Irooki ....

Yuji Iwasaki ....

Kazuya Higuchi ....

Fuka Toma ....

Chikomichi ....

S T A F F   L I S T

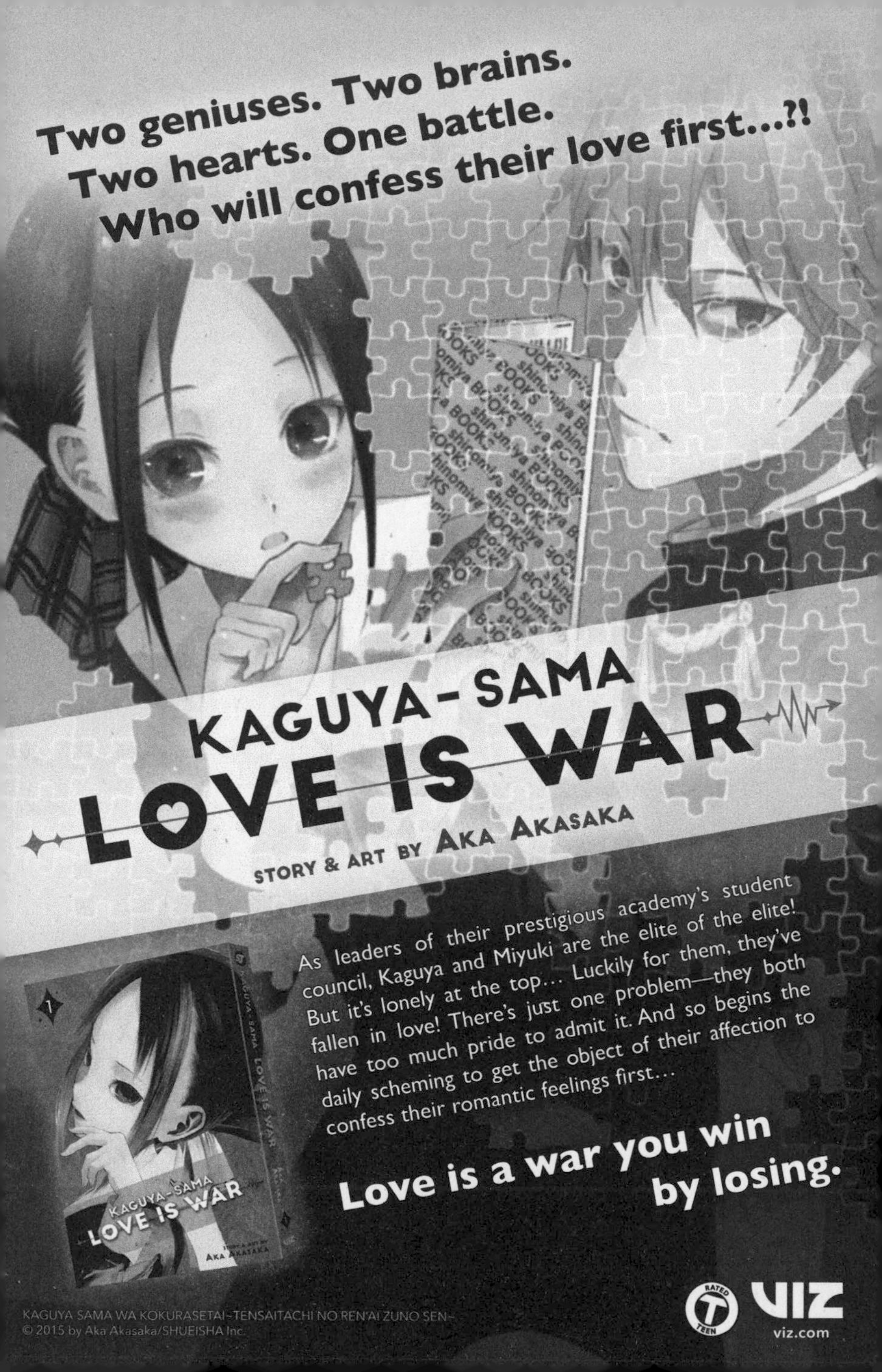
Two geniuses. Two brains.
Two hearts. One battle.
Who will confess their love first...?!
KAGUYA-SAMA
LOVE IS WAR
STORY & ART BY AKA AKASAKA
As leaders of their prestigious academy's student council, Kaguya and Miyuki are the elite of the elite! But it's lonely at the top... Luckily for them, they've fallen in love! There's just one problem—they both have too much pride to admit it. And so begins the daily scheming to get the object of their affection to confess their romantic feelings first...
Love is a war you win by losing.
KAGUYA-SAMA LOVE IS WAR
AKA AKASAKA
RATED T TEEN
VIZ
viz.com
KAGUYA SAMA WA KOKURASETAI~TENSAITACHI NO REN'AI ZUNO SEN~
© 2015 by Aka Akasaka/SHUEISHA Inc.

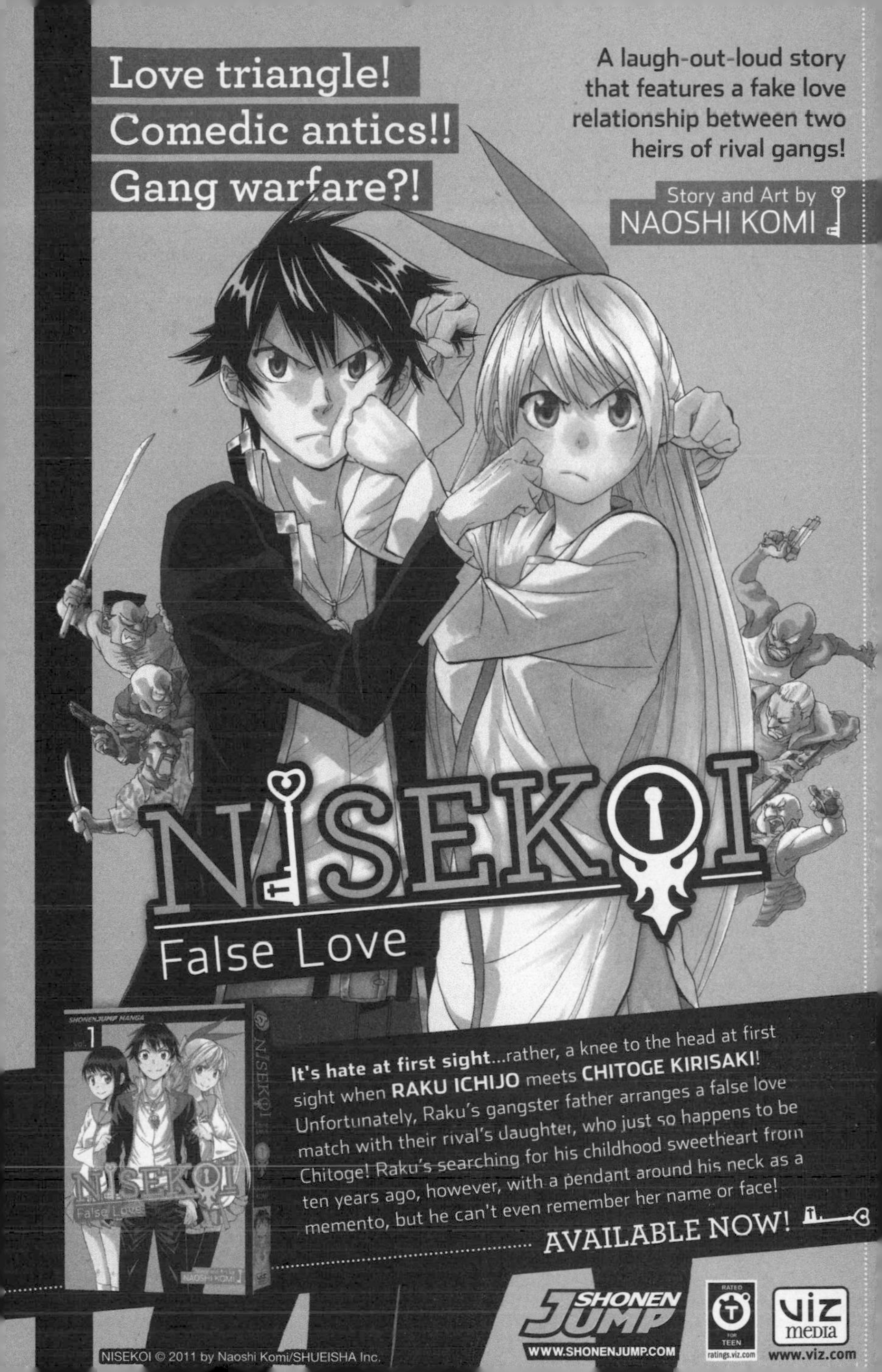

Love triangle!
Comedic antics!!
Gang warfare?!
A laugh-out-loud story that features a fake love relationship between two heirs of rival gangs!
Story and Art by
NAOSHI KOMI
NISEKOI
False Love
SHONEN JUMP MANGA
vol. 1
NISEKOI
False Love
NAOSHI KOMI
It's hate at first sight...rather, a knee to the head at first sight when RAKU ICHIJO meets CHITOGE KIRISAKI! Unfortunately, Raku's gangster father arranges a false love match with their rival's daughter, who just so happens to be Chitoge! Raku's searching for his childhood sweetheart from ten years ago, however, with a pendant around his neck as a memento, but he can't even remember her name or face!
AVAILABLE NOW!
SHONEN JUMP
WWW.SHONENJUMP.COM
RATED
T
FOR
TEEN
ratings.viz.com
viz media
www.viz.com
NISEKOI © 2011 by Naoshi Komi/SHUEISHA Inc.

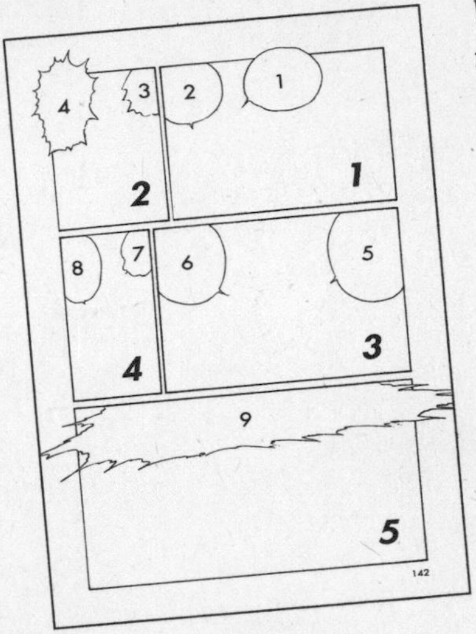

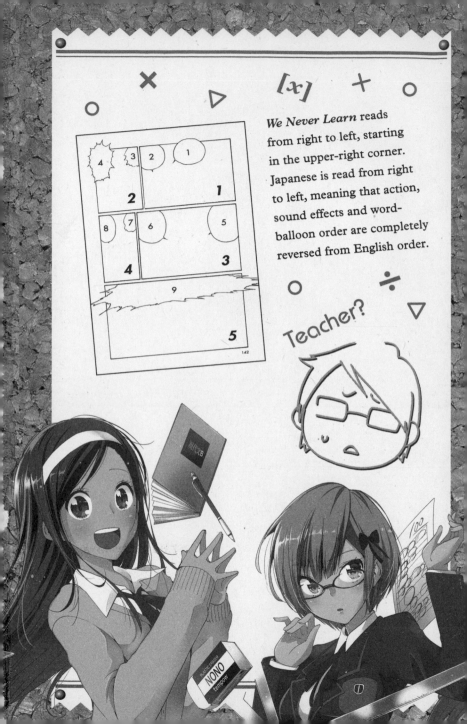

We Never Learn **reads from right to left, starting in the upper-right corner. Japanese is read from right to left, meaning that action, sound effects and word-balloon order are completely reversed from English order.**

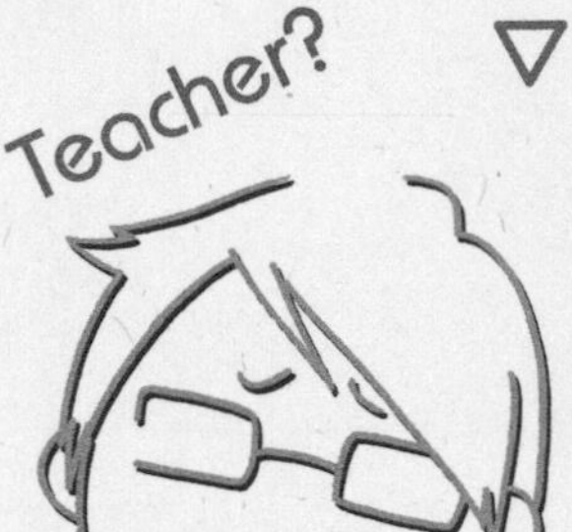
Teacher?

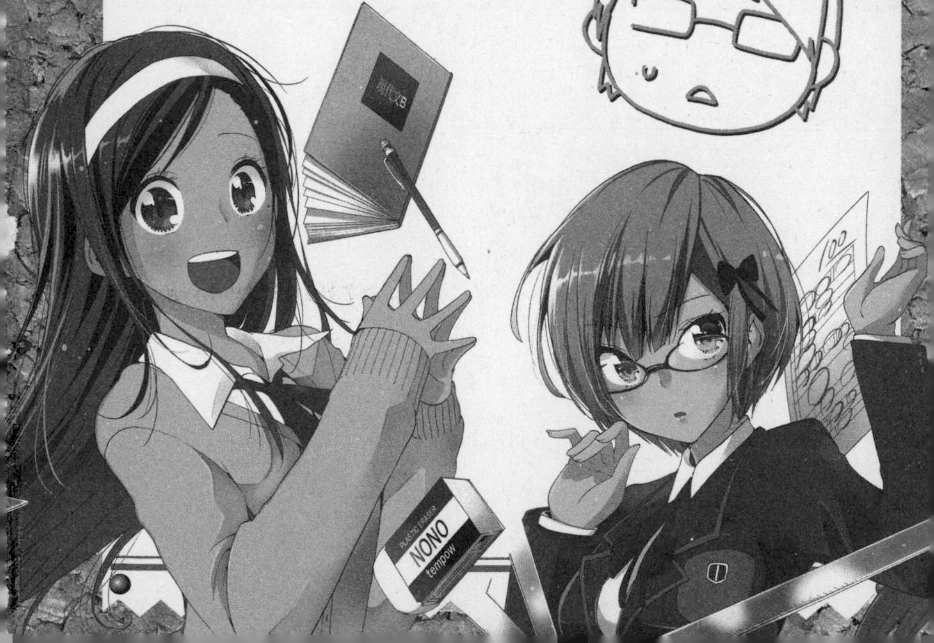
NONO
tempow